FOLLOWING THE WATERS

~

FOLLOWING THE WATERS

"Ideals are like stars.
You will not succeed in touching them
with your hands.
But the seafaring man who
follows the waters, follows the stars.
And if you choose them for your guides,
You can reach your destiny!"

—CARL SCHURZ (1829–1906),
German-American legislator, reformer, and journalist.
Quoted by John F. Kennedy in 1960 campaign speech
in Wisconsin where Schurz had lived.

~

Astrid Tollefsen's

FOLLOWING
THE WATERS

~

Voices from the
Final Norwegian Emigration

*An oral history & personal perspective on the triumphs
& tragedies, adventures & lifestyles of
Norwegian emigrant fishermen & their families
during the Twentieth Century.*

*From Norway to Brooklyn & New Bedford,
Seattle & Alaska, & often back to Norway.*

A LEIFUR PUBLICATION
Cape Cod, Massachusetts 2004

FOLLOWING THE WATERS,
Voices from the Final Norwegian Emigration
An Oral History

Published in the United States of America, 2004
Leifur Publications, Box 150, West Barnstable, Massachusetts 02668

Library of Congress Control Number: 2004095080
Tollefsen, Astrid, 1937–
    Following the waters: voices from the final Norwegian emigration: an oral history & personal perspective on the triumphs & tragedies, adventures & lifestyles of Norwegian emigrant fisherman & their families during the 20th century / Astrid Tollefsen. — 1st ed.
    p.   cm.
    "From Norway to Brooklyn & New Bedford, Seattle & Alaska & often back to Norway."
    Includes bibliographical references.
    LCCN 2004095080
    ISBN 0-9746515-5-9
    1. Norwegian Americans—History—20th century.   2. Norway—Emigration and immigration—History—20th century.   3. United States—Emigration and immigration—History—20th century.   4. Norwegian Americans—Massachusetts—New Bedford—History—20th century.   6. Fishers—United States—History—20th century.
I. Title.
E184.S2T65 2004   305.83'982073'0904
    QB104-800011

Permissions for copyrighted and professional materials:
Cover painting: Sailing into Skudeneshavn 1902, Gunvald Falnes. Owner: Dr. Inge Gilje, Haugesund, Norway
©Photography: Gunleif Wilhelmsen by James Nachtwey/VII, Paris
© Selected fishing vessel photos: Steve Kennedy, Wellfleet, MA.
©New Bedford scenes: Arthur Moniz, Arthur Moniz Gallery, William Street, New Bedford MA.
©Illustrations of USCG Ships. George E. Bieda, Windjammer (Naval and Aviation) Arts, Silverdale, WA.
Chapter 6 Cover, Waiting for Papa. © artist: Magne Adolfsen, Kvitsøy, Norway
Custom designed Norwegian Motifs: Evangeline, Santa Barbara, CA
Rosemaling Motif: © Joan Dahl, www.rosemal.com "Norwegian Trolls & Rosemaling Vol.1"
Music: © Ballad of the Midnight Sun, Tønnes Olsen, Aleksander Hauge, Karmøy Norway
Design and typesetting: Publisher's Design and Production Services, Inc., Sagamore Beach, MA 02562-1480

FIRST EDITION

DEDICATION

To: Momma, Papa and my son, Kristian

～

*This book is also dedicated to
friends and relatives
who believed in me
and inspired me
throughout my life.*

With Deep Appreciation

~

To: Individuals who supported this book because they care about preserving Norwegian-American culture.

Ralph Brown	Toni Isaksen Johnson
John & Ellen Isaksen	A Norwegian friend
Spencer D. Knott	Ingrid Nilsen Climis
Arnleiv Jensen	Joan Gallop Currie
Robert Bendiksen, Ph.D	Dr. Kristian T. Simsarian
Doris Bendiksen	Cate Corcoran
Harald Mannes	Per Heidenreich
Ann Draper Arthur	

To: Individuals who supported this book in loving memory of a friend or family member.

IN MEMORY OF

JOSEFINE & HALLVARD STOL	*—from Lise, Mery, & son Jakob*
OSKAR MANNES	*—from son, Sverre*
NILS ÅDLAND	*—from son, Magne*
MAGNE & KARRY RISDAL	*—from daughter, Linda*
TORE ASKELAND	*—from friend, Christine A. Balboni*
SARAH BONNAR STONE	*—from grandson, Ralph Brown*
MARIE TOLLEFSEN BERG	
& KRISTIAN BERG	*—from Gunnar & Martha Berg*
CAPTAIN DAVID TOLLEFSEN &	
CAPTAIN MARTIN & SUSANNE DAHL	*—from the family*
SIVERT & EMILIE TOLLEFSEN	*—Carol Tollefsen-Hoaglund & family*
CAPTAIN SIGVART TOLLEFSEN &	
MURIEL CASWELL TOLLEFSEN	*—from grandson, Kristian*

To: Norwegian organizations who, in keeping with their mission, graciously supported this book.

THE ROYAL NORWEGIAN CONSULATE, NYC
NORDMANNS-FORBUNDET, *The Emigration Fund of 1975*
SONS OF NORWAY, *General Heritage and Culture Grant*
KARMØY KOMMUNE, *Skole-og kulturetaten*
CITY OF STAVANGER, NORWAY, *Chief Municipal Administrator*

~

With Deep Appreciation

To: My expert, long-suffering, tireless, generous, patient, and tactful editor, William J. Breisky, a very special man, who encouraged my work, offered invaluable editing assistance, and took me under his wing, along with his kind family, as a friend. They all enriched my life and this book very much!

To: Volunteer, Linda Risdal Knott, daughter of a fisherman, for her patience and precise copy editing skills

To: The New Bedford Standard-Times for their generous cooperation and open-handedness to me for the use of their materials. Special thanks to William Kennedy, President and Publisher, for his interest and generosity in sharing the resources of his newspaper. My personal thanks to former waterfront writer and editor, Brad Hathaway and current waterfront writer, Jack Stewardson for their accurate and exceptionally well-written waterfront stories.

To: Norwegian newspapers: *Haugesunds-Avis* and *KARMØYBLADET*. American newspapers: *Norway Times (Nordisk Tidende)*, *Mattapoisett Wanderer*, *The Advocate*. Fairhaven, *The Barnicle*, New Bedford, and *Western Viking*, Seattle for their support. And also to TV Haugaland, Haugesund, Norway.

To: Individuals, now living or dead, new friends and old, and family members, both in America and Norway, who participated in the interviewing process and/or offered me encouragement, help, publicity, moral support, a smile, sometimes lodging, editorial support and always background information. Without this generous help from so many, this book would not be a reality today.

Contents

~

~

Contents

Foreword

~

BY LARS FURE, SENIOR ADVISOR, NORWEGIAN
MINISTRY OF FOREIGN AFFAIRS, OSLO

On 17 May 2001, I had the great pleasure of taking part in the Norwegian Heritage Day celebration in New Bedford, Massachusetts. As head of the Norwegian Information Service in the United States at the time, I already had some experience of the Norwegian-American way of celebrating 17 May, Norway's national day. However, I knew in advance that the Norwegian Heritage Day in New Bedford would be celebrated in quite a different way from, for instance, the traditional and spectacular parade in Brooklyn, New York. The mere fact that it was a long time since there had been a 17 May event in New Bedford made it very special.

Why this renewed interest in old cultural and family ties between Norway and the New Bedford/Fairhaven area, and why take an interest in the Norwegians and their mark on this local community? I already knew the answer: Astrid Tollefsen and her book project. The more I read the rich material that she has collected and put on paper, the better I understand the immensity and sincerity of her efforts, and the more I appreciate the value of her ambitious undertaking. Norway and America share a history. But not all parts of this shared history are equally well documented. There has been a great deal of focus on the large number of Norwegians who immigrated to the Midwest. And in 2000, His Majesty King Harald V of Norway opened an exhibition on Ellis Island, which reminded us of the Norwegian immigrants' impact on New York and the large community they built in Brooklyn. So the time has come to add another chapter to the book of Norwegian-American relations to include those who "followed the waters" from Norway to Brooklyn and then on to the shores of Massachusetts. Some of them even went further on to Seattle and Alaska and made significant contributions to the development of the American seafood industry.

The ocean has been central to Norwegian-American relations since day one. To many it was more than merely a transport route; it was a route that both separated and united. To those Norwegians, mainly from the Karmøy area in Southwestern Norway, who settled in New Bedford/Fairhaven and

~

often went back and forth between their two homelands, the ocean provided a means of livelihood and became, in turn, a way of life. It is their history that Astrid Tollefsen has set out to tell us, as well as that of the local Norwegian-American community that they made into their American home. In many ways it is a personal history of a girl who was, and then again was not, part of this community, due to the early and tragic loss of her Norwegian father. The way I read it, the author's search for her own identity must have been an underlying motivation for writing this book.

The book is a personal history, but it is much more than that. Through the author's experiences in childhood, adolescence and adulthood as well as the many compelling personal histories that she has collected, we learn a lot about the socio-cultural history of New Bedford/Fairhaven. Like the Norwegian community, the area's ties to the sea are fundamental to its existence and development.

Of course, to Norwegians and Norwegian-Americans it may be a matter of pride to have the influence of their fellow countrymen and women on a mighty country like America documented for posterity. They, too, are part of America's history and the local history that is such an integral part of the identity of a community and its inhabitants.

We all know that roots are important, and so is pride in these roots. Since we live in a world that is changing so rapidly, we need to pause sometimes so that we can nourish these roots. Astrid Tollefsen's contribution in this regard is significant, not only for the Norwegian-Americans who still live in Fairhaven/New Bedford, and their descendants and relatives in Karmøy and elsewhere, but also for all of us on both sides of the Atlantic who, by reading her book, will come to understand a little better the deep roots of the Norwegian-American relationship.

The nature of this relationship is indeed complex and not always easy to understand. I often recall the words of the elderly New Bedford woman who was honored on that Norwegian Heritage Day on 17 May 2001. She had been separated from her Norwegian-American husband by the onset of World War II, and spent the difficult war years in Norway. At that celebration of the Norwegian national day, although she was full of praise for Norway, she ended her remarks with "God bless America." That's how it is to have your heart in two places.

You, Astrid, have certainly put your heart into this book. Your work deserves our blessing and our sincere gratitude.

~

Two Houses: Two Shores

—Old Skudenes print

The Sivert Tollefsen house (right center with the gambrel roof). My father, Sigvart, grew up here and his youngest brother, Mandius, drowned in front of the house.

TODAY TWO HOUSES STAND DEFIANTLY against wind and weather in two different countries—near two different seas—with two different histories. Yet, they are eternally intertwined, because they have both provided the setting for the lives of our ancesters. One is now inhabited by a young family, and the house, intact, proudly overlooks Skudenes harbor in Norway. The other, built several hundred years ago in Fairhaven, Massachusetts, stands alone as a relic of the past and is surrounded by a jungle of once lovingly-tended plants. It overlooks a playing field, once a fresh water pond, where the youth of the town still flex their muscles. It gets too much attention

~

from the wandering neighborhood kids and stray animals of all description, and it is a lonely house whose past may be all that it will ever have.

There is yet another house, or part of one, that has ties to these two houses. It used to stand on a hill in a particularly lovely part of Karmøy, Norway, named Håland, where the breezes join from two peninsulas and give continual fresh air. This was a summerhouse for the same family. It was a house of sunshine, carefree days and merriment, and largely untouched by tragedy. All that is left now is the foundation and a few timbers used to build a nearby shed by its present owners. The view from this location is extraordinary, up the west coast of Karmøy, with its stark rocks, fine ocean spray and pink heather.

The Skudeneshavn (Skudenes harbor) house was once one of the largest houses in this lovely town and was near the family farm, called Høines. My grandmother, in the early 1900s, was fondly remembered by a former neighbor as "always knitting and wearing a white stiffly-starched apron over her dress while she walked home from town after doing her shopping." She remembered the whiteness of her apron shining in the sun.

Henriette Emilie Hanssen Tollefsen, called Papa'sma or Mor by her future grandchildren, was a stern disciplinarian and very strong. Her husband lived most of the year in Brooklyn, America—as a fishing boat owner and skipper out of New York City—and he sent money home each month for the family. He returned home almost every Christmas by working his passage on a boat and stayed a few months to help his family before he returned to America to work.

He was a very tall, hefty man, and everyone liked him. Handsome, imposing, intelligent, gentle and caring, he was a special man. He began taking his older sons and daughters with him to America, when they were about fifteen or just past confirmation, but he had one young daughter who had had a stroke when she was an infant, and the parents knew they would always have to provide for her at home.

—AT photo

The Tollefsen house with built-on porches in the early nineties.

Grandmother was a bit different from many others in town as she was of German/Danish stock, and some of her forebearers came from the town of Wyk on the island of Föhr—now German but formerly Danish—on the Jutland penninsula. Her family sailed alone in a very small boat to Kvelland, on the island of Hidra in Souhern Norway, in the late 18th century. A long lyric poem about this boat trip was memorized by my grandmother, but it was lost

—*Tollefsen archives*

Papa'sma and her young family about 1913. *Left to right:* Marie, Sigvart, Ellinor, Emilie with baby Hans, and Ellen Gurie.

to the ages when she died. She always reminded us of her German heritage, although she had much Norwegian blood.

Her husband was Norwegian, and his family lineage dated back to the first recorded data in Ferkingstad on Karmøy. Most of his ancestors lived in the Skudeneshavn area, but there had been periodic new blood infusions from other areas of Norway by mariners who returned home with brides from their journeys to Southern Norway.

The sea had always been at the core of life for those living in Skudeneshavn, but even with that history, my grandmother in the 1920s could never have imagined that she would soon lose her youngest son to the sea in front of her home in Norway or that in a few years the sea off the east coast of America would take her son, Tobias. She could not know then that her oldest son's first child would die at birth at the same time her husband lay dying of pneumonia in New York. This would have been incomprehensible to this God-fearing woman. She had no idea that she would come to America

—*Tollefsen archives*

The family in Norway in the twenties. Ellen Gurie is on left next to a woman who might be her grandmother and David Tollefsen and Marie with nephew George Christiansen are to the right. Back row are unknown family members.

—*Tollefsen archives*

A Tollefsen formal family portrait with three of the ten children, circa 1926. Left to right: Grandfather Sivert, Hans Andreas, Emilie Henrietta (Pappa'sma), my father Sigvart and Ellen Gurie.

—AT photo

View of Skudeneshavn from my father's childhood home, 1991.

to start a new life, and that her oldest son, Sigvart, would die at sea a few years later. And as soon as she fought her way through those losses, her son-in-law would perish at sea in the mid-century, and then a few years later lose yet another son, Arnleiv, to a storm at sea in 1964.

How was it possible for one woman to survive all of this tragedy and yet still maintain an absolute faith in God? Her faith grew throughout the years despite this pain.

Today her house in Skudeneshavn is still called Mille's house, and I know her old house in Fairhaven as Papa'sma's house. This house shared her life, her good times and her bad, her family joys, children, grandchildren and perhaps great-grandchildren. It shared her sorrows, her hopes and her dreams, her days serving coffee and waffles to family members, her robust health, her energy, her pain and her death.

—AT Photo

Pappa'sma in Fairhaven, circa 1970. She loved to hear of our adventures and travel and kept all the photos of our awards and achievements safely protected in her Bible.

Now the house sits alone, and we wonder if its days are over, or if someone will come and breathe new life into this town landmark; one of the first houses to be built in Norwegian-beloved Fairhaven.

Granddaughter Carol Anne Tollefsen-Hoaglund, my cousin, remembers: "I look at the house now and think of it as a monument to our past—something that is frozen in time. Although it is in disrepair and empty, I revere its strength, as Mor's strength, which persevered. The house is a symbol of the struggle. And, even now, through the overgrowth of vines and brush, I remember sitting in the yard under the makeshift hut with grapevines winding through the rails. I can smell the white lilacs and honeysuckle and remember drinking Kool-Aid, eating sweet waffles, and chomping on her gooseberries. I was mesmerized by our grandmother and her remarkable presence."

—Tollefsen archives

The family summerhouse in Håland where happy times were shared.

These houses bear the print of our family, all ten children, two parents and many in-laws, as well as cousins, brothers, sisters and grandparents. These houses are my gift from the past. I want to learn from them and to hear their stories. I hope to discover some of life's secrets from the wisdom hidden in their walls. I have always wondered why some families are singled out for great pain and others for success and joy. Do these walls know the answer?

As I stand in front of the house in Norway, I see my grandmother and hear the children and try to visualize my father and what he might have said or done. I heard from a cousin that one of my uncles in his youth had sneaked up to the summer house with some friends. While partying and dancing in the main room, one of the guests looked out the window and spied my strict grandmother walking up the hill in her white-starched apron and carrying her Bible. I was told they all jumped out of the back window and crawled up the hill so she would not see them. How many such family stories are lost forever to the grave?

This book tells the story of many emigrant lives, as it resurrects life events, shares memories, and weaves diverse experiences into a unique community profile. In doing so, it gives all of you the flavor of the Norwegian-American experience during the twentieth century.

Vær så god! (Vaer saa god) Enjoy!

The Baptismal Waters

Emigration medal celebrating the emigration sesquicentennial. *"They came from Norway and helped build America."*

THE EMIGRANTS COME TO AMERICA

THE KINGDOM OF NORWAY is blessed with people who possess great loyalty, strong love and allegiance to their country—a land that is deeply imbedded within their hearts and souls. Given a choice, few would leave their homeland except to visit friends and families in other lands or enjoy the sun on a vacation.

Norway is also blessed with extraordinarily beautiful scenery, a rock-bound coast and islands, deep fjords, forests and mountains. It is a country of great contrasts, with nature in all of its glory and all of its bleakness. It is all dark; it is all light. The land is barren; the land is forested. It is flat; it is mountainous. It is basically rock with a bit of land. One can see seaweed and experience tides sixty miles or more inland by the saltwater fjords.

In general, the people are blond and blue-eyed but some also have jet-black hair and deep brown eyes. There are churches everywhere, but too few people attend them. The people today are pietistic, respectful of religious teachings but basically secular. They are very happy; they are very sad. There seems to be no middle ground in the Norwegian's makeup. It is a country of black and white with no time for gray. Today this is literally true: black oil from the offshore rigs, white ocean foam.

—Courtesy Børge Solem

The Norwegian American Line's ship *Stavangerfjord*, at home in Stavanger before heading out to sea for New York City.

As recently as the sixties, it was rare to have a telephone. Now there are satellite-positioning devices for exact locations in the taxis and everyone, it seems, has a mobile phone. Until the sixties most Norwegians were very poor. Since the exploitation of North Sea oil, these same people enjoy one of the world's highest standards of living. For hundreds of years, maybe thousands, people left Norway to bring wealth home. Now other people come to Norway to bring wealth back to their homelands.

The elements of the country's beauty were also the elements of its poverty. Only a small percentage of the land is arable and even this land is rocky and thin and not able to support Norway's large families.

It is a country where a boat is accessible to most of the land because of its enormously long coastline and fjords, but there are mountainous areas and areas of interior farmland and forests where transportation and communication had been a problem until recently. National cohesiveness did not develop easily, and even today, there are some cultural differences. Much of this condition resulted from natural geographical barriers where isolated communities fostered strong local loyalties as distinct as the many dialects. Norwegians are apt to trust those from their local areas first, their region second, their country third.

Norway is a small country of about four million people. It has more than ten thousand islands and is shaped somewhat like an elongated teardrop. Its people have experienced their share of tears over the centuries

Personal communication is not the Norwegian's strongest asset. It is often difficult for the Norwegian as well as other Scandinavians to divulge

—*AT photo*

Typical Hardanger Fjord rural scene, 1991.

more in any discussion than is explicitly requested, especially in a group. Norwegians like to make decisions by consensus and avoid disagreement within groups at all costs. This method prevents one from being in a "superior" position and therefore does not violate the *Janteloven*, a set of cultural laws that were codified in the mid-twentieth century by a Dane, Axel Sandemose, who lived in Norway much of his life. They had been a deeply imbedded cultural pattern within all Scandinavian cultures for generations, but adopted most heartily, some feel, by the Norwegians. Many outside the culture find this to be a formidable communication barrier and the decision-making process can become very frustrating and seemingly slow.

Norwegians tend to have strong opinions, however, and like to have their own way on a one-to-one basis. As one Norwegian friend once said, "We are not always right, but we are never wrong." The *Janteloven* influences communication and may preclude total expression. These "laws," which stress that everyone has the same status regardless of talent, experience or education, may be an outcome of the arguing and conflict of bygone years or they may have been developed as a way to avoid confrontation or a byproduct of long-term dominance by another country. In any event, they are sometimes criticized for stifling spontaneity, creativity and innovation.

PENDLING

THE GEOGRAPHICAL FEATURES that have aided communication are the fjords and waterways. They provided a way for news, information and rumors to be spread by ship and boat, especially the mail boats. The native landscape makes Norway, and its people, unique in this world. And this uniqueness may have contributed to *"pendling,"* another cultural pattern that influenced emigration to a high extent. *Pendling*, as explained by a reporter, Bjarte Amble, from the *Haugesunds Avis*, a newspaper on Karmøy, is a coined word borrowed from a clock's pendulum that goes back and forth, or as the Norwegians say, "forth and back." The expression connotes going forth from their native land and then going back repeatedly. *Pendling* became the standard by which many coastal Norwegians lived. They often left Norway's shores to go to other shores for wealth and then brought their riches home to support their families in Norway. This practice was evident with the Vikings and continued throughout the many years of emigration. Almost all emigrants return to Norway whether to live or visit. Such people known to *pendle* are called *pendlers*, and they helped to keep Norway economically alive throughout the centuries until oil was discovered off her shores.

Because of this established pattern of *pendling*, I have chosen to call such people "emigrants" rather than "immigrants" throughout this book. They never truly left Norway behind, and spoke, ate and lived essentially Norwegian lives with many thinking of the day when they would return to their homeland.

The industrial revolution in essence bypassed Norway in the nineteenth century, except for the establishment of textile factories and engineering workshops. Between 1850 and 1880 the size of the Norwegian merchant fleet increased dramatically. There was a great emigration of farmers from Norway to America's upper Midwest also at that time.

The twentieth century emigration drew somewhat more from the fishermen living on the shores and islands of Norway. The North Sea fish supply can be unreliable, and those who made their livelihood from the sea most often migrated at times when fishing was poor in Norwegian waters.

Similarly, although Norway is known for its great merchant fleet, only so many positions exist aboard her ships, and technology, over time, took over much of men's work. The children had to eat and many merchant seaman and fishermen were forced by circumstance to leave their families and go off alone, following the waters to America's fishing grounds. Sometimes the family followed; other times the father simply returned each year to visit. Some families, of course, left as a unit, especially if they had relatives who had already emigrated.

DECISIONS!

ONE PONDERS THE DECISIONS that had to be made by these emigrants. Where to go, what to bring, how to raise money for the passage? And when the family was a large one, how to decide which of the children to leave with which relatives? Many brought practical things that really mattered to them; others brought treasures that had been in their families for generations.

A 1998 cultural exhibit, curated by Severin Haines—son of emigrants from Karmøy, was held at the New Bedford Art Museum. It featured personal treasures brought over by Norwegian emigrants—many forms of *bunad* (the Norwegian regional attire), silver, jewelry, needlework, woolen sweaters, musical instruments, cutlery, dishes, cooking utensils, and an assortment of Norwegian paintings and handiwork, all lovingly used and cherished over the past century.

—*Courtesy, Dreyer Bok, Stavanger*

A Cunard Line passenger contract from Stavanger to New York in 1902 and signed by K. Torgersen.

Tysvaer in Southwest Norway, famous as the community that sent the first emigrants from Norway to America, has a small museum dedicated to the Norwegian emigrant. It tells the story of one family and its passage to these shores. It vividly shows the expatriate life of the Norwegian and features the famous trunk that so often is a symbol of emigration. Emigrants today look at that trunk and remember their own trunks filled to capacity with the simple treasures they moved to America.

Leaving the extended family behind is difficult under the best of circumstances, but in generations past it was complicated by the conditions aboard ship, dangers at sea, and poor communications. Unless men could work on the ship, and thus help pay their and their family's passage, they generally had to travel steerage class, later third class, which often was not a pleasant experience.

Sometimes they traveled directly to America and other times had to change ships in a port such as Liverpool, England. Saying goodbye and not knowing if the family would ever be reunited was extremely difficult for all

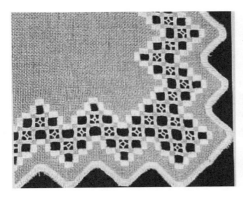

Sample of Hardanger embroidery.

—*AT photo*

Emigrant trunks. Promise of America exhibit, Tysvaer Culture House, Norway.

—*AT photo*

Children's toys brought over from Norway by Norwegian emigrants as displayed at the New Bedford Art Museum in 1998. This cultural exhibit was beautifully developed by Severin "Siggy" Haines.

—*National Park Service*

Advertisement for White Star emigrant ship from Liverpool to New York. Often Norwegians took a Norwegian ship to Liverpool and then a White Star liner to New York.

involved and also for their communities. The women had to carry on alone, and many towns in Southwest Norway, especially the island of Karmøy, became populated largely by women and children without men to help maintain the households.

GOODBYE-HELLO

WHEN AN EMIGRANT SAID GOODBYE, he also said hello to an uncertain future in a country known to him largely through rumors, letters and stories from others. It was often a heart-wrenching experience for all concerned, and for the people of Norway, it was one that had been repeated again and again since Viking days.

A first step in the emigration process was the trip to the port of embarkation. In the early days this might encompass a combination of horse-drawn carriages, ferries, small boats, wagons and walking. When the travelers arrived in the port city, arrangements had to be made to "settle in" until the ship arrived.

—*Photo by Dr. Hans-Eirik Aarek*

Cathedral of Saint Swithun, Stavanger, Norway, 2003, during a peace rally.

The day the ship was to sail, there was a special worship service at the historic Cathedral of Saint Swithun in Stavanger, to ask God's blessing on those who were leaving. Emigrants tell of passengers and friends, led by a clergyman, walking in a solemn march from the church to the departing ship.

Norwegians never resented those who left. They loved their countrymen and felt sad that they had to go elsewhere to survive. The emigrants were never considered quitters or thought of in any negative way. Quite the reverse—they invariably were considered Norwegians who lived in another country because their native land was poor and couldn't support them. Thus they were welcomed with great love when they returned home alone or visited as a member of a succeeding generation.

A contemporary Norwegian poet, Aleksander Hauge, describes this feeling in his beloved poem, "Song to Karmøy":

> *"If you've been away,*
> *we welcome you home!*
> *You'll still hear the ocean*
> *whip the rocks with foam*
> *and see Utsira, shielding the land,*
> *juniper meadows, the heather and sand."*

The passengers waved to the sobbing loved ones left behind on the quay. Flags flew from the ship and dock, but they grew apart as the ship left the harbor and became smaller and smaller on the western horizon to the refrain of their beloved national anthem, "*Ja, vi elsker,*" in Verse one:

> *"Yes, we love with fine devotion, this our land*
> *that looms rugged, storm-scarred over the ocean*
> *with her many homes.*
> *Love her, and in our love recalling those who gave us birth."*

As the ship steamed farther and farther out toward the North Sea, the music became fainter and fainter until all that could be heard was the lashing of the waves against the bow of the ship and the steady drone of the engines.

Then the music stopped altogether and the passengers could see the tiny, costumed figures pack up their musical instruments and leave. This was the moment when the passengers knew they had indeed left their beloved country and families behind. So, looking to the future, they turned to the work of unpacking and preparing their living space for the long journey ahead. And perhaps they had a cup of coffee together.

THE EMPTY HOME

FOR THOSE LEFT BEHIND, the loss of these friends and relatives now sailing into the North Sea was also becoming a reality and this reality was even more painful when they opened the doors to their empty homes. Often it is a small thing that symbolizes the shock of a loved one's absence. It can be the simple task of washing the cup last used that leads to tears. Surrounded by the remnants of packing and shipping, there was weeping, pain and emptiness of spirit in addition to many prayers and supplications—and perhaps more than a cup or two of coffee that evening.

The passengers on board had conflicted feelings: sad at leaving friends and loved ones, but also excited about their futures. In the early days, they did not speak the language of the Americans and they knew little about this land of opportunity. But one certainty when they stepped onto their ship was that they would see the Statue of Liberty when they entered New York Harbor and a near certainty was that they would live in the Bay Ridge section of Brooklyn. That was where Norwegians most often lived when they followed the waters to join America's commercial fishermen in the early part of the twentieth century.

CHILDHOOD MEMORIES

CHILDREN HAD LITTLE CHOICE in emigration; they had to go with their parents, or be left in Norway with their mother or another relative. I have often wondered what it would be like for such children. What were their feelings, their fears and joys?

Arnleif Jensen, born in Skudeneshavn and who now lives in America's South, remembers much of his early life in his personal memoir.

"I can't recall exactly when I learned that we were going to leave Skudeneshavn and go to live in America, but it had to be about the time of my eighth birthday, the end of January 1927. I vaguely remember Mother (who he called Mamma) and *Bestemor*, my grandmother, talking in hushed tones so

The Jensen family passport portrait taken in Skudeneshavn just before they emigrated, 1927.

my brother Aleck and I couldn't hear what they said. Then Papa showed up, and that's the time we learned what was going to happen. A flurry of activity started getting things packed or sold. And I understood Papa was making arrangements to sell the house to the town barber. Mother and *Bestemor* had to make arrangements for *Bestemor* because she was not going to travel with us. I believe Tante Gjertrude, my aunt, was going to give her a home. Aleck and I were told to continue at school until almost the day of departure, probably to keep us out from underfoot. Some big boxes and trunks were sent ahead to Stavanger, to be stored for loading on the *S.S. Stavangerfjord*, a passenger ship of the Norwegian American Line, which was expected to arrive in Stavanger in the latter part of March. I remember Aleck, Mother and I had to go to a photographer's shop to get a picture for the passport.

"Finally the great day came. We took the ferry from Skudeneshavn, each of us carrying suitcases and bags of stuff. The ferry terminal was near the Stavangerfjord berth. The minute we got to its main deck, we had to start down again as we could not afford first class, second class, or even third class. We had steerage tickets, the lowest class you could buy. I didn't realize the difference until I tried, without success, to explore the higher-class territories. But as I remember, it didn't really bother me to be in the cheapest territory; the thing that really was offensive was that we couldn't explore the upper-deck public areas. We could go on the main deck, but that was about all and we got to know that very well.

"Finally the ship got under way. It was a raw, cold day, but there were crowds of people on the dock to wave goodbye. Our ship backed away from the dock with the help of a tugboat. After turning around, it headed out of the harbor with several blasts of its deep bass horn. This had to be the most exciting thing that had happened in our young lives. And we remained on deck until we no longer could see land. The weather that first day wasn't too bad. When we had lost sight of land, the wind picked up, the waves got higher, and the ship began to roll a bit. It was a big ship so it wasn't bothered by the waves very much at that time. But during the night the wind had picked up even more. The next morning we went to the dining hall for steerage passengers and it was a large place, probably seating a hundred or more people. One of the stewards taking breakfast orders came to our table and we gave him our order: soft-boiled egg, bread and milk. When the egg came, and I cut the top off to eat it with a spoon, there was barely any white showing. I can't believe it had been in boiling water for more than a minute. We had been taught that we were to finish everything on our plate, but this time even Mother found it hard to set an example for us, so we all passed on the eggs and got by with the bread and milk. I did try one spoonful and almost gagged, and that was it for boiled eggs the rest of the trip. I never got seasick on any sea journey but the spoonful of almost raw egg brought me close.

"The weather continued to be bad: windy, rainy and stormy, which was typical of the North Atlantic at that time of year. The North Atlantic is hardly ever decent, weather-wise, but is especially bad in the winter and spring, according to Papa. The wind was strong and that made the waves high, and that made the ship roll. There were no stabilizers on passenger ships in those days, and people got sick. I think Mother was not feeling well for a day or two, but Papa and we boys didn't have any trouble.

"Some of the fascinating things that we found in the evenings were our very first movies. They were silent, of course, and didn't even have the piano accompaniment that silent movies had in America in those years.

"The next major event on our journey was the stop in Halifax, Nova Scotia. It was a Sunday, and when a newspaper vendor came aboard selling papers, Papa bought one. It contained a Sunday comics section. Aleck and I asked for that and we spread the paper out on the bed and 'read' the comics.

"It must have been the very end of March when we departed Norway and it took us two weeks to arrive in New York. That date was April 13th, Mother and Papa's anniversary."

THE EARLY DAYS

WHILE THE "SLOOPERS," the sailing ships that left Stavanger beginning in 1825 bound for the New World, took more than ninety days to reach New York, ships later in that century took about a month. The trip generally ranged from a minimum of eight or nine days into the mid-twentieth century. As one retired fishermen, Jacob Jacobsen, recalls: "I came from Torvastad on Karmøy and traveled alone to America in 1936. We went to Kopervik in my cousin's car and took the boat to Stavanger. I remember packing my confirmation suit for the trip to America. I was sixteen years old and was sad to leave, but since my father was in America, I looked forward to seeing him again.

"The boat went from Stavanger to Bergen to pick up more passengers and then went out in the North Sea to America. Almost immediately the weather got worse and worse and then came the storm, the worst they say in history, the storm of April in 1936. I was sick the whole time and we tried to lay out the storm for two days. I thought we had had it, but then came Easter morning and I heard the hymn with words referring to 'ending the sorrow' and I knew we would make it. And we did."

THE STATUE OF LIBERTY

AS THE EMIGRANTS APPROACHED New York Harbor, they could see, just off the bow to the starboard side, their new home—Bay Ridge, Brooklyn. As their ship moved into the harbor, "Miss Liberty," who reigned in torch-lit majesty on her own island, welcomed them. Her presence seems to dominate the whole harbor area and in many of the emigrants' eyes, she was also a close relative because she too was, indeed, a product of Norway.

The emigrants from Southwest Norway knew that, although the statue was a gift from France to America, it also represented Norway. On the windswept northwest coast of Karmøy lies the town of Vigsnes, a small, rocky and wildly beautiful village with several museums and a heather center. In the late 1800s, Vigsnes housed the largest copper mine in Northern Europe. The mine was owned by Charles DeFrance of Belgium and later by a French company. At its high point, it employed eight hundred miners and more than three thousand people lived in the town that developed around the mine. The copper from the Vigsnes mine was shipped to Belgium and then sold to France, where some of it became the skin of the Statue of Liberty. Although this story was always believed by Norwegians to be true, it was later proven at New Jersey's Bell Laboratories after they studied the Vigsnes ore and its

—*Courtesy of Aleksander Hauge, Vigsnes Copper Mine Museum founder*

The copper that originally sheathed the Statue of Liberty came from the Vigsnes copper mine on Karmøy, Norway. There is a sample of the ore attributed to Vigsnes at the statue today.

—National Park Service Photo

Lady Liberty.

properties. Thanks to the foresight and work of a grandson and son of a miner, poet Aleksander Hauge, there is now a museum at the mine site that both tells the story of the mine and its contribution to the Statue of Liberty.

Arnleif Jensen remembers the first time he saw the Statue of Liberty:

"We were approaching our goal, New York Harbor. Most of the passengers were out on deck for the exciting scenes and action coming up. I can remember looking at the southern coast of Long Island and wondering about the land. I could see beaches and some trees, but we were not close enough to see buildings, until we got farther in, approaching the Rockaways and Brooklyn. Someone pointed just off the port bow and then we could see the Statue of Liberty in the distance. It was a thrilling sight. Papa had told us about it. Of course, we were not headed for it as a destination, but for Ellis Island. This was the port of entry for most immigrants from all countries. People who traveled in first class went through customs at the dock in Manhattan, where the ship was to be berthed. Passengers like us had to go down a gangway to board a boat that carried maybe a hundred people at a time to Ellis Island.

"We were herded into this huge building, and into this very large room where there were dozens of desks. We were formed into lines, each one heading for a given desk. Because Papa and his family were citizens, we were told to go to a desk near the end of a big room. This was a privilege non-citizens were denied. The line at this desk was much shorter than the others. The clerks quickly perused the passports, compared the pictures in them with the faces before them, and asked a few questions. Papa answered these. But when it came time to write the names in his register, the clerk was, at Mother's request, changing the spelling of my first name, which in the passport was 'Arnleif.' Mother thought that sounded too foreign, so she thought she would do me a favor by changing it to 'Arnleiv,' which she thought would sound more American."

THE LIMPING WOMAN

One Norwegian woman just missed being shipped back to Norway. Her daughter, Toni Isaksen Johnson of Maine, tells it this way:

"My mother's name was Helga Marie Trondsen and she was raised near Oslo. She was offered a scholarship for college in 1910 when she was sixteen, but was too adventuresome and decided to come to America with her girlfriend, Clara. Before the ship landed, everyone was examined by the doctor and if not physically fit a chalk mark was put on the back of their clothing just before they got to Ellis Island. This 'X' meant they could not enter the port and would be sent back to their homeland. My mother was limping and the doctor checked her several times and could not find anything wrong with her leg. One day she was in the medical office and only the nurse was there. My mother asked if there was a shoemaker on the ship so that she wouldn't limp anymore as she had lost the heel on her shoe. The nurse could not stop laughing and thought it was so funny. Mother did not want to go back to Norway!"

Another Norwegian emigrant, my late aunt, the former Ellen Gurie Tollefsen, traveling on the *Aquitania*, recalled quite a pleasant passage to America: "I came over in the twenties on a luxury liner in one of the upper classes. Although it took me years to pay back the loan, it was a wonderful trip. When I got into New York, I was a whisked right through and two of my brothers met me, no trouble at all, and we went right to Brooklyn."

ELLIS ISLAND

ELLIS ISLAND was in service exclusively for immigration from 1892 to 1954, and those who came in this final migration from Norway often experienced Ellis Island before airlines took over as the favorite means of transportation.

Ellis Island was beset by many problems related to understaffing, politics and attitudes of the day, in addition to the changing, more restrictive quota

—*National Park Service Photo.*

Ellis Island today as seen in aerial shot showing shoreline of New Jersey at photo top.

laws. It also served as an internment center for foreign enemies during the war years and as a detention center for those who would be deported. Before the onset of World War I, almost a million immigrants came through each year. After this unpopular war, immigration was at a high point but new immigrants now had to face a more stringent and longer immigration process.

THE WASHTUB

STEPHEN SMALL, grandson of a Norwegian woman from Haramsøy in Northern Norway who arrived with her children to meet her fisherman husband in the mid-1920s, recalls the family story of his grandmother. "My mother was very excited about the trip, but my grandmother was never happy about emigrating. She didn't want to leave home. Besides luggage and clothing, she brought all her cherished possessions—including a galvanized washtub filled with dirt and plants. The Ellis Island officials told her she couldn't take plants off the ship, so a seaman threw the tub over the side and it floated on the waves. They watched it float away—their own piece of Norway in New York Harbor, and that became a moment of sadness and worry about what may come next."

At that time, emigrants had to pass a literacy test and a medical exam, offer evidence that they would not become a burden to the state, and be within the immigration quotas. The rules changed constantly, and one deficiency could send the would-be immigrant back to his native land.

Henry Curran, who served as commissioner of Ellis Island for three years, was very concerned about the immigration process because of the thousands of people who were returned to their countries. As he watched them being sent back on the very ships that brought them, he wrote: "Day by day the barges took them from Ellis Island back to their ships, back to the ocean to what? As they trooped aboard the big barges under my window, carrying their heavy bundles, some in their quaint, colorful native costumes worn to celebrate their first glad day in free America, some carried little American flags, most of them quietly weeping. They twisted something in my heart that hurts to this day."

The quotas became more and more restrictive. Another commissioner, Frederick Wallis, proposed that the inspection process be transferred to American consulates overseas. After 1924, the immigration process was moved to the American Embassies and overseas consulates where the emigrants were required to obtain visas and permits to work in America. After this change, only about half of the new immigrants passed through Ellis Island, and others entered through other seaports. The last documented

—*National Park Service*

Inspection card required for entry into America
at Ellis Island. This one is for a passenger sailing
from Christiana (Oslo) on the *Oscar II* in 1910.

"guest" on Ellis Island was in 1954 when a Norwegian seaman who had
outstayed his shore leave was detained before being shipped back on the ferry
to Manhattan.

AUTOMATIC CITIZENSHIP

IN THE EARLY PART OF THE CENTURY, those who had Norwegian
fathers who had become American citizens became citizens automatically. To
be a captain of a fishing boat, a man was required to be a citizen, and those
who aspired to skipper a boat took out American citizenship papers. Their
families then were "grand-fathered" in" under this process. Later years
brought different legislation, but in the first quarter of the century, this was a
principle that made a great difference in the lives of many Norwegian
emigrants. My own family was part of this process.

A retired fisherman recalls: "I was standing on the deck of the ship and a
friend of my father saw him waiting for me on the pier and pointed him out
to me. Since my father was a citizen, I was able to walk right through and not
have to go through Ellis Island."

It should be noted here that some Norwegians who were seamen took a
more unorthodox route to America. They came on merchant ships and
became assimilated into the Bay Ridge community. No one knows how many,
but there are stories of those who did just that—many of them young men
who "tried out America." Most who became serious about emigrating went
back by merchant ship and then returned the legal way. A few slipped through

Embarkation card issued to each emigrant by the ship's captain. Without it an emigrant could not leave the ship.

—National Park Service, Ellis Island Collection

the cracks. Such "creative immigration" appears to have been rare after Ellis Island became a reality, but it is said to have happened during World War II, when many Norwegian seamen were displaced. They often chose to join the American military and at the end of the war, it is said by emigrants, many were awarded American citizenship. Others married Americans and were granted citizenship because of the marriage.

—Courtesy Børge Solem

The *Stavangerfjord* leaves New York Harbor with the Statue of Liberty and Brooklyn Bridge in the background.

THE WELCOME

THE NEXT STEP after landing for most Norwegian emigrants was finding their relatives among the assembled crowd and then traveling to their first home, Bay Ridge. An appreciable part of Bay Ridge was Norwegian in language, churches, clubs, food, schools and culture, and it housed a large Norwegian community made up of fishermen, merchant mariners, those who worked on yachts and others connected to the sea, as well as carpenters.

Arnleiv Jensen remembers:

"After finishing the formalities at Ellis Island, which included a cursory health check, we were directed down to a dock where a ferry pulled in and we got on, with all our baggage. The ferry took us to Brooklyn, and I believe relatives met us. I think they hired a taxi to take us to Tante Malene's and Uncle Jack's house. Anyway, we finally arrived at their house at 7223 Sixth Avenue, and there we met cousins Vivian and Jackie. Theirs was a row house, and they lived on the second floor, having the first floor rented out. I can remember Jackie leading us upstairs with Aleck and me close behind. Jackie was trying to talk to us in English, and, of course, we didn't understand. To confound the situation, Aleck and I conspired and started jabbering in what we thought might be a fair imitation of English.

"…. We crowded in with the Johnsens for a few days while Mother and Papa were out looking for an apartment for us. I can remember being impressed by Vivian playing the piano, and hearing music on their Victrola, a hand-cranked one.

"Finally, Papa told us he had found an apartment around the corner on Seventy-second Street. It was a three-room place—small kitchen, living/dining room, a small bedroom for the parents, and a bathroom! This was luxury for us. Aleck and I had cots in the living room. And the school was right across the street, almost. This was a four-plex, and we managed fairly well. There were grocery stores a block or two away on Fifth Avenue, and McKinley Park was just another block away. And, of course, Mother had the support of Tante Malene and Vivian, who was twelve years old. We found the area fascinating because it was a big city place instead of the rural village we

Bay Ridge, Brooklyn. Third Avenue at Seventy-Fourth Street. Circa first third of twentieth century.

—Old photo

—Toni Isaksen Johnson archives

The Martin Isaksens.

had come from. Until we had to start school, which wasn't that long, we explored all around the neighborhood."

Toni Isaksen Johnson, now of Maine, remembers her mother's story when she arrived in New York from Norway: "My Mom already lived in Bay Ridge and she met my father, Martin Elias Isaksen, there. He came from Farsund, Norway, when he was seventeen. My Mom went back to Norway in 1916 to visit her family before she married. She got this trip instead of an engagement ring. It would be almost forty years before she was to visit there again. They married in 1916 and moved to New Jersey.

"They had nine children. My father was a deep-sea scalloper and his boat was named the *Cristeen* and built in 1883 as an oyster boat. He bought it in 1936 and rebuilt it into a scalloper. He was well-respected by other seamen and was called 'Captain Martin.' "

LIFE IN BROOKLYN

IN THE "History of the Norway Times (*Nordisk Tidende*), by Judy Gabriel Vinje, Norwegian emigration is described. "In 1900, Greater New York counted about 11,000 Norwegians, a number which rose quickly to 63,000 in 1930. The majority of them—23,000—lived in Brooklyn, the borough directly across the East River from Manhattan. The metropolis quickly became the most urban center of Norwegians outside Norway. The colony came to be affectionately called *myostkolonien*—after the Norwegian cheese *myost*."

Living in Brooklyn were carpenters, boat-builders and construction workers who labored on many of the great projects in a burgeoning New York City, such as the Brooklyn Bridge, skyscrapers and the subway system. The Brooklyn Navy Yard was a favorite place of employment for Norwegian emigrants who had shipbuilding skills.

According to the *Esso Perspektiv*, published in 1997 by *Esso Norge AS:*

"Norwegian-born engineers became famous for their work on skyscrapers, bridges, tunnels and subways. For example the Woolworth Building was designed by engineers Gunvald Aus from Haugesund and Kort Berle of Halden, and the Queens Midtown Tunnel in NYC was planned by Ole Singstad from Lensvik, Trondelag."

Women who worked had jobs as child-care workers, cooks, maids, nurse's aides and sometimes secretaries. Some of the enterprising young women took language courses and attended specialized schools. It was fairly easy to get a good job before the Depression. Scandinavians had the reputation for being good, loyal, honest and undemanding workers. They were considered to be very desirable labor who, in many cases came with skills already highly developed or, in other cases, were more than willing to learn new skills. They quickly found jobs and adjusted to their new lives. Their biggest adjustment was to city living with its inherent complications. It was as though folk from all over Norway had been rooted out of their simple villages, islands and farms and dropped into this huge foreign city. Bay Ridge, however, was as about as Norwegian as one could get in another country. Language, food, churches, clubs, bakeries, delicatessens, craft shops, social activities—all Norwegian.

Friendships were not only exclusively Norwegian but were drawn from those who shared the same region or town. People from Bergen befriended people from Bergen and joined the Bergen Club and their lives revolved around friends from their hometown. So it was also with those from Stavanger, Karmøy, Sørlendinger (people from the south of Norway), Oslo and Northern Norway. That is not to say that there was no "cross-pollination." Women and men from different sections of Norway did indeed meet and marry despite their differing dialects. Some even went so far as to marry a Swede, a German or an American. But Norwegians were preferred and the more local the better. If one family knew the other family or knew someone who did, that was *"fineste sort,"* a popular expression in Norwegian meaning "finest kind." Often the men went back to Norway to meet a prospective bride because so few women in America were considered suitable. Others were considered "foreigners."

To the American, the Norwegian was the foreigner; to the Norwegian in Bay Ridge, the American was the foreigner. Because parts of Brooklyn were so immersed in Norwegian culture, many Norwegians had limited contact with American cultural traditions and mores. The Bay Ridge women had the most contact with American culture in their work as housemaids, nannies or cooks. They learned about American taste, particularly the tastes of rich Americans, and that, indeed, added a great deal to their expectations in the culinary, home decorating, fashion and child-raising worlds. One recalled that for the first time she experienced foods such as "artichokes, fancy fruits and special cuts of meat." She learned to cook from the lady of the house, who introduced her to a whole new world of good food.

In those days, most Norwegian women who worked wore neat, attractive uniforms, were proud of their work and shared their experiences with each other while walking the children in their care through the lovely parks of Brooklyn and Long Island. But these young women also looked forward to shopping in the big city and seeing all the sights of this new world. The young women's weekend evenings were often shared with the Norwegian men at the local Norwegian clubs organized by people from different areas. They enjoyed picnics and dances and other activities that young people have always loved including many visits to Coney Island, the great amusement park of that day.

And much of this more protected social life occurred in the so-called "flapper era," which meant Prohibition, dancing the Charleston, and a bit of danger in Manhattan itself, as organized crime was rampant there.

The Norwegians met, dated, married, and started new families and sometimes moved on to other areas such as Long Island—and, if they were fishermen, to New Jersey or New Bedford. Some returned to Norway. Many Norwegian women were especially lovely by American standards and sometimes married the people for whom they worked. That was vividly illustrated in the 1950s with the marriage between a Kristiansand-born employee and a Rockefeller son. That was not the first such marriage, and not the last.

BAY RIDGE

MY OWN MOTHER and father lived in Bay Ridge for a while during the early years of their marriage. Mother vividly remembered her life there, after moving from her native New Bedford: "We were married in my family's home, located up on Acushnet Avenue, a mile north of Lund's Corner in New Bedford, and then we took the steamer from Fall River to New York, which in those days was an overnight trip. That was the favorite way to go to New York then. I had my honeymoon on that steamer, and the next day we got to Brooklyn, and I wondered if I were still in America.

"Everyone spoke Norwegian and I was in this big city with so many people and couldn't understand a word that was being said. We lived with Sig's family for a while, but because of the language and cultural differences and because we wanted our own private time and lives, we rented a little apartment for ourselves in a house owned by a lady from Nova Scotia, Mrs. Bickett. She was so nice and kind to me. I used to sit on her front porch and knit and talk with her when Sig was out fishing. Soon I was pregnant and went through my pregnancy in Brooklyn. Sig was out to sea most of the time, and I would walk down to the park to see if I could see his boat coming into the harbor. No one believed that I could find his boat, but I always did, and then I could estimate the time it would take him going into the Fulton Fish Market and then over to our apartment. He was out to sea so many days, and we saw so little of each other.

"That was the best time for us—when we could be alone together. It was a whole new world in Brooklyn and it was hard, very hard for me to be alone there in those days. I was desperately lonely and was a stranger in my own land. Except for Mrs. Bickett, I hardly heard English spoken."

People's lives often revolved around the activities at the church and there were two Norwegian churches to choose from—both Lutheran. One had a service in Norwegian and one appeared to be more pietistic than the other. Children went through Sunday school each Sunday to prepare for their confirmation and the church activities filled the lives of many Norwegian people during the first half of this century. One former Bay Ridge resident, Dorothy Olsen (Mrs. Ivar) of Troy, New Hampshire, said that while she was growing up her "life centered on the church, and her family did not participate in the social activities such as dancing, picnics and parties." It was like that for many pietistic families.

THE NORWAY TIMES (*NORDISK TIDENDE*)

THE NORWAY TIMES, then based in Bay Ridge, Brooklyn, was a vital link for the Norwegian community. In "The History of the Norway Times, From Seaboard Tabloid to Cultural Treasure" by Judith Gabriel Vinje, it is explained: "Like all immigrant newspapers of the time, it was a vital tool for newcomers. Besides serving as a guide to American life, opening windows to new experiences and hopes, it also kept alive the Norwegian connection, assuring contact between the old country and the new, and thereby lessening the immigrants' sense of dislocation. On a grass roots level, it promoted Norwegian cultural expression, helped foster the growth and activities of groups and organizations, and gave everybody something to talk about over *kaffe*. Sometimes that talk might grow quite heated, for the community was regularly involved in cultural schisms on issues ranging from politics to religion to alcohol. *Nordisk Tidende* reflected and sometimes even helped generate the heat in its columns.

"It also was a helping hand. Throughout all those early years, its pages provided many practical services, such as printing lists of boarding houses offering cheap room and board for newcomers. It fostered causes, it filled meeting halls, and it furthered literature, publishing poetry and works by new writers. Its church page carried inspirational messages, as it still does, and its ads were eagerly scanned for information vital to a new life, from the mundane to the crucial. In its pages were recorded the milestones of human life, from arrivals to departures, from births to deaths.

"Immigration from Norway dwindled to a mere trickle in the late 1920s and 1930s, and the use of the Norwegian language declined with the passing of each generation, but not in Brooklyn, the biggest Norwegian city outside

Bergen and Oslo. The connection to Norway was as close as the harbor, with Norwegian ships in port, and many residents who worked in shipping. The colony was often referred to as a suburb of Oslo or Bergen. At its height, there were clubs, choirs, festivals, churches and institutions. Norwegian was the language of the street, and *Nordisk Tidende* was the paper of record.

"The Brooklyn community was oriented to the sea and seafaring. There was always a strong whiff of the briny sea over the Norwegian colony in these early days," noted editor Andreas N. Rygg, editor and part owner of *Nordisk Tidende* from 1912 to 1929, and author of a history of the Brooklyn colony. Most of the people encountered had either been or still were sailors, or they were employed in shipyards, on harbor vessels, or in business having to do with shipping. In consequence thereof, a strong atmosphere of the sea prevailed.

"They (the Norwegians) went about their new lives 'with Norway in their hearts,' a phrase that summed up the blend of memories and sentiments that they experienced on the deepest level," according to historian Christen T. Jonassen.

THE DEPRESSION YEARS

FISHERMEN WORKED HARD during the Depression. Fish was in high demand because it was affordable, but the prices were low and no one had a lot of money. Emigrants were still coming into Brooklyn and money was difficult to come by for most other trades. Many good jobs were lost because construction slowed down or ceased. Those who had worked on yachts were left without work, as the rich lost their yachts after the market crash. Many of the rich who employed domestic staff lost their businesses and their homes. The poverty started to trickle down to Bay Ridge. It hit the settled Norwegians hard but conditions were almost impossible for the new emigrants. They had come with very little and that was used up quickly. The jobs normally available were no longer there for the asking. This was the Great Depression, the dramatic collapse of countless new dreams. Millions of Americans could not meet their housing costs and friends had nothing to give them as they were also in great distress.

One Norwegian woman, the late Margie Gustafson, remembered the horror of seeing many Norwegian women "sitting with their children on the sidewalk, surrounded by their furnishings, in front of their former homes." They were now homeless after being put out on the street for non-payment of rent. For those who had run out of options, the only place to live in Brooklyn during those awful years was in one of the shantytowns that were springing up all over America.

—Skudeneshavn, Norway, 1998. AT photo

My late cousin, Otto Olsen, with painting of a long liner in full sail out of New York City. He and Sadie Ben were onboard, circa 1930.

Many were called "Hooverville" or "Hoover City," after the president many blamed for the collapse of the economy. But the Norwegians had another name for Brooklyn's Hoover City. It was called "*Ørken Sur*," meaning sour desert. Here the new emigrants made makeshift homes out of boxes and pieces of metal and lived under the most primitive of conditions while they cooked what little they had to eat out-of-doors, regardless of the weather conditions. One former Bay Ridge resident remembered visiting a Norwegian friend there one day and was "appalled at the conditions." She remembers that Norwegian families were "sitting outside their makeshift homes in their old clothing" and were disillusioned with their emigrant experience and missing their homeland. "They had nothing," she remembers with pain. She recalled the smells of the cooking, and some less welcome smells as well. Although this place was not limited to Norwegians, many Norwegians had gathered there. The sight left an indelible impression upon all who saw it in those days.

One Norwegian widow, Serine Matland, now living in Fairhaven, remembers: "The fishermen were getting only half a cent a pound for yellowtail in those days and some skippers just went back out and dumped their catch."

THE FISHING GROUNDS

IN THE FIRST THIRD OF THE CENTURY, the whole commercial fishing industry was centered at the Fulton Fish Market, which was the central market on the East Coast. The fish were brought in on many types of

The *Cristeen*, once owned by Martin
Isaksen, is now restored and owned
by the Oyster Bay Historical Society,
New York. Now spelled *Christeen*,
she is the oldest fishing boat in
America and still used for special
events such as marriages.

—Photo courtesy Toni Isaksen Johnson

boats—long-liners, draggers, scallopers, and day-trippers. These were the
days before there was reliable refrigeration and fish was brought by boat from
other fishing ports to New York. There were good fishing grounds off New
York and south to Virginia, but the most reliable and fertile grounds were at
Georges Bank, located off the Massachusetts coast. Here the fish were
abundant because of the food produced by a unique combination of shallow
water, light and temperature, which was influenced by the reliable Gulf
Stream.

During fishing expeditions to Georges Bank, the fishermen were apt to go
into other ports such as Nantucket, Boston, New Bedford or Gloucester for
provisions, anchorage or repairs.

Writes Toni Johnson, daughter of the Norwegian skipper, Captain
Martin Elias Isaksen of the sloop *Cristeen* that fished out of the Fulton Fish
Market in New York, "When my father was out to sea, he planned on being
there for two to three weeks. He loaded the boat with two tons of ice for meat
and the scallops. In the summer he would be away for six weeks, as he'd go
where the scallops were. He would go to Cape May, New Bedford and
someplace in Maine where he would sell the scallops and load the boat with
supplies and enough food for eight men. He made his money in the summer
and had a good reputation. All winter long my Mom bought her food on
credit and cash was kept for emergencies. Then the first trip out after winter
my father was able to pay the whole bill."

COMING TO NEW BEDFORD

THE MEN WHO FISHED OFF GEORGES BANK stopped more and more in
the port of New Bedford because they found New Bedford to their liking, and
eventually buyers came into this port and as refrigeration improved, the
fishermen could sell fish there rather than go into New York. Then one or

two of the fishermen asked their families to come and visit them while they were there, and they did. They came, they saw, they liked and the families started to come up in the summer to New Bedford-Fairhaven in the late twenties and early thirties, rent an apartment or a house and enjoy this corner of New England with its beaches, fresh air and parks. After the heat and row houses of Brooklyn, the lack of green space and privacy, New Bedford-Fairhaven with its summertime treasures was a bit of heaven for them. And very important to the thrifty Norwegians was the cost of housing in the New Bedford-Fairhaven area. They could rent one floor of a house or a whole house for a fraction of what they paid for a smaller place in Brooklyn. Rent averaged five dollars a week in New Bedford and it was at least five times that in Brooklyn. New Bedford-Fairhaven looked better and better to them, and as more and more Norwegians came, it became the place that most preferred to live.

A Norwegian fisherman named Kris Olsen, known as "Kris Pase," now deceased, recalled in 1996: "In 1932, I fished out of Brooklyn, did long-line fishing for cod and I brought them back alive. In 1933, I came up to New Bedford. Six scallopers were already there, including *Anastasia*, *Valencia* and *Isabelle*. I lived in a rooming house near the docks where the telephone company is now. It was owned by a Mrs. Frankel and was about five dollars a week. Later had a place that was seven a week with two rooms together. I found work at the barrooms and met people there."

Also, there were elements of New Bedford-Fairhaven that reminded them of Norway—especially the narrow streets, old buildings, wooden houses, gardens, and water views everywhere. The city's residents were friendly and accustomed to people with accents. Yes, the Norwegian fishermen and their families liked New Bedford, but they loved the small town across the river, Fairhaven, even more.

A GRANDSON REMEMBERS

STEPHEN SMALL RECALLS a typical story of this change in location.

"In the late twenties my grandfather, Hans Haram, made arrangements for his family to go to New Bedford. He and another guy bought a lobster boat and lobstered out of New Bedford. He worked very hard and eventually bought a dragger. They dragged from the sides using old fishing schooners. The boat designs were less refined then."

As the fish refrigeration processes were refined and fish could be shipped to New York, the men began to fish out of New Bedford-Fairhaven more often, and the families, who had once visited and enjoyed New Bedford-Fairhaven, now came up there to live all year and encouraged their relatives and friends to come as well.

—AT photo.

Serine Matland of Fairhaven, Massachusetts: A twentieth century emigrant and widow of two Norwegian fishermen, she still has her lovely smile and gracious demeanor.

Serine Matland, the widow of two skippers, recalled her move to Fairhaven during her first marriage. "We married in Brooklyn, but fishing was bad and we needed to make a living, so we came to New Bedford. We lived in six rooms in North Fairhaven for only five dollars a week. The building had several floors and was over a bar, but they didn't bother us at all. My mother lived on one of the other floors. Later we bought the home I live in today for $3,300. Everyone was so close in those days and we all knew each

—The Otto Olsen Archives, Skudeneshavn, Norway

The New Jersey branch of the family. Uncle Karl Sigvart Tobiassen, second from left front, our Santa Claus, and owner of the *North Star*, shown here with cousin Otto Olsen and Norwegian friends.

other well. We walked the baby carriages to the dock and met the boats there, and we talked with each other and caught up on the news."

My family, who in the twenties lived in New Bedford part of the year and Brooklyn the other part, fell right into this pattern. This also was the time when the Norwegians became very involved in the scallop industry and fished for scallops in the summer on Georges Bank. By the late thirties, there were many Norwegian families throughout the New Bedford-Fairhaven area, and Fairhaven increasingly was the town they came to when they came from Norway to fish.

The other port frequented by Norwegians was Atlantic City, where there was an enclave of fishermen from Karmøy. They also fished out of the Fulton Fish Market and sometimes summered in New Bedford-Fairhaven where the families visited relatives while their husbands fished on Georges Bank. I remember one summer when I visited my great-uncle from Atlantic City who had rented a home on Arnold Street, across the street from my mother's sister's home.

Norwegians soon found that as their expenses decreased as a result of moving to Massachusetts, their savings increased. Support services started to develop, such as a Norwegian-owned ship supply store, a Norwegian-owned bakery, and eventually a Norwegian-owned propeller shop and other marine-related shops. New Bedford-Fairhaven became the port-of-choice as many of the fishermen and the families settled happily there and prospered. They then started to dream about the futures for their children—their education, their church and all of those community activities that made life cohesive, productive and happy for the Norwegian. Life looked very good for them in New Bedford-Fairhaven, *Amerika*, and letters were sent to Norway asking that more relatives come over and help out because everything looked "*fineste sort*," "finest kind."

But it would not be "finest kind" for all in the years to come. The terrible price paid in human life for this new prosperity would be more than any community could afford.

Legacy & Folklore

NATIONAL ANTHEM
OF NORWAY

Ja, Vi Elsker Dette Landet

Ja, vi elsker dette landet,
Som det stiger frem,
Furet, værbitt, over vannet,
Med de tusen hjem.
Elsker, elsker det og tenker
På vår far og mor
Og den saganatt som senker
Drømme på vår jord, Og den saganatt som senker
Senker drømme på vår jord,

Norske mann i hus og hytte,
Takk din store Gud!
Landet ville han beskytte
Skjønt det mørkt så ut.
Alt hva fedrene har kjempet,
Mødrene har grett,
Har den Herre stille lempet,
Så vi vant vår rett, Har den Herre stille lempet,
Så vi vant, vi vant vår rett.

—*AT photo*

Antique homes in Skudeneshavn, Norway

Ja, vi elsker dette landet,
Som det stiger frem,
Furet, værbitt over vannet,
Med de tusen hjem!
Og som fedres kamp har hevet
Det fra nød til seier
Også vi når det blir krevet,
For dets fred slår leir, Også vi når det blir krevet,
For dets fred, dets fred slår leir.

—AT photo

Skudeneshavn waterfront view looking out to the former Tollefsen home.

Yes, We Love This Country

Yes, we love this country (land) which rises up, rugged and weathered, above the sea, with its thousands of homes. Love it, love it and think about our mothers and fathers and the saga of past ages that sends dreams to our earth, and the saga of past ages.

That sends dreams, sends dreams to our earth. Norseman, in house and cabin, thank your great God!

It was His will to protect the country although things looked dark. While fathers fought and mothers cried, Our Lord quietly opened the way.

So that we won our right. Our Lord quietly opened the way So that we won, we won our right. Yes, we love this country which rises up, rugged and weathered, above the sea, with its thousands of homes. And as our fathers' struggle has raised it from distress to victory. We also, when called upon, will strike a blow for its peace. We also, when called upon, will strike a blow for its peace, its peace.

First performed in 1864. Eight verses
Words by Bjørnstjerne Bjørnson, 1832–1910

2

Yesterday's Tides:
Norway and Straumfjord

A CHRONOLOGICAL PERSPECTIVE

—Courtesy Arthur Moniz, Arthur Moniz Gallery, New Bedford

New Bedford's historic waterfront showing the view of New Bedford that the fishermen saw just after coming into port. The New Bedford Ship Supply on the right was owned by Sally and Rasmus Tonnessen and was second home to many Norwegian fishermen as well as the source for all their gear. Rasmus (Ray) often put up the guarantee for the young men to come to America and Sally and Ray felt a responsibility for these young men while they were here.

STRAUMFJORD

THE FINAL NORWEGIAN EMIGRATION, as it is known, occurred between the mid-twenties and the late sixties in the twentieth century. But it was not, according to some thinking, the first Norwegian emigration to Buzzards Bay and its environs, which includes the Greater New Bedford area.

—*AT Photo*

The first emigration to America from Norway in 1825 was celebrated by the issuance of this special American stamp in 1925, featuring the slooper, *Restauration*. It marked the one hundred year anniversary of the sailing.

The slooper, *Restauration*, is displayed at the Norwegian Emigration Center, Stavanger, Norway by this model.

Author Paul Schneider points out in his historical treatise on the Buzzards Bay area, "The Enduring Shore," that in the last part of the first century: "The Vikings, say those who believe they actually sailed this far south, called the whole Buzzards Bay-Vineyard Sound area, Straumfjord, or Bay of Currents." This concept, which is from one of the many interpretations of the Norse Sagas, is cited in "The Story of Cuttyhunk" by Louise Haskell.

Indeed Straumfjord was well named as these currents, storms and inevitable unpredictability caused Norwegians many problems over the years. Nineteen centuries later in the very area their forbearers may have explored, the fishermen of the final twentieth century migration sailed out to the abundant seas to ply their trade. Their work produced great wealth and great loss, great joy and great sorrow, great success and great failure, great courage and great waste, great faith or loss of faith.

NORWAY

Despite their cultural and geographic differences, the Kingdom of Norway and the Massachusetts southeast coastal area of Greater New Bedford have many common ties—the influence of the Quaker religion, a mutual maritime history, oil, and strong, independent women whose skilled seafaring men were away for long periods of time.

Norway is a relatively young country in terms of national identity and was isolated from much of European history—the Roman Empire, the various conquests and wars that divided Europe, and indeed the Renaissance and the Industrial Revolution. Its isolation is best evidenced by the lack of castles and grand homes.

The people of the land, now known as the Kingdom of Norway, made their mark over most of the known world for several hundred years by sea. During the last part of the first century A.D., The Norwegian Vikings had an important role in the development of the British Isles, including Ireland, England, Scotland and the Northern Islands. Vikings also settled what is now Normandy, France (Normandy meaning Men from the North), and their explorations and settlements influenced the history of Iceland, Greenland and North America.

The first known ancestors of today's Norwegians were prehistoric hunters and farmers who arrived in what is now Norway after the last Ice Age and intermarried with others who settled there through the sixth century A.D.

800–1050: Norwegian Vikings began almost three hundred years of raiding, settling in areas of Western Europe and governing in the British Isles. Southern and western Norway were overpopulated and it was from these areas that the Vikings sailed. In fact, they sailed from some of the same waters and islands that the emigrants did when they sailed to America some nine centuries later. Many emigrants to New Bedford came from the island of Karmøy, between Haugesund and Stavanger in Southwest Norway, where the last Viking king died.

The Viking story was often told from the vantage point of those who were defeated, but we should also remember that the known world in those days was a violent place. Vikings were berated in history for their raids and destruction of life and property as well as their theft of valuables and capturing of peoples. Little else was known except for stories from the Icelandic Sagas because many artifacts from those pagan days are said to have been destroyed by early Christian monks in Norway.

Recent excavations, however, are beginning to show more about the way people lived and they portray a more domestic side of Viking life. An article on Vikings in the May 2000 edition of National Geographic Magazine pointed out that: "Many scholars now believe that the Vikings actually enriched rather than eroded established European civilizations. They raided monasteries because that was where the money was. But the Norsemen were also astute merchants and politicians who expanded European horizons. They were craftsmen, shoemakers, blacksmiths, poets, and aesthetes who designed ships of noble proportions. They founded towns, created settlements, ruled in areas of Ireland, England, Scotland and Iceland and explored parts of the North Atlantic."

The area around York, England—near the original home of many of the Pilgrims who settled Plymouth, Massachusetts—was basically Viking territory for many years. People from that area still boast of their Viking ancestry and Nordic features. There is a restored Viking settlement in York, and many Viking artifacts have been found in the area.

Ireland has a three hundred year history with the Vikings. A popular belief shared by present-day Norwegians is that: "The Vikings brought back the most beautiful Irish women for slaves and that is one of the reasons why the Norwegian women are so lovely today." Norwegians founded Dublin, Ireland, and many people from coastal Ireland can trace their ancestry to the Norsemen of old.

Irish slaves brought by the Vikings to Iceland later intermarried with the Norsemen and are genetically linked to Icelanders of today who show much Celtic blood in their DNA.

Up to this time, there were many unrelated Viking kingdoms in Norway. Harald I conquered several such kingdoms and united Norway. The climactic battle was in the Hafrsfjord near Stavanger.

985: Eric the Red led Viking settlers to Greenland. A few years later his son, Leif Erickson, whose name is spelled in many different ways, became the first European to explore North America. According to the May 2000 edition of the National Geographic, "Leif wintered in a place he called Vinland (Vineland) where he found grapes, salmon streams and pastures, then returned to Greenland in the spring. His brother Thorvald launched his own journey years later. He was the first European to encounter native Americans, whom the Norse called Skraelings, and the first to die at their hands, shot with an arrow. His last words allegedly were, 'We have won a fine and fruitful country, but will hardly be allowed to enjoy it.'"

990: King Olav I was converted to Christianity in England, and subsequently converted his countrymen in Norway by force. His successor, King Olaf II, continued his work.

1349–1350: An outbreak of plague killed more than half the people of Norway, weakening the country severely and making Norway more dependent upon other countries to feed its population.

1397: Norway came under Danish rule.

1536: Lutheranism became the official state religion.

1814: After 417 years of Danish rule when Danish was the official written language, Norway was ceded to Sweden as a prize of the Napoleonic Wars. Sweden crushed a revolt aimed at Norwegian independence, but the Norwegians wrote their first constitution on May 17 and that is regarded as their first step toward independence from rule by neighboring countries.

1821: The beginning of Norwegian emigration to America.

CLENG PEERSON

Important events in Norway's history seem to originate in the Stavanger area, and emigration was no exception. According to the Norwegian Emigration Center in Stavanger, "The Quaker community from Tysvaer, just north of Stavanger, sent Cleng Peerson (also known as Klein Pedersen Hesthammer, born on May 17, 1783) and another man, Knud Olsen Eide, who died after arriving in America, to learn about opportunities for the community to settle in America."

Peerson's Quaker group had decided that the New World might be a place where he and his fellow members of the Society of Friends might practice their faith without persecution. It was not an original thought, but one that had occurred in the minds of many oppressed people with the discovery of the new world. The Pilgrims from England founded Plymouth, Massachusetts, with the same ideal, to have freedom of religion and freedom from a state-dominated church.

In 1824, Cleng Peerson, who became known as the "Father of Norwegian Emigration," went back to Norway and spoke of the good prospects he had seen in America. It was decided that a group should travel, and Cleng went back to America to prepare for their arrival. On July 4th, 1825, fifty years after America's independence: "The fifty-four-foot sloop *Restauration* set sail from Stavanger, bound for New York, USA. Almost three months later, on October 9th, the sloop and its fifty-two passengers from the southwestern part of Norway anchored in the port of New York. The Sloopers, as these pioneers of Norwegian emigration are called, because they sailed on a sloop, were Quakers and Haugeans who were persecuted for their religious beliefs in Norway and sought freedom in America."

According to Michael Holmboe Meyer, a writer in Stavanger, Norway, "People thought it was pure madness when the fifty-two emigrants set out from Stavanger harbor July 4, 1825. They left on the *Restauration* for their ninety-eight-day voyage to the New World. There was a rumor of sea monsters and other things in the Atlantic Ocean. But they made the journey. It is said that there was no drinking water by the end of the voyage, and by chance they found a barrel of wine in the sea." This wine sustained them for the trip and, in essence, may have saved their lives.

According to the Norwegian Emigration Center, Cleng Peerson came from Tysvær, and met the Sloopers when they landed in New York on October 9, 1825. They moved to northern New York State and settled in Kendall Township on land purchased by Peerson. The settlement became a stopover on the way to the Midwest, where most of the Sloopers established a colony in the Fox River Valley of Illinois.

Peerson's role in bringing Norwegians to Texas is discussed in a report in "News of Norway," provided by the Norwegian Royal Embassy. An article in the September, 1997, issue tells of festivities in the city of Clifton, south of Dallas: "The first immigrants settled west of Clifton, founding the Norse community in 1854. When eight couples arrived from east Texas, they traveled to this part of the country that greatly resembled the 'old country' and where free land was offered. Peerson is buried in the Norse Cemetery by Our Savior's Lutheran Church."

Emigration continued throughout the century, with the majority of Norwegians settling in Minnesota, Wisconsin, the Dakotas and other Midwestern states. But a considerable number of merchant seamen, fishermen and carpenters, most thought to be from Norway's coastal areas, settled in Brooklyn and Manhattan. There was also a great need for carpenters and other laborers in New York.

In the hundred years that followed the voyage of the *Restauration*, some 800,000 Norwegians immigrated to the New World. Today there are more people of Norwegian descent in the United States than in Norway itself, where the current population is more than four million.

1905: Norway became an independent nation, separating from Sweden's rule. Denmark's Prince Karl was invited to be King of Norway. He accepted, taking the name Håkon VII. The present King Harald V is his grandson. Their independence was achieved from Sweden by threat of war. Many young men in Norway were part of a standoff with Sweden on the Swedish border when a war for independence loomed. According to my father's cousin, Tobias Høynes, of Skudeneshavn, Norway, my grandfather, Sivert, was one of them.

Just about this time, when Norway finally became independent, there was also a great shortage of fish in Norwegian waters. Men left their homes to go to America to fish and live in the Brooklyn community. They commuted back and forth to Norway, as did my grandfather a few years later.

King Håkon VII, Norway's first king after independence from Sweden in 1905. His great-grandson Crown Prince Håkon will be Norway's next king and he will be followed by the first queen in hundreds of years, the Royal Princess Ingrid Alexandra.

LA REINE DE NORVÈGE
FILLE DE ROI D'ANGLETERRE

—*Photo of unknown origin*

Queen Maud of Norway was married to Håkon VII, first king of Norway after its independence from Sweden in 1905. She was the granddaughter of Queen Victoria of England and daughter of Victoria's son, The Prince of Wales (later King Edward VII) and Queen Alexandra (formerly of Denmark). Queen Victoria's many grandchildren became part of other royal families throughout Europe. Maud and Håkon were the parents of King Olaf V, who is the father of the present King Harald V. Consequently there are strong ties between the United Kingdom and Norway.

1920: After the First World War, Norwegians, many with relatives in America, emigrated to Brooklyn, and later to New Bedford. The fishing industry grew there, and the scallop industry developed and flourished.

1940: Germany invaded Norway and quickly controlled the country. King Håkon VII and the cabinet fled to London, where they maintained a government-in-exile, and a pro-Nazi government was installed in Norway. During this time some members of the royal family lived in exile in America, including the present King Harald and his sisters, the Princesses Ragnhild and Astrid. They summered in South Dartmouth, Massachusetts, just outside New Bedford.

1945: Germany surrendered and Håkon VII returned to Oslo in triumph. This was the beginning of the largest immigration to New Bedford. There are no accurate figures because of the habit of going back and forth (*pendling*). Estimates are based on the number of boats, the size of the families and people making shorter stays. It is believed that as many as five thousand Norwegians passed through or stayed in the New Bedford area from 1924 to 1975. One fishing boat owner and captain who was active in the community estimates that as many as fifteen hundred Norwegian fishermen and their families lived in or around New Bedford at any given time in the 1960s.

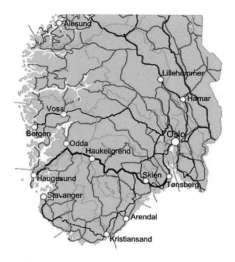

Late 1960s–1970: Norway's economy expanded greatly as a result of petroleum and natural gas production in the North Sea. About one-third of the Norwegians in the New Bedford area returned to Norway, one-third went on to Seattle/Alaska, where enterprising Norwegian fishermen found ways to make much more money, and the other third stayed in New Bedford.

South, Southwest, and Western Norway, home to many emigrants. Some were from islands in the North, but many were from the area between Stavanger and Haugesund.

The emigration stopped. The need was no longer there as Norway was now a very wealthy country and able to invite refugees and immigrants from other countries to live there. Some of these new citizens were the children or grandchildren of Norway's emigration to America, but others came from Eastern Europe, Asia, the Mideast and a few from Africa.

NEW BEDFORD, MASSACHUSETTS

MY MOTHER'S HALF OF OUR FAMILY had deep roots in New England, dating back to the Pilgrims in Plymouth and Ben Franklin's maternal grandparents, the Folgers of Nantucket. I have heard stories throughout my life about the world of the early Yankees—a world focused more on religion than anything else. Wealth never seemed very important to them; living righteously did. Mother's family had Unitarian, Quaker and Congregational roots and was fairly typical of New Bedford-area people of that time. Mother always told us that we had ancestors who whaled and were on schooners. She often recalled childhood memories of sitting on the knee of the legendary "Captain Jeb" Tilton who would come to visit her family and who was always covered with coal soot from his boat. He told her many stories of the sea. But she also remembered that her mother had to clean and clean after he left. Everything seemed covered with coal dust. And there were many stories about

—*Old postcard*

Pleasant Street, New Bedford, first third of twentieth century, looking north. It looks much the same today, except for the traffic.

the Seamen's Bethel where both grandmother and grandfather sang each Sunday. There were seafaring men on both sides of our family.

When one thinks that New Bedford's architecture itself was modified to provide a vantage point for families of seafaring men—the so-called "widow's walks"—one can appreciate the importance of the sea to early settlers in New Bedford.

NEW BEDFORD MILESTONES

Early 1600s: British Captain Bartholomew Gosnold explored the shores, rivers, fields of the area where New Bedford and its suburbs would exist in the future. The land at the time was inhabited by the Wampanoag Indians.

1620: Pilgrims settle in Plymouth, Massachusetts.

1652: Colonists from Plymouth Colony purchased more than 115,000 acres of land along the Southeast coast of Massachusetts from the Wampanoag tribe.

1664: Old Dartmouth was established and consisted of farms and scattered villages that comprised what are now Acushnet, Dartmouth, Fairhaven, New Bedford (then called Bedford Village) and Westport.

—*Courtesy Ralph Brown*

Scrimshawed scene of Union and Purchase Streets, Old New Bedford, on 8½-inch whale tooth. This tooth was adjacent to the whale's tooth buried with President Kennedy and is part of the Ralph Brown collection.

1700s: Bedford Village, as part of Old Dartmouth, was located along the banks of the Acushnet River and by the 1750s it had become Old Dartmouth's

45

business center. Many Quakers stayed and became leaders of the town. In 1765, Joseph Rotch, a Quaker from Nantucket, moved to Old Dartmouth. He and Joseph Russell provided capital to spur the whaling industry forward.

It is ironic that the first Norwegian emigrants to America were Quakers in search of religious freedom and that another group of Quakers sought religious freedom from Puritan oppression to settle in Bedford Village in the seventeenth century. All of them cherished religious liberty and did not want to pay for the maintenance of a state church. Quakers were individualists who were hard-working, thrifty and encouraged business. Such traits are typical of Norwegians as well. The Quakers were largely responsible for the development of the waterfront, shipping and fishing out of New Bedford, and the Norwegian emigrants followed these same pursuits when they began arriving almost three centuries later.

New Bedford officially became a town in 1747 and the hundred thousand acre tract of Old Dartmouth became three towns: Dartmouth, New Bedford (which still included Acushnet and Fairhaven) and Westport. The Revolutionary War and the War of 1812 slowed its growth. During the Revolutionary War the British marched down Union Street—burning as they marched.

The 1800s: Melville wrote, "New Bedford rose in terraces of streets. Huge hills and mountains of casks on casks were piled upon her wharves, and side by side the world-wandering whale ships lay silent and safely moored at last." But the British blockade of American ports during the War of 1812 prevented whaling ships from leaving New Bedford Harbor.

New Bedford broke away from Dartmouth and Acushnet and was incorporated as a city in 1847 during the height of its prosperity as a whaling center. The New Bedford Standard-Times refers to Melville and those days: "Here he found a prosperous port (population 12,000) and a waterfront that throbbed of rough-and-tumble sailing types from around the world. Of seven hundred fifty vessels registered in the harbor, probably two hundred fifty were whalers." Whaling was the source of New Bedford's great prosperity

—*Courtesy Arthur Motta, Director of Tourism, New Bedford*

The Official Seal of New Bedford showing its identification to the harbor as well as its churches. The motto "We diffuse light" is thought by most to refer to the whaling industry supplying whale oil to light the lamps of the world, while others feel it may refer to the Quaker religion.

during its glory days in the early 1800s. Whalers sailed all over the world and their trips lasted up to seven years away from home.

New Bedford became a city populated by women with families to manage alone and, as in Norway, the Yankee women in New Bedford became very strong, independent, hard-working and self-reliant women. Noticing New Bedford women, Melville wrote, "The women of New Bedford, they bloom like their own red roses. But roses only bloom in summer; whereas the fine carnation of their cheeks is perennial as sunlight in the seventh heaven."

They became independent because their husbands were away for such long periods of time, were sometimes seriously injured and/or didn't return. Dr. David S. Martin, formerly of New Bedford, recalls the adventures of one whaling ship. "I once did an analysis of the log of a whale ship—the *Emily Morgan*, sister ship of the *Charles W. Morgan*. They (the whalers) left New Bedford in 1859 and returned in 1863—went out to the Pacific up and down a couple of times and ended up in the Sea of Okhotsk, facing the east coast of Hokkaido, in Northern Japan, survived a near-mutiny, and had someone fall from the rigging to his death in heavy seas in the South Atlantic."

Quakers at this time were also largely responsible for the growing Underground Railroad movement of the mid-1800s, when slaves were brought up through the northern states to Canada.

I remember as a child hearing stories passed down since the Civil War about the cave at the top of Durfee Street in New Bedford, at the junction of Rockdale Avenue. The legend was that this cave was part of the Underground Railroad and that slaves had been hidden there waiting escort to their next stop. We were afraid to go into the cave but it was discussed very often and we felt that made New Bedford an important part of history. We loved biking to that street because the Durfee Street hill was the one low-traffic hill that was high enough and safe enough to speed down without touching the handlebars.

David Martin recalls these youthful adventures: "I remember the cave vividly and riding my bike up to view it and finally screwing up enough courage to really crawl inside, even though it was only a bit more than a few inches above the head if you were on your belly. Of course, I have no documentation of it being part of the Underground Railroad, but remember it being told to me as such."

In a New Yorker magazine article of April 23, 2001, Louis Menand described the New Bedford of the mid-1800s as "an enviable city." Menard declared: "Two characteristics distinguished the principals in the New Bedford whaling firms: They were mostly Quakers, and they tended to intermarry. Quakerism conduced thrift; intermarriage conduced to acculturation; and the consequence was that, by the 1850s, New Bedford was the wealthiest community, per capita, in Massachusetts, and one of the wealthiest in the United States."

—Old Map

New Bedford's bustling waterfront at the turn of the century. Note combination of both masted vessels and power-driven vessels.

David Martin also recalled that some of his family were Quakers. "My paternal great-great-grandmother (who lived in the mid-nineteenth century) was a faithful Quaker, as was her daughter, my great-grandmother, Emily Frances Sisson, who married my great-grandfather, Henry Martin, and wore a Quaker bonnet to 'meeting' each Sunday. I have a photograph of her and her daughter, my great-grandmother, sitting in Apponegansett Meeting House on Russells Mills Road in Dartmouth, posing for a picture, with her wearing the black bonnet. When my father passed away, we had some family heirlooms, including that very beautiful shiny bonnet and her wedding dress, which was gray."

In our family, we would often hear stories about New Bedford's grandeur. I remember my grandmother talking about the beautiful parks of the late 1800s, and there were stories from her mother and father's recollections dating back to the mid-1800s. She told of huge mansions that had since burned down, beautiful parks and opulent gardens. There was a sunken garden at Buttonwood Park, and even in our day the gardens at Hazelwood Park were impressive. Melville wrote of New Bedford's beauty in those days: "Nowhere in all America will you find more patrician-like houses, parks and gardens more opulent, than in New Bedford. Go and gaze upon the iron emblematical harpoons round yonder lofty mansion. Yes, all these brave houses and flowery gardens came from the Atlantic, Pacific and Indian oceans."

Many of New Bedford's residents lost their lives fighting in the Civil War. The whaling industry also declined due to the sinking of many of its ships in Charleston Harbor where they were loaded with rocks and sunk to make it difficult for the Confederates to enter or leave the harbor. They were known in history as the "stone fleet."

Many sailors also deserted the fleet for the gold rush and the ships were simply abandoned on the West Coast. In addition, much of the fleet was frozen in the Arctic. The discovery of oil and the consequent decline in the demand for whale oil marked the end of New Bedford's glory days.

New Bedford has as its motto, *"Lucem diffundo"* ("I diffuse/spread light") and indeed for many years, New Bedford's whale oil lit the lamps of the world. Some feel that the motto also means that New Bedford set a fine example to the world.

NEW ERA

TEXTILE MANUFACTURING took up the economic slack left by the decline of the whaling industry, and new immigrants arrived to compete for the new jobs. Groups of newcomers arrived from England's mill cities, such as areas around Liverpool. They clustered in the South End of New Bedford near the ocean. New Bedford, a long narrow city following the course of the Acushnet River which emptied into the Buzzards Bay and unlike other early American cities because of this design, became a city of ethnic neighborhoods, with Yankee, English, Irish, Canadian, French, Polish and Portuguese (mainly from the islands) inhabitants, complete with their own churches, schools, culture, language and stores.

New Bedford and Lowell became the centers of the state's textile industry in the late 1800s and early 1900s. As the industry grew, it literally reshaped New Bedford. From the waterfront one can still see New Bedford framed by its mills and the tenements where its mill workers lived. There was also an influx of Roman Catholics from several European countries, and their ornate churches with the tall steeples started to dominate New Bedford's skyline.

The 1900s: New Bedford had seventy textile mills in the early twentieth century, but the Great Depression of the 1930s devastated the textile industry and one by one they headed south, closer to the source of materials, along with their management talent. And if that was not enough to change New Bedford forever, 1938 brought a legendary hurricane that

Old postcard showing New Bedford's vital downtown area at night. Looking south from William and Purchase Streets in the first third of the twentieth century.

destroyed numerous homes, killed many people and devastated the water-front. It severely damaged whole neighborhoods and industries near the shore and throughout the city. It hit at high tide and there was a large tidal surge. We all heard stories of how the whole downtown area was flooded and we saw the remnants of the houses and other buildings that the water had taken so ferociously out to sea.

The National Weather Service reported in its "Summary of the 1938 Hurricane": "The hurricane was responsible for 564 deaths and at least 1,700 injuries in southern New England. Damage to the fishing fleets in southern New England was catastrophic. A total of 2,605 vessels were destroyed, with 3,369 damaged. Sections of Falmouth and New Bedford, Massachusetts, were submerged under as much as eight feet of water."

Those of us who grew up in the 1940s remember the destruction we saw everywhere. It was very common to see the remains of a fireplace standing by itself in a grassy field, or crumbled sea walls at the beaches, or a broken roller coaster, bleaching in the sun like a fractured sea monster, in what was once an family amusement paradise called Acushnet Park, near Fort Rodman.

Fishing became an important industry after the 1920s, and scalloping, New Bedford's specialty, flourished under the expertise of the Norwegian fishermen. Sailing schooners and wooden boats eventually gave way to today's steel, diesel-powered draggers and scallopers.

1940–45: During World War II there was no emigration from Europe to America, but the New England factories supporting the war effort were

—Old postcard

New Bedford High School on County Street. As we walked up these front steps each morning we never knew that this building resembled the Royal Palace in Oslo.

working around the clock and there was a dramatic influx of women on the nation's assembly lines. German submarines infested the waters around the New Bedford area and the Atlantic sea-lanes causing a severe threat to the fishermen and shipping. Many Norwegian fishermen took an active role in spotting submarines and reporting them to the U.S. Navy. Many had families stranded in Norway under German occupation.

1945–1969: After 1940, according to an EPA study, "The Post Textile Period had high unemployment in the first half of the period, a decline in population as workers left to find jobs elsewhere, and diversification of industry. New Bedford responded by refocusing on its connection to the sea. The commercial fishing industry expanded during this time. Although the commercial fishing fleet was active in New Bedford in the second half of the nineteenth century, those boats depended on sail, and thus could not get fresh catches back to port quickly. Several changes occurred during the beginning of the twentieth century that allowed the fishing industry to expand into a major industry in New Bedford: motors on the fishing boats, use of trucks to transport the catch, modern refrigeration, and a freezer plant built in the 1940s that added to the port's ability to process fish. The port of New Bedford became a major fresh-fish processing center on the East Coast and the major scallop port on the northeast Atlantic coast. In 1984, the port of New Bedford ranked number one in the nation, based on value of landings."

In the post-war years, although there was a steady decline in optimism about New Bedford's future for those living there, the city seemed like a paradise to those coming in from other lands. This was the time of the greatest Norwegian emigration to New Bedford and the growth of the fishing industry, particularly the scallop industry, which would eventually make New Bedford the most important fishing port in America.

1970–2004: New Bedford had its ups and downs during this period but is finally optimistic about its future with the realization of new projects such as the New Bedford Whaling National History Park and an expanded Whaling Museum. There are many plans for a revitalized downtown area and its many adjoining neighborhoods are becoming fashionable once more. There is also talk that the Boston train may run once more to New Bedford and if so,

—AT photo

Some of New Bedford's waterfront area today: cleaned up and preserved for the future.

—Old Postcard

The famous Whaleman Statue in front of the distinctive New Bedford Free Public Library and across the street from New Bedford City Hall.

that would open many commercial possibilities and opportunities for population growth.

The fishing industry has continued to grow and has placed New Bedford as the number-one fishing port in the USA. New Bedford continues to prosper under the strong local government leadership.

FAIRHAVEN

WHEN I WAS A CHILD, and it was time to visit our Norwegian relatives, Mother would put on her hat and say, "We are going to Fairhaven today." Fairhaven meant Norwegians, and we were off to visit for a few hours. That is all I thought of when I heard the name Fairhaven—Norwegians. We would sometimes walk to Fairhaven, crossing over the bridge and looking down to the water through the grate in the movable part of the bridge. It was a long walk, but I always liked Fairhaven as it seemed more restful, and children were playing outside on the streets and sidewalks.

The homes were very different from New Bedford's two- and three-deckers, but in the forties it was not a particularly well-kept town, and I think some of that was the result of damage of the Hurricane of 1938, coupled with the austerity of the post-Depression years and the war when so many men were away. My memory includes images of damaged buildings here and there and many huge and vacant mansions. Much work needed to be done on these homes before they could be restored to their previous greatness and termed as landmarks, but with the hurricane and war years such work just had to wait until there were better days.

FAIRHAVEN LEADERS

EARL B. DIAS formerly of The Standard-Times wrote, "Unquestionably, Fairhaven's most famous native son is Henry Huttleston Rogers, the Standard Oil magnate who became one of the most powerful tycoons of his day. Born in 1840, Rogers lived during his childhood and early youth in the house at 39 Middle Street, which still stands today. A member of the first graduating class of Fairhaven High School, Rogers, after completing his secondary school studies, worked as a clerk in a grocery store, then as a baggage master for the Old Colony Railroad, and, at the age of 20, left to seek his fortune in the oil fields of Pennsylvania." By the time of his death in 1909, he had amassed a fortune of more than $100,000,000, but despite his rise in the world, he never forgot Fairhaven, which he once called "the dear old town which for 200 years has been the home of a continuous line of some of my ancestors."

During his lifetime he spent many happy hours in Fairhaven at his elaborate eighty-five-room mansion near Fort Phoenix, and he bestowed on the town the magnificent Fairhaven High School, the town hall, the beautifully appointed Millicent Library, the Rogers Grammar School, and the magnificent Unitarian Memorial Church.

These eclectic buildings distinguish Fairhaven from every other town on earth. They vary in architectural period and design and may be a bit startling to the first-time visitor as they appear to some to have emerged from a fairy tale. This architectural confection was designed by a single architect, Charles Brigham, and set a standard for the town in many ways. The neighborhoods are very neat and tidy and seem to compete for garden design. European influence is very pronounced throughout the town as contrasted to surrounding towns like Mattapoisett, which are colonial American in character.

—Courtesy EURO Ship's Store

The ornate Fairhaven Town Hall is a good example of Fairhaven's eclectic architecture.

—*Old postcard*

Fort Phoenix in an early photo.

—*Old postcard*

Fort Phoenix bathhouse and pavilion before the 1938 Hurricane. The beaches and views here have delighted many generations of native residents and emigrants.

Fairhaven was incorporated in 1812 and has tree-lined streets, fine old homes, and a working waterfront. It is a friendly town, a hospitable town, and an enviable town. One place I remember well was Fort Phoenix with its great rocks, cannons and places to hide. In my childhood days there was a hurricane-damaged grand pavilion with a fountain and gardens and a great picnic area up in the woods behind it, a place where it was cool and friendly and where we could eat our egg salad sandwiches. The views from Fort Phoenix were lovely, and we could see most of New Bedford, the lighthouse, and, out to sea, the Elizabeth Islands. We didn't know then that periscopes from enemy subs scouting the harbor might also be observing us.

Fairhaven has always been a community of seamen, at one time whalers, later fishermen and often pleasure boaters and has had the sea at its core. The views from Fort Phoenix are still spectacular. Now a state park, the fort once protected New Bedford Harbor and played an important role in the Revolutionary War and War of 1812 against the British. Although readied for the Civil War, it was not used then. Norwegians loved "The Fort" and it often was the last thought on a fisherman's mind when he left the harbor and headed out to sea.

Mabel Hoyle Knipe, of Fairhaven, wrote in 1984 that Fort Phoenix was offered for sale and then bought for the residents of Fairhaven in 1926 by Cara Leland Rogers Broughton, daughter of Henry Huttelston Rogers. Greatly distressed that the historic fort might fall into the hands of developers unmindful of its history, the then Mrs. Urban Broughton wrote: "I am quite sure that my father with his love for Fairhaven would not wish to feel that Fort Phoenix with its traditions should go to anyone outside the town. I am relying on you to secure Fort Phoenix for me." The British title of Baron Fairhaven of Lode would be bestowed upon her husband posthumously in 1929 and therefore by royal decree Cara Leland Rogers Broughton became the first "Lady Fairhaven." Through her generosity, Norwegians have indeed enjoyed Fort Phoenix.

NORWEGIAN INFLUENCE

EVEN TODAY ONE CAN SEE Norwegian flags flying proudly from many homes, and a look through the Fairhaven phone book will show countless Norwegian names. There is the Trinity Lutheran Church built by the Norwegians, and there are Norwegian-American shops, restaurants, beauty parlors, fishing boats, yachts, ship's stores, propeller shops and other Norwegian-owned stores related to the fishing industry.

Norwegians still love to visit Fairhaven on their trips to America as they will most often have a memory, a friend or a relative in this town. One visitor told a would-be hostess in another town that he wanted to stay in Fairhaven because he had heard about it all his life in Norway and wanted to "roam its streets for a few days." Fairhaven has been good to the Norwegians and the Norwegians have been good to Fairhaven.

Late 1960s: Oil discovered in Norway. Emigration ended.

The Greater New Bedford area and Norway had both religion and a seafaring life in common, and oil also played a great role in their common history. The discovery of oil in America led to New Bedford's decline as a great whaling port and ended her great prosperity. And the discovery of oil in the North Sea led to a new and wealthy Norway. Quakers were responsible for beginning an emigration that eventually made the New Bedford area far more viable. Quakers in Norway began the emigration process to America. Whaling and fishing were critical industries in both countries. Carl Wittle in his 1939 writing, "We Who Built America," described Norwegians as "a strong, resolute, stubborn people. Practically all are Lutherans, and combine a Lutheran piety and sense of duty with a strong desire for material advancement. They are thrifty and eager to acquire a homestead. They are strong and stubborn individualists, lovers of freedom, law-abiding, and vigorous defenders of their Church."

There was enough in common on the two shores of Norway and Stromfjord to make the Norwegian emigrants feel at home and allow them to contribute constructively to life in both countries.

They did!

Legacy & Folklore

ADVICE TO A SON

"Make your ship good to look upon,
then skillful men will come and the
ship will be well manned.
Make your ship ready for the sea
when the summer starts,
and navigate in the best part of the summer.
Always have reliable ropes on your ship,
and do not stay on the sea in the autumn
if you can help it."

—*The King's Mirror*
An ancient book of advice
from Norwegian Viking fathers to their sons.

3

Charting New Waters

THE CROSSCURRENTS OF AN AMERICAN-NORWEGIAN MARRIAGE

—Courtesy Arthur Moniz, Arthur Moniz Gallery, New Bedford

The Seamen's Bethel, left, and Mariner's Home on Johnny Cake Hill, New Bedford. Momma's father and mother sang in the choir here, Papa's name is on a memorial plaque, and it is here where Momma's memorial service was held.

HOME WATERS

IT WAS IN THE NORWEGIAN COASTAL TRADITION—since the mid-1800s—to come to America, live in Brooklyn and fish out of New York.

In the summer it soon became a habit for many in New York to come up from Brooklyn with their boats, take rooms in New Bedford and fish on Georges Bank. (According to author William MacLeish, Georges Bank made its first appearance in history as "St. George's Shoal at the beginning of the seventeenth century. Familiarity gradually secularized the name, and in time laziness claimed the apostrophe." They brought their dragger/scallopers to

New Bedford and were largely responsible for developing and managing the soon-to-be-burgeoning scallop industry in the New Bedford area.

My grandfather, Sivert Tollefsen, came from Skudeneshavn on the island of Karmøy shortly after the turn of the century, following Norway's independence from Sweden. (Karmøy is about one-half the size of Cape Cod and is one of Norway's largest islands. It is located between Stavanger and Haugesund, some forty minutes north by ferry from Stavanger or faster by the swift boat. Now one can drive over a bridge from Haugesund to Karmøy, but prior to the mid-fifties, there was no bridge.)

He came to America to fish in order to support his family in Norway, because there was very poor fishing in Norway at that time. Each Christmas he would go home to Norway and stay for several months to visit the family. Then he would return to America. This was the established pattern for many Norwegian fishermen in those days if they could afford the trip home.

Many wondered how my grandfather had the money to do this so often. We were to learn later that because he had advanced merchant marine papers, he had worked his way "forth and back" by providing the maritime skills the captain of the liner needed for assistance and relief duty. One of my father's cousins, the late Tobias Høines, recalled: "Uncle Sivert was a pilot also. Members of our family were pilots for many generations in Skudeneshavn. They just traditionally became pilots."

In the tradition of the Norwegian seaman, my grandfather brought a large trunk home each year from America, filled to overflowing with clothing, toys and various necessities for the family. And when he was home, he instilled in

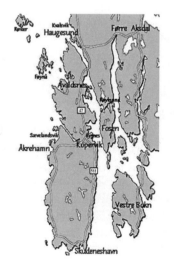

Map of the island of Karmøy and its surrounding islands, with Haugesund to the north. Idyllic Skudeneshaven is at the southern tip of the island, and Avaldsnes (Viksnes) with its copper mine is north. The Haugesund airport is located just across the water from Avaldsnes near the "A" on the map. The bridge to the mainland is at the narrowest point in the northeast of the island. The center of the population and shopping is around the Åkrehamn and Kopervik areas. The most beautiful drive is north from Skudeneshavn to Kopervik on the east side. (This map does not show the scenic Burma Road, which is about half way to Kopervik and across the island from east to west.) Haugesund is a city with major shopping, hotels and restaurants.

each of his ten children the desire to come to America. His son David, who followed in Sivert's path, often said, "I felt I was an American. Father was. I always knew I was too, and it was natural to come when I was old enough. I was going home to America."

Many men, during this break from fishing in America, did some fishing in Norway in addition to caring for home, family and property. It is said that come the next autumn in Karmøy, when so many men were back in America, the birthing rate so overwhelmed the midwife that she was not able to get to all of the homes in time for the births. As one former Karmøy resident recalled: "The midwives were tired and rundown, because they could not rest from one delivery to the next. It was unbelievable how so many babies were born at the same time, especially in Skudeneshavn. It just about drove the midwives crazy."

My grandmother had ten children and like the other families of Skudeneshavn, many were born in the fall. During the pregnancies and births the men were not with their families, but when they came home, there was almost always a new mouth to feed. This pattern bred very strong and independent women on Karmøy in Rogaland, Norway. The fathers never really knew their children well until they were older. When the children reached their mid-teens, after confirmation, many would come to America, one by one, to find work. One of my grandfather's sons said, "I couldn't wait to take the ship over. It was all I thought about and prepared myself for—to go to America."

NEW BEDFORD

THE YOUNG WOMEN coming to America would often care for children or work as housekeepers or cooks. The men would fish if they came from that background; most of the others worked as carpenters. And so it was with my grandfather's family—each year the older children came over and lived with their father, a new American citizen, in Brooklyn. In the summer he would come to New Bedford to fish in Georges Bank's fertile waters, rent a house or one floor of a two or three-storied house, and his children would be with him for the summer before returning to Brooklyn. It was during one of these annual migrations in 1928 when his eldest son—my father, Sigvart, eighteen—and his younger brother Tobias, sixteen, came with their father to New Bedford, a city very different from the New Bedford of today.

Herman Melville once wrote: "Nowhere in America will you find more patrician-like houses, parks and gardens more opulent than in New Bedford." Indeed, New Bedford was, in the mid-nineteenth century, the country's oldest and most prosperous whaling port.

But even decades after Melville's death, in the first third of the twentieth century, New Bedford was an enviable city, resplendent with beautiful parks known for their elaborate gardens, uncrowded warm-water beaches, elegant homes in stately neighborhoods, a bustling waterfront, excellent schools, ornate theaters and a busy downtown area.

Factories producing textiles and other goods replaced the whaling industry, but there was still shipping in and out of New Bedford, usually Yankee-owned and operated. Most of the fishermen were day-trippers, but the city was seeing the beginnings of a thriving commercial fishing industry manned by Yankees, Newfoundlanders, Latvians and eventually Norwegians and then even later, Portuguese from the islands. The city's workers had pride in their jobs and their multi-decked homes, locally called tenements. Despite the later Depression and general lack of money, New Bedford retained an overall feeling of solidity. The lively downtown area was well illuminated in the evening by gaslights, and the stores, restaurants and theaters were a beacon to emigrant Norwegian fishermen accustomed to the small towns and villages of Norway. For them, it was an ideal port city, proud of its whaling heritage and seafaring history.

People strolled at night along Purchase Street and danced in the downtown places where young people gathered. One such place was a building that future generations would know as the State Theater, and later as The Zeiterion. But in those days, it was a popular place to dance in a real ballroom, and it featured dance floors on different levels with at least two live bands. It was there that young women and men gathered each Friday and Saturday evening to dance fox trots and waltzes on one floor while others danced the Charleston or whatever music was "in" on the other. There you met your friends, future husbands and wives, and if you were a lucky young woman— because in those days no one had much money—someone would buy you a Coca-Cola and walk you home.

The single Norwegian fishermen, who did have some money, enthusiastically frequented this community ballroom when they came in from a trip. Norwegians generally are quite musical, and the fishermen were known to be wonderful dancers, have good manners, and come from respectable Protestant homes, essential to most of the Yankee women of that day. And if they didn't drink too much, they were considered potential husband material. It was here that my mother, Muriel Caswell, and her girlfriends spent many of their weekend evenings after working all week in the stores, factories and offices of New Bedford.

As Florence Tripp Lekom, my mother's best friend, nostalgically recalled of the Norwegian fishermen: "They looked like young blond gods, and they were such wonderful dancers. We just loved those boys. We had so much fun in those days at the dances."

THE NEW BEDFORD YANKEES

AT THAT TIME, New Bedford was primarily Yankee with a smattering of French, English, Irish, and a few Portuguese emigrants. Most of them kept to their own ethnic groups in the early part of the twentieth century. Each group basically had its own churches, neighborhoods, schools and clubs. The Yankee families were often descendants of the early settlers and like my mother had roots back to the Mayflower and some of the founding fathers as well as the whalers—in my mother's case both the Pilgrims and Benjamin Franklin's family.

They were very set in their traditions, their lifestyles, family roles and relationships. Many were poor, but for most of them the accumulation of wealth was not a life goal and conflicted with their religious beliefs. Their religion was generally an evolved version of Puritanism and Quakerism, but there was a smattering of Episcopalians as well. The most distinguishing characteristics of the Yankees, especially the Congregationalists and those from Quaker backgrounds, were that they were religious, thrifty, proud of their traditions, and teetotalers. In those days, New Bedford had many thriving Protestant churches filled every Sunday to overflowing. Most of the Yankees—many from families that had been in this country for two to three hundred years—considered themselves to be true-blue American, with English and Scottish roots, and they expected newcomers to adopt their ways.

The young people would go dancing on the weekend evenings with stern instructions from their families to behave properly. And so it was that my mother, who was very musical and loved to dance, met Tobias, who, according to her, was the best dancer in her world. He had a brother named Sigvart, but she was initially interested in Tobias because he danced so well. So they became friends, looked for each other each time there was a dance, and danced the night away.

She recalled sixty-six years later: "It was so wonderful to dance with him. He was so kind and gentle, and, well, he just knew how to dance so beautifully to the music. He was so tall and I so short, but we whirled around that room until I was dizzy. He was such a wonderful man."

THE MYSTERIOUS WATERS

TOBIAS, BEST KNOWN AS TOBY, was a fisherman, and in 1931 he was fishing on the *Mary*, a relatively new boat and larger than most of the fishing boats out of New Bedford. On one of her trips, the *Mary* simply did not come back. The Coast Guard searched. Fishing boats searched. Friends and relatives waited and waited. People came to the house and prayed with

Mother's family. My uncle took out a boat and searched Buzzards Bay. But they waited to no avail. Nothing was ever heard from the *Mary*. No wreckage was ever found, and Toby was gone.

It was Sigvart who came to Mother's house to comfort her, and they mourned together, both of them close to this man whose company they had so enjoyed. And it was Sigvart my mother began to know, understand and love in their mutual grief. She always said that Toby and Sigvart were very different and that Sig couldn't dance like Toby, but that he was a wonderful man, and she loved him. He was very handsome, with blue-gray eyes and reddish-light-brown curly hair, quiet, gentle, sincere, responsible and hard-working. He had that wonderful flirtatious smile—a twinkle in his eyes, with just a hint of sadness—that many Norwegian men have and that many women find so attractive and compelling. The look that says: "There are wonderful mysteries about me that you could perhaps discover—if you have a bit of patience."

Sigvart as the eldest son felt responsibility for his family, his brothers and his mother. He also had a wonderful sense of humor and was a practical joker, a trait shared by many Norwegian men. One of his sisters said years later, "He was an angel; no one could ever find any fault with Sigvart." The family loved him, and he would play his accordion with glee while Mother played the piano and sang. Mother was an accomplished singer and played the piano beautifully "by ear." Music was very important in their lives and absolutely central to hers. Maybe he was thought of as an angel by his sisters, but he also was a practical joker and loved to tease people, especially my mother's mother. He was forever untying her apron, and it would fall down at inappropriate times.

While Muriel and Sigvart were dating, they were caught "necking" on the living room sofa one evening by her father who asked what was going on. She answered innocently, "Sig is teaching me Norwegian." "That must be quite a language," my grandfather responded critically, "if he has to get halfway down your throat to speak it."

The next year they married in a simple home ceremony and took the overnight steamer from Fall River to New York—that was their honeymoon. I once asked my mother what she thought about the day she married, and she replied, "I was so glad not to be a burden on my family anymore because of the

—*Tollefsen archives*

Papa about the time he met Momma, circa 1931.

Depression and so happy to be with this gentle, handsome, kind and loving man. He made me feel so very special."

BROOKLYN, AMERICA?

THEY LIVED FOR A TIME IN BROOKLYN with his father Sivert—whom my mother called "a gentle giant, so light on his feet and so kind"—and some of the siblings. Bay Ridge was incomprehensible to Mother, who was a small-city woman. Brooklyn with its tall buildings, crowds, row houses, and many languages was confusing. But so were the Norwegians. So many Norwegians speaking Norwegian, eating Norwegian, thinking Norwegian. It seemed mysterious to her that in America she could feel she was in a foreign country. And to make it worse she, being married to a fisherman, was alone most of the time. She felt lonely, isolated and desperately homesick. Eventually they found rental rooms for themselves and were afforded

Miss Caswell Is Married at Home

Bridal Couple Will Live in Brooklyn, N. Y.

The ceremony uniting in marriage Miss Muriel Mabel Caswell, daughter of Mr. and Mrs. Wallace Caswell and Sigvart Tollefsen, son of Mr. and Mrs. Sivert Tollefsen, Brooklyn, N. Y., took place at the home of the bride's parents, 2355 Acushnet Avenue, at 3 p. m today.

The Rev. Leslie C. Greeley officiated, using the single ring service. The home was attractively decorated with ferns and cut flowers. The bride, who was given in marriage by her father, was gowned in royal blue faille crepe with a shoulder bouquet of white roses and lilies of the valley and wore a blue transparent velvet hat.

Mrs. Ralph Saltus, sister of the bride, was matron of honor and wore a rust sheer crepe gown with accessories to match and a shoulder bouquet of talisman roses.

Ralph Saltus, brother-in-law of the bride, was best man.

A reception was held at the Caswell home after the ceremony and a buffet lunch was served. Mr. and Mrs. Tollefsen took the New York boat and will make their home at 579 46th Street, Brooklyn, N. Y.

—Tollefsen archives

Momma's wedding announcement, in the New Bedford Standard-Times. Marriages were often held in the home during the Depression years and bridal gowns were an unaffordable luxury. Mother wore her signature color blue.

more privacy. Mother, now pregnant, would walk down to a park by the ocean every day, knit, and watch for my father's boat to enter New York Harbor. She was close to her father-in-law, whom she considered to be the kindest man she had ever known, but was not to become close to the Norwegians in general.

Her girlfriend, Florence, traveled to Brooklyn one day to visit her. Florence remembers: "I was Muriel's best friend from childhood and was living on Long Island at the time. We talked on the phone, and I decided to go and see her. So I went into New York City by train and then by subway to Brooklyn. She was so glad to see me, as she felt totally lost in New York. Sig was out fishing most of the time, and Brooklyn was like a foreign country to her. Everyone was Norwegian. She had a small apartment, and we gabbed and laughed all afternoon together—just like old times."

My mother did help new emigrants with their English and got to know many Norwegian women in this way both in New York and later in New Bedford, but the close friendships she had hoped for never materialized. She felt a bit let down in these attempts at friendship.

My father, the eternal practical joker, had a joke backfire on him one day. He had taught Mother a Norwegian song to sing for his father's birthday and he practiced and practiced with Mother until she had all of the words right and then had her sing it to his father. She was so proud that she had this special gift to give her beloved father-in-law, and bursting with pride she began to sing in her lovely church-soloist voice. She recalled that as she sang his face got redder and redder, and he seemed to be ready to explode. She couldn't understand what was happening so she kept on singing, and only when she saw his face start to turn purple did she stop. He took her husband out of the room and she heard them shouting. My father with his practical jokes had taught my Mother a naughty song as her first debut in Norwegian, and she never truly forgave him for it. This proper, well-intentioned Yankee was very embarrassed that day.

She never could understand why the Norwegian "foreigners" didn't embrace American ways, and they couldn't understand why she didn't embrace theirs. Often my parents were at a stalemate, and somewhat frustrated when it came to each other's expectations and customs. Other Yankee women who married Norwegian men had similar experiences, but it seemed easier for the brides whose ancestors had less distant ties to the continent. Mother, for instance, never understood the Norwegian importance of serving coffee to guests before talking and visiting, and the Norwegians never understood why she wasn't more hospitable. It was in the Yankee tradition never to have coffee after noon and to serve tea at other times. To Mother, it was outrageous to have coffee in the afternoon "when everyone knew that one was to drink tea."

—*Tollefsen archives*

Momma shows her unforgettable smile—a rare photograph, as she almost never smiled when her photo was taken. This looks like Papa, but also looks like his brother, Uncle Hans Tollefsen. I think she is smiling beside Hans at Papa while he takes the photo on the boat.

Sigvart and Muriel moved back to New Bedford when Sig and his father decided to bring the boat "up" to this port. The move did not bring the happiness she had anticipated. Her newborn daughter died after a devastating seventy-two-hour delivery. A four-foot-eleven woman had some difficulty delivering large Norwegian babies. She was struggling for life herself at the same time her beloved father-in-law lay dying of pneumonia. So life began to take a tragic turn for her and her husband early in their marriage.

GOING HOME TO NORWAY

THE DAY SIVERT TOLLEFSEN was buried was a sad day for the island of Karmøy because its people had to acknowledge that, although a better life was to be had in America, it could also mean tragedy for the families left behind. America might be a land of riches, but it also could be a land of death. Older people in Karmøy still talk today about that tragic day when Sivert Tollefsen came home to Norway, a man who died in a hospital rather than being lost at sea. They say that he was the first Skudenes emigrant to die in America and come home this way. The whole island, somehow, participated in this bitter event. To many, that day was a defining event in their lives, and one that reshaped the image of America as a perfect dream.

My grandfather's casket came by ship and finally home to Skudeneshavn, and was placed on a horse-drawn wagon and brought to the church and graveyard. People remember many mourners walking behind the casket with my grandmother Mille, whom we knew as "Papa'sma," leading the mourners all the way to the church. They say she stoically walked with some of her remaining children, dressed all in black and looking very regal. The whole town of Skudeneshavn and many from other parts on the island turned out that day in 1934. They say the casket from America was so big that it took extra men to lift it. Sivert was a very large man. He was buried in the grave by

—Høines archives, Norway

Great-grandfather Tobias
Tollefsen Høines,
1846–1918.

—Høines archives, Norway

Great-grandmother Ellen
Gurine Tollefsen Høines,
1850–1931.

—Høines archives, Norway

Great-great-grandmother
Johanna Evensdatter, born
1816, Flekkefjord, Sokn.

the church, where he rests today with Papa'sma and many other family members.

They are together now but were often apart for long periods of time. One cousin of mine read a letter Sivert had written to his wife while he was in America. He had signed it, "Your Friend." The women of Southwest Norway lived lives of loneliness, work, and responsibility—with too many children. The monthly letter from America became the only link with their husbands. Unfortunately, this was the rule rather than the exception.

STARTING OVER

"Moons waxed and waned. The lilacs bloomed and died,
In the broad river ebbed and flowed the tide,
Ships went to sea, and ships came home from sea,
And the slow years sailed by and ceased."

—Henry Wadsworth Longfellow,
"Lady Wentworth"

AFTER THESE TWO TRAGIC DEATHS—the baby and the father—Sig and Muriel rented one floor of a house in New Bedford's West End on Armour Street near Buttonwood Park. At that time the fishing business was thriving, and Sig now owned and skippered the fishing vessel *Valencia*, which he had bought from his father. After two devastating tragedies, life gradually began to be more optimistic, and things were going well for them. I was born in 1937 and Mother often said that was the happiest moment in her life—especially after losing her first daughter.

Traditionally, parents in the West End with babies took them by carriage to Buttonwood Park and showed them off to their friends, walked around the gardens, viewed the pond, fed the animals and enjoyed the sights and sounds of a lovely New Bedford afternoon. I remember this carriage well and how much I enjoyed being pushed in it with several toys strung across the top. Momma & Papa in 1937.

—Tollefsen archives

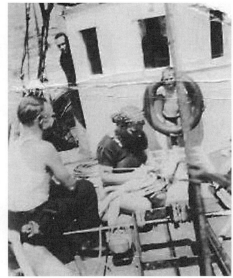

—Tollefsen archives

—Tollefsen archives

I am happy, secure, loved and joyous on Armour Street, before the troubles.

My mother's brothers-in-law, my Swedish Uncle Carl Johnson and Yankee Uncle Ralph Saltus, with her cherished sister Winifred on an outing on the *Valencia* with unidentified child, possibly one of the Saltus brothers, circa 1932.

During those days they attended the Elim Baptist Church with many other Norwegians, because Swedish was spoken there and Papa understood it. There was no Norwegian church, and they both felt comfortable there. Mother was a Congregationalist and Papa a Lutheran, so the Baptist church was a comfortable compromise. They enjoyed their church life together, and I was to continue there off and on into my teen years.

Mother often said, because "Papa was either fishing, repairing the boat, or entertaining a relative or friend who had just come over on the last boat," that they had very little time together alone during their all-too-short five years.

But they sometimes had picnics on board the *Valencia* with her family, and all of her brothers-in-law and sisters really enjoyed Sig, his boat, his charming way of speaking and his practical jokes. He was fun to be with, and he took some of the edge off the too-serious Yankees. They also spent some wonderful days at my aunt's borrowed summer home, "Fox Hill," on a hill overlooking the Slocum River in nearby Dartmouth. Here they would take a small boat out to Deep Water Point and swim and picnic or sometimes row to Russell's Mills for provisions. Fox Hill was an estate owned by the Hawes family and lent to my aunt and uncle during the summers. We were all to spend many wonderful summers there while we were growing up. With its large house, bathhouse, beach, tennis courts, stone well, rose arbor, boathouse and private dock as well as many acres of land for blueberrying, we were very blessed to be guests there, and my father especially loved it. I have heard that the men would go down to the boathouse and sneak a beer now and then, well away from their tea-drinking Caswell wives.

My cousin David Saltus, who spent many happy days with them at Fox Hill, wrote his Harvard freshman essay about his Uncle Sig. He loved his uncle and totally enjoyed his company. He wrote nostalgically of the happy times they had had together and how he had visited the boat, and Sig's struggles with the language. He wrote about how much fun his uncle was, how Uncle Sig had paid attention to him when he was a boy, and how much he missed him when he died. In turn David, as we were growing up, paid much attention to us and I especially loved him for his kindness, gentleness, intelligence and humor. He always made me feel special and loved.

My mother's family had a great sense of "wicked" humor, a type of humor that had to be "acted out" and left us all in hysterics. It was out of character for their upbringing but very like their distant descendant, Ben Franklin. They loved to laugh, but their attitudes toward life were generally very serious and apprehensive. Momma's best friend, Florence, remembers, "When we were with Mooie and Sig, we were always laughing. Sig had the most wonderful sense of humor. He loved a good joke, and he and my husband, who was an emigrant from Lithuania, had so much fun together laughing. I also remember that he was always hugging Mooie, her familiar name, and that he was very good to her. He loved her a lot."

NORWAY COMES TO ARMOUR STREET

"I couldn't bring myself to go into the house because I knew how things would go. One thing was clear to me: My mother-in-law was in charge— she didn't have to ask anyone."

—Gro Holm, "Life on the Listol Farm"

MY YOUNG UNCLE DAVID "came over" to live with us just after I was born and before striking out on his own, and my mother enjoyed him. My grandmother, whom we called Papa'sma, followed his visit.

My grandmother's role in the life of the household, where my father was the eldest son, was neither explained nor discussed with Mother and it differed considerably from American traditions. But one day "Sig's mother," as Mother always called her, arrived from Norway and moved in with them and was more than a little skeptical about this American bride. Sig promptly went

Again at Buttonwood Park, Papa with his youngest brother, David, who came to live with us for a while. David was about fifteen when he entered America on the day I was born. They both had reddish curly hair but David was taller. After Papa died and David would visit, I would run up to him and say, "Papa, Papa, No, not Papa" and then run out of the room. I sometimes feel I spent my lifetime waiting for Papa to come home. Papa's death was very hard for a boy of David's age. He loved his oldest brother very much.

—Tollefsen archives

out to sea for fourteen days and left them alone. One spoke no Norwegian and the other no English. Mother was to tell us in later years how impossible it was to get her to eat. She would eat "nothing I gave her," and would continue to talk to Mother in Norwegian, and Mother simply couldn't understand what she wanted. It was an enigma from both points of view.

One day Mother left the house to walk me in my carriage up to Buttonwood Park, and when she came home some of the furniture had been moved around and many of her decorations, pictures and mementos had been put away. In their place were Norwegian memorabilia, doilies and photos. Sig's mother had arranged things the way she wanted and the way she felt her son would like it.

—Tollefsen archives

Papa'sma, with Papa and me when she was living with us. This photo was taken in front of Auntie Bea and Uncle Ralph's antique home north of Lund's Corner at 2421 Acushnet Avenue in New Bedford. Here we enjoyed family outings, sweeping lawns, hills to roll down, woods, apple tree swings, farm animals and several gardens.

This presumption was something Mother would never forget, and her annoyance tended to grow over the years. Grandmother had asserted her place as head of the family, and the lines had been drawn. When Sig got home, both women confronted him at the door. Later that day, Papa'sma gave him a shopping list, and when he got home with the goods she spent the rest of the day making Norwegian fish balls, which, my mother exclaimed, were the best thing she had ever eaten.

In defense of my mother—for I do believe that Papa'sma was well-intentioned and

—Tollefsen archives

Papa and me circa early 1938 when I was about one year old. The spots are age on the photo. This is how I remember Papa.

following traditions of her day—I must say that Mother already had a very domineering mother of her own, so she was not looking for more people to tell her what to do and especially not a woman. Mother was what I call a "man's woman"—she liked to wait on a man and for the man to make decisions. She was feminine and dependent and had been taught to wait for her mother or husband to decide what she should do. One thing that still surprises me in all of this is that my two grandmothers never went head-to-head over issues. I'm still astonished at that because Mother's mother was very outspoken and domineering and not one who took anything from anyone.

Papa'sma eventually got her own place, and in time the two women grew to respect each other, although they were never close. Mother knew from the beginning that a Norwegian bride would have been much preferred in the family and that everything she was to do would be open to criticism and contrasted to what a Norwegian woman might do. The one thing they had in common was Bible reading, and that one thing gave them a tentative bridge of understanding. To Mother, she and her husband loved each other, and that was that!

Momma and Papa had almost two years to enjoy their baby daughter, to whom he gave much attention and, in the Norwegian style, freedom.

As I got older, he allowed me to run on the sidewalk and gave me the kind of responsibility and freedom that frightened Mother. My mother's sister, Winifred Johnson, used to remember nostalgically: "I would look out the window and see Sig and Astrid in those pretty Norwegian sweaters and hats coming down Arnold Street. Astrid would be running a few feet in front of him as fast as her chubby little legs would take her, and he would be following and laughing. I remember those beautiful smiles, her dimples, rosy

—Tollefsen archives

The Caswell sisters—Winifred, Beatrix and Muriel—in the early thirties. Close sisters and wonderful aunts to us all.

cheeks and curly hair. What a lovely, happy picture they were, and he was so proud of her. He used to toss her up onto his shoulders while he laughed and waved at me. He would talk to her in Norwegian, and she would answer. Those two were so close! He was such a wonderful man—so handsome, so much fun. I'll never forget those days."

THE GREAT 1938 HURRICANE AND ITS AFTERMATH

THEN MOTHER BECAME PREGNANT with her son, Thomas, who was to be delivered in late August of 1938 and whose early days were somewhat over-shadowed by the "Great 1938 Hurricane." That September hurricane was the most destructive in New Bedford history. Stories are still told about that fateful day with its tidal wave, winds and incredible damage. Most of New Bedford's fishing fleet was damaged or sunk at the docks of New Bedford and Fairhaven.

My father's boat, the *Valencia*, a fifty-two-foot dragger/scalloper, was tied up in Fairhaven on the dock's leeward side between two other boats and took

—*Origin unknown.*
What a hurricane can do to a fishing boat.

—*Tollefsen archives*
Papa's last picture. The *Valencia* was being repaired and overhauled but sank on its next trip.

—*Tollefsen archives*
The *Valencia*, a western-rigged fishing vessel home-ported in New Bedford and New York. Circa 1936.

71

quite a battering during the hurricane. But Papa made a short three-day trip with the *Valencia* just after the hurricane and had no trouble.

A few weeks after the hurricane, the *Valencia* narrowly escaped disaster. On that trip, just off the Nantucket Light, they were fully loaded, and the boat couldn't take the weight. Its seams opened, and she began to fill and sink. "They set off flares and burned mattresses when no one paid attention to their signals," my mother recalled to the Standard-Times in 1938. "In just the nick of time, a boat turned back and towed them to New Bedford." The *Valencia* was dry-docked and thoroughly gone over and repaired at the boatyard in Fairhaven.

"He was very careful and always saw to it that things were all right as far as he could tell," Mother remembered.

⌒

"Wait, Gudrod, 'til the storm is past!
Loose not thy long-ship while the blast howls overhead so furiously,
Trust not thy long-ship to the sea,
Loose not thy long-ship from the shore;
Hark to the ocean's angry roar!
See how the very stones are tossed
By raging waves high on the coast!
Stay, Gudrod, 'til the tempest's o'er—
Deep runs the sea off the Jadar's shore."

—Harald Hårfagre's Saga, "Heimskringla"

THAT TERRIBLE DAY

MURIEL AND SIG prepared for his next trip as usual but with one difference. This time they sat down and sang hymns together with the piano and accordion.

She later said he was very unhappy with one of the crew, whom she said was not Norwegian. She told me she had never seen Papa so upset before. And when he left, reluctantly, that unhappiness was to be her last memory of him. Papa went out New Bedford Harbor into Buzzards Bay, through the hole, into Nantucket Sound and to Georges Bank as usual with the *Valencia*. They fished successfully for a few days and started to return home. They were by the Nantucket Shoals, low in the water with a full load of fish, when disaster struck.

There are many stories about how the *Valencia* went down. But after examining newspaper articles, the death certificate, official reports, as well as talking to the survivors and their offspring, a clearer picture emerges.

Valencia was returning home after a very good trip. Everyone was feeling happy because they were now to have the money they lost when the boat was in dry dock. They depended on that income, and none more than their

⌒

skipper, Sig, who had a new son, very high hospital bills and new repair bills on the boat. They rode heavy and low in the calm water about thirty miles southeast of the Nantucket Lightship by Nantucket Shoals when suddenly a freak northeasterly gale and lightning storm hit with full impact. The waves pounded the boat, which had been weakened by the hurricane, tossing it violently as the men were deafened by the thunder. Suddenly a bolt of lightning hit the mast and traveled to the hull where it burned a hole in the side. *Valencia* began to sink quickly.

(My brother, retired Commander Thomas S. Tollefsen, USN, a small-boat expert, explained almost sixty years later: "When lightning strikes a boat, the voltage flow is downward to the base of the mast, then a leap to a through-hull valve or engine block to the shaft and into the water as a ground. The force is such as to blow out the sea valve and open the interior to rapid flooding. That is a possibility here.")

Papa put the dory over the side, and the crew got into it hurriedly. At the last minute, in maritime tradition, Papa decided to try to save the boat by setting blankets afire on the mast as he had done so successfully before, hoping that another boat or the Coast Guard would see them and come to their rescue. Perhaps he was thinking of his bills, perhaps of his pride in his boat, perhaps his duty as a captain, or perhaps of his men. We will never know what his last thoughts were as he climbed steadily to the top with a kerosene-soaked blanket to set the mast afire. The mast was slippery, wet and shaking violently. He could not hear the men in the dory calling to him through the thunder of the waves hitting against *Valencia*, his love and pride. He reached the top of the mast, now at a perilous angle to the sea, and exhaustedly lit a match. Then on the top of this rain-soaked, wind-tossed mast with slippery hands wet from both kerosene and rain, he slipped and fell onto the unnaturally tipped deck and into the frigid sea. The men rowed to the spot where he fell and pulled him out, but it was too late.

Nils Aadland (Ådland), according to his son, Magne Aadland, pulled his dying captain into the dory and placed him in the hull of the boat for ballast.

Nils Ådland, the brave and caring Norwegian fisherman who pulled my father's body from the sea so that he could be buried at home. He injured his back doing so and was to suffer from back problems all his life. He never forgot this tragedy at sea and the loss of his young skipper, and how they all almost lost their own lives.

—Magne Ådland family archives,
Karmøy Norway

Magne told me in a telephone conversation from Norway that his father pulled a muscle in his shoulder doing this and for some reason it never healed and he always lived with pain from that fateful day of November 15, 1938.

The coroner's death certificate for my father stated that he died from "asphyxiation by immersion"—drowning. People who saw his body said he was very bruised. He was just twenty-eight years old, the ship's captain, the oldest son, the proud father, the loving husband, the brother, the uncle—the Norwegian emigrant.

THE CREW

THE CREW ROWED FOR THIRTY-SIX HOURS in a fourteen-foot dory, guided by the Norwegian sailors using traditional Viking navigation skills: following the sun and the North Star. They finally found the Nantucket Lightship and were exhausted, dehydrated and beyond speech. One man, who sat next to my father in the boat, was, so it is said in Norway, to spend most his remaining years ill from this harrowing experience—many hours beside a dead body.

The New Bedford Standard-Times, November 17, 1938, reported: "First word of the tragedy came at 10 p.m. when the light vessel notified Coast Guard headquarters that she had picked up the dory and three survivors. No details of the sinking were received. Listed as saved were Jack Knutsen, George Jacobsen and Nils Aadland, all of this city. The skipper and owner of the *Valencia*, which left this port last Thursday, is Sigvart Tollefsen, 28, of 128 Armour Street, this city.

"While the Coast Guard did not name the dead man as Captain Tollefsen, members of his family expressed the belief that it must be him. Mrs. Muriel Tollefsen, the former Muriel Caswell of this city, said her husband had taken the *Valencia* out on a fishing trip last Thursday. 'His trips generally lasted only three or four days or at the most five days, but when we didn't hear from him Tuesday we began to worry,' she sobbed. 'He always called us by telephone when he reached Nantucket.' Mrs. Tollefsen, mother of a nine-week-old son and 20-month-old daughter, said her husband's crew usually consisted of five to six men, but she was uncertain as to how many were on the last trip. Two of Tollefsen's brothers had drowned at sea, she said, adding that her husband had come from Norway in 1929 and had married her five years ago.

"Coast Guard officers said that apparently the survivors had rowed in the bitter cold from the spot where the vessel sank twenty-five miles southeast of the lightship, which is forty-four miles off Nantucket. The *Valencia* had alternated this city with New York as her home base. The skipper had made his home here for about six years."

Later the Standard-Times reported: "The survivors had battled the wintry seas for thirty-four hours in a fourteen-foot dory, steering by the sun and stars for the Nantucket Lightship when they pulled alongside their goal at ten last night, exhausted almost beyond speech. Drawn, weary and oppressed by their tragic experience, the men filled in the gaps in the story, which was sent by radio to the Coast Guard Headquarters at Boston by the superior officer of the lightship. 'The *Valencia* sprang a leak in the storm which battered her Tuesday,' the men related. They tried to bail her out, but she filled faster than they could bail. The weight of the water was splitting her bottom as Captain Tollefsen climbed the mast to hoist a blanket as a distress signal. He lost his balance descending and was knocked unconscious by his fall to the deck. There was nothing they could do for him, they said, and he died within a few minutes. So rapidly was the *Valencia* sinking, the spokesman continued, that they had to launch their dory without losing a moment more than was required to lift their captain's body into the craft. (Later recollections were that they were in the dory when they lifted his body out of the water. Death by drowning would reinforce this version.) They had neither food nor water during the day and a half that they plied their oars toward the lightship. About three thousand pounds of fish went down with the *Valencia*. The men, fed and warmed and given beds last night on the lightship, were taken off at 6 a.m. today. Captain Tollefsen's body in the dory, which alone was saved of his ship, also was aboard the cutter. It was claimed upon arrival by Ralph E. Saltus, 2421 Acushnet Avenue, a relative."

There was no account of the non-Norwegian crewmember whom Papa considered to be a troublemaker. I would prefer to think that he didn't go on

Momma is gaunt and still recovering from a caesarean section and emergency surgery after giving birth to her large son, Thomas Severt, six weeks before. This was the last day of my secure, carefree and loving childhood. As this photo was being taken, Papa died at sea and life would never be the same again. I remember the angora hat, gloves and lovely warm coat trimmed with fur. This is in my memory as the last pretty clothing I had, except for the red dress, until I learned to sew my own.

—Tollefsen archives

that trip, as he was not mentioned in any newspaper or Coast Guard accounts, but Mother swore up to her last day that he was with the group who came to her house to tell her about the Papa's death and she was always very suspicious about him. I really feel that she was too upset to remember exactly who was there, and it is clear that the crew were all Norwegians and all his friends.

My mother had two babies, one twenty-two months old and the other just nine weeks old, when the Coast Guard officer came to notify her of Papa's death. She went into shock that day and began a life filled with worry, bad health and perceived insurmountable obstacles to overcome. As her friend Florence told me, "Mooie was different after Sig died. Her life revolved around her health, and she talked about it all the time. She was not like that before."

Mother had two babies and four dollars. My father stubbornly had not taken out life insurance. She had no idea what she would do, and she would not even look at my dead father at the funeral; she was still weak from her caesarean delivery. They were in debt from her large medical bills and his boat repairs; she didn't know how she would buy milk for her babies. She often said that when she went to the cemetery for the burial and saw hundreds of dollars of flowers there, she had wished that those who had sent the flowers had sent money to her babies instead.

Her best friend recalls, "It was such a cold, wet day—that day of the funeral. I remember it as being so very sad and so very cold. It was so hard." A Norwegian woman remembers leaving the funeral home and standing next to my grandmother. It was a bitter cold and wet day and my grandmother, Papa'sma, looked into the skies and said, "Today the whole world is crying with me."

Our family is very indebted to the crew for honoring their captain enough to bring his body home. Unlike many others families, we had a grave in the cemetery to visit over the years.

THE AFTERMATH

WE MOVED INTO MOTHER'S sister and brother-in-law's home—already cramped because my maternal grandmother and their daughter also lived there. My aunt's Swedish-American husband insisted we come to their home as he had grown up very poor and understood our situation. We lived there for some time, quite a few months, until Momma regained her strength and courage and found some support. In those days there was no seamen's union, no Social Security for self-employed fishing captains, no programs that helped widows except for some very small funds from the city. The City of New Bedford gave us a small check every two weeks, called Mother's Aid.

Mother was totally committed to staying home with us and raising us well. Raising us well meant surrounding us with books and knowledge so that we could have a vision, and succeed in life. She wanted us never to be in her circumstances. She read to us constantly when we were young, and we read to ourselves when we were older.

The years after my father's death were very worrisome. I should have been too young to worry, but I did. My age did not preclude my mother sharing her burdens, as she had so few people to talk to. Mother's health was always poor. She was fragile, lonely and sad, but most of all, I think she was frightened. Her one consolation in life was her beloved music, and she spent hours playing the piano in her lively way and singing along with her beautiful voice. It was a hobby she carried throughout her life, and it brought joy to her and many others.

She strongly felt she should remain at home, surrounding us with security and love. I remember Mother being very timid, a stark contrast to the traditional coastal Norwegian women who were seemingly unafraid and understood the risks of this lifestyle. They had been trained for hundreds of years, in a country with men on the sea, to be self-sufficient and in charge.

Mother was dependent on others in many ways, and she did what she was told by other family members. She was very concerned that she might somehow become very ill, and lived in fear that her children would be taken from her and put into an orphanage. She struggled to become more independent, but had little self-confidence. She lived in dread of criticism, so we had to be perfect. We could not make a mistake because "they"—the city—might take us away or her own mother might be angered in some way. Unfortunately we were to grow up only one block from the orphanage, so that made such fears very real for us.

Mother, although she had many fears, had really good common sense. She could understand other people and their motives very quickly and could cut to the quick when it came to relationships. She hated conflict of any kind and always had the demeanor of one who was sweet and accommodating. She was noted for her lovely smile and extraordinary blue eyes, her compassion and her sense of humor, as well as her love of music. And she was almost always right in her assessment of people.

She knew her life would never be comfortable again, but she did her best for her children so that they would live easier lives. Soon after my father died, my Norwegian grandmother visited and made a well-meaning suggestion that further put terror into Mother's heart. She proposed that Mother give up her son for her to raise "Norwegian."

Mother took that as a threat rather than as an offer of help. Her "No!" was adamant and precluded future trust. She always said that Papa'sma wanted her son but not her daughter, and Mother always thought me to be the

Norwegian one, in that I was independent and strong-willed from the beginning. "She is just like the Norwegians," I would hear her family exclaim. I also had the dimples, the characteristic space between my front teeth that is seen so often in Norway, and the green-gray eyes. My brother had the very blond hair and deep blue eyes and large front teeth. He was as quiet as I was outspoken, but he was really more confident. I was very shy inside despite my outward demeanor. We looked Norwegian and were much larger than our Yankee cousins. Mother was less than five feet, so we towered over her when we were quite young.

Some mothers went to bars to meet men. Mother would not do that. She was a religious woman and felt that her place was in the home watching over her children. To my knowledge, in all of our early childhood, she went out three times in the evening.

LOW TIDE

IT IS NEVER EASY TO BE POOR. One is reminded of it every moment of the day. Being poor in a middle-class environment had special problems. There was pain in being poor. I remember in the sixth grade, a classmate told everyone from the top of a staircase landing in the Rodman School that her mother had told her we took charity and that we were "no good." A beautiful Jewish girl from New York named Paula, who became my hero, came to my rescue and told the whole group that this girl was a very nasty person and to ignore her. People liked Paula and for good reason. After the sniggering kids left, she came to me and said, "You do have insurance, don't you?" I didn't know. All I knew was that my father was dead and that the city helped us to survive, and, except for some gifts at Christmas from family members, that was it. (I learned that unpleasant day, also, that a woman from a different faith could be more loving and caring than one from my own church.)

Mother got sixteen dollars every two weeks, but her expenses were higher than that. There was absolutely no money for clothing, transportation, medications, school supplies, household supplies, winter clothes, toys and doctors. School field trips, a warm winter coat, good boots, dress-up clothes, pretty Christmas presents and other such luxuries were out of the question.

She would sit at the kitchen table when the check came, with scraps of paper and bills pieced by her little spiked bill-keeper, and with little piles of change in rows before her. She counted, recounted and changed the height of each pile with a very worried look on her face, trying to decide how much she could pay on each of her bills. I can never forget those evenings as I watched her through the crack in the bedroom door, at our home at 58 Lindsay Street, when she tried to balance her accounts and couldn't. Mother was always in debt to the grocer and tried to pay it off by caring for sick people, baby-sitting, and later housework—all illegal within the system. Even my baby-sitting earnings were deducted from her paltry check, when the city knew of it.

To my recollection, we rarely had seafood at our house, even though all of my father's relatives were fishermen. And it was against Mother's upbringing to ask for it. I cannot recall, after about age eight, our being invited to Norwegian celebrations, nor did we see our relatives unless we went to Fairhaven. Basically we didn't know them very well. I always felt that no one wanted to be seen with us because we had such poor clothing and theirs was so nice. All the Norwegians seemed wealthy to us. They all had full refrigerators. I felt they were ashamed of us. I always remember, as does my brother these sixty years later, that our refrigerator was mostly empty and little was on the shelves except for the day when "the check came."

Mother always managed to get meals on the table, but there were no extras. She used to read "Five Little Peppers and How They Grew," a story about very poor children, and that made us feel rich, and she also made us give our old usable clothing to the poorest of the poor to make us feel that we were not on the bottom and to feel herself, I think, that she had Christian charity. When we were older and she could get away, she did housework for several people in town and we worked, of course. The welfare lady looked the other way. She told Momma we were the only case she had that she felt would make it somehow. Thank God for her, but Mother was always under the threat of a neighbor, a relative or someone who might call the welfare office. The worst came in our early teens when we had to live in a housing project. That was the bottom of the pit, but it was a motivator for building better lives for the future. If we didn't succeed and go on to college, it would be the "5 and 10" for me, and for my brother, the factory and this kind of housing.

Luckily we were to spend the rest of our teen years in a very old but lovely home next to my aunt's home north of Lund's Corner in the extreme North End of the city. These houses were part of the Hawes estate, as was the summer vacation home of our early years.

—AT Photo

Momma on a freezing day in 1954. She was settled at 2405 Acushnet Avenue, working as Girl's Director at the Dennison Memorial in New Bedford, her daughter was about to go to college and her son was later to enter the United States Merchant Marine Academy. This was a happy time for her.

The Hawes family owned the Acushnet Sawmill where my uncle was the manager. The day we moved there and Momma saw the new wallpaper, paint and lovely views from the windows, she just sat and cried with joy. She was so thankful to Mrs. Hawes and even though there was no hot water and the house was very cold in the winter, to us it was a wonderful house. It sat in a good neighborhood with woods, gardens and fields in the back and my aunt and uncle next door. And best of all, we could bring our friends home without shame.

The City of New Bedford and the taxpayers were the ones who paid for us and to them I am eternally grateful and humbled. Thank you! I hope we have paid it back with interest and with service to our country. We are here today because of Mother, friends and relatives, the schools, the "Y's" and scouting, the churches and the citizens of New Bedford. I are indeed indebted to them.

LOVELY EARLY-CHILDHOOD MEMORIES

I STILL REMEMBER THE LOVELY CLOTHES I had worn as a small child before Papa died. I remember the house we lived in and Papa playing his accordion. I remember his love, his fishing boat smell, his warm touch and voice, but I can't remember his face except as a frozen image in a photo.

I just remember being loved, accepted, secure and happy with him. He made me feel that he was proud of every little thing I did, and he gave me so much attention that Mother often said she was a bit jealous. Her Yankee background was one where children were to be in the background, seen but not heard, whereas the Norwegian children were given prominence in the home. He spoke to me in Norwegian, and I answered him.

I remember the wonderful feeling of my velvet coat, a suede jacket and leggings, a fur-trimmed hat with a fur muffler, as well as the Norwegian sweaters sent from Norway. His aunt, Tante Serine Tobiasen, made me the most beautiful dress. It was red taffeta with bands of ruffles, and when I think of myself at

—A Tollefsen photo

My father's accordion. He would play his accordion and Momma would play the piano and together they would sing the Norwegian songs he loved and also many hymns. They sang together just before he took his last trip.

—*Tollefsen archives*

Two years after Papa died I wore the beautiful bright red taffeta dress made for me by Tante Serine Tobiassen when I was born. It made me feel pretty, secure and loved all at the same time.

two to three years of age, after he died, I see myself in Tante Serine's wonderful dress.

All the clothing felt so good to the touch in those days when Papa was there. Later, when we had to make do with so very little, the dream of once again having a nice home and soft-feeling clothing became a goal in my life.

Papa, after his death, became the family stories
of his life in five years of marriage.
I never learned any more about his life before that.
A few photos of him on his fishing boat,
And a name on a gravestone, visited too often.
I used to look at the grave
and think that he would talk to me if I stood there long enough.

Captain Sigvart Tollefsen, 1910–1938

His memory became wearing a white carnation on Father's Day
when all the others wore red.
He became the reason for seeing Mother sitting alone
at all our special times and graduations,
and his death, the reason why we couldn't be like the others.
He was that void I always carried in my heart,
an emptiness that was never to be filled by another man.
I always thought of him when I heard Norwegian accents
or heard my name pronounced properly.

*I could feel him near me when I traveled and saw the fishing boats
come into many ports around the world,
or inhaled the peculiar smell of the fishing docks.
I thought of him the day I had my ensign bars
pinned on me in the U.S. Navy,
and the day I got married and walked up the aisle alone.
I never forgot him. His memory gave me a lifelong desire to know
everything I could about Norway and the Norwegians.
His death also gave me a lifetime fear of abandonment.
His genes gave my brother a lifelong love of the sea
and a life on the sea.*

SUNDAY IN FAIRHAVEN

WE VISITED THE NORWEGIAN FAMILY in Fairhaven, especially my grandmother, Papa'sma, on some Sundays in the earlier days. We really enjoyed her a lot and loved to go there. She and Mother had a cordial, correct relationship but not a warm one. There was always that little tug here and

—*David Tollefsen archives*

Uncle David Tollefsen, an emigrant from Skudeneshavn, Karmøy, marries Marie Dahl, whose father was a Norwegian fisherman in Rhode Island. Her grandfather was the famous Norwegian painter Hans Andreas Dahl, from Northern Norway, and her grandmother's family were from Åkrehamn on Karmøy. Her grandparents met when he was doing the art work inside the church. Uncle David and Tante Marie were a handsome couple and to me, then a young girl, she looked like a princess in a fairytale book.

there for learning the Norwegian ways, which my mother resisted. We were never alone with Papa'sma, and outside of having coffee and waffles on our visits, I don't ever remember having a sit-down meal with her or any of the Norwegian aunts and uncles. We were not invited for "overnight stays" as we so often were with my mother's sisters. My mother's sisters were almost our extra mothers. We freely went back and forth to their homes and stayed as long as we were welcome.

I do remember the beautiful Norwegian wedding of my Uncle David Tollefsen and his beautiful bride, Marie Dahl. There was dancing and wonderful food. Mother was very sad that day—happy for David and Marie, but she missed my father very much. It was hard for her to see his family and hear their accents.

I also remember that there were frequent visits from the Norwegian relatives right after Papa died, and I especially remember that everyone would cry the whole time. One of my uncles would bring fish when we were very young, and we were very grateful for that because food was always an issue. But he stopped his visits when he married and had his own family.

I especially remember that it was always pointed out that we were half-Norwegian and that made me feel that we weren't quite good enough to be totally part of the Norwegian family. In fact, it worked the other way too. I never felt that I totally belonged to Mother's family. Somehow we were different, just half of two wholes.

I recall that Papa'sma always offered us coffee on our visits and that upset Mother, who thought children should not have coffee. So before we went into Papa'sma's house, we got the "coffee lecture" in addition to the "do not touch anything" lecture and the "do not ask for seconds, because they will think I don't feed you at home" warning. "If Papa'sma offers you coffee, say no thank you and have a glass of milk instead, because coffee will stunt your growth." (I knew I was far too tall already and Norway was a country of coffee drinkers and tall people.) And so Papa'sma would offer us a cup of coffee, knowing full well that Mother did not approve, and we would always shyly say, "Yes," with a smile, as we loved the coffee.

Well, I said, "Yes." I don't recollect what my brother said. Papa'sma would smile shyly, but triumphantly, and pour it for us with lots of cream and sugar. I can see my mother now as she tried to stifle a look of disappointment. I knew I would "get it later" and I didn't care. I thought it was O.K. if Papa'sma offered it, and I liked to drink her coffee, as it was so good with her waffles and wonderful bread, cheese and lingonberries.

I remember she was supportive of our achievements, and our pictures sat on her dining cabinet. And I remember a dollar bill or two being put into Mother's pocket or given to her in an envelope sometimes before we left. In those days it was very helpful. And a few dollars were sent to us for graduations and special days in our lives such as birthdays, especially when we were young.

My Norwegian relatives appeared to us as very rich. I found out much later that they were not. The one thing I really remember about Papa'sma's family besides the tears is that when we would visit they always spent much time scolding us for not coming more often, and were seemingly quite annoyed. We never seemed to talk about anything except "Why don't you come more often?" Mother liked to have a specific invitation rather than a general "come anytime," which didn't seem sincere to her. "Come Sunday at two" would have made more sense to her. But without a phone we could walk all the way over to Fairhaven and find no one at home. We children were embarrassed at these conversations and would squirm in our chairs and look around the room, sometimes fastening our eyes on Papa'sma's cuckoo clock and hoping the bird would come out and divert attention from this question. Cultural differences and misunderstandings permeated our lives and relationships during those days.

THE BLUE DRESS FROM "WINGS" DEPARTMENT STORE

ONE OF MY NORWEGIAN AUNTS, Tante Ellen, took me on a surprise shopping trip one day when I was in the seventh grade and bought me a beautiful blue dress. My aunt was very attractive and glamorous, and I shall never forget that day. A new dress from a good store—"Wings." That was all too rare in my life. I met her downtown, and we walked together to the store. I remember how excited I was. I wanted everyone to see me that day doing what the other girls did. On that day, I wasn't so different.

On very special or totally impromptu occasions, aunts both here and in Norway would give me silver—beautiful old silver spoons and forks and elaborate serving pieces handed down through the family, which I love and treasure today. One of my tantes just before her death told me that of all the children in the family, I somehow was the most Norwegian in temperament, mannerisms, looks and interests. I took that as a great compliment.

"You are youst (just) like us," she said, and I smiled as she handed me a piece of silver, saying, "I am giving this to you because I know you will love it and appreciate it." That was the last time we were to talk before she died.

UNCLES

ONE UNCLE, whom we really didn't know at all, bought us bikes one Christmas and that was much appreciated. When we were teens, another uncle took us driving in his new car and let us drive it on a back road. Before he married and had his own family, he also would visit us and bring some fish with him. That was really great, but they were never to be uncles who were a part of our lives; these were just occasional treats, not the relationships we yearned for and needed. My brother and I needed male role models since our father was dead, and I have always been sad that my Norwegian uncles were not closer to us. I would have liked to have known them better because in knowing them, I might have known a bit more about Papa, as well as knowing more about men in general. I was very fearful of men and very shy around them, as are most girls who lose their fathers. I would have loved, for instance, to have visited a fishing boat with an uncle so that he could tell me all about my father's life. Truthfully they never mentioned Papa and when Papa'sma and my tantes mentioned him, there would be tears. Perhaps my uncles didn't mention Papa because they were all too vulnerable to the same fate. Indeed, one of them was "lost" in 1964.

They were also very disappointed that they could not talk to us in Norwegian and often asked us why we hadn't learned it. We always answered, "How?" No one volunteered to teach us, and we rarely heard it. One uncle on his deathbed asked me that question. I felt terrible, and still do, that I cannot converse in Norwegian. At least now I can read it a bit and understand some.

I vividly remember my great-uncle Karl Sigvart Tobiassen who would visit each year from Atlantic City and would send us twenty dollars every Christmas, so that Momma could buy us some gifts. For a few years Mother did just that, but as the years went by, the Christmas money had to pay for coal and other necessities. My brother still remembers with loathing the yearly flannel shirt that was his best Christmas present.

I remember a conversation with another uncle in the middle of my senior year of high school. I was visiting his home and he took me aside and said, "I hear you are going to college to become a big shot. I suppose you will not see us again as you will be so much better." I was amazed that he said that to me and simply didn't understand what he meant. I believed we should be all that we could be. One Norwegian-American woman has a different point of view on this. She wrote to me that "Norwegians stayed to themselves—they were so embarrassed and ashamed of their broken English. I think your uncle was telling you that he was ashamed of his lack of education."

I look back now at those family relationships and realize many of the problems we experienced were the result of misunderstandings related to language and cultural differences. For example, until the day she died, Momma believed that Grandmother owned a large herring factory in Norway. I didn't understand why she believed that so strongly, but she always said that Papa had told her that the family had wealth in Norway. I asked about that very thing when I traveled there after Papa'sma's death many years later. The answer surprised me. "Yes," they said, "Mille had a herring factory. We all did. The fish would come in and we would dry it in our basements. We thought of it as our own factory." So again, the difference in language and understanding led to great differences and misconceptions among the American brides who married Norwegians.

ALWAYS THE COFFEE ISSUE

AND THERE WAS ALWAYS THE COFFEE ISSUE. Mother didn't serve it, and the relatives felt insulted. Simple cultural differences and expectations—so small and yet so important to people's lives and relationships.

One tante, before she died, told me that she and Papa'sma would visit and bring a pound of coffee to our house. My mother would thank them and put it away. Next time they would walk the several miles with coffee, cream and sugar, and Mother would thank them and put it away. At times they also brought pastries or waffles, and the same thing happened.

"So we stopped coming," she said. They took it as being not wanted; Mother took it as a simple gift. I only wish they had said, "Muriel, let's make coffee." Mother just never thought of serving it; that wasn't her tradition and in all of her life she never felt comfortable entertaining guests. It just wasn't her way, not even for her own sisters. So I did it in later years because I loved it. And Mother would say, "There's Astrid entertaining again. I just don't understand that girl."

Mother felt generally ignored by the Norwegian women, some of whom had been friendly when father was alive, but I think this was more of their fear of Mother's situation than their dislike of her. She recalls seeing one woman who had been a guest at their home in New Bedford when this woman lived in Brooklyn. Her husband was very close to my father. Momma recalled fifty-five years later, "After your father died, I saw her coming down Purchase Street, and I smiled and started to wave, and as soon as she saw me, she turned and walked the other way. I never forgot that. It hurt me very much."

Mother did explain to us that had we gone to the Norwegian church, people would have been friendlier to us, but she was a Congregationalist and her church meant a great deal to her. She sang in the choir, was often a soloist, head of the Sunday school, had a Brownie troop there, and for her it was a second home. Lutheranism, in those days when the service was conducted in Norwegian, seemed to her very elaborate and "Catholic." To her it was a foreign faith. Her ancestors were the Pilgrims, and she was not to break faith with them. In later years, as an adult, my brother became a Lutheran along with his wife and two of his sons.

Several people who had been my father's friends—one a Swedish man with a German wife, the Seabergs—were kind to us in those years, and we visited often. They would give us the clothing their children had outgrown. It was always lovely, but often didn't fit. We would visit there also and play with the children and delight in all of their toys.

NORWEGIAN CHRISTMAS

THE NORWEGIAN FRIENDS living on our street, my father's friend, Rasmus Tonnessen and his Yankee/Irish wife Sally, were very active in the Norwegian community, as they owned a large ship's store where my father was the first customer. Papa and Ray had been close even in Norway most of their lives and these dear people made sure that Mother received some gifts and a yearly fruit basket that had an envelope with money in it. I remember Momma crying when that arrived.

The Tonnessens saw to it that we were invited to the yearly Christmas party given by the Norwegian fishermen and their families in the early days. I remember how beautiful my aunts and other wives were and that the families seemed so glamorous compared to my mother's relatives. We would look at all of the pretty clothes and finery and be embarrassed that we did not have that. Mother was very embarrassed about all of our worn clothing, including her own hand-me-downs from her sister.

—Bill Olden Archives

Sally and Ray Tonnessen (rear) a few years after my father's death. They were good to Momma and always remained her true friends. The also had a Norwegian-American marriage and they understood Momma's predicament well. They were caring, generous and loving people. Ray was quiet and said little. Sally was more outspoken and very open. I really liked her.

—A Tollefsen Archives

Sally Tonnessen, left, with Momma the day Tonnessen Park was dedicated. I wore my Norwegian hat and am towering over them. Harriet Didriksen, Sally's devoted niece, is next to me, and my German friend Karin Michaelis Reynolds is at right. I saw Sally after my mother died and Sally said to me, "Muriel was a good woman. She took good care of her children. She was a good woman."

Those parties were wonderful, and I remember the abundance of food and the colorful Norwegian dresses, but most of all I remember that we had to sit very still and be perfect, while the other children ran, danced and played while having a great time. The Norwegian children were given the freedom to run around, play tag, and make noise. We were half-Norwegian and that half wanted to play, but the Yankee half prevailed, and we sat. Mother was very protective and would give us dire warnings before we went in—to take care not to embarrass her in front of the relatives. It was important to her that they see us as obedient, good, well-brought-up children. I think now that the Norwegians saw us as sad children and wondered why we didn't play with the others. In fact, they would come over and ask us why, but Mother would answer their questions.

As we grew older, we saw less and less of our Norwegian family. They were busy with their own lives and tragedies as well as their own expanding families. We always visited Papa'sma, however, catching her up on our lives and achievements. In adulthood, we are friendly with the various cousins. I got to know many of my aunts and uncles later in life, and I enjoyed them very much and have great love for several of my aunts. And my mother was right— we are very much alike. One of my aunts understood me implicitly, and I felt she could almost read my mind, and another shared my mannerisms. One relative showed me Papa'sma's Bible after she died, and it was filled with newspaper articles about our accomplishments and us. I was so happy that she did that.

GROWING UP AMERICAN

Mother was very lonely, particularly after the war, when all the men came back to their homes, and her friends became preoccupied with their husbands. She did her best and did it well, but I remember life then as sad and different from all the other relatives and friends we knew. She saw to it that we went to church, scouts and the "Y," that we learned new skills and were with people who would set good examples for us. She had the American approach to the value and role of church and community agencies. She was very proud of us and we always saw her smiling face at our childhood events. One thing I remember vividly: No matter how poor we were, we would "make do" somehow and trust in God. It was important to Mother to show the Norwegian side of the family that she could raise her children well.

As we got older, we were instructed never to walk or bike below Purchase Street near the waterfront and never go down to the docks. Mother was very fearful that my brother might take it in his mind to become a fisherman—and, God forbid, that her daughter might meet a handsome Norwegian fisherman and have to live as she did. We heard about that a lot in our teen years. She tried so hard every day of her life to bring us so as to not repeat her life of pain. I know some of that was because she felt she had to be both mother and father.

For example, she was afraid of the water, so she saw to it that both my brother and I became good swimmers, so good in fact that we were both life-guards and instructors for many years. Both of us also taught boating skills and boat safety in our late teens and early twenties.

I don't ever remember Mother telling me that my goal in life was to be attractive, marry, keep a house and have a family. She just kept talking about having an education and career and that a man coming into my life might interrupt that. Clothing had to be very discreet and nothing could flaunt or otherwise distract. My mother applied a negative label to girls who dressed to please boys.

"You must be very careful," she would say so often, remembering her own situation. "Get an education first, no matter what. Later, after you have your degree and a career, you can think about men." I was thankful for this deter-mination, because at one point in my life an uncle who was not Norwegian tried to persuade her to make me quit high school and work in a factory. I remember his words: "She is just a girl. Education doesn't matter for her. You need her to support you, Mooie." And for the only time in her life, she stood up to him. I remember standing on the stairs listening in terror that somehow he might persuade her, as he usually did. Her tragedy of being widowed prevailed over her obedience to him, thank God!

One day I was talking to a Norwegian-American woman, and she told me that I was very lucky to have grown up in this manner. She said that both her mother and father were Norwegian and that she grew up with one goal only—to meet a man to marry, to have a neat, lovely home and raise children. She lamented how she knew nothing else, basically, and would have loved to have some options in her life. "So in a way if your father had lived," she told me, "you would have had the same mentality and mind-set that we all grew up with—marriage, home and family." She emphasized I was lucky to not have married at nineteen as did she and most of her friends. How she envied all of my travel and adventure that somehow my mother through her deter-mination had enabled.

We always struggled to be the most we could be and had faith that if we tried hard enough, it would happen. At thirteen I took a job in a fruit store. I sold fruit to the customers and was so pleased I had a few dollars to buy some school clothes. One day after I had worked there for about a month, Papa'sma came into the shop. I went over to wait on her, and she gave me a frozen look.

"What are you doing in here?" she asked. "You are not supposed to be in here." I remember just standing and staring at her. I was so proud to be working, and she seemed so upset and ashamed of me. She gave me a very disapproving look, left her fruit and walked out haughtily. The owner of the store came over and told me that she was one of his oldest customers, and I was to blame for her walking out. He was quite angry. "It's my grandmother," I said. The next day he told me they couldn't use me any longer. I think now that Papa'sma felt sad and powerless that day and worried about my future.

—Tollefsen archives

Momma's proudest day, my graduation from college. A few years later she was to have a graduation of her own.

Some family members on both sides felt we wanted too much in life, but then they had not been in our position; we had no place to go but up. Both my brother and I went to college, I at seventeen, through our own initiative. And we also earned master's degrees. My brother followed the Norwegian tradition of the Merchant Marine and graduated from the United States Merchant Marine Academy at King's Point and then had a career in the Navy. I went into teaching, became an officer in the Navy and an executive and consultant in the nonprofit field. Together we had approximately fourteen years of university education. Mother was very proud of our achievements, as was Papa'sma.

Later in Mother's life, after serving as the Girl's Director at the Dennison Memorial for many years and shortly after she turned fifty, she traveled to Washington, D.C., and attended and graduated from the Hannah Harrison School for Women. Career opportunities then opened up for her and she became a professional administrator, specializing in dormitory/residence management. This gave her the opportunity to have many new college-age daughters each year. She later remarried and she and her Italian-born husband started a successful business together.

She always encouraged us to rely only on ourselves, reminding us how she had been left alone with little help. It was a lesson we were to learn for life.

HOMEPORT

M OTHER HAD A VERY DIFFICULT LIFE because my father had decided to climb that mast in the tradition of the sea. In my heart of hearts, I wished, of course, that he had thought more about us and just let the boat sink. But with his youth and financial responsibilities, he felt he must do it and trusted that nothing would happen to him. But it did, and when he died a part of all of us died.

And to make things worse, Papa'sma would eventually lose four of her six sons and a son-in-law to the sea. It was more pain than anyone should ever bear.

THE END

IN THE MONTHS PRECEDING Mother's death in 1998, when I was caring for her and she was very ill, she became much closer to the remaining Norwegian relatives. Several of them visited her quite often, and I served the coffee and food. There was real warmth and understanding, and I remember Tante touching Momma's face and saying, "God bless you, Muriel." There had been so much pain and so much loss, and very long, lonely, tragic years for these two widowed women.

A few days later my mother died, and the one thing I remember well at her funeral at the Seaman's Bethel was a middle-aged man sitting alone in the back row. I approached him and asked if he were a friend of Mother's. "Yes," he said, "I was your paper boy, and I will never forget Mrs. Tollefsen because of the beautiful smile she gave me when I brought the paper." I thought to myself 'that was over fifty years ago' and then I remembered him. Each week he would knock on the door to collect the paper money. I don't recall that he ever spoke. He always looked down and simply put his hand out. We were poor but perhaps rich by his standards. Momma had one of her big smiles for him, and I think it made him feel better. He remembered her after all those years. That was Momma and that is why my father loved her and why we will never forget her.

Sally Tonnessen, a good friend of my mother's into her late years, upon hearing of my mother's death, said, "Muriel, she was a good woman. She gave up everything for her children." My mother would have loved to have heard those words. That is what she wanted to be remembered for. Her life was her children. I recently went to Sally's funeral and said to her silently, "Sally, thank you for always remembering us when we were children."

TODAY

NOW THEY ARE TOGETHER, Momma and Papa, buried alongside one another on very cold and wet days, in the Acushnet Cemetery and still guarded over by my mother's mother in the plot next to them. Mother and I visited that spot for so many years and planted many flowering plants there each spring. As children we would run around and be too noisy. I continue to re-experience our many stages of growth when I visit there. I can hear the voices of our childhood and our relatives scolding us or telling us to fetch the water for the plants. I can see my relatives' tears at the grave. So much time had passed and so many tears have been shed. Recently some heather was planted on the grave by a Norwegian friend from my father's island as a symbol of Norway. I knew my father would love that. I planted heather also on my grandparents' grave in Norway.

Now on Karmøy, there is a fisherman's memorial with an altar and bell tower looking out to the west. My father's name, the names of all of my uncles and other men who were lost to the sea in America are listed on this memorial. I feel today that they and their parents are all together in spirit once more. They are home again.

> *"Here he lies, where he longed to be;*
> *Home is the sailor, home from the sea."*
>
> —Robert Louis Stevenson, "Requiem"

CHAPTER

4

The Explosive Waters

THE WAR YEARS: 1940–1945

Gunleif Wilhelmsen, later a New Bedford fisherman, is in the boat on right preparing to land on the beach in France, on D-Day 1944. Note size of shell, top of photo.

NEW BEDFORD

THE MOST SIGNIFICANT EVENT of the mid-twentieth century—World War II—made an indelible mark on the lives of all who lived through those epochal years. As children growing up in New Bedford, we remember the dark city, the black shades, the schools' regular gathering of

93

children and teachers for mock air raids where we sang patriotic songs and prayed. We collected newspapers, had victory gardens, saved cans, knitted afghans, mailed fudge to the soldiers, saved our pennies for war bonds and stamps, and learned to assemble margarine from a white lard-like substance which we colored with a small ball of deep orange material. We children loved to knead this mixture and can still remember the yellow stains on our hands after we had made the color uniform so that it would resemble the scarce butter. It certainly didn't taste or smell like butter to us.

We remember having to eat all of our food because there were starving children in Europe, and we remember that we were raised in a community of mostly women due to the absence of young men away in the wartime effort.

The church bells did not ring, as a tribute to our men fighting the wars. The car headlights were painted half black, and people were generally anxious and worried. The newspapers carried stories that frightened us as children and photos we weren't supposed to look at. At the beach, our mothers would tell us not to go out too far because an enemy submarine might be lurking there. We looked for periscopes in the water, and we were sure we saw them during those warm summer days at Acushnet Park or Fort Phoenix. And, indeed, submarines did prowl those waters.

We were never to draw swastikas on the playground because if we did that or called someone a Nazi or Jap we were sent to the principal's office. Some of our friends' parents who had German accents, we were told, could not leave the city and were watched and often suspected of being spies. We

—*Detail of early map*

New Bedford's West End in the forties—from the waterfront to Buttonwood Park. Many fishing families lived in this area.

—*Courtesy of the late Alice Bell Brown*

During the war we would stand in line and bring our dimes to the teacher. She would then give us stamps to put into a book, which eventually would be turned in for a defense bond, called war bonds. We were told this helped our soldiers win the war.

remember planes in the sky, huge dirigibles practicing their anti-submarine reconnaissance work, and in Dartmouth at my aunt's vacation house on Slocum River, we used to see gliders practicing for combat missions in Europe. We would hear fragments of conversations—hushed rumors about Colonel Green's estate and secret military work there, and scary stories about German prisoners in a camp on Cape Cod.

I remember visiting a family friend's home one day where we ate lobster, which her fisherman husband had brought in from his last trip. It was a special treat for us, but when I looked up I saw her tears. She was German, and that day the Americans were bombing Berlin where her sister and family lived. I never forgot her tears and pain that day as she bravely tried to entertain us with this special treat. She said, "We have so much, and they are starving. I feel so bad, and I don't know if they are dead or alive." Her anguish taught me that there are decent people on both sides in a war. She had been very generous and loving to us as we grew up, and her Swedish husband had been my father's true friend.

Our Norwegian relatives worried about the family in Norway as well as their husbands and brothers out to sea here. There was secretive talk about submarines and Norwegian fishermen. For the children there seemed to be many secrets and shrouded talks during wartime—things we weren't supposed to hear, see or repeat.

My cousin Toralf Tobiassen, who lived in Atlantic City, appeared at our home one day in uniform. He was very handsome, kind, and proud to serve in the United States military. My mother, who adored him and his family, cried bitterly after he left. His mother, Josefine Serine Isaksen Tobiassen, known as Serine, had been my mother's closest Norwegian friend before her tragic early death just a few months after I was born, and my mother loved her very much and missed her greatly. Therefore, Toralf, had a special place in Momma's heart. One day, a year after he left, my Aunt Alice ran up the street

Domei News Agency Reports:

JAPS SURRENDER

The Standard-Times EXTRA

NIPPONESE WILL ACCEPT POTSDAM PROCLAMATION

Silent on Emperor; U. S. Is Mum

—New Bedford Standard-Times

The end of the war. VJ Day.

and called to my mother from the gate. My mother went flying out of the house to see what was wrong. I heard her wail—a sound never heard from her before—and it frightened me. My mother and aunt came into the house and told us that Toralf had been killed when his plane exploded over Long Island during a training exercise. My mother was never to get over this tragedy. Shortly after there was another loss when her young cousin was killed in Africa in a train mishap, while serving with the Army.

I remember my mother telling my uncles to be very careful when there were rumors of German submarines offshore. What we didn't know was that many fishermen were carrying out anti-submarine intelligence missions for the government while they were at sea.

I remember Momma going through the house and smashing everything that read "Made in Japan" on Pearl Harbor Day. I also remember the day when President Roosevelt died, that the streets were filled with sobbing people as they poured out of their homes trying to comfort one another. It was frightening for us to see the adults so upset. We felt the end of the world was at hand—surely Hitler would capture us now, we thought.

And who could forget the joy at the end of the war? V-J Day was celebrated with a parade on Purchase Street; church bells ringing and filling the air with joy; decorated autos with their horns blaring; people running and shouting with happiness, and street dances in front of city hall with women and children dancing together. The general euphoria helped us believe that life would be O.K. again, and our brothers, husbands, sons and boyfriends would be home soon. And shortly after that we had our first taste of bubblegum which was nonexistent during the war years.

The war had really ended.

—*William Olden archives*

Norwegians of the New Bedford area at a Christmas banquet just before the war. Rasmus and Sally Tonnessen, at upper right, most likely organized the party.

NORWAY

THE WAR YEARS AFFECTED US ALL dramatically, but we didn't know then what was happening to our friends and relatives in Norway. The war had a profound influence on the Norwegians and their later emigration to America. Those who came after the war were very different than those who had come before. Money was their goal, and there was never enough because memories of poverty and deprivation during the war years shaped their thinking throughout their lives.

THE BIG SURPRISE

DURING THE POST-DEPRESSION DAYS of the late thirties, while Norwegian fishermen were making good money and expanding their fishing fleets on the Atlantic Coast, Hitler was gaining extraordinary power in Germany and Europe. Most of those in the Norwegian expatriate community, and their families in Norway, took little note. Life went on as normal, and the Norwegians felt they were protected by British naval presence in the North Sea area and the official neutrality of Norway.

—*German photo, courtesy Dreyer Bok.*

Germans arrive by bus on Karmøy circa 1940.

The fishermen went back to Norway at Christmas on the *Julebot*, Christmas boat, usually the

Stavangerfjord, spent the customary two to three months at home with their families, friends and neighbors, and returned to New Bedford each spring. Babies were born in Norway in the autumn. Some fishermen saved their money to buy houses here so that their families could follow them to America. Others just sent money home for their families in Norway and didn't plan for them to emigrate—decisions made by mutual consent.

As Hitler became more and more powerful in Europe and began his aggression against his neighbor countries, the Norwegians were still not concerned because they felt that their country was not of great strategic importance. Because they were so closely related to Germans in language, culture and religion, they felt they would not be regarded as an enemy. They also believed that they could maintain their neutrality as they had done in World War I. They made an agreement allowing Great Britain to charter a portion of the Norwegian Merchant Marine and in return Norway was to be permitted to maintain its pre-war level of trade with Germany. So it was a total shock to those in Norway and to Norwegians in America, when Norway was invaded and occupied by the Germans on April 9, 1940.

And it was a particular shock to the New Bedford fishermen's wives and their children who were visiting relatives in Norway at the time, and to the many wives and families of Norwegian-American fishermen still living in Norway. Their husbands were frantic.

Norwegian fishermen in America had a number of choices once Norway was occupied. They could join the United States military and fight the Axis powers, or they could join the Norwegian or American Merchant Marine to help win the war by delivering critical war supplies to the European theater of operations. If neither of these choices were possible, they could go on fishing and volunteer to serve as intelligence agents for the United States government. This was a dangerous and courageous choice made by many who could not join the conflict but who wanted to do their best to help their native land, friends and families, and assist their adopted country.

During these war years, Norwegian fishermen in Massachusetts had virtually no contact with their families in Norway and some didn't see the babies, who were born in the months after their last Norwegian winter there, until many years later. Some didn't even know that they had new offspring until after the war. Most did not know if their families were dead or alive because little or no mail was able to get through the German net over Norway. But they could and did raise money for Norwegian relief societies, and they could listen to their short-wave radios to try to pick up news from Norway.

It is interesting to note that the family of Norway's Prince Olav summered in South Dartmouth during the war years. Years later the king, as the honored guest of Norwegian-Americans in the Greater New Bedford area, recalled his days in South Dartmouth during the war. His son, the little boy who played on the shores of South Dartmouth, is now King Harald of Norway.

THE WAR YEARS IN NORWAY
TIDES OF PERIL: WINDS OF CHANGE

"The German strategy was to occupy both Norway and Denmark and leave Sweden neutral. During the First World War the German Fleet was locked in the Baltic Sea and the Germans remembered that vividly. They needed ready access to the North Sea and Atlantic Ocean, which the Norwegian ports and deep fjords could provide. These ports would provide ideal naval bases to launch their war at sea, and their submarines would have ideal hiding places. This strategy proved sound as the war developed."

—ODIN, Official Documentation and Information from Norway.
Article "Norway and World War II," Tor Dagre, abridged

A MASSACHUSETTS NORWEGIAN-AMERICAN WOMAN, Janna Isaksen, who was visiting in Southern Norway when Germany invaded, reflects on that time. "I saw the last ship leave for America in March, and then the Germans came in April. We didn't know that it was to be the last ship, but it was very crowded. The North Sea was mined and a Norwegian flag was painted on the ship. The Norwegian flag was flying high so Germans knew what ship it was as Norway was neutral. The lifeboats were hanging outside and waiting for the people to get in—ready to go immediately into the water in case they hit a mine. It was very frightening for the people on board as they stood outside until the ship had cleared the minefield. The Norwegian national anthem played when the ship left. It was very emotional even though no one knew that this would be the last ship. So many were stranded in Norway, and we didn't know the Germans were coming. I was going to take my mother with me to come back to America later. I started to go and then my father died, and I had to stay longer. My son who was very young was with me."

THAT AWFUL DAY IN APRIL, 1940

"A huge fleet departed from German ports with troops and materiel. Nearly the entire German Navy, six army divisions and a large air force contingent, took part in the attack. The first targets were eight Norwegian towns and cities along the country's lengthy coast."

—ODIN

A NORWEGIAN-AMERICAN FROM BERGEN, Gunnar Berg, remembers: "I think about it now, and I can't understand why we were so surprised. The German merchant vessels lay off our shore for at least a week. We all saw them, and we knew there was something strange going on because our island, the windward side of Bergen, had horse droppings accumulating on the beaches. Why would merchant ships carry horses? And then one morning there they were. The German ships docked at the piers in Bergen, and we were invaded by German soldiers and their cavalry. Why didn't we know or suspect? We thought it was just the merchant fleet."

THE INVASION AND OCCUPATION

—German photo, courtesy Dreyer Bok

A German soldier looks out to "his" fjord during the war years.

AN OSLO TEENAGER, Oddvar Solstad, who was to become a fisherman in New Bedford, recalls the invasion: "There were lots of airplanes, and there was total confusion. No warning at all! A total surprise. I was sixteen years old. They came in the middle of the night, and we all went down into the basement because we didn't know what was going to happen. There was bombing around Oslo but not in the city. They landed at the airport outside Oslo. Our military tried to defend but had no experience or manpower.

"A huge German warship by the name of *Blucher* was sunk almost by chance in the Oslo Fjord, which is a narrow fjord. The *Blucher* sailed up the fjord where there was a fort with a few old cannon. The 'Old Moses,' a fifty-year-old cannon with equally old cannon balls, fired and hit the ship directly, igniting its ammunition and fuel oil. It sunk almost immediately, killing most of the military and civilians on board. But other ships could still get by it.

"The next morning there was fear because we were afraid the Allies would bomb Oslo. Everyone who could left the city. My dad was in retail fish and had a truck. We drove to a farm forty-five miles away and stayed there for several weeks until we knew what was going on. Everything was total confusion. No one we knew had information. The Norwegian forces were trying to prevent the Germans from going north as the king was fleeing north. Norway's gold bouillon went out to England on fishing boats, and that helped with the war effort from England."

A Norwegian-American wife, Janna Isaksen, stranded in Norway with her son, tells of her fright at the time of the invasion: "The Norwegian flag came down and the German flag went up. We were occupied. There was fighting, and they almost got the king. He was sailed out on a Norwegian ship and then to England. His family then went to America. He went out through the north

—*AT Photo*

Janna Isaksen pours coffee at her home in Dartmouth, Massachusetts, 1997, as she relates her story.

of Norway from Oslo, and a boat picked him up there. The Germans came on airplanes, trains and boats. Bodies kept coming onto our Island of Hidra in Southern Norway, washing up on shore from the fighting out to sea. We couldn't have lights at night—we had to have heavy shades so that the allied bombers wouldn't see us."

The late shipping entrepreneur Lauritz Eidesvik, from Bømlo, an island north of Haugesund in South West Norway, was a child when the German invaders came. "I knew we were at war because at the cemetery one day, while our neighbor was being buried, I saw the German planes coming over. My father was called to fight against the Germans. I was in the second grade and believed in God. I fell on my knees and prayed for my father to return, and he did. We had less food during the war and lived on potatoes and fish. We also had a farm and a pig. The Germans occupied the school, and we were free from school. We didn't like them but had no problems on our island. We knew by the color of their uniform if they were dangerous. The SS was dangerous."

A man from the island of Karmøy, Kaare Ness, shared his memories of the early days of the war: "We were just young teenagers when the war broke out. There were many Germans on the island. They had foxholes and bunkers, and there were many guns. They came in ships, showing up in different places on the same day. The coastline is very long, so the invasion had to be carefully planned. No ships to Karmøy; they came into Haugesund. The first German I saw was near the ninth of April when I had to go to my grandmother's house and had to cross the main road from where I lived. A truck came from the north going into Skudenes, a regular Norwegian truck with two German soldiers sitting on back of the truck with guns. No one resisted because there were no soldiers there defending. Norwegian soldiers were in Oslo and Bergen.

"Later on there were lots of Germans on the islands, and they put up camps in different places. We traded eggs for cigarettes and sometimes got a meal from them. We didn't think much of it, and we as kids didn't have the sense to know that they had invaded us and taken all our rights away."

German bunker in Åkrehamn, Karmøy, Norway.

—AT copy of a photo in their home.

Karl and Martha Berg in the early days of their marriage.

THE DISLOCATED FAMILIES

MANY MERCHANT MARINERS were not in Norway at the time and had to find ways to fight the Germans outside their homeland. Most operated out of England and didn't see their families throughout the war. One such seaman, Karl Berg, whose wife Martha was stranded on the island of Fedje—just north of Bergen, remembered: "I was in England and got my Norwegian seaman's papers translated into English, and the Americans accepted me right there. A union man said, 'This guy is Norwegian but holds American papers,' and he talked them into accepting me into the American Merchant Marine. 'The American flag will take care of you,' he said. I was so proud that the American Merchant Marine wanted me. I had no choice during the war. I had to go.

"I was in the invasion of Normandy and made seven trips from Southampton to the beachheads and two trips to Italy as well. I sailed from New York to England and was in convoys. It was very dangerous, but I am still here; I don't know why."

THE NAZIFICATION OF NORWAY

"After the German troops had conquered the allies in Norway, the Germans started reorganizing Norwegian society to comply with their needs. This involved anything which could contribute to the progress of the German military, but changes which served Nazi ideology also began to surface. In addition to a German commander in chief, Norway was also burdened with a political commissioner. While the population was being terrorized and oppressed, Norway entered a state of semi-paralysis for five long years."

—ODIN

ODDVAR SOLSTAD FROM OSLO explained: "After a few weeks, life began to take on some normalcy. The Germans had a stranglehold on Norway. After about a year, they confiscated the radios, and we had to turn in all heavy boots, blankets, clothing and bedding for their troops. Food became scarce, and pressure was getting stronger on everyone. During the occupation the

Germans would seal off the streets and search everyone on the street when you were walking or riding on the streetcar to see if they could find weapons and other contraband. Grini, the concentration camp, was west of Oslo. Our school had been taken over by the Germans as they used the classroom for the troops, and we had to study in private places in the community. I graduated in 1941."

President Franklin Delano Roosevelt addressed Princess Martha of Norway and Americans at the presentation of a new submarine chaser to the Royal Norwegian Navy, September 16, 1942, with these eloquent words:

> *"If there is anyone who still wonders why this war is being fought,*
> *Let him look to Norway.*
> *If there is anyone who has any delusions that this war could have*
> *been averted, Let him look to Norway.*
> *And if anyone has doubts of the democratic will to win, again I*
> *say, Let him look to Norway.*
> *But the story of Norway since the conquest shows*
> *that while a free democracy may be slow to realize its danger,*
> *it may be heroic when aroused.*
> *At home, the Norwegian people have silently resisted the invader's*
> *will with grim endurance.*
> *Abroad, Norwegian ships, Norwegian men have rallied*
> *to the cause of the United Nations, and their assistance to that*
> *cause has been out of all proportion to their small numbers."*

ATTEMPTS TO HELP THE NORWEGIANS

MANY ATTEMPTS WERE MADE in America to help the besieged Norwegians by shipping foodstuffs and other life necessities. Various support groups and U.S. officials made many plans but each plan seemed to be thwarted. When all the relief groups finally merged into a collaborative effort, monies became more available, and more than a million dollars was collected in the later war years from individual Norwegian-Americans and organizations. Most of the monies collected were used to support the Norwegian military, including prisoners of war and merchant mariners.

One program that succeeded was the Norwegian Seaman's Christmas and Relief Fund, which was supported by Americans and Norwegian–Americans. Bent Vanberg writes in his book published by the Sons of Norway, "From So Many . . . For so Few": "From the fall of 1941 until the spring of 1946 about 90,000 Christmas packages were distributed. Of these about 64,000 went directly to the Norwegian crews aboard ships in the Port of New York, to all the seaman's churches and institutions in New York, as well as in larger ports in America and Canada. About 26,000 packages were sent to England, Iceland, Italy, Egypt, India and other places where Norwegian ships sailed. In addition, watertight bags to preserve the seaman's personal documents were distributed, as well as clothing and necessities for hospitals and other institutions servicing the seamen.

It needs to be remembered that neutral Sweden harbored many smuggled Norwegians during the war years. Sweden was a place for Norwegians to hide, and the routes taken by such escapees might be compared to the so-called "underground railroad" of the American Civil War. Most Swedes remain very proud of these deeds, which often involved great risk. Relations between the two countries have been sometimes awkward over the years, but many Swedish people still tried to help their Norwegian neighbors when they were in danger.

—*Published in Brooklyn for Norwegian-Americans.*

King Håkon sends his Christmas message from exile to his people on the cover of a wartime edition of "NORGE." The message says, "I send all Norwegian Women and Men the best for a *GOD JUL* (Merry Christmas)."

MEANWHILE IN NORWAY

MANY NORWEGIANS SPOKE OF FOOD being the paramount problem during these difficult years. Fishermen would travel inland to trade fish with the farmers under the cover of darkness, but they faced constant danger from the Germans.

Martha Berg, a wife alone on an island in Norway near Bergen, recalls her life while her husband was in the American Merchant Marine: "Life in Norway in those days—well, we tried to survive, learned to survive. We had whale meat in summer, and we grew potatoes. Many Germans were on our island. There were barracks and an observation tower. If you kept away, the Germans left you alone. They were young boys. We weren't friendly.

"After the First World War, things were very bad in Germany, and German children came to Norway to live and be fed. I heard a German soldier speak Norwegian to me one day very well: 'Did you eat yesterday?' he asked. He was one who had been here after 1918. I didn't answer."

One former harbor pilot told of the problems with the German Navy and how they, the harbor pilots, actually had some power during the war years. He remembered that the Germans needed their cooperation to enter the rocky harbors with their ships and that they, the Norwegian pilots, could sometimes barter with the Germans because of this need. Such bartering often improved the quality of life for the townspeople.

Egil Ellingsen, now living in Seattle, recollects the days of his youth. "The Nazi military filled the coast of Norway with minefields to obstruct any allied submarines or vessels to get through the fjords to help our country. Fishing captains were given sketchy maps outlining where the mines were located so that we could still fish and hopefully survive. Those were anxious times of navigation. In 1943 when I was twenty-one, my Uncle Didrik and I purchased a fishing vessel together. We were both young to have accomplished this feat, as Didrik was only twenty-nine and closer than a brother. To this day, we are still close, even though he lives in Ferkingstad, Norway, and I am in America.

"The Nazis confiscated all radios from the people and cut off all communication sources. Our ship radio was registered with the Nazis and signed out to me for the fishing season only. It was to be returned to the Nazi Office at the end of each season. Not returning the radio or being caught listening to the BBC from England was punishable by death. Young and loyal to my country, I kept the radio and hid it in our ship, listening to BBC and providing true information of what was happening in the war as part of the Norwegian underground."

LOCAL SYMPATHIZERS VS. NORWEGIAN DETERMINATION

"As in all the other occupied countries, the Nazis benefited from the support of local sympathizers. Vidkun Quisling proclaimed himself the new head of the government and ordered the Norwegian armed forces to stop battling the Germans. But Quisling's intervention backfired and only stimulated the resistance. Following an initial period of shock and confusion in the summer of 1940, Norwegian determination to resist grew. The Nazification of society was countered at every turn, especially in the church and the schools. Thus, Quisling's Nazi Party only got a modest grip on the people's soul, and could only exist under the protection of the German armed forces."

—ODIN

20+30 NORGE

The Nazi-endorsed Norwegian collaborator Quisling put his face on this wartime postage stamp.

RECALLS GUNNAR GUNDERSEN, who emigrated to New Bedford after the war: "There was no money from my father in America after 1940. It was very difficult on the women alone. I was twenty years old when the war came. The Germans tried to recruit Norwegian boys, and the worst was the uncertainty and the fear that they would take us to fight on the Russian front. When I heard Quisling talking on the radio, I was sick to my stomach because he was now prime minister."

Another post-war emigrant from Norway, Kaare Ness, recalls, "The boats were given official papers by the Germans, and these papers had to be shown to the German officials before a boat could go out to sea. The underground took boats to London occasionally, and the Germans needed to keep track of the boats to prevent this. There was no bombing on Karmøy, but the waterway between Karmøy and the mainland was a dangerous place and critical for transportation. Sometimes the English planes would come over and drop mines to close the waterway. We saw planes shot down a few times but didn't see any other fighting."

A Haugesund native, Kitty Ellingsen, relived her teenage days during the war by explaining: "We had air raids constantly in Haugesund, and British and Canadian planes flew over and bombed the port. We prayed that the pilots would not be shot down, and we also prayed that their bombs would not hit us. One day a Canadian pilot was killed, and when we tried to bury him, the Germans wouldn't let us.

"There was one particularly frightening day which I remember vividly. I had a pair of shoes for my sister who was living and working in Stavanger, and I decided to take a ferry there so I could give them to her. The Germans were on all of the boats. Just as we were leaving Haugesund there was an air raid, and British and Canadian planes came and bombed and sunk the boat next to us. It went down stern first, and we could see the soldiers on board. But we kept going, and I saw another boat hit and sunk. While running from Kopervik to Stavanger, another wave of planes came over, but we were able to maneuver away from them.

"I went to get a life jacket, but a German officer took the last one, so I didn't have one. I was about sixteen and just held onto my New Testament and prayed the whole time. We got to Stavanger OK and my sister got her shoes. I risked all of that for a pair of shoes to give to my sister."

The *Vindafjord*, bombed by the Germans between Skudeneshavn and Stavanger. From: *"De som dro fra Karmøy til America"* (They went from Karmøy to America).

Kristian Berg, my late uncle from Bergen, recalled in 1992: "We had hidden a radio in the basement and were careful not to tell anyone. We could occasionally hear the news from England. But it was frightening when the Germans made house searches."

The Reverend Dr. Gordon M. Torgersen, whose father came from Stavanger, remembers a story he heard on a family visit to Norway. "I always get a chill when I think of one of the relatives who ran a hardware store. Secretly, he kept a forbidden radio in the basement of the shop. He would go to work early and listen to the British broadcast, make notes of the war news, and have it available for a friend who would come in and get it, then make a newspaper account available for others so that they all came to know all the available news about the war."

CIVILIAN RESISTANCE

"Underground military groups were established in parallel with civilian resistance, and a prime objective was to assist in the Allied and Norwegian intelligence operations. The groups were useful in reporting the movements of German vessels and the transport of troops and materiel. In November 1944, Norwegian intelligence was heavily responsible for the sinking of the 41,700-ton battleship Tirpitz. When progress was eventually made in arming the underground Norwegian groups, often by parachute drops

from Allied aircraft and supplies from the Shetland bus, the military groups became more of a problem for the Germans, particularly for the Gestapo. Toward the end of the war, the home front carried out sabotage against the transport infrastructure. Armed clashes occurred all across the country."

—ODIN

ODDVAR SOLSTAD

ACCORDING TO ODDVAR SOLSTAD: "During that period of time we had to be careful in class because we didn't know who might be a spy—some Norwegians liked the Germans. Some belonged to the Nazi Party in Norway, and they would snitch on the others. Some of the teachers of English and history were outspoken and tried to keep up the Norwegian spirit. One of the teachers was picked up by the Gestapo and interrogated. He jumped out of the window and killed himself—because he might have had knowledge that he didn't want to share, he killed himself.

"My dad had contacts with the underground and started after the occupation to stop the Germans. One group was called *Milorg*, military organization, and, the other, *Civorg*, civilian organization. In the winter of 1944, I asked my dad in my last year of high school about the resistance. I and my buddies were anxious to get into something against the Germans. He didn't commit himself, but I got a message I should meet with a person in the corner of a graveyard at such and such a time and when I saw this person there I should give him a certain question and he would answer with a known phrase. That would be my contact. So I went and met the guy and established contact and that man was the only man I knew in the underground, and he asked me if I could organize a group.

"I contacted other kids I knew, who had been Boy Scouts with me, and a couple of others, who were close neighbors to me. We organized our own little group and through this one contact we were instructed where to meet to get instruction. Over a period in

—AT Photo

Oddvar with his scrapbook reminisces about his days as a resistance fighter and as a New Bedford fisherman, as he looks out to Marblehead where he makes his home.

the winter of 1944, we were given instructions on basic training. Instructors came in either locally or were parachuted in from England to instruct. So we had basic training given in attics or basements in Oslo and also trained outside Oslo in a huge national park where people ski and hike. We knew this area well because we had been there with the Boy Scouts, and the Germans didn't go in there. So one by one we would go up to that area and meet in a particular place for training. We did this during the winter until spring.

"In spring I was asked by my main contact to be a saboteur, and I had to check with my boys. We all wanted to do that. So, in addition to weapons training, we got more intensive and more frequent training which was more dangerous. We were young and didn't consider the danger of it. I was twenty. As part of this training, we frequently had to move explosives around the city and we moved them on the subway or car and carried weapons under our coats. We hoped no one would stop and search us. Many of the women were serving as couriers, carrying explosions on their bodies, sometimes disguised as being pregnant. After the initial training as intelligence/saboteur, we were given jobs such as scouting out areas that would be destroyed by other saboteurs. In response, the Germans had this poster placed all over Norway, which tried to frighten the people:

"You will be unemployed because of the saboteurs."

"This poster had little effect, even though the people were without much food or warm clothing. When the war ended, the underground resistance forces, *Milorg*, consisted of 44,000 soldiers."

"Already in 1940, the first Norwegians were sentenced to death in German courts of war, and execution squads were active from 1941. Starting in 1942, more and more Norwegians were shot in reprisal. At the same time, thousands were jailed in Norway or sent to concentration camps in Germany, Poland and France."

—ODIN

PERIL AT HOME

A NORWEGIAN-AMERICAN MOTHER, Janna Isaksen, relives her desperate plight: "I came to Norway in 1938 with my small son to help my mother who was worn out from caring for my sick father. My Norwegian-American husband in America was drafted because he couldn't show he had dependents, as we were in Norway. He fought in the South Pacific.

"In about two years the Germans took Americans living in Norway to exchange for their prisoners on a ten-to-one ratio. America wouldn't cooperate, so the Germans took us to Grini Concentration Camp. We were about thirty-five people. They took the Jews to Grini also and then sent them to Germany to death camps. "Although Grini was a concentration camp, we were told we were 'guests,' but we knew we were prisoners. It was a hard time. Johnny was staying with my mother, my husband was in the South Pacific and I didn't know if he were dead or alive. I missed my boy and was numb with fright.

"Any pity for the civil population is inappropriate." —Adolf Hitler

"The Germans planned to send us to Germany; everything was ready. We were packed and the routes planned. We were going by boat and we would have been in the bottom of a boat for many days. My family had hired a lawyer to help. Then, suddenly, I was let go when the lawyer's letter came in. The courts had officially declared me 'a woman without a country.'

"That was a happy day! I went to Oslo and then home to Hidra with another woman. My family knew I was coming. We were all happy and celebrating. No problems from the Germans after that. They didn't stay on our island as it was a bitter cold winter."

Her son John relives that time also. "Mother was in concentration camp because she was an American citizen. The Germans wanted no collaboration. She was in Grini for nine months. My grandfather was an American citizen and worked in the states when they were young. He worked on bridges in Chicago. My father was in the American Navy. His ship got torpedoed, and he ended up on one of the Pacific Islands. I lived with Grandmother and *Filletante* (aunt by marriage). I lived in three different places but with Grandmother most of time. It was hard for her to have a young kid hanging

—Old print

Janna's other home during the war years: Grini Concentration Camp near Oslo.

—*AT copy of a photo at the Isaksen home.*

The Island of Hidra, where Janna and John Isaksen lived during the war years.—Some of my ancestors came from there also.

—*AT photo*

John Isaksen in 1996, ponders the terrible war years in Norway for him and his mother.

around. I didn't understand. All I knew is that they took my mother. She was gone. That was all. My mother never talks about it."

IN AMERICA: NORWEGIAN FISHERMEN AND THE U-BOATS

MEANWHILE, NORWEGIAN FISHERMEN in Massachusetts and along the Atlantic coast were scouting German submarines and reporting them to the Navy when it was safe to do so. The fishing boats were unarmed. Some had special radios supplied by the Navy Department and others, some retired fishermen stated, used homing pigeons for messages. The radios were hidden in leaded bags for a quick toss overboard in case of a German boarding. Only one person on board knew the code to contact the Navy.

The boats weren't allowed to use any lights while running, but they would see the submarines alongside, and it was at times quite frightening. Often there were bombs and other military hardware in the fishing nets.

There were many German U-boats off the coast of New England as it was ideal for them to hide in the many bays and inlets while having a safe spot from which to sink cargo ships traveling in the sea lanes along the Atlantic Coast. Admiral Doenitz of the German Navy, commander of U-boat Waffen, was delighted with these conditions on our coast. One such boat sunk the British warship Cyclops off of Cape Cod in 1942. The coast was very long and the naval ships too few to adequately protect this sea frontier; so information from the fishermen was very valuable. The U.S. Navy under Admiral King was trying to protect the Merchant Marine ships carrying war-winning supplies to our military and allies. During 1943 there were 300 German U-boats and they sank forty-one Allied ships in just one month, two-thirds of which traveled in convoys. The subs traveled in "wolf packs" at sea and the Germans were building them at the astonishing rate of about forty per month. The Germans lost more than half of their U-boat fleet and seamen in this campaign.

—The History Channel, paraphrased

NEW BEDFORD FISHERMEN AND THE SUBMARINES

As REMEMBERED by New Bedford fishing captain Jens Isaksen: "The Navy put a radio onboard. Only American citizens could use it, and as captains we had to be citizens. We had official charts and marked them if we saw something. We saw several German subs, marked them on charts and radioed them in after they went under the water, so they would not hear us. One day right by us, a sub surfaced and we could see the conning tower and periscope. Didn't feel too good about that! I have a certificate from the Commandant, Eastern Sea Frontier, and also, the Navy gave me a photo of the leaded bag we would use to throw the radio overboard if we were caught. We did spot and report German ships. My four brothers were all in the American service but I was on the boats here."

A New Bedford fisherman, Jacob Ostensen from Northern Norway, told his story about these days: "We ran with no running lights and had a U.S. Navy codebook on board, but only one of us could use that. One boat from Maine spotted a sub and called in. The Germans heard the signal, came aboard and sunk it. All the men were killed. It made you think twice before

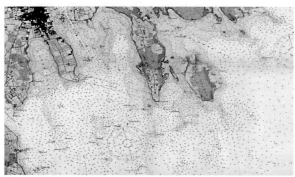

—*US Government map*

A mariner's map of the approaches to New Bedford Harbor. Massachusetts' ragged coast makes for ideal harbors and, in the case of the Second World War, ideal hiding places for German submarines.

—*AT photo*

A Norwegian skipper and boat owner, the late Jens Isaksen, recalled the days when he left this same New Bedford Harbor to fish for scallops and site enemy submarines, while his family was stranded in Norway for five years without a word.

reporting any sighting. We were supposed to report anything suspicious to the Navy, but we would think about it seriously. They had guns; we didn't. After the war, the observers got certificates from the American government for their work. I was the observer, but the skipper got the certificate. I was not happy about that, as I was the one responsible for the codes. We also picked up three bombs one day in a net and another day seven bombs."

A Fairhaven fisherman, my uncle, David Tollefsen from Skudeneshavn. reminisced about his dangerous days as a submarine spotter. "I was an observer. We saw subs but we had to keep silent about it all at home. The Germans had sunk a Dutch boat by torpedo, and we found the Hollanders on two lifeboats. There were about twenty of them, and they were covered with grease. We gave them to the Coast Guard in Massachusetts and kept silent about it all."

The son of a Norwegian fisherman, Henry Pedersen, remembers: "My father, Arne Pedersen, originally from Northern Norway, reported two or three submarines he saw on trips. He saw the periscope and didn't know if they were German or American but reported them anyway by the special radio. He said after he reported them he 'took off fast.' Such sightings cost him 'some good fishing,' he told me, as he was on good fishing grounds when he had to leave and then couldn't find the fish again. Both he and my uncle had plaques from the government commending their work."

Fairhaven Norwegian-American Serine Matland tells of her family experience off New York: "My brother spotted a submarine and called it in to the Navy. He marked the spot with a buoy. He then waited for the plane to come, and the plane sank the submarine. Some of the sailors got out, were rescued and put in prison. My husband went to visit them, and one of them said, 'If we had thought that your little fishing boat was spying on us, we would have sunk you.' The fishermen got an award from the Navy."

Another recalls her husband's adventure: "My husband was a skipper during the war on a fishing boat out of New Bedford. One night he was off watch and sleeping when the first mate burst into his cabin, ashen. A German sub had pulled up near the boat. They got their fishing boat out of there as soon as possible and called in the sighting on the radio that had been given to them. My husband said very little, but it was in the newspapers. The one thing he did say was that he would never forget the look on the mate's face. He had never seen anything like it before or after."

(When I asked an elderly fisherman about the secret code for inclusion in this book, he answered emphatically: "*Nei, nei.* It is a secret and I will never tell anyone, not even you, even if you were a naval officer.")

Norwegian-American cooperation was not limited to dangerous submarine spotting. The government needed boats, many boats, and, in at least one case, bought a soon-to-be-launched fishing boat from its owner, although the transaction was not entirely voluntary on his part. They paid him reparations with interest and the Navy converted it into a patrol boat.

KARMA OF THE SEA

JOHN ISAKSEN RECOLLECTS: "Before my father was drafted into the Navy, he was skipper on the *Malvina B.* On his first trip as skipper, he picked up a crew from a Norwegian ship that had been sunk by a U-boat. I think that the name of the ship was the *Norness.* Later he was to serve in the American Navy in the Pacific, where his own boat was sunk by Japanese torpedoes. He was rescued and served the rest of the war on shore duty on an island in the Pacific."

—Isaksen family archives

The *Malvina B.* was skippered by Magnus Isaksen who fished out of New York City. On Isaksen's maiden voyage as skipper, he rescued the crew of the Norwegian ship, *Norness,* which had been torpedoed off of Long Island. Later he was to be rescued under similar circumstances in the South Pacific where he was stationed during the war.

From a deceased skipper, "Kris Pase" Olsen: "I went into the Army and went to landing craft school. I trained in Cotuit. Because I was Norwegian, I was asked about the beaches of Norway and my language ability. I was excited about going to Norway and using this skill. There were two groups; one went to Europe and one to the Pacific. Wouldn't you know the Army shipped me out to the Pacific where I made three invasions. I won the Bronze Star in August 1945 but lost my hearing from a bomb exploding nearby."

One retired boat owner—Jacob Jacobsen, now living in Florida— explains: "I went up to Boston to enlist for the war and signed up for the landing boats. Then I had one more trip before I went into training. So I went fishing just like any other time and the rigging came down and hit my head and face, almost shaving off part of my face. I was a long time in the hospital after that and still have the huge dent in my head. That was a terrible accident, but I think about it now and say it saved my life. I would have been on a landing craft in the invasion of Normandy and probably would have been killed."

NORWEGIAN POPULATION TERRORIZED

"The Germans arrested a huge number of Norwegians. Teachers, officers and students were collectively arrested. And many were captured for their resistance to the occupation and for anti-Nazi activities. A sizable number were sent to German concentration camps where they perished. A total of 40,000 Norwegians were imprisoned by the Germans."

—ODIN

A KARMØY MAN, who later fished out of New Bedford, reminds us of the danger in those days in Norway: "One underground man on our island had a wife who was a teacher in the school. He was in the resistance, and he made a secret trip to England, although we didn't know about it until later on. He came back with radio equipment for communications and kept it in the school-house where she was teaching, but it was found and he was arrested. He was found guilty and sentenced to be killed and was sent to Grini Concentration Camp near Oslo. The English flew there and dropped some bombs on a factory and some bombs didn't go off. So the Germans gave him and some other prisoners a chance to defuse the bombs in exchange for their lives. He was successful and then was sent to Germany. When he came home after the war, everyone was there to greet him and welcome him home to Norway."

CIVILIAN DEPRIVATION AS SEEN THROUGH CHILDREN'S EYES

"Aside from the political and military oppression, daily life in Norway was marked mostly by the lack of food and other supplies during the occupation years. With its low degree of self-sufficiency in food production, Norway had relied for years on imports. Imports plunged to a minimum during the war years, and supply problems were compounded by the 400,000 Germans on Norwegian soil. Per capita, Norway was actually the country which had the most German occupiers on its territory."

—ODIN

The children who grew up during the war years in Norway have vivid memories of their dangerous childhoods. These memories of the occupation are colored by their youthful experiences.

John Isaksen from Southern Norway remembers: "We heard about damage in Bergen from bombs. We only had three bombs in our area—maybe accidentally from the bombing of Knaben near Kvinestal. I was lying on my bed and I had a piggy bank of top of my bureau. When bomb went off, I was showered with money. I jumped right over Mother and ended up with my grandmother downstairs.

"I knew some of the German soldiers. They would come and make inspections. One of them gave me chocolate. I really didn't know what was going on. We made up a play boat, with sail, cabin and a Norwegian flag. The flag stayed up there, and they never said anything to us about it. I think it was the only Norwegian flag flying in Norway at that time. We took four Germans and ferried them across the four hundred feet to the other island and they gave us an *ore*. We thought that was wonderful."

"The German soldier was O.K.—but not the SS. My grandmother went out and gave the soldiers something hot one time when they were freezing outside. She felt sorry for the young boys, but got upset when they came into the house. They never did anything bad to us except arrest my mother and put her in Grini Concentration Camp."

Another retired fisherman who was a boy in Southern Norway during the war years remembers: "We grew up in the war, and my town was occupied by the Germans for five years. I remember the German soldiers. They took over the schoolhouse, and one season I couldn't go to school because they had the school building. We had food during the war because my father had a store. We were given cod liver oil every day at school.

"I remember the bombing. The English were bombing the mines producing molybdenum, a silver white element used in alloys and in the armaments industry. The mines were about five miles away, and during the bombing the sky was filled with planes. I never saw so many planes as in March of 1943. The sky was dark from so many planes. One girl at school lost two brothers in the bombing at the mine. They didn't stay in the bomb shelter. They were too curious.

"The soldiers came with big Polish horses, huge horses, six or eight for one carriage

—Courtesy of Dreyer Bok

Germans inspect bomb damage to the mine at Knaben, above Kvinesdal, Norway.

pulling milk, food, and supplies for the soldiers. We were too young to be afraid, and the soldiers were friendly with us. I used to like to walk on my hands when I was young, about seven, and I never fell. One day I was walking on my hands near the German soldiers who were lying on the ground in the summer sun after lunch. I walked along and all of a sudden I fell right on the top of a sleeping soldier. He jumped up and pulled his gun with bayonet on me, and I was so shocked—just ran as fast as I could. I was so lucky that day but that was also the last day I ever walked on my hands near the soldiers.

"Generally speaking they stayed to themselves and so did I, but they were young also, and treated us as just as kids in the neighborhood pretty much. But I knew there was danger there."

FROM AN ENTERPRISING TEEN

GUNNAR HAINES REMINISCES about his youth during the war: "We lived outside Stavanger. Pa was a pipe smoker, and without the pipe he was in misery: The pipe was his life. I remember one Sunday morning, it was a beautiful day, and Pa had the pipe and no tobacco. I wanted so much to do something for him, so I went out in the kitchen and took a rutabaga and cut it in an odd shape and then smeared on some grease and put it in paper and then into a brown box.

"I had a spot picked out to wait, and down the highway came a German officer and a woman who was also in uniform. They stopped and were talking. So while I was sitting and waiting, I asked them if they would like to trade butter for some tobacco. He saw this good-sized package. '*Ja*, but I have to take the butter with me.' So I said O.K. and I gave him the rutabaga against my best judgment. Then I thought I would surely get into trouble because he would see it was not butter. But I waited because I was thinking of Pa and his pipe. I saw them coming back and as they got closer and closer, I thought he was just playing cool as he knew it was not butter. But I sat it out and he gave me a big smile, the tobacco and also some chocolate because they both said I was such a nice boy. And I said, 'No, I don't want any chocolate.' 'Yes,' they said, 'Take it, take it.' So I took it all and went home and gave it to Pa. They didn't come after me but so many times I thought about it and the trouble I could get into.

"Before the war ended, the Germans came and occupied two rooms upstairs. They were there because, in case of an invasion, they could involve civilians. It was a cowardly way of doing it."

Kirsten Lindoe Smedsvik, who lived in America during part of her youth and who, when she was younger grew up in Haugesund during the war years, recollects: "There were many troops in the area. I remember one day when the Germans were using our road for maneuvers and rifle practice. I had to walk down that road to school, and when I came home in the afternoon it was dark, and I was afraid. I was about eight years old. So when I approached that point in the road, a German officer came over and told me in Norwegian not to be afraid. He said he had a pretty little daughter in Germany like me and he would help me. So he walked with me and protected me from the others right to my home. I never forgot that kindness to me."

Germans are remembered for instances of both kindness and cruelty as another man from Karmøy recalls bitterly: "My cousin was out playing with his friends, and the Germans came by and told them to leave as they were to begin their target practice. My cousin had a bad knee and limped and couldn't keep up with the others. The Germans didn't wait, began their practice and hit him with a bullet, which killed him. I will never forget that."

Germans are also remembered for what they took with them, as recalled by a New Bedford fisherman, the late Didrik Didriksen: "We had a beautiful white 'fjord horse' that we treasured, but the Germans came and took it away one day. The German horse farm was just below us, and we would go down there to see our horse and also look at the king's personal horse. It had the crown emblazoned on its side. But one day we could not find our white horse. We looked and looked. We never got it back after the war. My father believed that it had been sent to Germany and was on one of the ships that had been sunk. We needed that horse as it did the work on the farm. It was the best workhorse. Sometimes the German soldiers would give us candy. They were pretty nice to the kids on the island, but we needed our horse."

Another retired fisherman in Norway, Alf Isaksen, remarked: "The Germans used the fields behind our house for their daily practice and maneuvers. We could see them clearly. That is how we grew up—watching the Germans learn how to destroy."

Several remembered nostalgically that the German soldiers loved to eat rabbit meat. "They would always ask us to hunt rabbits for them and they would buy them or trade them for things we needed. After a while one soldier got quite ill and they investigated and found us out. We had been selling them the stray cats of Karmøy. After that, they would say: 'We want rabbit meat and no cats.' It became a legend here on the island, those words: *Keine Katzen.*" ("No cats.")

Deprivation continued throughout the war and the Norwegians learned to "make do" with what they had available. Gunnar Berg, a Fairhaven emigrant from Askøy, an island off the coast of Bergen, remembers: "We had very little of anything during the war years, but I remember best the homemade shoes. They were made out of fish skins and narrow wooden slats. They worked O.K. until it rained, and then they dissolved. If you know Bergen, you know that it rains just about every day."

One Haugesund woman who would emigrate to New Bedford and Seattle, Kitty Ellingsen, remembers her days as a teenager during the war

Soviet prisoners in Karmøy area during the war years. They and others like them built the Burma Road across Karmøy and made birds for the children out of small pieces of wood.

—German photo courtesy Dreyer Bok, Stavanger

when her family had to survive with so little: "We needed thread very much to repair our clothing and to make new clothes. Sometimes we took two old garments and made a new one of them. One day there was a notice that thread would be available. So I stood in line for a spool of thread from eight p.m. and all through the night until it was my turn in the wee hours of the morning. A simple spool of thread was that important to us."

THE PRISONERS OF WAR

THE GERMANS PLACED 44,000 Russian prisoners of war in Norway where they were virtual slave labor. They did the laborious work needed to build the German military infrastructure such as building roads and other arduous tasks. Many were in South West Norway.

Norwegians remember their youthful experiences with the prisoners and still reminisce about those days. They would give the Russian prisoners food as they marched along the road to their work, and the prisoners would give them beautiful birds, which they had carved out of a solid piece of wood. Many of the children on the island of Karmøy and surrounding areas had those birds. They would try to hand the Russians a carrot or a potato or something, as they knew the prisoners were starving. The Germans didn't generally bother the children.

An American fisherman, then a child in Norway, explains: "There were Russian prisoners on our island, and they had to build all of the facilities for the Germans as well as a road across the island, called now the 'Burma Road,' as it was built with slave labor. The prisoners had little to eat, and one day a Norwegian gave one some food, and the Germans killed the prisoner immediately with a blow to the head and just

—AT photo 1998

Kirsten Lindoe Smedsvik with a carved wooden bird made by Soviet POWs in the Haugesund area. They gave the children these birds in exchange for scraps of food.

119

quickly buried his body outside the camp. Some of us kids thought that he was buried alive."

Kirsten Lindoe Smedsvik pointed out in an interview in 2000, "I still have the bird a Russian prisoner made and gave to me."

Kitty Ellingsen also recalls the Russian prisoners and her family's successful plan to assist them. "We had Russian prisoners in Haugesund, and we tried to help them when we could. It was a bitter cold winter, and they had old shoes but no socks, and they had to work outside all day long. So we fashioned socks for them out of an old quilt and then had to get into the camp to give the socks to the prisoners. We had been given some coarse grain meal sent from the Ukraine, and mother made a thick soup out of it. Then we walked to the camp with the hot soup and cups and first offered it to the Germans. When they turned their backs, we went into the camp and gave some to the prisoners who were starving and very happy to get this food. As children we were allowed to do some things."

THE SURRENDER

"As the German collapse drew near, there was fear that the Germans would fight rather than surrender. The German commanders followed the capitulation orders, which they had received, from their superiors in Germany on 7 May 1945. A day later, an Allied mission flew into Oslo, followed by Allied and Norwegian military detachments. The Norwegian Government returned home from Great Britain and on 7 June 1945, King Håkon followed."

—ODIN

"ODDVAR SOLSTAD, the Oslo saboteur, explains: "On May 8 there was tension because there were rumors that the Germans would not accept the surrender and would fight to the end. There were very many Germans there and we had to protect our intelligence office. They decided not to fight and it was over. At the end of the war my group, called an action group, was assigned to headquarters, and I was given two more groups. On May 8 we were to protect the intelligence office. After the Germans surrendered, they were under house arrest, and then they were shipped back to Germany."

Another future American on Karmøy remembers: "I was fishing, and I looked up and saw the flags waving. I knew the war was over. I came in so fast."

A boy in Southern Norway fondly recalls: "I was coming home from school and I saw a flag going up and I knew—we were free."

His mother, the former concentration camp prisoner from Hidra, recalls: "We were out in the fields putting in potatoes and saw a boat with a

Norwegian flag, and we knew that the war was over. All the flags went up on the island. During the war they wanted us to fly the German flag. All the flagpoles were lying underneath the houses, and they went right up."

A former teen from Karmøy recollects: "At the end of the war, few had radios. The Germans took them—sealed in a room in a storehouse. Everyone ran to the store to get his or her radio after it ended. My dad and uncle were fishing lobsters on an island and didn't know the war was over till they saw the Norwegian flags flying on the mainland. The underground took over the camps and captured the Germans."

—*Solstad archives*

Oddvar Solstad Moe with his resistance group at the end of the war.

"The German capitulation was carried out in an exemplary and peaceful way, but it took months before all the German troops were repatriated. It also took some time to repatriate the 141,000 foreign nationals, which the Germans had brought into Norway. These included 84,000 Soviet prisoners of war and 13,000 conscripted laborers."

—ODIN

A resistance fighter on Karmøy, who later became a very respected New Bedford fishing boat skipper, Ragnvald (Ray) Haines was at the German surrender on his island. His son, Severin Haines, recalls his father's memories of his life at that time. "My father was in the resistance on Karmøy and he also worked on a fishing boat. He had been in the Merchant Marine before the war but in the resistance he only knew two other people: his brother and a friend. That was done so he couldn't reveal names if they were captured. He didn't say much about their work there, but at the end of the war he went to the German Command with his brother for the surrender. They had not had new clothes for many years so they went in their regular old clothing, in marked contrast to the German regalia. The Karmøy German commander formally presented himself and his troops in surrender with all traditional German military ceremony. I was born exactly nine months after V-E Day and I will always feel that I was part of the end-of-the war celebration."

"After the war, legal proceedings were initiated against those who had betrayed their country. About 46,000 persons were punished for treason. Among these, 18,000 were sentenced to prison terms and 28,000 were

fined and deprived of their rights as citizens. A total of 45 Norwegians and Germans received death sentences; 37 of the executions were carried out."

—ODIN

The saboteur, Oddvar Solstad, points out that: "After the peace was officially signed, we remained attached to the intelligence headquarters. We found the Nazi headquarters building and went down to the building, got into the headquarters and found all the records of the Norwegian Nazis. We called the police, and they came and picked up the records. Our group was then assigned to pick up all of the Norwegian Nazis. We brought the Norwegian Nazis into the headquarters for interrogation. All of them were tried, of course, when we had proof they had been Nazi collaborators, and a few were shot. Quisling was tried and shot. We were in charge of the group that protected Quisling while he was being tried."

A Karmøy resident reminds us that: "The women who fooled around with the Germans were punished after the war. Their hair was all cut off and they were shown to the community. We never forgot those who were too friendly. After the war many others were shunned because they had helped the Germans."

One son of an emigrant remembers: "While visiting Norway I met fifty-four relatives, but there was another one I did not see, for she had dated a German, and the family would never have anything to do with her after that."

"When the human costs of the war were estimated in Norway, the tally showed that 10,262 Norwegians had been killed, including 3,670 seamen. The Germans had executed 366 and tortured 39 to death. Among political prisoners and members of the underground, 658 died at home and 1,433 abroad. About 6,000 Norwegians had volunteered for the Germans, and 709 of them had fallen in battle. During the years of occupation, the Germans had absorbed nearly 40 percent of the gross domestic product. In addition, there was the considerable material destruction. An estimated 16 percent of the national wealth had been lost, and the outflow to Germany had been twice as high per capita as it was, for instance, in France."

—ODIN

THE NORWEGIAN NAZIS

THE NORWEGIANS WHO VOLUNTEERED to help the German cause were most often shipped to the eastern front in Russia where they were put in the front lines and used as cannon fodder for the enemy. A young man in

Stavanger suffered such a fate. A very intelligent young man, who was influenced by his political employer, despite his family's pleas to the contrary, went over to the German side. He was killed and buried in Russia. No one knew why he did this, except he was young and had been persuaded that this was the right cause for him. He gave his life for his belief that he was protecting Norway from the communists and thought himself a patriot, but he brought much anguish to his family and later generations.

Janna Isaksen, in Southern Norway, reflected on those days: "I remember so well what happened in our town. There was a man who lived above Flekkefjord and he was very friendly with the Germans. We hated him because of that and shunned him and his mother in town and especially in church. He was always partying with the Germans in his house and he had all kinds of good food, liquor and other gifts from the Germans. He and his mother had to sit in back of the church because no one wanted to see them.

"One day he told his mother that his life was in her hands, and she must believe that things were not as they appeared. Toward the end of the war, a German ship was sunk in the Lafjord, near Flekkefjord, and the Germans figured out that perhaps he had something to do with it. He heard them coming for him and fled the house, running for his life from farm to farm, seeking shelter. No one would help him, and he was turned away from each farm. At one point when the Germans were so close, he actually went into the fjord to hide, even though it was winter. Now he was icy, weak and too cold. Finally one farmer let him go into the barn to dry out and get some warmth, and thus he evaded the Germans.

"He was not a traitor as we had all thought but a true patriot who had risked his life by being in touch with the English all through the war and giving them vital intelligence information. He had a good view of the Lafjord and the countryside from his home and a good ear for much German talk at his parties.

"So after the war was over, he and his mother came into the church and sat in the back row once more. The pastor invited them to sit in the first row and as they walked up, everyone rose in salute to his mother, him and his bravery. I never will forget that. I realized later that by hating him and shunning him, we had actually made him safer."

IN APPECIATION

IN AMERICA, Norwegian-American U-boat "spies" off the American coast including Captain Jens Isaksen of Fairhaven, Massachusetts, were thanked by the United States Navy for their service with a certificate such as the one below:

123

HEADQUARTERS
Commander, Northern Group
Eastern Sea Frontier
North Station Office Building
150 Causeway Street, Boston, Mass.

12 May 1945

Mr. Jens Isaksen
14 Elm Street
Fairhaven, Mass.

Dear Sir,

As Commander Northern Group, in immediate charge of frontier forces in the District, I take great pleasure in forwarding to you the attached certificate which you so well deserve.

At the same time, I wish to thank you for the valuable assistance, which you have rendered to the forces under my command during the Battle of the Atlantic, World War II.

Yours very truly,

Felix Gygac, Rear Admiral, U.S.N.
Commandant, First Naval District
Commander Northern Group, Eastern Sea Frontier

IN NORWAY: FREEDOM!

THE END OF THE WAR WAS CELEBRATED everywhere in Norway by the flying of flags, music, parades and gatherings. Although there was little food and the deprivations of war had taken its toll on the people, there were smiles everywhere.

The island of Karmøy produced a commemorative spoon showing a man rising from broken chains and reflected the feelings of the population at the end of the war.

The collective post-war feeling of the Norwegian population was: The war is over! The king had returned! We can get back to living again! We can see our families again! And now the 17th of May.

—*AT Photo*

U.S. NAVY Certificate of Appreciation
given to Jens Isaksen and other skippers out
of New Bedford for their heroism scouting
German submarines during the WWII.

—*Courtesy Dreyer Bok*

The war is over in Norway. Free at last!

THE 17TH OF MAY, 1945

THE TRADITIONAL NORWEGIAN National Constitution Day on the 17th
of May will never be celebrated with quite the same spirit and meaning as it
was on that unforgettable day in May of 1945. This holiday is very profound
for the Norwegian and celebrated with more patriotic enthusiasm and joy
than, for instance, the American Fourth of July. But in 1945 the Norwegians
had been captives for five years, and now they were free! They celebrated in
every manner possible, given the limitations of food, drink and new clothing.
Flags were flown everywhere; every town had a parade; national costumes
were taken out of their hiding places and cleaned, ironed and adorned. Silver
and other valuables were rescued from their secret places and polished until
they gleamed; the best dishes were brought out, even though there was little
to put on them, and traces of the Nazi occupation were destroyed where
possible. The national anthem was sung over and over, and other Norwegian
patriotic music took on new feeling and meaning.

Eli Mannes Syre, now of Fairhaven, recollects her grandmother talking
about that wonderful day on Karmøy: "The Norwegian flag had not flown,
and the national anthem had not been sung for five years, so the 17th of May
of 1945 was an incredible celebration and a day my grandmother would never

forget. She went up to the second floor of her home to take a photo from a window. She said when she looked out all she could see were flags and people . . . one huge wave of people, more than she had ever seen together, and they were waving their flags, shouting and singing, ecstatic with joy. It was a picture that will be in our minds and hearts forever."

Life was Norwegian once more, and these proud people were optimistically smiling again as they started to plan for their lives as free citizens. There was a scarcity of everything and very little money, so letters were written to friends and family in America, and the phone lines were much in demand—when phones were available at all. Similarly, their families in the States were trying to get in touch with them, or traveling to Norway to see if their relatives there were still alive. Families needed to be reunited—and men needed to make money in America.

Jens Isaksen of Fairhaven remembers: "My wife was alone with our small son during the war in Norway. We had no contact at all, and I was very concerned about her. I saved my money wisely. When I had saved enough money to buy a house, I bought one for my family. I came on the first boat to Norway after the war with many others who were trying to go home to find their families. We had to have some shots before we traveled and I was very sick from the shots when my wife met me. I had never seen my son who was now almost seven years old. We had sent packages when we could get them through. I was very excited but felt so sick."

Commemorative silver spoon Norge, 1945, celebrating the end of World War II. Each area had its own special variation of the spoon. On Karmøy the inscription can be interpreted as "imprisoned but not broken."

Jen's wife Malene responds: "I can't put it in words how I felt. I met him in Kopervik and he was sick. I had saved three precious eggs and we ate them to celebrate his return. He asked if that was all we had to eat and I answered, 'Well, there are none tomorrow.' We had the same clothes all that time, no fabric to buy or even old clothes to redo them. We had nothing."

If the families in the towns, villages, cities and islands of Norway were to be reunited with their relatives living abroad, contact needed to be made. Once they made contact, large packages started to arrive from the states filled with chocolate, hams, canned food, precious coffee, cigarettes, toys for the children, and new clothing.

My cousin, Gunnar Berg of Bergen, describes his reaction to these packages. "I remember just after the war a large box arrived at the house. The relatives in Fairhaven had got together and sent us clothing, cans of food and all kinds of wonderful things we needed."

Kaare Ness from South West Norway stated: "After the war ended, people in the states sent food and clothing to us. War rations came also, and I remember the corned-beef hash—really a feast for us. After the war I was in the Norwegian Merchant Marine and others who had been stranded in Norway went back to the states."

BACK HOME TO NORWAY

THE MERCHANT MARINER Karl Berg, who served in the American Merchant Marine, recalled his attempts to return to Norway to be with his family and that he "was so homesick after the war; I wanted only to go home. Could've got American citizenship immediately but all I could think of was to go home to Norway and see my family. I went to the Norwegian consulate in New York and there were many Norwegians there and the officials said, 'Where did you come from?' I said I was on an American ship, but the officials put me aside because they didn't know if I was Norwegian or American."

During those days when he was trying to get home to Norway, Berg had only seven days to report to the local Merchant Marine union and didn't want any problems with that regulation, so when his name came up, he thought, "Finest kind," as his assignment was to load foodstuffs. He thought for sure he would go to Europe "as they were starving there." But instead the ship was sent to Panama to pick up some PT boats, and then they headed for the Philippines. He remembered that he "just wanted to jump over the side of the boat." He was in the Philippines for over a year and the only good thing about it was that he was now able to write to his wife.

His wife Martha remembered those days well, saying, "The war was over before we knew he was still alive. Not a word for five years. One Christmas we got a Red Cross letter—otherwise no connection."

Karl relived this day by stating: "I told a man I had heck of a woman in Norway," and he said, 'You mean your wife is still married to you?' Believe me, that wasn't easy. I tell you. I hope nobody else goes through that. When I got back to New York, I went to the dock where the *Stavangerfjord* was leaving New York for Norway. I had trouble getting a ticket. I went to the Norwegian American Lines office, and there was a young man there who told me 'the ship is full.'" He remembered emotionally, "I lost my temper and control. I was away for so long and wanting to come home to Norway. I said to this young man: 'Do you know where I was during the war? I was on convoys all during the war. I haven't seen my family in years and you tell me it's all full?' I lost control over myself. I didn't know what I was saying or doing. An older man came out and saw me shaking. I was completely out of control, and I'm not ashamed of saying it now. I said to him, 'You have been sitting here all during the war, and you tell me I can't go home to Norway?' The old man calmed me down and told me 'although the ship was full, one woman hadn't paid yet,' and asked if I had the money. I did, and he gave me a ticket for her berth. 'Finest Kind!' But I didn't want to see that young man again.

—AT photo

Karl and Martha Berg tell their story from their garden in Dartmouth Massachusetts, 1996.

"The boat came to Bergen. Six long years away and then I saw my wife. She was waiting for me on the pier. Kind of strange when we saw each other. My son was now a big boy, and just a small kid when I left. When he called me 'Daddy,' I was so careful and scared because all those years nobody called me 'Daddy.' But I am still here. With God's help I am still here. I tell you I always loved my wife and I always will."

—AT photo

John Isaksen, my second-grade almost-friend in 1996. A man in love with his boats, family and work.

—Isaksen archives

Janna Isaksen with new child five years after the war.

The former concentration camp inmate Janne Isaksen, now a resident of Massachusetts, remembers: "After the war the Americans notified us to be in Oslo right away, and they took us to America on a troop ship. It still had all the guns and military equipment on it."

Johnny Isaksen, her son, reflected: "My mother had to find the money to pay for the passage back to America, and that wasn't easy with my father still in the South Pacific. After the war, the war brides went to America free and somehow that didn't seem fair that we, after so much hardship, had to pay the fare."

THE MARSHALL PLAN

HELP CAME TO NORWAY in the form of "The Marshall Plan" which went into effect on June 3, 1948, with $241,000,000 allocated to Norway and another $1M for exchanges and study groups. The Marshall Plan, which is universally recognized as the plan that enabled Europe to recover after the war, gave food-stuffs, metals, machinery, tobacco, oil, fabrics, and fodder. In the end, Norway received $460,000,000 with $357,000,000 being a direct gift. As soon as this program took effect, the country started to recover, and the families began to make their plans.

The saboteur, Oddvar Solstad, now living in Massachusetts, recalled: "After the war the 17th of May was incredible. We were discharged in September 1945, and I wanted to continue my education. The Germans had closed down the universities, and there was a backlog when they reopened. I heard about American scholarships so I came to America to Tufts University in

—Solstad archives

Letter to Oddvar Solstad Moe from King Olav, thanking him for his work during the war years.

Boston and fished in New Bedford in the summer. They knew about my work in the underground, and it helped me to get accepted."

In other cases, life simply went on, people seeking to live life as normally as possible as Lise Stol from Karmøy reminds us. "I was born right after the war, and there was no material for my christening dress; so mother found a parachute that had been dug up on the island and made a dress out of its silk. It was a very special dress."

AMERIKA

IN WESTERN NORWAY, where many had relatives in America, the post-war plans often contained the word: *Amerika*. For it was America that beckoned as the land of opportunity and promise. It was in America where there was plenty of everything, and many Norwegians wanted to have a part of it.

Many had relatives in the States with established homes and connections to work. "Why not go to America now?" they thought. "It is in the Norwegian tradition to be a *pendler*. We can give it a try and see if we like it. There's good money to be made, things to buy, adventure to be had, relatives with homes to visit and most of all work and the opportunity to buy a big car. And, of course, if things don't work out, we could return to Norway at any time. We would never have to be poor again."

—*Courtesy Serine Matland*

Norwegian wives in New Bedford during the forties.

On the island of Karmøy, it is said that almost every family had a relative in America, particularly in New Bedford, and that after the war some of the towns were practically without men. Many made plans to begin their new lives far from the poverty of the war years and with dreams to make it "big" fishing in New Bedford, America.

Egil Ellingsen, now in Seattle, recollects those days vividly: "I was called into the Norwegian military after the war was over. Since I had captain's papers, experience on the ocean and expertise in navigation, I was recruited by the Navy. As captain, I was assigned the command of a PT boat with four crew members and we were trained how to destroy the drifting Nazi mines and other explosives along the coastline of Norway to make the waters safe for freighters and ships. Once a mine was located, we launched a rubber raft with two men and explosives to attach to the mine. The explosives had a nine-minute timer before they would explode, so we had to work carefully and safely. Once the explosives were set, we quickly took aboard the men and raced away as fast as possible in the PT boat. This was an extremely dangerous and life-threatening assignment and I am grateful God kept me and my crew safe during our tour of duty. This PT boat operated out of Arendal with its homeport in Kristiansand. While I was serving in this capacity, my parents, ten-year-old sister Lillian and I applied for visas to immigrate to the United States.

"In the spring of 1947, our visas came through. As a result, with this opportunity to go to America, the Norwegian military gave me an immediate honorable discharge to pursue this new adventure. Together with my family, I boarded the passenger ship *Venus* in May, leaving Stavanger for Newcastle, England. We took the train to London overnight and the next day traveled to Southhampton to embark on the *Queen Mary* with our next stop, New York!

"New Bedford had numerous opportunities in the scallop fishing industry. An established Scandinavian community in New Bedford welcomed me into their arms, especially Rasmus and Sally Tonnessen, the owners of New Bedford Ship Supply. They were hospitable, caring and like family to the young fishermen, including us in holiday celebrations and helping us to feel at home in a new country. Establishing roots in the New Bedford area, I attended church in the Oxford Chapel with other Norwegian families in Fairhaven.

"All during this time I corresponded faithfully with a beautiful young nurse, Kitty Ulland, from Haugesund. So in December of 1948 I boarded the Christmas Ship, *Stavangerfjord*, in New York to take me back to visit her. She has often said that her first thoughts as she met me at the pier and scanned the faces of all the men on the ship was that the most handsome man of all was hers! We became engaged that Christmas Eve and decided that our future life together would be in America. And so, in April of 1949, I boarded the *Queen*

Elizabeth alone to return to New Bedford to work and save money to marry Kitty and bring her to New Bedford. Working and saving every penny, I was able to return to Norway in December of 1950 for Christmas with her and her family. We were married on February 3, 1951, at *Vaar Frelsers* Church in Haugesund and traveled to America together in April 1951 on the *Oslofjord*. What a wonderful blessing it was to have Kitty to share my life with. Kitty established a loving home, welcoming and guiding many Norwegian fishermen and their families over the years in the New Bedford area.

—Old postcard mid-fifties

The type of postcard most often received by families in Norway from their sons, daughters and husbands in New Bedford. No wonder more wanted to come to New Bedford, "Amerika."

Mery Stol Vilhelmsen, who spent many years in New Bedford but now is living in Sevlandsvik, Karmøy, wrote a poem, *Amerika*, in 1999 about the dream of coming to America in those days after the war and of its reality.

Amerika

Amerika kva er nå vel det
   Drømmelandet me lengtar å få se
Me gjorde oss tankar og fanteserte
Korleis det blei om me immigrerte.

Når krigen her hima endelig tok slutt
Tyskerane reiste med kuler og krutt
Ja, nå må me jammen komma oss vekk
Så lånte me pengar og kjøpte billett.

New Bedford var målet me satsa på
Der vat det visst å masse av scallop å få
Vemodig det var å avskjed taavskjed
   ta.
På den lange turen til Amerika.

Ute på havet var stille og storm med
   lange vakter og i dårlig form
Men når me fekk sjekken vanlivet top
   Og hjarta det gjorde rit ekstra hopp.

Men åra på fisket og havet et tøft
Med mye frysing og tunge løft
Men tyngst av alt er når budskap oss
   når
Om dei som sin gravplass der ute får

I dag vil me minnast dei kjente og
   kjære
Som måtte for alltid i havet være
Men Gud har gitt oss eit håp her på
   jord At vi møtes igjen i Himmelens
   kor.

America

America, what in the world are you,
   really?
Are you that dream-land which stirred
   our imagination with thoughts and
   fantasies about what it would be like to
   emigrate there?

When the war here at home finally ended,
   and the Germans withdrew their
   instruments of death,
yes, that was our chance to get away.
So we borrowed money to buy tickets to our
   dreams.

New Bedford was the destination of our
   hopes.
We knew many scallops could be caught
   there.
Bittersweet was our farewell
when we left for the long journey to
   America.

Our first taste of life as fishermen was
   tough with storms, long watches, and
   our own poor condition.
But a good paycheck sent our spirits soaring
   and our hearts beating with joy.

But years of fishing at sea is hard, getting
   cold and wet to the bone.
But hardest to bear is the message that
   comes with news of those gone to their
   grave out at sea.

Today we remember friends and loved ones
   who remain buried at sea through
   eternity.
God has given us hope here on earth
   that we will meet again at heaven`s
   gate.

Poem by Mery Stol Vilhelmsen
Translated in part by Aastein Aase

A new and large emigration began from Norway to America with people who had been conditioned by poverty, accustomed to hardship and hard work and raised as virtual prisoners. They, like Scarlet O'Hara in "Gone With the Wind," never wanted to be poor again but would always carry the feeling within them that they were not totally secure in their new-found riches. This generation of emigrants was like no other from Norway. Some would achieve more materially than they could ever have imagined, while others would lose more than they had ever contemplated.

> *"Liberty is the air America breathes . . . In the future days, which we seek to make secure, we look forward to a world founded upon four essential freedoms . . . freedom of speech and expression . . . freedom of worship . . . freedom from want . . . freedom from fear."*

> —Franklin D. Roosevelt

EPILOGUE:
THE ATTITUDES TODAY

TODAY IN NORWAY the war is just a memory to some, and to the young people, it's ancient history. There are still strong feelings among the older people about these difficult years, and some artifacts of the German occupation still remain. These conflicting perspectives are inherent in some of the conversations and observations of the Germans.

German tourists often relate their perspective of Norway as a place they love to visit because of the great beauty, cleanliness and good fishing. And a German war veteran in a German-Norwegian Veteran's Club in Germany told a Norwegian publisher in Stavanger: "We can never forget those wonderful sweet years of the war stationed in Norway. We were so lucky to be in such a wonderful country—beautiful. We will never forget those days!"

But some Norwegians have a different attitude: "They (the German tourists) come here each summer and bring their own food and equipment. They don't shop here at all. They fish and fish and then they freeze it all and take it back to Germany. All they do is take. I hate to see them here on our soil. When I see German flags flying here, I cringe."

Others are inclined to remark: "Well, they are people too, but I still have a bad feeling about them and those years. Our children feel differently because they did not live through it. There are German tourists driving on the Burma Road—the road they built with slave labor through our beautiful moorland."

Some feel that: "Those who come as tourists may have been the occupiers or their relatives. I would rather not know. We cannot ever forget."

A former prisoner in a German concentration camp reflects: "If I go to Norway and see a German flag anywhere, I am very upset. How can they fly Germans flags after all we went through in the war?"

I remember a telling conversation I had in 1992 in Balestrand, Norway. I said to the innkeeper: "I was wondering why I see so many German and Japanese flags in the towns here, yet no American flags. I used to see many American flags here." "Yes," he answered, "Germans and Japanese are the ones who have the money to travel now."

And I recall in 1998 on Karmøy when I said: "I would like to take a photo of the German bunkers . . . do you know where they are?" "Oh," answered a friend, "they are everywhere, but overgrown . . . nothing much is left of them now. Nobody cares and nobody takes care of them and nobody takes them down either."

And one man remarked about the dreaded German bunkers: "We used to go up to the bunkers and drink beer when we were kids. They were great hangout places."

AUTHOR'S POSTSCRIPT

TODAY, AS I LOOK BACK AT MY LIFE THEN, I feel it was in those days right after the war when I knew I was different, that I was not to have a father like the other girls did. Even though the war had ended, we were going to continue to be poor. My friends' fathers came home after the war. Whereas during the war years those kids were like us, growing up with a mother alone, scrimping, saving and making do with what they had, now it was all different. These tall strangers were living in their homes and buying new clothes and gifts for my friends, celebrating birthdays with parties and presents and going on trips and other such wonderful things we did not do. It was then when I saw families together in the church, after school, and in the neighborhood, that I really knew how different our lives were.

Death is not understood well by the very young, but at that point I knew that Papa was never going to come back. He was killed on a fishing boat, and he was never going to walk with me, give me a ride again on his shoulders, hold me in his arms, sing to me, show me how to count in Norwegian, or rock me to sleep. We would not be able to buy the things we needed to be like all the others. Even Mother suffered more now, because her girlfriends were with their husbands. She must have felt particularly alone and different those years after the war. Reality had set in and our limitations exposed to the world.

The positive thing I knew after the war was that I could dream about eventually going to Norway and meeting my relatives and seeing my father's land. That idea was very exciting to me and got me through some long and difficult times.

Legacy & Folklore

FIGHTING THE WATERS

"As I stepped off the dock onto the boat, I stopped living.
I knew that for the next ten days,
I would be working over twelve hours a day
preparing scallops day and night
on a rocking, slippery deck,
rain or shine, warm or icy cold,
in calm or rough seas.
I was damp, wet and cold most of the time
and just one wrong move could mean
a serious injury or my life.
I always tried to get on a ship with at least a toilet,
but usually didn't.
The first time I went out as a teenager,
the captain saw that I was left-handed and hit me.
He ordered me to open the scallops with my right hand
to get the best meat. I did it, but my hands
were often rough, cut or chapped throughout my career.
I fought the waters for thirty years
and was lucky; I came home.
But I saw too much, lost too many friends,
and can honestly say,
I hated most every minute of it."

—From a retired fisherman in 1995

CHAPTER

5

~

Sailing a True Course

THE NOBILITY OF OLAF BERG
& HENRY SIMONSEN

Early stone Viking carving showing the vital
relationship between man, fish, ropes and boat.

RENOWN
All men are mortal.
Words of praise
Will never perish,
Nor a noble name.

—"The Havamal,"
circa 900 A.D.

NOBILITY, WITH ITS TWIN meanings of dignity and decency, can surface at unexpected times in one's life—often in times of challenge or crisis. Ordinary people who have lived ordinary lives can rise to an occasion

~

without thought for themselves. They make a conscious or unconscious decision, based on their values and upbringing, on what they feel is the decent or right thing to do.

Generally speaking, the typical Norwegian will follow the group and not take a bold stand unless he is led. I have often heard Norwegian friends say, "I don't want to get involved." This reaction may again be traced to the *Janteloven* and its implication in their lives.

Olaf Berg and Henry Simonsen were typical Norwegian-Americans, who lived their lives harvesting the sea. Yet both, in a time of challenge, more than rose to the occasion.

> *Olaf Berg gave his life for the principle of decency.*
> *Henry Simonsen led his crew in a heroic feat that saved lives*
> *and brought international acclaim.*

THE OLAF BERG STORY

WAY BACK IN THAT SINGULAR PLACE where I store long-ago impressions and hazy recollections of pleasant events, there is a warm, sunny backyard bordered by shrubs and flowers. The year, I believe, is 1940. I am a toddler, playing with some toys alongside a pretty little girl named Beverly, while her big sister Betsey and a friend amuse themselves in the yard, and our mothers relax on lawn chairs and chat.

Our mothers were old friends from childhood. Both had married Norwegians, and they had much to talk about. My mother was a recent widow, and Momma's and Aletha's husbands had been friends. Both families attended the Elim Baptist Church every Sunday, and Beverly and I were in the "cradle room" together. Beverly was a part of my life for many years. We went to school together through upper grammar school and high school and visited several times in college. We were baptized together when we joined the church; we graduated from high school and college at the same time and became teachers. We kept in touch, but not a lot, and when my mother died many years later, Beverly came down from central Massachusetts to be there for me. Our lives have intersected during many rites of passage, and our friendship has always held a special place in my life.

Beverly wore colorful Norwegian sweaters to grammar school, and with her blonde hair, high cheekbones and friendly manner, she seemed to represent everything beautiful about Norwegians. She also had a warm and friendly family and her life seemed stabile, happy and secure. I often wished I could be more like her. Then one day, there was a news report that her father had been killed on his fishing boat. I remember my mother crying and saying, "Poor Aletha, this will be so hard for her and she is pregnant again." I didn't see

Beverly until school started again, and by then all the shine was gone. Suddenly she was a slim, blonde girl who looked very pale and very fragile. I remember saying something to her about how lucky she was to have known her father, but she just looked at me and turned away without a word. Life had changed for Beverly and her family and was never again to be the same.

This is the Olaf Johan Berg (Olsen) family story as seen through the eyes of his daughters Beverly, Betsey and Nancy, with the help of some old newspaper articles that have been lovingly saved in the hope that some day the story of Captain Berg's life and death might be more fully appreciated. It is also a mystery story, possibly a murder mystery. A reader of this book may have the clue that solves it.

FOLLOWING THE WATERS
FROM NORWAY'S LOFOTON ISLANDS

OLAV JOHAN BERG OLSEN was born on the island of Flakstad in the Lofoton Islands in 1894. As the oldest of ten children and with money scarce, he had to work very early in his life, as did most Norwegian boys of that day. They had two choices: fishing or farming. Fishing seemed much more exciting to a young boy, so just after confirmation and completion of school at about age fourteen, Olav shipped out on a fishing boat as a cook. His cooking consisted of making coffee and boiling fish and potatoes. Later he was to be in the Merchant Marine and by the time he was eighteen, he had been around the world.

OLE OLSEN?

OLAV PROVED TO BE A MAN of courage at a young age. As a teenager he was a member of the Roald Amundsen expedition to the South Pole. His first wife's daughter remembers him talking about it and has seen him in a group photo of that great adventure. And after circling

—Circa 1915, Berg archives

Early photo of Olaf Berg (left) and his brothers in the Lofoton Islands.

—*Dirksen-Berg archives*

Olaf Berg at Buttonwood Park, with Betsey Berg in the baby carriage in background.

the globe, as many Norwegians were prone to do, he settled in Brooklyn—but not before there were some dramatic changes in his life.

His name was Olav Johan Berg Olsen the day he entered the United States at Ellis Island, but it wasn't Olsen when he went ashore at the Battery. As told by his daughter, Betsey: "The immigration official listed his first three names only. Dad realized the mistake but didn't speak English and figured there probably were too many Olav Olsens (Ole Olsen) anyway. At that time he officially became Olaf Johan Berg."

In Brooklyn, where he was a fisherman, he married a widow with a small daughter, Ingrid, and he worked and lived there until his wife's sudden death a few years later. The daughter went to live with relatives in Norway, and he moved to Massachusetts and fished out of Nantucket. It was on this resort island and former whaling port that he met Aletha Damon, a New Bedford Yankee with a college education, who had trained as

a teacher. She was working on Nantucket that summer as a waitress at one of the hotels, a job that many college girls and teachers sought during their vacation months. It was a lovely community away from home with great beaches, sailing, social activity and many opportunities to meet boys of similar age.

Aletha was an attractive woman with a big smile. She was a large, capable, friendly person who radiated warmth and easily could have passed for a Norwegian woman. And it came to pass that she was as attracted to this older Norwegian fisherman, Olaf Berg, as was he to

—*Dirksen-Berg archives*

Schoolteacher Aletha Damon's engagement photo. circa early thirties.

—*Dirksen-Berg archives*

Olaf Berg and his Yankee bride Aletha
Damon Berg on their wedding day.

her. As told by her daughter Beverly:
"Mom had told us that they had been
very much in love but that he didn't
propose until he met my grandmother. It was very, very important
to him to know her before
proposing." They courted while he
lived with another fisherman, Arne
Pedersen, also from Northern
Norway, whom he had met on
Nantucket and who would continue
to be his close friend throughout his
lifetime. He and Aletha married and,
after the wedding, his first wife's
daughter returned from Norway and
moved up to New Bedford to live
with them.

THE FAMILY

IN ADDITION TO HIS FIRST WIFE's daughter and his first mother-in-law,
as well as his new family in New Bedford, his family in Norway required
support from their eldest son and he received numerous letters asking for
specific items to be mailed to Norway. He faithfully sent packages throughout
his lifetime but was never to return to his home in the Lofoton Islands. His
daughters relate that "these frequent requests were sometimes difficult to
meet with a burgeoning family
on a tight budget, but he never
failed in his responsibility to his
parents in Norway."

He and his family, now
consisting of his wife, three girls
and his former wife's daughter,
attended the Elim Baptist
Church on Middle Street in
New Bedford, then known as
the "Swedish Church." It had
specific Scandinavian traditions
such as the "*Jul*" service on
Christmas Eve and a New
Year's Eve service that the

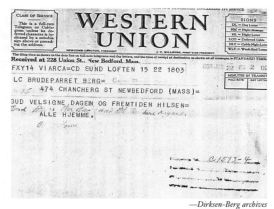

—*Dirksen-Berg archives*

Wedding greetings from Lofoton sending the
bridal couple best wishes from all at home.

community enjoyed and was a warm reminder of home.

Remembers his daughter, Beverly: "Dad and all of the other Norwegians we knew couldn't pronounce the 'J' sound. At home for Dad it was always 'orange yuse, yump rope,' etc. It seemed strange to me as a little girl that he and his fishermen friends would not tell us why they did that. Following church one Sunday, my father was talking with some of the fishermen and he called to one of them, '*Yohn, Yohn*, we go to check the *Yanet* and *Yean* before we go home.' We socialized with other Norwegian families, mostly people who went to our church, and most of them were from Northern Norway."

The Norwegian fishermen in the area had a club, and they would put on a yearly Christmas party, something that is fondly remembered by all Norwegian children who lived through those years. This colorful afternoon with folk dancing, *bunad*

—Dirksen-Berg archives

Olaf and first daughter Betsey Berg, circa 1936.

(Norwegian regional attire), music, gifts for all and wonderful food was something we all looked forward to each Christmas. Olaf Berg's children remember these Christmas parties vividly, and they also remember that he loved Christmas more than any other time of the year. Beverly recalls that he once told his family, "If I have to work at Christmas, I will get another job."

Like many other Norwegians, he belonged to the Masons and was essentially self-educated after graduating from the *folkskole* at age fourteen. He traveled widely and read a lot. Beverly remembers that "Dad taught himself to read English and always had books with him when he left for a fishing trip. His favorite books were historical novels in English. Imagine how difficult these books must have been to read and yet he managed to teach himself to do it." Shortly after he arrived in the U.S., knowing no English, he went into a luncheonette to eat. He later told his family, "The man next to me ordered 'ham and eggs and coffee,' so I repeated the same words and I ate the same thing, three times a day for many days."

"He was always working around the house when he wasn't on the boat," Beverly recalls, "and he especially enjoyed the spring and summer. Mom told us that the first time he went with her to a family reunion, it was held at a relative's farm. He got out of the car, and he rolled in the grass. She was upset thinking of the first impression he was making, but he was thoroughly enjoying himself and said it was 'yust' like home. His goal upon retirement from the fishing industry was to own a florist shop. He loved to walk into a shop and just smell the flowers. He loved nature, loved to be around growing things.

"Packages were periodically sent home to Norway. These always included coffee and sugar, among other things. My father was caring person who loved his life. He was proud of his wife and children, proud of being Norwegian, proud of being a good fisherman and proud of always standing for the truth. He had enormous pride in his work, home, family and himself. He and Mom once had an argument after the doctor had been to the house and ordered Dad to be hospitalized for a severe ear infection. He was so dizzy that he had to be helped to the bathroom, but he insisted he couldn't leave the house without shaving first. Mom insisted he go to the hospital immediately whether he needed a shave or not.

"Mom lost. He shaved—pride won."

THE SKIPPER

"He was," Beverly recalls, "helpful and easygoing at home, but on the boat, life was a different story. Like all skippers, he had to keep order and discipline. He told us how space was very limited on board the boat. For example, one day he twice told a new crewman to stow his gear. The third time he threw all of the man's belongings overboard. Loose items were a serious hazard to the crew. He took his work very seriously and responsibly. There was a great bond and loyalty between the men on a fishing boat, and their rules were unbreakable. No liquor was ever allowed on board. Anyone who tried was fired.

"This is not to say they didn't enjoy a drink or two on land. Dad always had liquor in the house. It was served to other fishermen who visited but never to their wives. Dad would not have a drink but would drink his coffee. Mom said none of the Norwegian fishermen's wives ever drank in their homes. Dad's saying was, 'A woman who drinks liquor will do anything.' Before his death, he was skipper of the *Stanley Butler*. Their trips lasted from six to fourteen days, and it was always like a holiday when he came home."

THE TRAGIC AND MYSTERIOUS DEATH
OF OLAF BERG

It is a mystery within a mystery, and the mystery deepens as it gets darker and then black. No one interviewed for this book admitted knowing anything about it, or even acknowledged knowing Olaf Berg. Most told me they had never heard of him, the family or the story. All clippings on the Berg family somehow have disappeared from the New Bedford Standard-Times newsroom library—and the Berg file should have been rather large because all four daughters had many achievements in their lives.

But the Standard-Times' articles documenting these last days of Olaf Berg's life have been lovingly and carefully preserved by Betsey, his eldest daughter, for more than fifty years, in the hope that one day the truth as she and her sisters understand it, might be more widely known.

The Standard-Times headlines jump out at the reader:

> *"'Forced to Dump Fish in Sea,' says Skipper"*
> *"Butler Crew Denies News of Cod Limits"*
> *"Suit Against Fisherman's Union Started in Court February 14"*
> *"Deaths of Two Fishermen are Checked for Foul Play"*

How did the seemingly benign act of being ordered to dump fish at sea lead to the suspicious death of two fishermen? Were these events related or merely a coincidence?

To start at the beginning: The *Stanley Butler* was a dragger out of New Bedford, but she often unloaded fish in Boston, as was the custom of many New Bedford boats. The men belonged to the Fisherman's Union in New Bedford where they dealt directly with their local New Bedford union representative. They were unused to the intricacies of the fisherman's union in Boston and probably assumed that the rules were the same.

But for one reason or another, it was the beginning of the end for Olaf Johan Berg when he sailed into Boston Harbor with a large load of fish one cold March day in 1947. He and his crew happily anticipated unloading, getting paid for their 118,000 pounds of cod, and going home to their families with another good trip under their belts and good pay in their pockets. No one on that boat that day expected problems, and certainly no one dreamed that within a few months their skipper, and one other fisherman out of Massachusetts who testified against the union, would die under suspicious circumstances.

The Standard-Times clippings preserved by the Berg family relate that a union official met the boat at the dock in Boston and told them they were permitted only 5,000 pounds of fish per man, or a total of 55,000 pounds, and that they had to go back out to sea to dump the rest. None of the men on board had heard of such a rule and didn't like being told this. So the eleven men protested and were led up into the union hall for a hearing and as a result of the hearing were forced by the union to dump their fish.

Such rules, many believed, raised the price of fish artificially. The Massachusetts attorney general's office charged that by limiting the catches of fish, the Atlantic Fisherman's Union was in violation of antitrust laws.

—*Photo by Albert Cook Church. From the estate of the late Aletha Berg,*
wife of the skipper of the Stanley Butler.

The F/V *Stanley Butler* on a cold winter's day in the
forties.

Captain Berg, skipper of the *Stanley Butler*, was asked to testify at this trial, and
he agreed.

At the trial, another crewmember testified that a union official told him
"they were restricting catches to keep the prices up and that was for the
protection of the industry." He told of having to go to a union hearing in
Boston for breaking union rules—rules that, according to the union official
there, "should have been learned in the bars." The crew of the *Stanley Butler*
denied that they knew such a rule existed.

Captain Berg also told the court that a union official from New Bedford
came to Boston while the crew was on trial and further told them that he did
not know of any limitation. The New Bedford official said he had come up to
Boston "to be sure his men would not be railroaded." Olaf Berg acknowledged, however, that the union in New Bedford voted to limit the weight of
their catches after this incident occurred in Boston.

THE PUZZLING PHONE CALL

OLAF BERG'S DAUGHTER Beverly recalled that after the court proceedings,
her father had planned to be with his family on June 30, 1947—the day he
died—and attend a New Bedford parade in the afternoon.

"Someone called that morning asking him to go down to the boat to do something. We never knew who made that phone call. The boat had been in dry dock and had been completely gone over, including new ropes in the rigging. He left saying he'd be back by lunch. Later that morning I answered the phone. It was Olaf Andersen, the owner, calling to tell Mom that Daddy had had an accident and was in the hospital. My grandmother kept us busy during the rest of the morning, and neighbors took us to the parade in the afternoon."

When Mrs. Berg finally came home, her husband was dead. Berg's daughters, as remembered by daughter Nancy, "cannot recall ever being told how he had died." "Later," says Beverly, "we learned that he had been carrying bricks up to the crow's nest. As the rigging had just been redone, the bricks used as ballast had to be replaced. The rigging broke, and he fell to the deck. He was the only one on the boat at the time. A crewman later told Mom that he felt certain the rope had been cut almost through. He said there was no fraying, and there was a blunt cut where the break was."

July 31: New Bedford Standard-Times headline: **"Deaths of Two Fishermen to be Investigated."**

The Standard-Times reported the "possibility" that two fishermen, Berg and a fisherman from Dedham, had died as a result of foul play and that the deaths were being investigated by the attorney general's office. Olaf Berg of New Bedford, they reported, was killed when he fell 20 feet from the mast of the *Stanley Butler* to the deck. And a cook named Godfrey Zimmermann on an Atlantic Coast Fisheries trawler died aboard a vessel as she was bound for home. The Standard-Times went on to say that "both Berg and Zimmermann testified against the Atlantic Fisherman's Union during hearings in Boston last month when Attorney General George Barnes brought suit to enjoin the union for alleged violations of the antitrust law in limiting catches of fish."

—Dirksen-Berg archives

Olaf Berg and his gang on the F/V *Stanley Butler*, circa late forties.

The Standard-Times further stated, "Dr. William Rosen, New Bedford medical examiner, said the death was accidental due to a fractured skull and fractured thigh. Berg was repairing rigging when he fell and other workmen who were in the area found him lying on the boat deck. The vessel was tied up at the Kelly and Son marine yards on the Fairhaven waterfront."

Berg's oldest daughter Betsey says today: "My father testified against the union, which we were led to believe was run by organized crime at that time. He and one other fisherman who testified lost their lives in suspicious accidents shortly thereafter. My father went to work on the boat while it was in dry dock, and the rope he would have had to stand on to repair something had been cut almost through and then turned over so it wouldn't show. He fell from the rigging when he was alone and fractured his skull. Mom was three months pregnant at that time with three little girls at home."

THE MYSTERY DEEPENS

"SHE HAD A VISITOR from the insurance company after his death," Betsey says, "who told her nothing could be proved, so it was better for her to take the insurance money which was double indemnity and not make trouble. And that is what she did; she had no choice."

A 1947 diary entry by Olaf Berg's widow reads: "Olaf J. Berg died in a fall from the rigging to the deck of the fishing boat, *Stanley Butler*. There was a suspicion that the rope had been cut on purpose as Olaf and another New Bedford fisherman, who was dead two weeks later, had testified in the Boston court."

Her daughter Beverly describes her mother as: "a wonderful woman who, after Daddy's death, was the rock for the family. Having my grandmother living with us made it possible for her to return to teaching. My grandmother had not had an easy life and I believe she had passed her strength on to Mom. One of Grandmother's favorite sayings was, 'God bends the back to the load.'"

The Standard-Times reported on August 3 that the Commonwealth of Massachusetts had brought an equity suit against the union and nine of its leaders, and after months of hearings the judge ruled that the union was a monopoly and in contempt of court.

SILENCE

NOTHING COULD BE PROVEN regarding Olaf Berg's death, but the family was convinced that it was not an accident. Was it just another unfortunate

—Dirksen-Berg archives

Aletha Damon Berg with her sister in the front row and with daughters Beverly, Betsey, Kathy and Nancy behind her. They all encouraged and supported each other throughout the years after Olaf's mysterious death.

event in the history of the New Bedford fishing industry or was it a signal to fishermen? Because of the uncertainty, fishermen might think twice before testifying in court against their union in the future.

And life in the Berg family would never be the same—but they were proud of their father—that he had been true to his values. Beverly remembers, "The Norwegian owner of the boat, Captain Olaf Andersen, thought of my father as a son and was very good to us throughout the years." And the four Berg sisters, despite their pain and their grief, matured in a church-centered life and have achieved a great deal in their lives—the result, they feel, of Aletha's perseverance and the inspiration and memories of Olaf Berg.

Three of his daughters, Betsey Berg Gillin, Nancy Berg Koroski and Beverly Berg Dirksen, will always remember the happy days with their father. The youngest daughter, Kathy Berg Pappas, never knew him except through stories. Many years later, all of them visited relatives in Norway together and one said: "It was as though we just belonged there." His daughters do not forget his legacy.

> *Olaf Berg was a Norwegian man who believed in the truth.*
> *He did what he had to do because it was the right thing to do.*
> *He died with a noble name.*

CAPTAIN HENRY SIMONSEN

"That Extraordinary Feat of Seamanship"

—From the U.S. Coast Guard report on the rescue of fourteen men
by Captain Henry Simonsen and his crew of the *Ike and Jens*

*It is every fisherman's nightmare and worst fear that he might be
cast into the ocean without a boat to rescue him. To be alone in the
water with no rescue in sight—to wait until the sea claims you as
another trophy—is a universal fear among all men and women
who make their living at sea. And because of this common fear,
there is a common response: to help one who is in trouble because
you, one day, may be in need yourself.*

THE CHRISTMAS SURPRISE

TEN DAYS BEFORE CHRISTMAS in 1961, the late Captain Henry
Simonsen was fishing for scallops on the *Ike and Jens*. But he found more than
scallops on that fateful trip. He and his crew found a place in history and the
eternal gratitude of thankful families and the Canadian government.
Christmas is a time for miracles, but miracles were very likely not on the mind

—*Isaksen archives*

The F/V *Ike and Jens*, owned by the late Jens Isaksen and skippered by Henry Simonsen,
circa 1959.

of Henry Simonsen on that trip. He was out at sea earning money for his and his crew's Christmas celebrations with their families and was trying to get back to New Bedford in time for shopping and holiday preparations.

> *"Oh pilot, 'tis a fearful night. There's danger in the deep."*
>
> —Thomas Haynes Bayly, "The Pilot"

When the skipper and crew of the Canadian scalloper *Aegir*, who were fishing in the same general area, first noticed the wind and seas coming up about a hundred and seventy miles east-southeast of Nantucket, they too most likely were thinking about their return trip to Nova Scotia and their own Christmas celebrations.

"Simonsen was jogging the same 60-mile-an-hour wind when he spied the *Aegir*," wrote the Standard-Times and quoted him as saying, "We were drifting off the fishing grounds and the winds were doing 60 knots and the sea was very heavy. I was in the wheelhouse with the mate. He looked out and saw the scalloper *Aegir* to the northeast. He then noticed that the vessel had just taken a very heavy sea and that several stanchions—upright supports—had broken from *Aegir*'s port side."

Captain Simonsen stopped his vessel, as he knew immediately that the Canadian boat was in trouble. According to the Standard-Times, he said, "We could see the crew of the *Aegir* on the deck waving life jackets and baskets at us, and the *Aegir* began to sink rapidly. Water had flooded her hold." Simonsen put out a Mayday call and then ran alongside the distressed vessel. The boat was "about 25 yards from us when we got off the first dory with six men and we picked them up. All this time the waves were breaking over us. The second dory held eight men, which meant that two were still on the boat. We had great difficulty picking up the men because of the weather and high seas. The eight got to us but just as they were getting aboard a large wave hit them and one guy tumbled off. Thank God he fell into the dory and scrambled back up. The *Aegir* sank shortly thereafter, after being struck with another big wave." (The name *"Aegir"* paradoxically has several meanings, one of which is: "The Norse god of the sea." The fishermen of the *Ike and Jens*, Norsemen, must have looked like gods to the men of the *Aegir* that day.)

> *"Anyone can hold the helm when the sea is calm."*
>
> —Publius Syrus, "Maxim 358"

One former crewman, Karl-Johan Melkevik, now living in Norway, remembers: "The last man we picked up was the cook. He had jumped off the boat, and we found out later that he had six or seven children at home. Our whole crew helped. Two men anchored themselves and reached over. The two boats were drifting back and forth as we tried to pull the men onboard. The sea and boats was rolling bad. We just thought about saving them. What else could we do? I suppose we were in danger, but we didn't think about that. We only thought of getting those men out of the sea and onto our boat. Simonsen was a very nice guy and a good skipper."

Captain Simonsen himself told the Standard-Times: "We saw the other two men rolling in the sea, but just then the *Barbara Jo*, another Canadian boat, came on the scene and took them aboard. It was providence that we were there. All but three of the men had families. One man, with tears in his eyes, put his arms around me and said, 'I have five children at home. You gave them the best Christmas ever.'"

The survivors all signed the back of a cigarette carton with their addresses before they were transferred to the *Barbara Jo*, which set out for Nova Scotia and home.

—Simonsen-Ferreira archives

Names and addresses of the *Aegir's* Canadian crew written by them on the back of a cigarette carton.

"They were on board waving at us and yelling (to us)," Simonsen said, "We couldn't hear (the words) but I think it was 'Merry Christmas.' Who could ask for a better present than that?"

The Canadians told the story of the rescue from their own perspective in the January 1962 edition of "The Atlantic Fisherman and Shipping Review."

An abridged version of that story reads:

"14 MEN RESCUED FROM SINKING CRAFT"

"Heavy loss of life was averted on Georges Bank when the New Bedford dragger *Ike and Jens* rescued 14 men from the sinking Lunenburg scalloper/dragger *Aegir*. Two men were picked up by the *Barbara Jo*. There was no loss of life. The storm that had lashed the area for several days was blowing itself out when suddenly a heavy sea hit the ship and filled the cabin, washing

some of the crew from their bunks, at 12:45
p.m. The *Ike and Jens* were listening on a
different frequency and didn't know that the
Aegir was in trouble and was steaming about
three miles away to windward.

—*Simonsen archives*
Ellen Simonsen at a later date.

"We blew our horn, waved and attracted
the crew's attention and the ship came on our
port quarter and stood by about 400 yards away.
Our first dory carried six men and made it
successfully to the *Ike and Jens*. The second dory
was swamped and the men were able to get back
aboard the *Aegir*. There was a gale of 45 to 50
miles an hour blowing and it wasn't easy to get over that short stretch of
water.

"The second try with eight men was successful, leaving two men on the
scalloper/dragger, which was settling low in the water. It was about two hours
since the first wave had swamped the boat. The *Ike and Jens* was still standing
by when the *Barbara Jo* came on the scene. The last two men were huddled
on the stern, the water lapping at their feet. They jumped into the water and
the *Barbara Jo* made the rescue. Two hours and ten minutes after the first
heavy sea, the *Aegir* went down stern-first.

"A few hours later, the Canadians were transferred from the American
boat to another dragger, the *Hansen*, just recently launched at Shelburne. By
this time the affair was taking on the appearance of a wartime combined operation. In Lunenburg, Captain George Crouse was contacting the Royal
Canadian Navy in an effort to have his men taken off the dragger. The RCN
frigate *Lanark* had just left Boston and was contacted by radio and the pickup
was made from the overcrowded *Hansen*. Both the Canadian and U.S. service
were on the job through the cooperation of Search and Rescue. Both had a
plane in the air and a ship under way on the first phase of the search when all
were recalled. The Coast Guard also had a ship standing by."

When Captain Simonsen returned home to New Bedford, he didn't say a
word to his wife, Ellen, about the rescue. She recalled in a 2000 telephone
conversation from New Hampshire where she now resides: "After he had
been home a while, the phone rang and it was an international news service
asking for a first-hand account of the daring event." She had no idea what they
were talking about and told them her husband would call them back. "The
phone," she remembers, "kept ringing from every newspaper imaginable."
Finally she and her husband decided 'to give Brad Hathaway from the
Standard-Times the story and others could then get it from him.'"

This was the first hint that their lives would change during the next few
days. She still remembers, "Letters and calls started to come from Canada,

—*Simonsen archives*

—*Photo: New Bedford Standard-Times*

The Simonsen-Simonsen family. Ellen seated next to sister Barbara on right, wedded Henry standing on left. Next to him are Ellen's parents, Pauline and Jack (Scarface Jack) Simonsen.

Captain Henry Simonsen with award for heroism.

thanking my husband and his crew for saving their husbands' lives and telling them that they would be eternally grateful to them." They received so many letters that they were unable to answer all of them. They were invited to homes, to celebrations in Canada, to testimonial dinners. But they didn't go. The Norwegian is shy and uncomfortable with praise. It seemed that all of Canada was expressing thanks for Henry Simonsen and his crew of the *Ike and Jens* for their bravery and courage.

The Canadians realized a fact that simply had not occurred to Captain Simonsen and his crew: The men of the *Ike and Jens* had risked their own lives and their boat to save the men on the sinking vessel, *Aegir*, without a thought to their own safety.

The owner of the *Ike and Jens*, Jens Isaksen, recalled in 2001 that the "rescue was a proud moment for me personally." He had known Henry Simonsen well from his boyhood days and said, "He was the best man I had." Jens Isaksen was "not surprised at Simonsen's and his crew's courage and bravery." "Simonsen," he said, "knew what he had to do that day."

The sea would not take Captain Simonsen's life, but he would die of cancer before he was fifty years old. He died with a noble name.

The courageous crew of the Ike and Jens:

Captain Henry Simonsen, b. Skudeneshavn

Peder Edvardsen, b. Åkrehamn   *Egil Ingebretsen, b. Torvestad*
Trygve M. Overdo, b. Torvestad   *Edvard Ingebretsen, b. Åkre*
John K. Kristiansen, b. Fyn   *Gjetmund Jakobsen, b. Sevland*
Sven Jacobsen, b. Åkrehamn   *Karl Johan Melkevik, b. Kopervik*
Nils Simonsen, b. Åkrehamn   *Jorgen Sandslett, b. Skudenes*

The men on the Aegir, according to their local records were:

Paul Rhuland, Acting Skipper   *Keith Parks, Riverport*
Gilbert Corkum, Mate   *David Knock, Riverport*
Everett Risser, Lunenburg   *Lloyd Whynacht, Stonehurst*
George Rhuland, Lunenburg   *Edwin Sabean, Blue Rocks*
Cornelius Vandertoorn, Lunenburg   *Arthur Weaver, Blue Rocks*
Herbert Peeler, Lunenburg   *Junior Herett, West Dover*
Perry Croft, Lunenberg   *Warden Mossman, Kingsburg*
Melvin Mossman, Riverport

Legacy & Folklore

JANTELOVEN
(The Laws of Jante)

IN 1933 THE DANISH WRITER AKSEL SANDEMOSE, who spent much of his life in Norway, wrote a novel called "A Refugee Crosses his Tracks." The story takes place in the imaginary town of Jante, where "the laws of Jante" clearly dictate social and moral standards.

The term *Janteloven*, which means the laws of Jante, reflects a code of conduct that pervades much of Scandinavia. But some feel that Norwegians adopted it most enthusiastically and that Sandemose simply codified that which was already informally in place. Some say he meant his novel to be seen as a farce, but that it was taken seriously. His book remains controversial because it is fiction based on the facts of life as he experienced them.

This code of conduct can help to discourage leadership, originality, creativity and competition—indeed, it can discourage a climate conducive to excellence. Its main purpose is to keep people in place and working together peacefully, and some think that it took root in Norway because Norway was ruled for so many years by Denmark and then Sweden. The idea is that being too smart or competitive is inappropriate in Norwegian culture. (Sports seem to be exempted.)

We should remember that this is Sandemose's interpretation of cultural tendencies and that these tendencies primarily relate to attitudes toward fellow Scandinavians; outsiders are often judged with more open and accepting attitudes. We also need to remember that Scandinavian artists and other creative people have had to work within these parameters, and despite this condition have succeeded—but not without taking risks and exerting much effort. According to one American friend who lived in Scandinavia for many years, "The Scandinavians don't really like these laws, but admit there is some truth to them."

Americans, on the other hand, generally teach their children to be proud of their individual differences, achievements and creative ideas. American children are rewarded for achievement with recognition, status and a sense of pride. Americans are conditioned to admire and strive to be like those who achieve, stand out and create. We tend to believe that all people are individuals and have gifts that need to be encouraged. Competition is apparent in our schools, and in the workplace.

The *Janteloven* pops up at the most unexpected times in Norway. But apart from this way of thinking, Norwegians and Americans are much alike in our behavior and attitudes.

One irony of the *Janteloven* is the outsider's assumption that this code would preclude a monarchy; yet all three of the main Scandinavian countries embracing this cultural code still have royalty. Indeed, the laws of Jante, do, it could be argued, lend themselves to socialism quite naturally. And that is an interesting sociological theory to ponder.

Janteloven by Aksel Sandemose as translated from the original Danish.

1. *Du skal ikke tro at du er noget.*
   You shouldn't think (believe) that you are special (anyone important).

2. *Du skal ikke tro at du er lige så meget som os.*
   You shouldn't think that you have the same standing as us.

3. *Du skal ikke tro at du er klogere end os.*
   You shouldn't think that you are smarter (wiser) than us.

4. *Du skal ikke bilde dig ind at du er bedre end os.*
   You shouldn't fancy yourself as being better than us.

5. *Du skal ikke tro at du ved mere end os.*
   You shouldn't think that you know more than us.

6. *Du skal ikke tro at du er mere end os.*
   You shouldn't think that you are more important than us.

7. *Du skal ikke tro at du duer til noget.*
   You shouldn't think that you are good at anything (that you will amount to anything).

8. *Du skal ikke le af os.*
   You shouldn't laugh at us.

9. *Du skal ikke tro at nogen bryder sig om dig.*
   You shouldn't think that anyone cares about you.

10. *Du skal ikke tro at du kan lære os noget.*
    You shouldn't think that you can teach us anything.

6

~

The Emigrant Wave

TESTING THE WATERS
1946–1965

—From a color oil painting by Magne Adolfsen, artist, Kvitsøy, Norway
Waiting for Papa

I LOVE TO TRAVEL. I love the adventure of discovering sights I have heard
about, seen in pictures or read about in books. I love to meet people from
other cultures and countries. I love the unknown and the discovery of new
ideas, thoughts and perceptions. I delight in the impromptu conversation and
in reflections of my peers who have lived life in the same times yet under
different governments, espousing different ideas. I love to listen to their
stories and views of their world, all of which is to me an opportunity for
growth and self-discovery. For me, it is more than a love; it's a need. I have
often wondered why I feel this way, and like to think that it is part of my
genetic makeup—this whole idea of travel, adventure and growth. I travel
alone in strange cities and on strange streets. I have that Norwegian love of

~

the unknown and do not feel fear but excitement and wonder when I travel to new places.

If I take those feelings and multiply them many times, I might begin to understand the sensations the Norwegian emigrants experienced throughout history, and particularly when they came to America. It takes a sense of adventure, risk and courage, and those who had it, loved their emigrant experience.

THE AFTERMATH OF THE WAR
& THE NEW *PENDLERS*

"Growing up in the war so poor, we wanted to do better.
We grew up in Norway, an underdeveloped country.
We were very poor, nothing there, not even a decent job."

—A successful entrepreneur remembers his youth.

THE WAR AND THE GERMAN OCCUPATION had left Norway impoverished. The eldest son often waited a long time before inheriting the family property or farm, and the remaining children, in most cases, had to find another home and work. Many were forced to emigrate to a country where there was more opportunity, such as America.

One woman, Kirsten Lindø Smedsvik, a young girl when she came to America just after the war, reflects on this period in her life. "My father came from a large family in Avaldsnes on Karmøy. His eldest brother inherited everything and there simply was not enough land there to support our family. So he started to fish and then went to America to fish. He had no choice. There was nothing else he could do."

Peder Eliasen, a historian from Karmøy, describes Norway in the days right after the war: "There were heavy taxes. We had to recover from the battles and build a new Norway. There were rich herring fisheries from January through March and a good living for a few months. Many fished in Iceland in summer and many went back and forth to Brooklyn and New Bedford—the stronger people could make a better living in America. In 1957 the herring disappeared. Merchant Marine sailors were fewer because although ships were bigger, fewer people worked on them with the more advanced technology. So work was a problem.

"During the fifties, there were lots of low-paying jobs in Norway because of much destruction from the war and the rebuilding efforts. We couldn't get a car for fifteen years and had to have permission from the authorities. We couldn't get a house on a reasonable loan. Bread and coffee were scarce. Our people had everything when they went to the U.S.A. It was like going to heaven—big car, central heating. The uncle in America picked up his nephew

—*Medhaug-Vilhelmsen archives*

Lise and Mery Stol in their Sunday best at Easter, just after arriving in America. After many years of deprivation, they were finally a family reunited.

—*Mery Vilhelmsen archives*

After many difficult years, the Stol family begins anew in America.

at the airport or dock in the big car and told his nephew to drive it. The nephew had never driven a car before or even seen a big car."

In the post-war years, even into the sixties, Norwegian living standards in towns and villages were comparable to those in rural America in the first half of the century. City life was somewhat better, but island and rural life was behind the times. Not much had changed over the years, and the war had made things worse.

TWO SISTERS REMEMBER

ONE EMIGRANT WOMAN, Mery Stol Vilhelmsen, remembers her life in Norway: "I was born in 1942. I was number four of a family of five children. We lived upstairs at our grandmother's house and didn't have much space at that time. We had no water inside. We had to go outside to do our duty, and get the water to carry in and out. We were lucky we had a river running by the house for fresh water, and on cold days when we were small, my mother used to bathe us in the sink tub, the same one she used for washing clothes. We had a bath every Saturday and a little wash-up other days.

"In the summer, we had a very good time in the river and bathed every day. All the kids in the neighborhood went swimming in the river as it was not too deep and was safe for the kids. Mothers and all the people around in the neighborhood had to take the water from that river to do all of the cooking and washing. People from far away came in carriages and brought barrels to fill up with water to bring back to the house for the animals and housekeeping. In those days we hardly ever went into a car or things like that. We were lucky to get the bus. When I was around seven, we moved into a new house. My father left for New Bedford in '47 and went fishing scallops."

Lise Stol Medhaug, sister of Mery Stol Vilhelmsen, remembers: "I was born in March of 1945 and in April, the war ended. It left Norway smashed. While mother was pregnant, there was hardly any food. People had money, but there was nothing to buy. Mother cooked herring and made a thick soup from it with flour. Our grandparents had chickens and a cow, so we got some milk. But they still had to use water for the cereal, and I lost my teeth early and had to get false ones because of the poor food my mother had when she was carrying me.

"It took five years in Norway to get back to normal. The government handed out stamps for the food. Each family got so much per person. Our weekend bath we did in the living room next to the oven and our naked rear ends got a lot of burns, as we had to be as close as possible to keep warm. My mother put stones in the oven, wrapped them in paper or clothing and put them in the bed before we went in—so we could keep warm.

"My grandfather had been to America farming in Minnesota for some years. I think he left Norway in the 1920s. He came home before the war in 1940. In 1946, my father left for New Bedford to try his luck at scallop fishing, so he could make money for a new house here."

NEW BEDFORD AFTER THE WAR

New Bedford had seen better times. The men were returning home from the war to a different city. The women had worked during the war. Many went back to their homes after the war, but none would ever be quite the same. The textile mills, which had been very busy in wartime, were never again to thrive at previous levels. One by one they closed and went south, where labor costs were lower, and New Bedford, now inundated with veterans and their new families, war brides as well as new immigrants, struggled to pay its ever-increasing costs.

Things were still clean, but it was simply not the same city that most of our parents remembered. There was still much 1938 hurricane damage evident in the beach areas, and we could see the broken skeleton of the huge roller coaster at Acushnet Park as we trod to the beach that was bordered by piles of broken concrete. After traveling there on the Sunday trolley, we would picnic in the grove, play in the water, watch the fishing boats pass the lighthouse, and listen to nostalgic stories from our family about the New Bedford that once was.

DOWNTOWN

There was still a very good downtown area, a respectable South End, and a North End shopping area. The downtown area around Purchase, Union and Pleasant Streets, dominated by the New Bedford Hotel and with elegant buildings such as the North Congregational Church and the Olympia Theater, still had good department stores, and some wonderful ice cream and coffee shops near the library.

It was there in the downtown area that we, as young people, would run into friends and chat in front of Cherry's Department Store, while we gazed longingly at the lovely clothes in the windows. We were surrounded by the aroma of roasting nuts from Planter's Peanut Store, where a costumed "Mr. Peanut," portrayed by my dear high school friend, Ronny Mitchell, might be working, and giving delicious peanut samples to us.

We would spend time at the library or see a movie for twenty-five cents on weekends at one of the ornate local theaters and, of course, have an ice

—Old postcard

Purchase Street looking northwest from William Street shows the distinctive Merchant's Bank (without the pigeons), a trolley car (also known as a street car), The Waldorf Cafeteria, Congregational Church and Olympia Theater. Everything past the bank, including these impressive buildings, was torn down for redevelopment. An amazing decision in the otherwise proud history of New Bedford.

cream soda at the "Five and Ten." No one who grew up then in New Bedford can forget the wonderful food at Lorraine's restaurant, where the floor was covered with sawdust, and we would sit on chairs with armrests while we smelled the coffee roasting—coffee with a wonderful aroma that in my lifetime, at least, has never been duplicated. How can any of us forget the Gulf Hill Dairy Restaurant that was quite elegant in a Victorian kind of way and was famous for ginger ice cream sodas.

Purchase Street, also known as Downtown, was the center of activity in those days. All the department stores were there. Some of the neighborhoods had the new supermarkets, but many of us preferred to shop in the local mom-and-pop store where they gave credit.

There was much home delivery in those days. The milkman delivered milk and milk products by horse and cart. Our grocer would deliver if mother's order was large, and the postman, in the forties, would come twice a day to the front door. The rent man always had a huge roll of bills for us to envy, as he would add our precious rent money very slowly to it. We would watch excitedly as the coal man sent the coal down a chute into our basement coal bin, while my mother worried about the price and that our order might not get us through the winter. We had the wood man, who would fill half of the basement with firewood for our big black stove; the insurance man, who would collect ten cents each week on a small policy for my mother and which was enough in the end to cover her funeral expenses; the rag man, who had a large, horse-drawn wagon and would shout, "Rags! Rags!" as he moved up the street leaving piles of waste behind him; the tinker, who would bring an assortment of delights to the door for purchase; the newspaper boy, who, fifty-five years later, would come to my mother's memorial service because he remembered that she smiled at him and was kind; the bread man, who always annoyed my mother by leaving things she could not afford; the gas man, the telephone man and the electric man who came when we had a problem—and, of course, the family doctor. Even the pharmacist made house calls in those days, and if all of us were sick, he would pass the medicine through the kitchen window.

In the summer we had the "pony boy" who would ring a bell as the pony pulled an ice cream cart topped with an umbrella through the neighborhood streets. We sometimes also had beggars or gypsies who knocked on the door and asked for food. One day a woman came and tried to sell my mother something, but she looked so hungry that Momma asked her in and she shared a meal with us. I remember that she wore many colorful shawls and that she didn't smell nice as she ate hungrily. After she left, Momma washed everything she had touched carefully and told us, "We have to be kind to those who have less than we do."

Somehow as I look back on growing up in New Bedford, I can re-experience the sense of safety and community we felt as the result of delivery people who also spread news, and, in a way, checked on us.

A CARING COMMUNITY

NEW BEDFORD STILL HAD little pockets of "old whaling money" as well as new professional money that enabled some neighborhoods to be especially lovely. The old Yankees and the new professionals could be found on the various corporate and nonprofit boards of directors in town, as well as on the governing boards of the churches, synagogues, private social service agencies and country clubs. They comprised the large corps of volunteers in the cultural and social service sectors and were generous with their time and philanthropic gifts.

Many were interested in the future of New Bedford and took an active interest in the youth in the community. I remember that they were very kind to young people who appeared to have initiative and drive, irrespective of their background, and would often be the ones to give us small jobs, volunteer a reference for college or help us plan careers. These community leaders admired young people who tried to better themselves and assisted in any way they could. Unfortunately, many of us who left to be educated in other areas didn't come back home to live in New Bedford.

A SAFE PLACE TO WALK

Hawthorne Street, where the thick canopy of beautiful trees almost obstructed the views of the old and gracious mansions, and its adjoining streets were the center of affluence and influence then. People walked often in New Bedford because it was a pleasant, safe and scenic place—above Purchase Street, of course. The man most famous for walking was our old Mayor Harriman who walked in a rumpled white suit at each parade, waving his broad hat to all of us. One would always find people strolling on weekends in New Bedford and see baby carriages being wheeled by mothers in groups with their children running alongside. Going out for ice cream was a favorite pastime for all of us when cars were still scarce. And Gulf Hill and Frates Dairy had the best ice cream!

New Bedford was slowly but surely going downhill in terms of "upkeep," but to the new Norwegian emigrant and *pendler*, having just gone through the war, it was a paradise and a place where good money could be made. The emigrant looked ahead to what the future might hold; the native would often feel frustration in what was and might have been.

—Norwegian American Line, Courtesy Børge Solem

Hands across America.

"Greetings to Norway
Greetings to my native land,
high up in the North!
I'm longing for your familiar shores,
the dearest shores on earth.
I am thankful for all you gave me,
which you freely give to the high and low,
and which I carry on-board with me today."

This principle may account for the fact that many emigrants did better financially, despite less education, than many of the natives. Or as Theodore Roosevelt put it: "The credit belongs to the man who is actually in the arena, whose face is marred by dust and sweat and blood; who strives valiantly, who errs and comes short again and again—who, at best, knows the triumph of high achievement; and who, at the worst, if he fails, at least fails while daring greatly."

EMIGRATION

THE FIRST EMIGRANTS FROM NORWAY to America in the nineteenth century came seeking freedom of religion, much the same as the Pilgrims did. They were Quakers. Later emigrants came for economic reasons, and others anchored here seeking adventure and discovery. Prior to the Second World War their goals were modest in nature. But after the deprivations of the war years, the emigrants' goals expanded, and many wished to make great sums of money and to have the power and security that went with it. It was a normal, healthy reaction to the poverty, deprivation and powerlessness of the war years in Norway. Many succeeded in this goal.

"The best people emigrated—those who had the most initiative.
The hardest workers left."

—Peder Eliasen, Personnel Director,
Hidra Aluminum Co., and Karmøy historian

A few landed on our shores for visits and study—and elected to stay. After the war ended, a young man named Oddvar Solstaad became such a person. He recalls: "After the war there were not enough places at the Norwegian universities for all the students, so I was able to get a Norwegian scholarship to study in Boston. My time in the Norwegian Resistance helped me qualify for this. In the summer term, I needed to support myself. I met a Norwegian

—Courtesy Lise Medhaug

NAL Stavangerfjord bringing its emigrant passengers home, circa 1960.

fisherman from New Bedford and he told me about the fishing boats there. So I went down to New Bedford a year after I came over in 1947.

"Someone told me to go to Rasmus Tonnessen's place, the New Bedford Ship Supply on the waterfront, and ask about work. I met Isaksen, the skipper, there and was told about a boat that had trouble getting her second engineer to show up because sometimes he hit the bars. That boat went into Boston. So I was told when the boat was expected to come to Boston and I went down from Tufts to Boston.

"I had to move out of the dormitory before the summer and put my stuff in storage and went to Boston Harbor where I found a place to room on Hanover Street with derelicts like myself—at thirty-five cents a night including breakfast. I waited for the boat from New Bedford, and when it came in, I talked to the captain and told him I was studying engineering. Of course, I knew nothing about it at that point, but it sounded good to him, and I waited the three days for the second engineer to show up. He didn't, so the captain took me on. Six hours on and three hours off. I was young; it was O.K. When you are young, you don't realize what you are getting into.

"I passed the test, I guess, because I was able to stay on. Whenever I needed a job, I had a reference, and that is the key—never had any trouble getting a job. I rented a room in New Bedford, spent all of my free time in the library and never went into a bar. I enjoyed it thoroughly—enjoyed being out on the boat. Most of the fishermen ended up in the bars, sad to say, and then they were terribly sick on the way out when they got on board the first day. When they got over that, they were great guys to work with and we all looked after each other's safety."

A young emigrant from Stavanger, Gunnar Haines, tells his story of how he became a fisherman and began a life on the seas of the world. He remembers with his innate sense of humor: "My father was not a fisherman and when I came to the States my mother warned me, 'Don't you go to sea!' In 1948 our family was poor and my future wife's mom and dad were living in America.

ABSTRACT OF LOG VOYAGE No. 6 East 1956. (305)
Norw. Amer. Line S.s. STAVANGERFJORD 13334 Gross Tons.
Captain IVAR GRØNBUKT
NEW YORK. Via Bergen, Stavanger, Copenhagen, OSLO.

Date	Lat.	Long	Miles	Weather etc.
June 22	41 - 48	65 - 30	391	SW. Llight breeze. Calm sea. Rain. Fog.
,, 23	44 - 36	57 - 33	388	SW. Light breeze. Smooth sea. Fog.
,, 24	48 - 28	50 - 02	390	NW. Light to moderate breeze. Slight sea. Fog. Overcast.
,, 25	52 - 25	41 - 57	389	W. Mod. to light breeze. Slight sea. Overcast. Light clouds.
,, 26	55 - 52	32 - 34	390	NE. Light breeze. Smooth sea. Light clouds. Overcast.
,, 27	58 - 16	21 - 37	385	NW. Light breeze. Calm sea. Overcast.
,, 28	59 - 43	09 05	398	NW. Light breeze. Slight sea. Overcast. Light clouds.
,, 29	60 - 08	E4 - 42	429	NW. Gentle breeze. Slight sea. Light clouds.

Left New York June 21st at 11.30 a.m.   Passed Ambrose Lightship 1.13 p.m.
Passed Marstein Lighthouse June 29th at 00.50 p.m. NST.
Distance 3160 n. m. Time 7 d. 18 h. 37 min. Average speed 17.00
Arrived Bergen June 29th at 2.40 p.m.
Arrived Oslo July 2nd at 9.00 a.m.   Total dist. 3973 n.m.

Log abstract of the *Stavangerfjord* from New York to Oslo, 1956.

Her family came to Norway and visited Skudenes and Stavanger. Their daughter was a nice-looking chick, and I decided she needed the best. So I made plans to go to America.

"My father was originally from Skudenes and was her dad's buddy. They came to our house so our fathers could visit and her father put up the guarantee for me to come to the States. I had always wanted to come to the States. First I went to Atlantic City, and then my uncle called: 'Could you come to New Bedford to work as a shacker?' (In this period of time a shacker was a man who did odd jobs on board and gathered up extra fish, such as lobsters, for sale later.)

"Someone wrote a note for the conductor of the train heading for New Bedford, and I got on the train and passed the note on to the conductor. I was picked up in New Bedford. It was December and was cold and dark. I remember the Fairhaven Bridge just before five o'clock, damp and cold and miserable. I got on the boat where I was to shack, threw the lines down, and went out."

And yes, they did get married. Gunnar went on to entrepreneurial success in maritime-related industries and traveled much of the world. He died in 2002.

A retired fisherman now living in Norway and America remembers his first days in New Bedford: "I was just sixteen when I came over to America. My father was born in Brooklyn in 1896. He served in World War I and was sent to France. His father and mother lived in Brooklyn for many years and then returned to Norway. My father visited Norway before the Depression in 1923 and met my mother and married. He came back to America and had three children here and lived in Brooklyn and then went back to Norway where he opened a store and stayed.

"I grew up in Norway and heard many stories about America. I first went to Brooklyn in 1952 when I was about sixteen and worked in construction on Long Island, but didn't like that very much. I heard that there were jobs in New Bedford and many Norwegians living there, so I came up here with the remaining money. Our home in Norway was in the mountains and I had never even seen the ocean or been on it, but I thought I would fish anyway. When I got to New Bedford, I was almost out of money and very tired. I finally found a room in a rooming house over a cafe near the waterfront. I was exhausted and fell asleep immediately, but in a few hours one of the biggest men I ever saw came into the room and tossed me out of the bed. It was his room and the landlady had let me stay there because he wasn't supposed to come back for a few more days. He let me sleep on the floor anyway, and the next day I went out for a job on a boat."

TWO BROTHERS FROM BØMLO: HOW TO BECOME VERY WEALTHY

SOME OF THE EMIGRANTS went on to great financial success, as did the Eidesvik brothers—from Bømlo, Norway. In the early fifties they lived life as economically as possible, sending everything they earned home to Norway. They are still a legend on the waterfront. Lauritz, in an interview in Haugesund, Norway, remembered those days well:

"In the mid-fifties the fish just disappeared in Norway, and there was no income. So we floated a loan for the family and had to make new money to pay it off. My brother and I flew to New Bedford separately and made a pact that if something happened to one of us, the other would take care of the families. We rented a room at 15 Kempton Street for six months. We wanted to send all the money home, so we didn't

—AT photo 1998

The late Lauritz Eidesvik, one of Norway's wealthiest men and founder of a maritime dynasty. He found ways to live on next to nothing in New Bedford and was grateful for the opportunity America offered him when he was getting started.

join the union although the union was very active then. The union tried to stop us from fishing, so we stayed on the dock till the boat left and then jumped onto it.

"We worked hard when we were out at sea and ate double rations there. When we came in, we went up to the North End to a bakery where they sold day-old bread. There we could get three loaves of bread for the price of one. We ate bread with sugar and butter when we were in port. Once in a while we had a 7-Up as well. We would spend no money whatsoever. We also did some painting for extra money and other odd jobs when we were in from fishing. We drank no alcohol, but would have two beers a year, if someone else paid for it.

"We sent everything to Norway. We never went into bars or had social activities, except we always went to church. Because of the union problems in New Bedford, we worked in Maine for another six months and then went back to Norway. We paid off the loan and had another seven thousand Norwegian Krone to begin our lives in Norway. That was a lot of money in those days."

Lauritz Eidesvik was managing director of Eidesvik and Co. in his native town of Bømlo. He was known as one of the most successful men in Norway and worked in the shipping industry as it relates to the oil industry off the coast of Norway. His company is very large, and his business card described his work as "supply, tugs, standby surveying, seismic vessels and operating base-ship repair," comprehensive services that cover most of the needs of the offshore oil drilling industry.

Said Eidesvik, "I worked hard when I was young, and now it is time to play. I give money to the church and to special things on my island. Many played when they were young, and now they have nothing. I have paid America back many times over in travel and in investment, and I like Americans but am not afraid to speak up to them. Sometimes they refer to my English, which is not perfect. So I just say, 'Well, how is your Norwegian?' "

Mr. Eidesvik died in the winter of 2002 while ice-skating. His obituary in the 31 January 2003 posting of Offshore Shipping Online, read:

"Lauritz Eidesvik, founder of Eidesvik Shipping, dies"

"Lauritz Eidesvik, Managing Director of Eidesvik Holding AS and founder of the Eidesvik Shipping Group, died December 17th. Lauritz Eidesvik was born on April 8th, 1932, and celebrated his 70th birthday in 2002. The daily operation of the Eidesvik Group was handed over to his son Simon in January 2002, but Lauritz was still an active player in the daily operation. He was a member of the board and managing director of the parent company Eidesvik Holding AS. More than 500 people took part in the funeral at a local church on December 23rd, 2002."

Sadly, Mr. Eidesvik worked all of his life and got very little time for the play he had planned. But as he was so devoted to his work and his large business domain, I truly believe that life without work would not have been as happy for him. From my interview with him and also talking with him once more two years later, I learned that he loved work, his wife, his family and his church very much indeed.

THROUGH THE CHILDREN'S EYES

Norwegians of that generation remember their childhood years and the war years well, and their experiences left an indelible impression in their hearts and minds. Says John Isaksen, whose mother had been imprisoned in a concentration camp during the war: "We came to America right after war on the *Stavangerfjord* when I was about eight years old. It was still a troop ship with gun mounts and other military hardware. My father was still in U.S. Navy. We went to Brooklyn first and lived with mother's sister. That is where I found out about America, and it was different—that's for sure. Lots of automobiles and noise.

"What I missed was the water and the boats. I missed my little boat so much, and I didn't like this big city. I used to take the boat out when I lived on the island. We would go outside the islands, and you had to learn how to handle a boat as a child or you didn't last.

"After father came home from the Navy, he became a fisherman. The boats fished out of Brooklyn and we came up to New Bedford in the summer. We settled here as it was more central to the fishing grounds."

(Author's note: I was in the third grade when a shy, slim Norwegian boy came into our class one day. I was very excited about that because of my Norwegian name. When I went home that noon, I told my mother that a boy named Johnny Isaksen was in my class. She told me that he was one of my father's relatives, and I was to help him adjust to school. So the next day I tried to find him alone. But he was always surrounded by the other boys—a bit of a celebrity, being from a different country and having grown up in the war. I finally saw him alone by the large tree in the playground and I went over to him and said, 'Hello, I am Astrid and my mother tells me we are cousins.' He just looked at me. He didn't speak English and he didn't understand, so he didn't answer. I thought if I said it louder he would answer, so I raised my voice the second time I tried to talk to him. Still no comprehension. The third time, he looked away when he saw me coming and the fourth time, he ran. I never saw him again until I interviewed him for this book. Needless to say, he didn't remember me.)

John Isaksen remembers the second grade well. "I was three years in the second grade. Kids had stars and I never got a star and I finally gave up. I should have tried harder. Mother had quite an accent and she would help me with the English words I brought home. I would have to bring them back and forth, and I never got them right. How come the teacher didn't know my mother had an accent? I made it into third grade eventually. I had Norwegian friends and spoke Norwegian with them."

(Author's note: When I was in the fifth grade at the Rodman School in New Bedford, a serious blonde girl in a Norwegian sweater and blue skirt entered our class one day. She was to be with us off and on for about three years. Her name was Kirsten. We all liked her and wanted to be her friend, but she was a bit shy and quiet and led her life in her own way. She was never personal with us, and we could not get close to her and chat as we did with others. I was disappointed because we had the Norwegian connection, but she stayed by herself. She was pretty, very smart, doing better than many of us even in English, and her work was neat and correct. She wrote her letters differently than we did, always wore Norwegian clothing and was especially well groomed and shiny clean. The teachers loved her at once because she did everything exactly the way they asked. Before she returned to Norway one year, we gave her a little going-away party. Then she reappeared the next year and we were very surprised. We never could understand why she came back and forth so often. We would have tearful farewells, and then she would appear again. I once asked her why and she simply said, "So my father can work.")

Kirsten Lindø Smedsvik recalls, in an interview in Haugesund: "I went back and forth to America often in the forties and fifties. First I went to Brooklyn and then up to New Bedford. I learned English quickly—went back to Norway and then came back to New Bedford, went back to Norway and then back to New Bedford. I was always a top scholar but there was too much adjustment to be made. There were no close friends and always new people and new houses. I graduated from Fairhaven High School and got a scholarship from an American university for a scientific education but had to go back to Norway because of my father's illness. I became a secretary and married and never went back to New Bedford. I was able to work using my English and that was good. I never want to be dislocated again."

And on Karmøy, Kaare Ness, who would become a future fleet owner in Seattle, recalls how he decided to emigrate: "I left Norway because I couldn't see any future there. My wife and son came over to New Bedford the same year. I saved my money and became a boat owner after nine years. We always saved money. Many didn't save money, but to be successful you have take care. I didn't drink. I put money in the bank. Many left for New Bedford after the war and many were single men. In the late forties and fifties, maybe seven to eight hundred men from our area came to New Bedford. Almost everyone came to New Bedford at one time or another. We were five brothers, a father and two sisters in New Bedford. About a third of those emigrants who came went back to Norway, and another third moved on to Seattle."

Many men came to New Bedford and left their families in Norway. Most were reliable, went home each year, sent money home regularly and were devoted fathers and *pendlers* in the best tradition. But there were also those who forgot their families.

THE CHILDREN LEFT IN NORWAY

AS RECALLED BY MERY STOL VILHELMSEN: "In 1950, when I was around seven, we moved into a new house in Stol on Karmøy. My father left for New Bedford in '47 and went fishing scallops and promised to send us packages of all kinds. I remember those packages, and I remember a beautiful doll and some nice winter clothes, candy and coffee, raisins and fruits. After the war it was hard to get things like that. We had to have ration stamps to go to the store and only so many stamps for each family. We used stamps for butter, coffee, sugar and chocolate. I saw my first ice cream after the war. They came with a bucket from a Skudenes bakery, and we had to eat it right away before it melted because no one had a freezer at that time. That was heaven—I had never seen anything like that and couldn't understand how they had made it. I also remember the first time I saw a banana—about the same time. My sister and I had to share one and everyone had to taste it. Every Christmas Eve we got an orange in our stocking. We used to hang up our stocking and that was the biggest surprise. In the morning, we had one orange and one apple and maybe a piece of chocolate and coloring books and maybe a doll.

"When we moved into the new house, it was nice, but no toilet inside. We had a little building outside with one seat and two holes, one for the grownups and one for the kids. We used to go to the toilet and sit and talk. That was the style. In the cities they had WCs in the houses. The rich people had bathtubs and toilets, but that was the rich. We were not rich. We made a well in the cellar and then didn't have to go to the river for our bath. Mother used to heat the water on the stove, and we would take our Saturday bath. Sometimes we went to our aunt's. She had a bathtub, and we were so lucky to have a bath there. (Author: This was true for some of us also in New Bedford. We never had hot water in our house and had to heat it on the small stove or go to my aunts' for a bath in a real tub.)

"We were always playing outside. It was safe to play outside day and night. In the winter we went ice-skating. We had only one pair of skates, so my brother and I were always fighting about who was going to skate. (Author: that was true for us also.)

"We had to help our grandparents with the barn. We had to bring the hay inside, and we had to help them pick potatoes and bring in the corn. We all had to do it because they were helping us, and they needed the kids to help them. My grandparents were old then, I thought, but in those days people looked much older. My grandmother was about sixty but looked a hundred to me. That was how they dressed and acted, but they were very good to us and she would sit with us and tell us stories and show us how to knit socks.

"As the years went by, we were always wondering why my dad did not come home, and we were waiting for letters—longer and longer—and he did not send money either. So one day Mother decided to go to New Bedford alone and the brothers were nice to her and gave her money and clothes, and we lived with our aunt. When I was thirteen years old, she left for New Bedford, by way of England.

"Mother sent us packages and money and did her best. It was hard for her. She had two big operations in the hospital and that cost her lots of money—money that would have been used to send for us. After two years she came home, and we were so glad to see her. She looked so good and younger than when she left and had nice clothes and things. She stayed home for a while and then left with my younger sister to go back to my father."

"SOMETHING WAS VERY WRONG"

LISE STOL MEDHAUG, now living in Norway, relives her life in those days. "In 1947 my father left for New Bedford to try his luck at scallop fishing. Mother was both mother and father with five kids. She also had to supervise the building of the new house and feed the workers. She had to carry the food about a mile a day with me the youngest hanging on her coat—back and forth.

"After living in our new home, I understood something was very wrong. Mother talked to the adults and told them she had to go out to work in the fields to make some money.

"At Christmas, other men came home (on the *Julebåt*, Christmas boat) with large trunks of dresses, beautiful toys, jackets, shoes and money. But what happened to our Daddy? He never came home. Some daddies just forgot to come home. Once my uncle came home with a big trunk by boat. He brought Christmas dresses to all of the relatives. I thought, Daddy has been in New Bedford, America, for seven years now and I can't wait till he gets home because he must have seven trunks now—one for each of the years he has been away. I can remember that Mom cried when I said that.

"My uncle told Mom what was going on with my father. He said that every time the boat came in, he cashed his check in the barroom and kept on drinking until there was no money left. My mother hadn't got a dollar for the past three years. My older brother and sister sent money. I was too young to be told. That spring my mother went to the bank to ask for a loan so she could leave to America to look up Dad. She got it and left with my uncle, leaving all of us home with my father's sister. I was happy and sad. But I was going to spend days and nights with my favorite aunt and uncle.

—Simon Vea archives

The *Stavangerfjord*, called the *Julebåt* (Christmas Boat), leaves New York for Christmas in Norway. The men returned to their families with gifts of all descriptions and often a new car.

"Mother sent a letter saying she had found Dad and had found a furnished apartment that she moved into. She said the city was full of Norwegians and families with babies. After a few months we got a package—clothing. Wow! I got my first doll, which I still have. My mother said she had been lucky and won it at Lincoln Park. She said she would be home at the end of the summer, and then we would emigrate and be a real family and live together. Summer came and passed, then fall and Christmas came when we got a nice package. Spring came and no Mom. What was going on? We got a postcard and a letter with dollars in it. Then summer came and a new Christmas. Mom still did not come home. Had she forgotten us also? I didn't understand.

—Simon Vea photo

Leaving New York on the M/S *Sagafjord* in 1965 are, left to right, Harald Hausen, Simon Vea, Tore Torsen and Lars Håland.

"Grandparents and aunts tried to cheer us up, and one day they let me know that she had been seriously ill after she arrived in the States but now she was fine and would come home in March. After two years apart, she came home.

"Oh, my! She wore lipstick and earrings and high-heel shoes. She looked like a movie star from California. I was so proud of her that I brought a load of kids home with me so they could look at my American mother. At that time, Dad got his feet on the ground because of the shock of Mother's illness and that was a good help for him. There was a lot of Norwegians that forgot they had a wife and kids at home and also they got a kind of *'solstikk'* (struck by the sun) and never came back home. That was an excuse for drinking alcohol and spending the check. In 1956, my mother and I left for Oslo for emigration papers at the American Embassy to come to America."

A TEACHER'S STORY

A MAN FROM SOUTHWEST NORWAY, Aastein Aase, now a teacher in Sandnes, Norway, decided to try out New Bedford for several years. He wrote nostalgically: "As a kid growing up on a farm close to the sea at Jæren on the Southwest coast of Norway, I had a dream to go and find out about some of my several relatives in America. My father and mother kept receiving Christmas letters from kinsfolk over there. Shortly after the war, my very first encounter with homecoming relatives was at Stavanger harbor, when Bernhard Pollestad with his family set foot on Norwegian ground. They had been living in North Dakota, owning a farm bigger than twenty average farms in my part of Norway. His youngest son, Barney, and I became pals, and I also became pals with other young Norwegian-Americans who came with their families to Norway after the war. After finishing upper secondary high school, my dream of going to America came true. The man who made this possible was my dear cousin Torger Tonnessen. His original name was Torger Aase (Åse) and in New Bedford, he was nicknamed 'Mickey Mouse.' Torger gave me a break scalloping on his boat where he was the skipper. He and his wife Maria also let me live in their home on Elm Avenue, Fairhaven, the first couple of months.

"Being a fisherman off New Bedford was a tough experience, even if I had had some experience fishing herring on the north coast of Iceland for two months during a summer holiday. I arrived in New Bedford in June 1958, and worked on several boats in New Bedford for nine months. Then a Norwegian friend of mine and I took off for Seattle to try our luck as fishermen there. 'Big money out west,' we heard. Unfortunately, Seattle was not as good for us as New Bedford. We lacked one important thing there: No connections, no relatives, and for several weeks no jobs.

"I finally got a job on a dragger as a cook, since cooking jobs were the only ones available. But I couldn't cook, and was asked to 'pack my sack' after the first trip. After walking around the docks for several days asking for a job, I finally got on a salmon boat bound for Southeast Alaska. The trip was supposed to last for two months. But bad luck again. I had an accident, fell overboard and was fished on board again with a fractured skull and ended up in Ketchikan Marine Hospital. After recovering, I decided to go back to New Bedford, and having a reputation there as an able fisherman, I had no problem getting a job.

"During those last nine months in New Bedford, I worked most of the time on a boat named *Dartmouth*, owned and skippered by Aksel Nærland, nicknamed 'Hurricane Aksel' because he used to go out instead of coming in when there was a hurricane warning—thus hoping for a top price on the scallops. I had intended to stay for only one year in America, to experience America, to get away from school, to earn money, to see relatives, to mature and then go back to Norway to study at Oslo University. It turned out to be two years, partly because of bad luck in Seattle/Alaska, but mostly because my last nine months in New Bedford proved to be the best period of my American experience. I had a steady job, made good money, got to know many interesting people, including a sweet red-headed American girl of seventeen. I was in doubt if I might well stay for a lifetime and become an American fisherman. But I made a compromise with myself: 'Let's go back to study in Oslo, and go back fishing in New Bedford during long vacations.'

"Fate decided I should not go back until forty years later, when I revisited Fairhaven for five days, staying at John Haaland's (Håland) home in Fairhaven in 1999. John Haaland used to be skipper on *Alpar*, and I had worked for him, and he and his wife, my cousin Magna, had treated me as a close family member. Strange thing to be back to recapture my lost youth."

"FORTH AND BACK"

AND WHILE THE EMIGRANTS were coming over on the *Stavangerfjord*, other Norwegian-Americans returned to Norway to visit their relatives and take care of business. They were proud of their newly acquired worldly goods, and it was a chance to go home to see the family, describe their lives, and perhaps boast a bit. The affluence they displayed made even more Norwegians think about coming to America.

The Rev. Mr. Henry Pedersen recalls his trip well. "We went back to Northern Norway as a family in 1947—a bit of showboating, I think. We brought our car over, and to get to the island we had to take one of two boats. We knew about the ferry, but we just assumed that both boats were large enough to take the car. So we went on the steamer. We had a big '47 Oldsmobile. They put oil drums down on the deck, put the car on them and tied the car down to bring it to the island. The roads on the island were very narrow. Ours was the third car on the island and if we met anything, we had to back up and let the horse and wagon go past. My father's family had done fairly well by Norwegian standards, and he felt he needed to show them he didn't make a mistake by leaving Norway. The children used to argue about who was more closely related to me. Everyone on the island, it seemed, was related in some fashion. Cousins often marry cousins still."

PAPA'SMA RETURNS

I REMEMBER THAT MY GRAND-MOTHER, Emilie, called Papa'sma by us, returned to Norway after the war to visit the family and property. While there she sold property in Skudeneshavn which would be very valuable today. She then returned to America. I remember it very well, because she brought us all beauti-fully handmade Norwegian Hardanger Bunad from Skudeneshavn. She also brought us traditional jewelry and gave me a souvenir spoon celebrating the end of the war on Karmøy. She returned with

New York City as seen on a menu cover of the Norwegian American Line's *Bergensfjord*.

my father's sister and we knew she would now settle in America permanently. She was never to return to Norway until her remains were taken there after her death in 1974.

THE AMERICAN-NORWEGIAN MARINER

AND THEN THERE WERE more complicated arrangements, such as this one from a dislocated merchant mariner: "We had one more child after returning to Norway from the American Merchant Marine. After our reunion, I was home for one and one-half years fishing. In Norway you had to have ration coupons for buying. In America you could buy all you wanted. I had the best of everything in the American Merchant Marine—steaks and all the best. I didn't know what rationing was as we got all the best food on Merchant Marine ships during the war. I didn't like rationing at all, and I wanted to go back to the States.

"I went to American consulate and was told that with American papers I could go back any way I wanted. Finest kind! In the States I could buy anything. But I was scared to bring my family over then with four children. My oldest boy was just confirmed, so I decided to go back to the States with him. He could go to school and college in the States. For four years I was alone with my boy. My wife was alone in Norway with three children, and I didn't visit them in Norway."

His wife responds: "I had been alone so much by then."

Her husband continues: "I bought a house before she came. Kind of scared to bring whole family over here. I was first in Brooklyn fishing out of New York and then to New Bedford for three years before wife came. I wanted to be sure to have a house and know I could support my family before I brought them over."

Wife: "We survived."

Husband: "I sent money back to Norway. I loved her then and I love her today."

Another Norwegian fisherman, so it is said, was married in another country and listed as dead when his merchant vessel was torpedoed. He had missed that fateful trip, however, so he took the opportunity to start a brand-new life and come to New Bedford to fish.

Many books and plays have been written about sailors' lives and loves all over the world. Certainly the "torpedoed fisherman" was neither the first nor the last seaman to live this lifestyle.

POST-WAR EMIGRANT LIFE IN NEW BEDFORD

THE NORWEGIANS WERE GENERALLY SAVERS, and much of the money from their "good trips" was put in the bank and used to buy houses or boats. But with some emigrants it was, too often, spent for escape and pleasure. There were so many unfamiliar choices and temptations in New Bedford for these young, unworldly men, and some, unfortunately made poor choices.

When the young men arrived in New Bedford, they had to make immediate decisions regarding their home away from the boat—the money they would save, send home or use for themselves; how they would spend their time on shore and with whom they would spend it. These all seem like easy choices, but to men who did not speak the language well, if at all, who were too young and mostly from families who had had so little during the war years, temptations plus too much money and too little experience often proved to be disastrous.

FOOD

MANY MEN NOW IN NORWAY talk nostalgically about the places they "hung out" when they were not in the bars. Some of these haunts were the restaurants of New Bedford, and a favorite of many was the Waldorf Cafeteria on Purchase Street. A cafeteria that served basically bland food was perfect for the Norwegian; there he could eat all the beefsteak, potatoes, carrots and bread he wanted. There was a huge choice spread out before them, and best of all there was unlimited gravy.

New Bedford children remember this place because they had to grab a coupon from a machine when they entered. There were tables and chairs near the front windows where the young fishermen could look out onto Purchase Street, which then was the heart of the city. There they watched people, especially the girls, stroll by. There they could meet their friends and perhaps some of New Bedford's residents. So the Waldorf Cafeteria is still spoken of fondly in Norway as the place "where we met our friends, hung out and ate good food." They also loved it there because if they didn't speak English, they could simply point to the food. One fisherman met a young woman there who was a Waldorf waitress and eventually married her.

The Bridge Diner, conveniently located on the bridge between Fairhaven and New Bedford, was a favorite fisherman's spot after an evening out and Norwegians could often be found there late at night for coffee and dessert or sobering up a bit after an evening of nightclubbing at roadhouses like the Hangar in Acushnet, the Orchid Room in the south end of New Bedford, or some of the better local dancing places such as Town and Country in the extreme northern part of New Bedford.

On occasion the young men might be invited to a friend's home for Norwegian fish cakes or fish pudding or some other special Norwegian food that they loved. They would be given scallops after a trip and often gave these to friends to cook for them. Many a girlfriend's mother cooked up scallops for her daughter and her Norwegian date.

Most Norwegians are not adventuresome eaters and generally, especially just after the war, did not like spices, herbs or foreign foods. Hot and spicy foods tasted like poison to them then, and to some, still do. They would go to local Chinese restaurants but would order American food, and often frequented the old Esquire Restaurant in the North End for late-night suppers. Sometimes they would have apple pie for dessert and always coffee. Some also ate in the bars, but a restaurant was a nice diversion from the bars. Also, many would frequent the downtown drugstores where they could get a sandwich or soda at the counter.

One such drugstore had a pretty young Norwegian girl, Lise Stol, at the counter and she loved to wait on the Norwegians. She recalls making "big tips" from them as they conversed in their native tongue.

The single men and the men away from their families usually did not cook at home, and most of the landladies forbade food in the rooms. Many Norwegians, especially the women now living in Norway, recall nostalgically the fried clams, clam cakes, fried onion rings, fish and chips and other typical foods of the New Bedford area. Norway does have fish and chips, but those cooked in the "English style" in New Bedford were deemed superior.

The fishermen's lives were basically lived downtown until they bought a car and ventured out as far as a dance hall, racetrack, roadhouse or Brooklyn to see their friends and relatives. Some went to New Hampshire to see the mountains or visit a racetrack, and men with families often visited Niagara Falls for a vacation. All looked forward to the summer, not just because it was safer out at sea, but because they could go to the beautiful beaches surrounding New Bedford. They loved the warm-water beaches more than anything here, and in the summer frequented as many beaches as they could find in the area, both saltwater and fresh. Photo albums in Norway will attest to the frequency and special meaning these well-loved beach days had for the emigrant.

At the beach, girls appreciatively noticed that Norwegian young men had strong, well-developed legs from walking and from living and working at sea on a moving, slippery surface. Many young women in New Bedford could be heard to remark, blushingly, not only on the "good looks" of the Norwegian men but also on their "great legs." Many Norwegian women remember that as teens they would go to their favorite beach at Fort Phoenix in Fairhaven to swim, dance at the pavilion or picnic up by the old cannons with their Norwegian fishermen friends. Fort Phoenix, which overlooks New Bedford Harbor, and was built as a fort to defend it, was once a grand beach and historic area with a dance pavilion, picnic facilities in the woods, a restaurant and great rocky areas for sitting, resting and viewing the lovely harbor. It played a pivotal role in the life of the Norwegian-American community. In addition to enjoying the facilities there, they could watch the fishing fleet coming in and going out.

CARS

CAR AND MORE CARS. The bigger the better, the faster the better. Price no object, cash sale, a convertible preferred, best loaded with every option! These cars were on show to their friends and screamed loudly, "I've made it!" The men would lend them to their girlfriends when they were out to sea, giving their girlfriends a type of prestige. (I remember at that time I had a '59 Volkswagen and my Norwegian friends thought it was just a toy. Why, they wondered, would I put money into that little toy?)

—*Stol-Vilhelmsen archives*

Norwegian-American bathing beauties at Fort Phoenix, early sixties.

—Mery Vilhelmsen archives

The Norwegian girls and young fishermen would meet at Fort Phoenix in Fairhaven for fun, laughter, swimming and music. By chance they might meet a prospective date or husband. Here is Mery Stol Vilhelmsen with her friends.

These cars could be seen in the parking lot at Lincoln Park—a large amusement park just outside New Bedford, and a favorite place for the fishermen, girlfriends and families—and at the drive-in theaters and the beaches on Cape Cod. These big, flashy cars with huge wing tails filled the holds of the *Stavangerfjord* on trips back to Norway, and sometimes the cars stayed when the men came back.

Their cars and body language told the world: "I've made it in America. I'm successful. See this car. Take a good look. I'm rich!"

Of course, many young Norwegian girls were met in this way and had rides in the cars, because these men were trying to make a grand impression as they looked for wives and new girlfriends in Norway. When they ran out of money, they sold the car, returned to New Bedford—sometimes with the new girlfriend—and bought another one.

Some of these cars are still on the road in Norway, taking up more space than is safe. They are kept up with great pride and now there are many American car clubs and even dealers specializing in used American cars. The cars look large by today's standards, but can still be seen shining outside Norwegian restaurants that are frequented almost daily by fishermen from the fifties and sixties. Many of these men dress now as they did then and speak with a unique Brooklyn-New Bedford-Norwegian accent, peppered with the vernacular of the fifties. Even when they speak Norwegian, many of the words come from their New Bedford days and with the New Bedford dialect.

—Courtesy Aleksander Hauge

Fisherman Magne Nes with his American car in the fifties. He was to spend most of his life living and working in the Seattle/Alaskan area.

—Serine Matland archives

Activities of women emigrants in the forties included their string band, shown here on an outing.

NEIGHBORHOODS

SOME MEN CAME TO AMERICA because family members sponsored them and they sometimes lived with these families. They were cared for in a familiar environment with family values. But many others were "on their own," with just some of their old neighborhood friends around. Some were barely sixteen—the age of the local high school sophomores. Others were older and had families to support back home. Some rented houses, when they had their families with them; others rented a floor on one of the two- or three-storied houses in New Bedford's west end. As soon as they saved enough money, they bought homes. Owning a home was very important to the Norwegian in this generation, and often they stayed in that home throughout their time in America.

Emigrants started to settle in favorite neighborhoods, forming clusters of Norwegians near relatives and friends and often not too far from the water. In the forties and fifties they settled in the west end of New Bedford, within walking distance of the waterfront and parks and in areas of Dartmouth bordering New Bedford but still near Buttonwood Park. Mostly, however, they were in Fairhaven.

Fairhaven was the favorite town of scores of Norwegians and already had been populated by Norwegians for several decades. There they had commercial piers for their boats as well as ship supply houses, boatyards and boat settlement houses, which settled the accounts from each trip and paid the fishermen their share of the settlement. Most enjoyed the beaches and scenery at Fort Phoenix, where they watched the fishing boats crewed by their friends leaving the harbor.

They loved the ice cream parlors, restaurants and ocean views from most of the streets. There they had their church, the Trinity Lutheran Church, as well as a Norwegian bakery and Norwegian neighbors. The size of their houses depended on their status as crew or boat owners, but virtually all were like the people who lived in them: clean, neat and sturdy. The Norwegian families are remembered by one of their neighbors, Margaret Urquiola Marquis, whose mother taught many of the Norwegian children in the local grammar school, as "those friendly and honest people who hung out their fish to dry on the clothesline." (Norwegians often dry their fish on clotheslines for their specialized ethnic dishes made with dried fish. This is still seen in Norway today.)

THE ROOMING HOUSES

Single and married Norwegian newcomers with families living in Norway most often rented rooms in homes in the downtown area of New Bedford within walking distance of the waterfront or lived with relatives. Before redevelopment, rooms generally were available in the multi-storied old homes, many typical of a style of architecture peculiar to New Bedford, along the narrow streets rising up from the waterfront. Streets such as Middle, Elm, Kempton, North, Pleasant, Mill and Hillman had many widows who rented out their extra rooms to the fishermen. They often preferred the Norwegians because they were reputed to be honest, clean and paid their rent on time.

Mrs. Sarah Bonnar Stone who was born in Glascow, Scotland, and whose son owned Albion Stone Jewelers, ran one such house at 844 Pleasant Street. She rented out nine rooms and preferred to have Norwegians, especially those who were nondrinkers. Her rooms were neat and clean and the environment hospitable. She took pride in her establishment and an interest in the lives of her roomers. Her house was located near the old fire station and was regarded by the fishermen as a premium residence.

Her young grandson Ralph Brown lived with her and his mother there while he going to school in New Bedford and remembers well the work he had to do to help his grandmother bring in the extra income. He now talks about all the scallops the fishermen brought them when they came in from a trip. Ralph said he never wanted to look at another scallop again in his life.

"The fishermen missed their own sons in Norway," says Ralph. They "took to him" and often would invite him to play cards with them. He liked these "great guys" and considered them his friends. He remembers some of the men living there as Gunvald Aadland, Aadne Mannes, Tonnes Schoen, and Sig Pedersen. One of them gave him his first shave and gave him fatherly instructions on how to do it for himself. He speaks of them now as his "main

—*Simon Vea Archives*

Norwegian emigrants in their rooming house on Elm Street. Left to right: Berdines Ferking, Jörgen Knutsen, Nils Nes, Karsten Brekkå, and Simon Vea.

male role models in those days" and vows to visit Karmøy soon and those men who are still alive.

Mrs. Stone charged four to five dollars a week rent for a room. It was Ralph's job to make the beds and clean the rooms for his spending money. He remembers: "My grandmother had large brass beds, and all nice stuff in the linen closet in the hallway. I made all the beds, and ironed on a mangle in basement.

"All the tenants paid on time—but I was so sick of scallops. I hated scallops. Mostly the Norwegians hung out in bars and the dog track. There were buses that went to the track. Most of them were married men and their families were in Norway. Many were from Karmøy and had come up to New Bedford from Brooklyn. When they came up, they would go to the New Bedford Ship Supply to see Rasmus Tonnessen, who would then recommend them to my grandmother. They would play cards and taught me how to play cribbage. We played a lot of cribbage. But they never came on the first floor where we lived—they had everything in their rooms.

"They were good tenants and were neat, very sincere and stayed for years. One was a Finn and he carried a knife. Finns didn't get along with the Norwegians. Grandmother was very tough and if anyone messed up, he was out. She was ninety years old when she gave up the rooming house and probably ran it for fifty to sixty years. It was a thirteen-room house, but redevelopment took the house. You know, I really liked these Norwegian men."

But all rooms in town were not of this quality, as another Norwegian fisherman relates. He went on to great success in Alaska and Norway but when in New Bedford, he took a room up on County Street. When Harald Mannes told his story, he settled back in his chair in Norway and smiled, saying, "This was quite a room. It was dirty, but I could clean it, wasn't worried about that. But I had also heard from the former tenant, a fisherman who had left New Bedford, that there were problems with mice and rats. That I didn't like!

"The first time I stayed there, I had just come in from a trip and decided to take a little nap. I was lying there, and I felt something moving under the sheets. Thought it was my imagination and dozed off again. But I woke up once more to this same feeling of something moving under me. And there it was! I could see this lump moving down the bed. It was a rat. Boy, I never forgot that!"

There also was a house with "rooms to let" run by a Norwegian woman from Skudenes. She was from the Høines area near the sea, the area where my family had originally lived. She was called "Anna by the Sea" and, as far as is known, was the only Norwegian who rented rooms in New Bedford to the Norwegian fisherman—although some Norwegians took in relatives or friends temporarily. I remember my grandmother taking young men into her home off and on over the years, most of whom were relatives or friends in Norway.

—Courtesy Ralph Brown, circa late fifties

Ralph Brown, a Yankee New Bedford boy with Scots roots, grew up surrounded and nurtured by Norwegian fisherman. He chose the Coast Guard for his career. His grandmother Mrs. Stone ran a boarding house where many Norwegian fishermen lived.

THE FISHERMEN'S LIVES AND WORK

Although they were beginning to have lives they had never dreamed possible, they also worked very hard and there was much competition on the boats as well as between the boats. There was pressure to make big money and to bring in money for the owner.

One fleet owner and captain recalls: "In the sixties, eleven guys were allowed to bring in one thousand pounds of fish each. Therefore, a skipper tried to bring in eleven thousand pounds on each trip. We stuck to it very well. It was a gentleman's agreement and no union rule. We always knew how many bags of scallops we had throughout the trip and one watch would tell another. The next watch would try to beat the last watch and there was always competition. If we had fourteen bags, the next watch (team) would try for fifteen so they could say 'we beat those guys.' One team had the skipper and the other the mate as the leader. They wrote all the figures down in the pilot house. In those days we didn't sort the scallops, and it was the same price for the whole trip.

—Names courtesy of Berit Nes. Photo courtesy of Aleksander Hauge given to him by a Norwegian friend

A crew of fishermen including Trygve Mannes, Captain Egil Ellingsen, Magne Nes, Samuel Samuelsen, Kaare Ness, Selmer Fagerland, Anders Andersen, "Snille Anton," and one unknown on the *F/V Lauren Fay* in the sixties.

"When we came in we went to the auction house, and they had a blackboard there. Same buyers would buy trip after trip. They had a watch that went off and had fifteen minutes to bid. Time up—end of bidding. If they really wanted your scallops, they bid faster. Sometimes they liked one boat owner more, and they bid on his catch.

"When we came into port, we tied up at the same dock. We also sometimes brought in yellowtail or lobster. This was called 'shack' (extra fish), and it was sold and the money divided among the crew. After you knew who would buy the catch, we would go to the fish houses to unload it and then back to the dock to tie up for a few days. You tried to time it so you came in early in the morning so you could unload early. The 'lumpers' would come in then and clean up. The crew did not want to stay on the boats in port." (According to "Lost at Sea," a Nova Scotian web site about the fishing industry, "Lumpers are people hired by the crews of . . . scallop draggers to unload the bags of scallops. At sea, the scallops are shucked, packed in bags and stored on ice in the hold. Upon reaching port, lumpers unload the holds, either by conveyor belt or by the bucket method. In times gone by, crew or lumpers would have to get down in the hold and manually throw the bags up to someone on deck."

Scallop bags are heavy and take some strength and skill in unloading. According to a scallop boat owner, there are about eighteen scallops to the pound, forty pounds to the bag, and the average take in 2003 per trip was 575 bags. That is a lot of scallops.

THE ROAD TO SUCCESS

As the emigrant fishermen became more experienced and skillful and saved their money, they were able to buy shares in boats—and eventually, with skill and luck, their own boats. Others inherited or bought the boats from their fathers. Many Norwegian fishermen owned shares in several boats and eventually owned many boats. There was a great deal of trust in these partnerships, often with family members or old friends from Norway, but sometimes these business transactions included an American who was not of Norwegian heritage.

Some men did not want the responsibility of boat ownership and remained fishermen working for others all their lives. Some tried ownership and didn't like it, and others tried being a skipper and didn't like it. So it basically was a matter of wanting the responsibility, weighing life's goals and also a bit of luck. Many of those who persevered skillfully, had good business sense and lived to tell the story, now have great wealth, power and resources.

THE EGIL ELLINGSEN STORY

Egil Ellingsen wrote about his early life as a New Bedford emigrant fisherman in a letter to the author. "In 1952 I obtained my U.S. citizenship papers which then allowed me to skipper fishing vessels. It was a momentous year in that our oldest daughter, Evelyn Margaret, was born on June 11, 1952. She welcomed her little brother, Kenneth John, on May 15, 1956, and on June 10, 1964, our youngest daughter, Erin-Joy, was born.

"In the fifties and sixties I skippered a number of scallop draggers, including the *Lauren Fay*, the *Bright Star* and the *Brighton*. Through saving and hard work, we built two homes during this period, and I acquired partnerships in the *Vivian Fay* and *Moby Dick*. It was during this era that an influx of Norwegian fishermen emigrated to the New Bedford area."

ROY ENOKSEN, ENTREPRENEUR

Olaf Enoksen, a Norwegian emigrant from Røst in the Lofoten Islands, emigrated in the twenties to Wisconsin where he worked on Great Lakes steamers. His daughter related that upon hearing that better money was to be made in New Bedford, he settled in New Bedford as a fisherman in 1938. He was one of the few emigrants from Northern Norway at that time.

Later his son Roy, after studying business and learning fishing skills, became a very successful fleet owner. Roy Enoksen explained the road to success in an interview with the Standard-Times in August of 1981: "When the chance to become a boat owner comes along, the man has to be prepared by having saved the money. The steps for becoming an owner are normally the same. You start out as a fisherman, then an engineer, a mate and a captain. Finally you get a chance to buy a vessel or become partners with someone." (Partnering is done because costs for one person became prohibitive as vessels become more sophisticated.)

Roy Enoksen graduated from New Bedford Vocational High School, a school many fishermen's sons attended because of the availability of practical information needed for the trade and also because their fathers decided it resembled the trade schools in Norway. He then went on to college where he studied finance. He was not intending to fish, although he had in high school, but he eventually did and in time owned many boats and also had a ship repair business.

He explained further in the Standard–Times interview: "In the earlier days, many boat owners did not go to sea but hired their own captains and fishermen. Now, most boat owners are fishermen. Today it is common to have a captain-owner and a shoreside investor-owner (also called dock captain or shore captain) because of the high cost of buying a fishing boat. It's big business, and if you are a fishing boat owner, you have to learn to live with problems. There are costly expenses to having a fishing boat, and you're always at the mercy of unpredictable weather systems. But it is a good business field. The opportunities are as good or better than in most other industries." He told this author that he believes "education is an asset."

There is formal schooling both here and in Norway for the required maritime skills that enable men to go from one level to the next. Some men returned home to Norway for this training and certifications and others, whose English was better, took classes in the States.

"Enoksen," according to an article in the Commercial Fishing News, "started out as a boy fishing summers with his father, Olaf, on the old eastern rig scalloper *Porpoise*. Later, he went on to own *Sea Trek*, another big wooden boat." He as "president of Eastern Fisheries has been a constant in the scalloping industry." Eastern Fisheries has grown over the years to become "a ten-boat fleet, with over $80 million in sales in 2000.

"Eastern Fisheries," according to Roy Enoksen, " . . . opened a new 'Fresh Division' scallop offloading and fillet house at the South End docks off Hassey Street, hoping to attract fish draggers as well as serve its own fleet. The North End Terminal will still be used for dockside repairs, dockage, and cold storage for imported product."

He remarked in my interview with him that: "The New Bedford waterfront from the early to mid-century was a rich culture. Redevelopment changed it totally." He expressed that it was a loss to the community.

Roy Enoksen is one of the few Norwegian fishermen who take an active role in the community of nonprofits and lend their time and expertise to try to solve community problems and help the New Bedford area achieve its potential.

And he is right about the waterfront. It was a colorful microcosm, a unique blend of nationalities, values and lifestyles and it all centered in a small area just north of the fishing docks—a place where merchants worked, supplying the needs of the boats, and where many men, young and old, sought their fortunes, adventures, good times, and new lives. And where relationships, wealth, families and futures were made or lost, where life-and-death decisions were made daily; and a place where, among the glut of many languages spoken by the men from several different countries, there was but one goal . . . realizing the promise of America.

Norwegians like Roy Enoksen and others built up the fishing and scalloping industry that made New Bedford the leading fishing port in the USA.

NEW BEDFORD, *AMERIKA*

MOST NORWEGIAN EMIGRANTS who came to New Bedford, Amerika, felt they had come to heaven. It had everything they had dreamed of and they had money to pursue the American dream. They had friends, new loves and

—Mery Vilhelmsen photo

Former emigrants Gunnar Gundersen with his wife Sigrid and daughter Anne Marie Gundersen Noll, at a 1999 Norwegian concert in Fairhaven.

—Berg archives

Cousin Gunnar Berg in the mid-fifties enroute from Norway. He brought typesetting skills for employment at the local newspaper, and later served in the American Army—after serving as a Norwegian with the occupation forces in Germany.

marriages, churches, savings accounts, stores and neighborhoods. They had everything that they had ever imagined and more.

But in some cases the dream became a nightmare. And there were the new dangers that came with married men living alone in American society. There was alcoholism, long separations from the family in Norway, and sometimes divorce. There was enormous wealth and success for some—but there was also danger, even death at sea, for others.

—*AT photo 1998*

Bjørn and Else Sjøen at home in Norway. They lived in New Bedford's West End. She was not sure she would like America after the first week, but adjusted to it and found friends at the Elim Baptist Church and in the neighborhood.

Legacy *&* Folklore

THE VIKINGS & THE FISHERMEN

VIKINGS LEFT HOME for long periods of time while the wife ran the household and managed the properties. The women developed into strong, independent people. So it is now with the fishermen's wives. Vikings often brought back women from other countries; so did the fishermen.

- Viking pride and attention went to the care and upkeep of their boats. So it is with the fishermen.
- Vikings had a strong attachment, love and respect for the sea interwoven with their religion. The fishermen have established superstitions about the sea and often have strong religious beliefs.
- Courage was the ultimate goal and achievement in the life of the Viking. Courage at sea is still a desired characteristic of the fishermen.
- Vikings settled in foreign lands from Russia to Greenland and often returned to Norway, thus originating the concept of *"pendling."* So do the fishermen.
- Vikings brought riches back to Norway. So do the fishermen.
- Vikings had an established code of conduct as indicated by the Eddas and Sagas. This code of conduct still permeates the fishermen's lives.
- Vikings were known to dip into the mead bowl generously. So it is with some fishermen.
- Vikings risked their lives in the pursuit of their work. So do the fishermen.
- Vikings had strong loyalties to their chiefdoms and tribes. Norwegians today have very strong attachments, loyalties and identification with their families, work gangs and hometown areas.

7

~

The Wild and Raging Sea

HURRICANE CAROL

—*Courtesy of New Bedford Standard Times*

Fairhaven fishing boats after the storm.

" . . . She battled out into the raging sea, now tossed on the tops of the mighty waves, now swallowed in the troughs between. Battered by the breaking crests, whelmed at times by 'green seas,' staggering like a drunken thing, and buffeted by the fierce gale, but never giving way an inch, onward, steadily . . . "

—R.M. Ballantyne, *"Battles with the Sea"*

~

THOSE WHO WITNESSED IT, as we did, will not forget the great storm of August 1954—Hurricane Carol. It was my high school graduation year and after the June ceremonies that marked one of our first passages into adult life came the traditional hustle and bustle of proms, parties, and preparations for college, coupled with summer jobs to help meet our college expenses. It was an optimistic, lighthearted summer and marked an end to our childhood years and the beginning of our first years away from home and our entry into adulthood.

It was a summer that started with joy and accomplishment and ended with sadness and tragedy. I was working at a day camp on Sconticut Neck in Fairhaven, and the camp had just ended when we heard that a huge hurricane was coming up the coast. The storm had already torn through areas just to the south of us, and we were expected to get the brunt of it. We were all worried that eventful August day when we sought to wait it out in one of the sturdiest homes in our neighborhood, a home that had withstood many New England hurricanes. I was a frightened seventeen-year-old, not knowing what to expect, as I sat peering out through a crack in the shuttered window at my aunt's antique Acushnet Avenue home, next door to our home in the far North End of New Bedford. As I sat there in her house on a little hill, I watched huge maple trees float down the street as if they were feathers. I could hear the great howls of wind rushing by the house while I listened to my family's stories about other hurricanes and the destruction in the city. We worried that some of the larger trees on the adjoining properties might not withstand the wind and crash into our houses.

The day went on and on, and I remember my mother with her Bible on her lap lamenting about the men at sea—hoping against hope that none would be out in this weather. Our fears worsened as the storm intensified, and we began to wonder if my aunt's gracious old house would survive this awesome day. It did—but many didn't, as my brother and I were soon to discover.

We got up early the next day and rode our bikes through tree-strewn streets and country roads to Sconticut Neck, a peninsula in Fairhaven. It was so quiet that day, an unearthly quiet, and we were surrounded by massive destruction that seemed unbelievable to us. The sea looked like glass with not a ripple on its surface, yet there was a great unseen power there. Few trees were left standing and hundreds of houses had disappeared. All we could see were the foundations and a refrigerator or two standing incongruously in the sand as beacons for their absent owners—and everywhere were piles of seaweed and pieces of wood that had once been homes.

I remember one story from that day describing a large house the hurricane had taken out to sea, leaving behind a refrigerator safely guarding a dozen unbroken eggs. Hurricanes choose frenetically who and what they will destroy.

Our camp was totally gone, and parts of the buildings were haphazardly transformed into seaweed-covered matchsticks about a hundred yards from the foundations of the original buildings. But what we didn't yet know was what had happened out to sea. The sea witnessed many acts of heroism that day by its imprisoned seamen, and there were many stories of survival, tragedy, loss and anguish. And like the refrigerators on Sconticut Neck, there were surprises.

> *"It's no fish ye're buying. It's men's souls."*
>
> —Sir Walter Scott

Acts of heroism at sea are often unknown to those onshore because lost ships cannot tell their stories. But it can be safely accepted as part of all tragedies at sea, whether ships are lost or saved, that men struggled valiantly to win the battle of man against sea. Heroism is an essential part of the Norwegian culture. It survives from pre-Christian Viking days, where it was the one cultural belief required from men who sought to tread the road to Valhalla.

> *"They, the heroes and heroines of early Viking stories, faced disasters. They knew they couldn't save themselves by any courage, or endurance or great deed. Even so they do not yield. They died resisting. A brave death entitled them, at least the heroes, to a seat in Valhalla, one of the halls of Asgard. This is their conception of life and death and underlies the early Norse religion."*
>
> —Edith Hamilton, "Norse Wisdom"

HEROISM

MANY ACTS OF HEROISM were carried out in the 1954 hurricane while the winds and waters devastated the fishing fleet in addition to whole neighborhoods in the New Bedford area. Jack Stewardson vividly and beautifully documented the courage of the men who fought that storm in his gripping 1996 report for the New Bedford Standard-Times.

"(The boats were) out to sea was when the late Magnus Kristian 'Big Kris' Olsen and his crew on the *Friendship II* were fighting for their lives. Hurricane Carol, which swept through the Caribbean and up along the Carolina coasts to New England to make landfall west of Providence, brought winds of 85 mph. Gusts up to 135 mph were reported at Block Island, R.I., a 10½ foot tidal surge along the coast and seas offshore that at times crested higher than 50 feet. In its wake, the storm would leave 68 dead along the Atlantic Coast and some $2.3 billion in damage.

—Courtesy of Sandi Demoranville, daughter of of "Big Chris" Olsen.

Photo of an extraordinary color painting by Arthur Moniz showing the attempted rescue of the *Friendship II* by the *Jacintha*. This gray photo is from the original color photo by Jack Stewardson for the New Bedford Standard-Times.

"But the Kris Olsen family will remember it as a time a husband and father came back from the dead. The family recently shared a video of Captain Olsen's recollections, taped on a Father's Day prior to his death in 1992.

"The *Friendship II* was five days out of port and carrying 6,500 pounds of scallops when she received word of hurricane warnings from Boston over the marine radio the afternoon of August 30. The boat was 90 miles southeast of Nantucket. 'There were a lot of boats to the eastward, fishing on the eastern part of Georges (Bank),' Captain Olsen would recall. 'We got a report of it coming up from Cape Hatteras. In those days we would put a buoy out when fishing. The *Friendship II* retrieved its buoy and began the long steam home.

"Another New Bedford boat, the *Flamingo*, saw the *Friendship II* leaving and called over the marine radio to ask why.' He said, 'Where are you going, Kris? You've got some more time left.' 'Yes, but we got a bad hurricane coming,' Captain Olsen replied. The *Flamingo*'s skipper said he would stay and keep a six-hour watch on the progress of the storm. 'Well,' I said, 'I'm going,' Captain Olsen recounted. 'I'm leaving right now.' So we left, and he said, 'We'll see you at the dock.' The *Friendship II* steamed westward, treading her way south of Nantucket Shoals, and by midday August 31 found herself moving into the heart of the hurricane. The storm had intensified as it moved up from Cape Hatteras, speeding ahead at a rate of 60 to 70 mph, and the *Friendship II* was about 30 miles south of Noman's land Island when the storm engulfed it.

"'We were almost home when we got caught,' said Mr. Olsen, who 20 years earlier had sailed aboard the J-boat *Yankee* in the America's Cup trials. 'The fog was thick and we didn't have the radar, like we have today, and the Coast Guard

—Olsen family photo from the New Bedford Standard-Times

Captain Magnus Kristian Olsen of the *Friendship II.*

said all the marker buoys were off station and you were bound to run aground. (We were) . . . not making any headway, but just keeping the bow to the wind.'

"By that time it was blowing every bit of 100 miles an hour. Captain Olsen 'was able to place a marine radio call home,' assuring his wife, Marie, and children everything was all right and that they were going to ride out the storm at sea. He had just hung up when it happened. 'So just then we took one big sea, and there was a crash,' he said. 'That's all you could hear, and there goes the doors on the pilothouse, one door on each side, and here goes one of our two dories over the side.' The ship's cook, trying to move forward along the deck, got caught in some of the debris and was swept over the side. 'His leg got caught in some of the wreckage there, but we managed to get him back over the side,' said Mr. Olsen, who was in the pilothouse at the time. 'The rogue wave also had ripped off the doghouse located at the whaleback hatch to the forecastle.'

"Shortly the engineer reported the 83-foot vessel had sprung a leak, and soon had three pumps going to try to stem the tide. 'I said, 'Get the buckets and get all the boys and bail the buckets,' Captain Olsen recounted. 'And they bailed.' The crew, however, was fighting a losing battle. The engineer, John Lund, came topside covered in grease, reporting he had tried everything but the pumps weren't pumping fast enough. The *Friendship II* was doomed."

"Similar life-and-death scenes played out that day throughout the waters of Southern New England. The New Bedford-based Coast Guard cutter *Legare* had been standing off Newport, R.I., when the storm broke. The cutter could make only a four-knot headway against the bucking seas, heading back for refuge in New Bedford, and finally sought refuge at Menemsha on the western tip of Martha's Vineyard. The *Amelia*, skippered by Captain Andrew Olden, a Norwegian from Northern Norway, talked to the mate of the *Redstart*, who said he thought they could make it 'around the corner' to safer waters.

"The *Amelia* and another fishing boat, the *Ursula M. Norton* (both Norwegian-owned boats), which had been trailing the former Navy minesweeper by two hours, later shifted course south to gain deeper water and never made contact with the *Redstart* again. The last boat to see the *Redstart* was the *Eunice and Lillian*, which reported passing the vessel about 45 miles south-southeast of Noman's land Island. Later in the afternoon the *Mary E. Deon* picked up a static radio contact from the *Redstart*, which reported being in serious difficulty, battered by 65-foot seas breaking over her pilothouse. There was no further contact with the *Redstart;* then one of the largest fishing vessels in the New Bedford fleet.

"A few days later the Coast Guard, searching for the overdue vessel, would report that wreckage, including parts of a mess table, pilothouse, rigging and rudder, splinters of a dory, lifejackets and pen board, used to separate fish in a hold, had been discovered within a three-mile radius of the Davis Shoal buoy south of Nantucket. It would be identified as from the *Redstart*. The splintered nature of the debris suggested the boat had been driven up on one of the shoal areas. In all likelihood, while the *Redstart* was in her death throes, the *Friendship II* was fighting her own battle with the sea."

As remembered by the late Gunleif Wilhelmsen, who was out to sea in that storm: "In the '54 hurricane, another vessel, the *Friendship*

Captain Sofus Mortensen of the *Jacintha*.

got lost. That boat—they were really hurt! They were filling up with water—taking a fair wind and heading right towards the beach. Going to the beach in that kind of weather was suicide. The engine room was over half-full of water right over the engine. The skipper had the American flag upside down on the rig. The *Jacinta* saw that they were in trouble. Turned around and followed them. Went up alongside and threw a line. Took a life raft and ferried it back and forth till they got all of the men off."

The Standard–Times reported, "Captain Olsen remembered several other New Bedford fishing boats, also standing south of Noman's land Island, feared trying to hazard a rescue of the *Friendship II*. The dragger *Jacintha*, however, decided to make an attempt.

Captain Sofus Mortensen, from Karmøy, who would pass away in 1995, maneuvered his boat about 300 yards downwind from the stricken scalloper. 'We got the life raft over and we drifted a barrel with 100 fathom of twine—line twine we called it—and it drifted with the tide over to the *Jacintha*,' Captain Olsen said. 'Then we hooked one end onto the life raft and three men jumped in and they hauled us to the *Jacintha*.' The seas were so heavy that the *Friendship II's* crew 'could see the keel of the *Jacintha* when she heeled,' and when she buried herself in a trough 'you couldn't even see her mast.'

"The rescue took two and one half hours. 'I never saw anything like it and I never want to again,' said Engineer Swain, of the *Jacintha*. 'I've been fishing 24 years and the hurricane was the worst storm I've ever seen.' He said, 'The raft was the only thing that saved the crew of the *Friendship*. A dory would have sunk, but the raft could keep buoyancy, even though the men were in the water.' Captain Olsen and his engineer, Mr. Lund, were the last to go across, but before he left his ship Captain Olsen decided to go below and retrieve the ship's papers. 'She was going down in the rear end,' he said. 'I went down and by that time there was water up to my waist.' He climbed up to his bunk and grabbed the papers, and then before returning topside decided he needed something else. 'I was thirsty all of a sudden, and I got a bottle of milk as I went up on deck.'

"By this time, the *Friendship II* was settling low in the stern, and her bow was standing up in the air. Captain Olsen and Mr. Lund climbed aboard the raft, whose wood-plank floor had been damaged. 'There was a great big hole in the life raft where the guys had jumped into it, so we had to sit on the edge,' Captain Olsen recalled. 'By then,' he said, 'the 100-fathom line must have been stretched near the breaking point. It was like a violin string, and I just touched it, and—boom!—it yanked us 10 feet in the water. That's how much strain there must have been on it.' When the life raft reached the *Jacintha*, there was one more difficult maneuver to complete in the 15 to 20-foot swells. 'When the raft went up, the boat went down, and when the boat went up, the raft went down, and they were trying to time it to grab the raft as it went by the railing.' They got the engineer off without mishap, but Captain Olsen, who weighed about 230 pounds, had trouble. 'I smashed my mouth when they took me over the rail,' he said. 'The first thing I did was go up forward to the forecastle and call down to find out how many men were aboard.' They said, 'Counting you, we've got 11.' I said, 'Good, that's all.'"

> *"God moves in a mysterious way His wonders to perform. He plants his footsteps in the sea, and rides upon the storm."*
>
> —William Cowper, "Light Shining out of Darkness"

The Standard-Times continued: "Mr. Olsen then went to the pilothouse to offer a 'Thank you, sir, God bless you' to Captain Mortensen, who, along with his crew would have their exploits written into the Congressional Record and be honored by the American Legion for heroism.

"The crew of the *Friendship II*, thankful to be alive, were wrapped in blankets and fed hot coffee down in the forecastle. They were not topside when the *Friendship II* took its final plunge beneath the waves. The *Jacintha* waited out the storm before heading into New Bedford.

"Back home in New Bedford, the Olsen family waited in their home, several blocks up from the waterfront. Late that afternoon, after the storm had passed, Mrs. Olsen walked down to the waterfront from her home, trying to find word about her husband. When she got to the docks, the National Guard was already there to police the damage, along with those searching for answers. A distraught, newly married wife of one of the crew-members of *Redstart* heard a rumor that the scalloper was lost. Mrs. Olsen also heard someone talking about the *Friendship*—the sister ship of her husband's boat—being lost, and then the name of the *Friendship II* being added to the list of casualties. Someone at the scene, who knew she was the wife of the *Friendship*

II's skipper, tried to shush the speaker. Mrs. Olsen called the owner of the boat, William White, and heard an ominous story. He said he had been told seven men had gotten off, but the others were gone.

"'The boat went down and they went with it,' she recalled being told. 'And I knew he was the captain so he would be the last to get off. He had to be dead. But I said no, I don't believe it. He's not dead. He's not dead.'

"The mind knows only what lies near the heart."

—Norse wisdom 1300, "The Elder Edda"

"Mrs. Olsen went back home and burned a candle in the window that night, waiting for her husband to come home. Around dawn, she heard footsteps coming up the outside stairs. 'Sure enough, he walked in the door, and his knees gave way,' Mrs. Olsen recalled. "I said, 'Are you hurt?'

"'No,' he said, 'I don't know what's the matter with me.'"

OTHER BOATS IN THE HURRICANE

THE FAMILY OF ANDREW OLDEN, skipper of the *Amelia*, remembers this hurricane also. His daughter Evie relates: "My father and crew of the *Amelia* were out in Hurricane Carol. I recall my mother on the phone while they were uncertain of the fate of those in the storm. I remember a close-knit group among the Norwegian fishing families, and the women and children were supported by each other when dangerous situations occurred. I recall my father telling us later that he had spoken with the captain of the *Redstart* and showed us pictures he'd taken of the wreaths he'd dropped at sea near the spot he'd last seen the *Redstart*. That made an impression on me that fishing is a dangerous job."

"There is nothing more enticing, disenchanting, and enslaving than the life at sea."

—Joseph Conrad, "Lord Jim"

Hurricane Carol was also a hazard to other coastal towns and villages in Southeast New England. Members of one family of Norwegians from Fairhaven were visiting relatives in Point Judith, R.I., during the hurricane. Carol Anne Tollefsen-Hoaglund recalls that memorable day and night:

"It was a breezy summer afternoon after a day at the beach, a stone's throw away from my grandparents' small and cozy gray-shingled house which we had just vacated to sleep at their new home which sat proudly on a hill. It was 1954 and I was seven years old. It was the year when my family spent the

—*Courtesy of New Bedford Standard-Times*

The aftermath: a tangle of wooden boats and masts.

last few weeks of the summer vacationing at my grandparents' house in Point Judith. Point Judith is a sleepy little fishing village complete with piers, pilings, fishing and sports fishing boats, and the Block Island ferry. The old house was perched at the dock's edge. My grandfather's fishing boat, the *Stars and Stripes*, was tied up right outside the front window, overlooking a deep channel of saltwater in Galilee Bay.

"That night, with no warning, Hurricane Carol roared into Southeastern New England with a vengeance. My grandfather got up in the middle of the night to ride out the storm on his small boat, and he battled both the waves and the fierce winds. All night and into the early morning he kept up the fight—man against mother nature at her worst. My grandfather saw something strikingly familiar float by him. It was his new refrigerator, along with parts of his old house—doors, windows and boards, torn stem to stern.

—*Courtesy of New Bedford Standard-Times*

The waterfront after the storm.

"Hurricane Carol had devastated the entire southeast New England coastline. Houses were torn from the shore, boats smashed at the docks, lives lost and memories washed away forever. Fortunately, my grandfather made it through the ordeal and returned to his new home on the hill where we were sleeping."

HURRICANE DESTRUCTION

AS REPORTED IN THE STANDARD-TIMES: "Hurricane Carol had left a path of destruction. The damage led to the drive to have the U.S. Army Corps of Engineers build the New Bedford hurricane barrier in the early 1960s. Damage to the waterfront alone was estimated in 1954 at $10 million. The entire New Bedford-Fairhaven shoreline was littered with wrecks of boats,

Braving the storm to see the boats.

smashed homes and cottages and debris from flooded waterfront plants, shops and boatsheds. Eighteen fishing vessels had been smashed or driven ashore in the harbor, and throughout the greater New Bedford area, hundreds of pleasure boats had been run aground or smashed into kindling.

"It was a great blow to the Norwegian-American fleet. The dragger *Jane and Ursula* sank at Union Wharf in Fairhaven. The *Pauline H.* had been beached near the Hathaway-Braley Wharf. The *Flamingo*, the fishing boat that had elected to stay behind, made it back safely."

The 1954 hurricane brought triumph and tragedy, destruction and despair to the Greater New Bedford area and its fishing fleet but the New Bedford area survived and made improvements to its harbor and its fleet. New Bedford had been devastated by hurricanes in the past and knew it would be again in the future.

But when the next one comes, New Bedford with her many fishing boats will have better tools with which to fight, knowing well that it is just one more part of life in a port city where, as Alan Cunningham wrote in the nineteenth century, "Our heritage (is) the sea."

Fishing boats stranded on a harbor island. Notice downed tower.

Hurricane Carol leaves boats stranded high and dry.

Legacy & Folklore

VIKING RULES FOR LIVING

Many of these precepts taken from the Sagas are still part of the cultural traditions and manners of Norwegians today.

- One should not laugh at the old and gray.
- You must have decent clothes. They need not be luxurious, but they must be clean and neat.
- If you have something to do, you must rise early in order not to waste time.
- Do not be a friend of your friend's enemy and always tell the truth.
- Nevertheless, it is permitted to reward a lie with another lie.
- If you come as a guest, you can tell interesting news, but if you have none you must listen silently to whatever the host has to say.
- Do not be greedy.
- Drinking is allowed, but not getting drunk.
- There is no shame in going to bed early.
- If you are receiving guests, you must be polite to them.
- You must offer water and towels also so they can wash themselves and offer them a place beside the fire so they can get warm.
- Do not laugh at guests. It is too easy to sit at your ease and make the tired traveler feel ridiculous.
- First and last: be honest!

CHAPTER

8

Discovering My Heritage

A VOYAGE OF FAITH

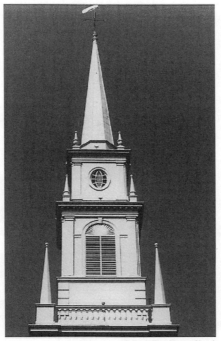

—Courtesy First Baptist Church

Steeple of First Baptist Church,
Worcester, MA

*"The lines are fallen unto me in pleasant places;
yea, I have a goodly heritage."*

—Psalm 16:6

IN A SCANDINAVIAN-AMERICAN MARRIAGE there is often a question related to the choice of a church. In my mother and father's case, she being a Congregationalist and he a Lutheran, the choice was made by virtue of language and friendship and what felt most comfortable. They chose to go to the Elim Baptist Church, which was founded by Swedish Baptists but also had as members many Norwegian fishermen and their families. Both my mother and father were fond of the minister, the Reverend Mr. Philip Backstrom, and I have many dear memories of life there when I was a young child. I remember a very sweet teacher in the cradle room named Rene, who was Swedish, and others who were very kind. And I remember the fishermen and their families. I loved hearing their accents and being part of their church life at the time. We continued there after my father's death, but then a new minister came and Norwegians were starting to leave to go to the Lutheran church.

My mother decided this was a good time to return to her church, named the Pilgrim Church, where she was happy as she knew everyone and could sing in the choir. She eventually became superintendent of the church school. I was not as happy there as a young girl because my mother directed the church school and that limited my freedom a lot, and also many in the church

The Elim Baptist Church Boys Choir, in the early forties, representing Norwegian, Swedish and Danish backgrounds. From left to right, third row: Carlton "Tommy" Johnson, John Drivdahl, Edmund Carlsen, Kenneth Hansen, Richard "Red" Harris and Robert Pearson. Middle: John Sorensen, Ray Potter, Edward Anderson, Gordon Baker, Thomas Helgeland and Russell Andrews. Front: John Birknes, Ole Midttun, William Olden, Philip Backstrom, and David "Sonny" Pearson.

were comparatively wealthy. I was very embarrassed that my clothes were not like theirs and the other girls seemed eager to point that out.

So I returned to the Elim Baptist Church when I was about twelve, and I spent my teenage years there. I felt some level of comfort surrounded by Scandinavians who, even if I did not have nice clothes, understood the reason why. But it had changed a lot and had become very strict. There were fewer Norwegians in the church and no social events. But there were still some Norwegian families with children my age and that made me feel closer to my father's culture.

Elim Baptist was in some respects a microcosm of the traditional Scandinavian hierarchy. Although the Swedes had founded it, the most vocal leadership was the Danes. The Swedes, and many there were, were content to be in the next hierarchy of leadership, being basically quiet and lending their money to God's work as they saw it. The substantial Norwegian membership took a negligible leadership role and simply attended and paid for what was needed. The Finns were very quiet and took a back seat. Now, looking back at it, I see that this leadership pattern reflected the relationships of the Norwegian people who were under Danish rule and then Swedish rule for so long. Leadership was simply deferred.

The Norwegians attended this church for many reasons, but in the beginning they attended because Swedish was spoken and the Norwegians understood it well. Also they liked the minister and the people. And there was, after all, no Norwegian church at that time. Those who preferred Lutheranism and had an unfailing allegiance to it went to services at the German church, an unpopular choice during the war years. (That decision during the war must have taken courage and more than a measure of faith.) Other Norwegians were scattered throughout the various Protestant churches in their towns.

By the time a Norwegian church was established in Fairhaven, many at Elim were entrenched Baptists, but others joined the Norwegian church which began as a chapel. Because it represented the church of their ancestors, (Lutheranism is the official, state-supported church of Norway and permeates much of the culture there), it is difficult to separate out what is distinctly Norwegian and what is Lutheran, inasmuch as Lutheranism is taught in the schools and supported by taxes.

I had formed most of my thoughts and beliefs about religion from youthful experiences at the Elim Baptist Church. We were told what to think and were often intimidated into accepting a belief system we didn't totally understand. There was much joy in the music and many wonderful people were "founts of kindness," but there were others, mostly not Scandinavian, who made Elim a rather frightening and judgmental experience. As one of my Sunday school mates, Henry Pedersen, now a Baptist minister himself, recently wrote: "It was my impression that the church of my youth just didn't want us to have a good time. It seemed to major in the things that it didn't want us to do rather than help us celebrate the things that God would have us do."

I remember vividly when our Sunday school teacher (who was not a Scandinavian) told us we would all go to hell and never should have been baptized because we had gone to our high school senior prom. That was the beginning of the end for me at that church. Even at seventeen, I knew we were quite innocent, and I understood God to be a loving God and not the entity this man proclaimed.

In the summer, however, I would attend a week's session at Camp Tispaquin in Middleboro. That was a special place and a wonderful place to meet other like-minded teenagers, have the counsel of dedicated ministers and "grow in the knowledge and love of God." It really wasn't a "camp" in that we did not camp out, and perhaps, more similar to the old-fashioned revival camp on some levels, but all in all, it was a lovely place and the music and friendships were a special experience. There we were not faced with church politics but were confronted with ourselves in relation to God—a good experience for teenagers about to enter college or the work force.

In 1954, I went on scholarship to Worcester State Teacher's College in central Massachusetts with a student body that was over seventy-five percent Roman Catholic. It was daunting to a seventeen-year-old in those pre-ecumenical years to feel so much antipathy from some of the students. I did not understand it at all, but the ecumenical movement changed these attitudes a few years later and future non-Catholic students enjoyed more acceptance.

I was working my way through college, so after school I would go to my residence, which was also my place of employment. I worked for an articulate Jewish family and cared for their six active boys as well as participated in their daily life including some of their religious traditions. I never forgot the Seder service and how they explained each moment to me and will always remember

—A Tollefsen archives

The Baptist General Conference's Camp Tispaquin, 1953, in Middleboro MA, where we had to wear dresses rather than camp clothes, and some wore even hats and gloves for outdoor services. It was a lovely camp on a lake where the days were devoted to Bible study, church services, and saving souls. One's status seemed to depend on how expensive, well-thumbed and organized one's Bible was. I learned a great deal there from some excellent ministers who took a real interest in "young people" as we were called in those days. I shall never forget the heartfelt music and singing. I remember the girls dedicating themselves to the mission field as nurses, while the boys planning careers in the ministry. Few considered women in the ministry in those days.

the beautiful expression on the Zoe Ostrow's face as she said the traditional words that evening.

I learned from all of these ecumenical experiences and broadened my levels of religious understanding but often felt loneliness for the familiar and accepting. One day a friend told me about a college-age group at the First Baptist Church of Worcester, an American Baptist Convention church, situated very close to Worcester Polytechnic Institute. I knew that my hometown Baptist church would not approve of this "liberal" church, but they had a very active agenda and met on Sunday evenings. Thankfully this was my evening off, and I gladly went and found a group of eclectic Christian college students from Worcester's many schools. For many of us, this was our "big evening" out when we prayed and sang, discussed the great issues of the day, danced, flirted, ate, made friends and grew in our understandings of faith and life. We formed many new friendships that were to last a lifetime and also many marriages resulted from meeting new people in this group.

> *"Thou wilt show me the path of life: In thy presence is fullness of joy. At thy right hand there are pleasures for evermore."*
>
> —Psalm 16:11

Many in the group attended the Sunday morning services together, including the president of our group, Harry Rydsrom, a handsome and personable Norwegian-American and Worcester Tech student from New York, and with whom I had a common link—our mutual heritage.

It was at the Sunday morning service where we found a very special home. It was an especially beautiful church with services that were near perfection in their presentation and dignity as well as warmth and artistic beauty. The music was unexcelled, and everything, it seemed, was done with precision, beauty and deep meaning. One soloist was a Swedish-American woman, Florine Solberg Barber, who took an especially kind interest in me and would invite me to her home on occasion for lunch.

But there was also another feature that was very significant to me—the minister, the Reverend Mr. Gordon M. Torgersen, a Norwegian-American from Minnesota with Stavanger roots.

—*Photo by LaPorte, Worcester*

The Reverend Dr. Gordon Melby Torgersen in 1965 on the occasion of my wedding day.

207

He was a man of courage and daring, humility and deep understanding, who taught us to think about our Christian lives in today's society. He showed us how to live as responsible Christians in our communities. He didn't teach judgment, hell or damnation. He preached love, peace and understanding. He somehow "put it all together" and influenced all of us in a special way. Even today, almost half a century later, old friends will say to me, "Remember Torgy's wonderful sermons and the great times we had at Solitaires (our college-age group)? There has been nothing like it since." He made us think about our lives and our faith.

There were times when we were allowed to participate in the service, and there were special conferences and gatherings that he encouraged us to attend with the church paying

—From a First Baptist Church publication

Part of the beautiful interior of the First Baptist Church Worcester. Many of Worcester's college students looked forward to services here each Sunday. It was always a total experience.

some of the expenses. We had a real community of friends, and our social lives were very active, with many connections to the other area colleges because of the interest taken in us. Gordon Torgersen inspired us, challenged us and taught us through his example. Gordon Torgersen lived what he taught.

During my last three years at college, I was lucky enough to work for and live with a family who were active Unitarians: Ann and Bill Arthur and their four wonderful small children, Karen, Sara, Janet and Scot, whom I grew to love very much. This dear family continued to be an important part of my life right up to the present. I am very thankful for them, their love, their influence and even further my understanding of differences in faith.

When I married, I traveled to Worcester to be married by Mr. Torgersen. I remember that I walked down the long aisle alone because of my father's death. My father, however, was there for me in that moment as the sanctuary was filled with the strains of "Eternal Father Strong to Save," also known as the mariner's hymn. His memory became part of the service.

> *"I have set the Lord always before me: because he is at my right hand, I shall not be moved."*
>
> —Psalm 16: 8

208

When the Vietnam War was raging and there was growing dissent, Gordon Torgersen took a firm stand against the conflict and eventually left the First Baptist Church because of his stance. But this action only caused many to respect him more. He went on to become president of Andover-Newton Theological Seminary, outside of Boston, where he influenced many lives and careers and enabled many women, who were just starting to enter theologically based careers, to achieve excellence in their work as clergy.

—Courtesy of First Baptist Church

The Reverend Dr. Gordon Melby Torgersen, now retired in Florida, in the pulpit of the First Baptist Church of Worcester.

I learned and I grew in my faith because of him and although he never knew it, he was my Norwegian role model. I developed pride in my heritage because this man of faith and courage was not only an exemplary and well-respected Christian minister, he also was a Norwegian.

When I look back over my life, I have to say that he was one of the few who really influenced me and made me strive for meaning in all that I do. Many years later I was working as Director of Christian Education at a local Congregational church in California and had several opportunities to give sermons. One day I brought a tape of one of my sermons to him at Andover—Newton while he was president. He wrote me a thoughtful note later and told me how much he liked it—my voice, as well as the delivery. Those were words I shall always cherish because if he liked it, it had to be good.

I spent most of my career working in Christian-centered organizations and most likely will retire in a United Church of Christ community for retired Christian workers in California. I feel that my experiences at the First Baptist Church in Worcester under Gordon Torgersen greatly influenced my life.

Thank you, Gordon Torgersen, for all that you did for me in my life and also for all the loving attention you gave my family. You showed me what a Norwegian-American could achieve in life by having courage, intellect, commitment and faith. *Tusen Takk* (thank you) for that very special smile that encouraged and gave support to me during my college days. May your life continue to be an inspiration and a blessing to others!

The Elim Baptist Church on Middle Street in New Bedford, which survived the city's redevelopment. It was known as the Swedish Church and is where most of the Scandinavian population attended church until the Lutheran Church was built. After the Scandinavian membership died off, it had several reincarnations and was once for rent as an office building. At one time the singing from this church could be heard throughout the neighborhood.

—*AT photo*

I returned to the Elim Baptist Church building a few years ago. It was being renovated into an office building and everything had been removed from the sanctuary except for the baptistery (large water tank) and a framed plaque on the wall. The tablet thanked about six Swedish families, founders of the church, for the donation of the pews. These families were the same group of people I remembered with great fondness. I thought of all the people I had known in the congregation and the church activities we shared and also of our youth group. I recalled when I was baptized there and, soaking wet, had fallen down the back steep staircase. Bruised from shoulder to ankle, I got no sympathy from my mother who felt it was God telling me that two baptisms in one's lifetime was one too many.

I recalled as a small child I had sung a hymn on this very spot, and I cried all the way through it. When I finished everyone in the congregation seemed to be crying with me. So on this day in the late 1990s when the role of this church had ended and it was about to become an office building, I, no longer a child, remembered the words from Matthew 26:30: "And when they had sung a hymn they went out. . . . " and I sang an old gospel hymn to the spirit of the people I remembered and, yes, there was still a tear or two.

> *"The Lord is a portion of my inheritance and of my cup.*
> *Thou maintainest my lot."*
>
> —Psalm 16: 5

9

~

Secrets of the Deep

The young Norwegian fisherman: strong, handsome, eager to work and skilled. The late Tønnes Kvinlaug, August, 1961.

"Mountain folk are quiet, soft-spoken and quizzical of eye, with no trace of arrogance in their makeup. Seafaring people have much the same look. It is the look of all people who live exposed to the elemental forces of nature and who know how powerless man is against them."

—Edna Ferber, *"A Peculiar Treasure"*

~

T HE DANGERS AWAITING the New Bedford fisherman at sea ranged
from the trivial to the terrible. Storms took a heartbreaking toll, but
beyond the storms there were other factors inherent to the industry that were
equally perilous. Natural phenomena, the vessel's structure and equipment,
debris from the ocean floor, and, of course, the sea life itself contributed to
loss of life or limb aboard fishing boats. Many incredible sea tales resulted
from the tears or laughter, merriment or misfortune foisted upon the boats
and their crews.

During the 1940s there was a children's Saturday morning radio program
called "Land of the Lost." It was a sea fantasy, and children loved it. But there
is a real land-of-the-lost at the bottom of the sea, and sometimes the Norwegian emigrant fishermen acci-
dentally discovered it. These
fishermen, particularly the
scallopers, who scoured the
ocean floor with their drags,
never knew what they would
uncover in the debris brought
up to the deck. They wanted
scallops with a minimum of
trash, but all too often their
drags would be loaded with
rocks, pieces of furniture,
skulls and bones, dishes and
pottery, guns and equipment,
and sometimes things that
spelled catastrophe.

—*John Isaksen archives*

John Isaksen's *Hustler*, the day it was launched.

One Norwegian skipper
brought up a bottle of cham-
pagne on his maiden post-war voyage out of New Bedford, and he went on to
great success in his fishing career. Perhaps as he looks back on his life, he
could regard this bottle as a good-luck omen for him—a special re-christening
for his boat.

A long-time fisherman and captain, John Isaksen, remarked, "We
brought up everything that is down there—typewriters, torpedoes, helmets,
garbage, and rocks. The most trivial was plastic heels for ladies' shoes. But
there were also bullets, shells and other military stuff, especially off of
Norfolk."

The daughter of a skipper out of the Fulton Fish Market recalls that her
father "often brought home pitchers and plates from well-known steamships
that crossed the ocean. During the bootlegging period, it was not unusual for
the dredges to bring up bottles of whiskey."

THE MYSTERY OF THE *MARY* AND THE STONE

IN ONE EERIE CASE, the sea rendered up a clue to the mysterious loss of a boat. My uncle, Tobias Tollefsen, one of four brothers who lost their lives to savage seas on separate occasions, was on the *Mary* when she disappeared in 1933. According to the Standard-Times of New Bedford, "The *Mary* vanished, along with her crew of eight, in the stormy March waters around Georges Bank. Captain Michael Smith had taken the *Mary* out on February 27, 1933, but put into Nantucket because of stormy weather. The crew attended Ash Wednesday Mass there on March 1 and put out to sea again. She was reported about twenty-five miles off Georges Bank when last seen on March 10."

Nothing was ever learned of the *Mary*'s disappearance. Tobias had had a painted stone, which he kept with him as a good-luck omen. His younger brother David recalled: "My brother was lost in 1933. One night, many years later, I had a dream that an ocean liner had rammed his boat. The ocean liners used to try to make speed records by racing and going out of the sea lanes in those days. Soon after my dream, I was out at sea and the stone he had painted came up in the net. We were near the shipping lanes. I feel the dream was real, and that is how my brother died."

David kept the stone as a final reminder of his brother and said, "It was almost as though he put it in the net himself for me to find, so I would understand what happened."

MARTIN ISAKSEN

A NEW JERSEY FISHING CAPTAIN, Martin Isaksen, would tell his children of his adventures at sea. His daughter, Toni Johnson, recalls: "We used to love hearing stories about the big waves and whales washing up on the boat. He would tell us of the close calls he had. One night a big steamer was heading right for the *Cristeen*, and my father was able to steer the boat away just in time to avoid being shattered. He said the steamer could have hit them and not even have known it. The *Cristeen* was a matchbox compared to the ship bearing down on her."

Some collisions were inevitable due to fog. Fog rolls in when warm water and cold air meet—or vice versa—and that happens often at sea. Untold disappearances can be laid to collisions, and those collisions to fog, especially in the years before reliable radar and modern forms of communication and navigational devices.

Icing of a vessel is another example of natural phenomena that makes fishing particularly dangerous in the winter. It has to be scraped constantly and if it is not removed, the weight if it can sink a vessel without warning. The daughter of the *Cristeen*'s skipper recalls: "The *Cristeen* made the New York papers many times in the winter because when they went into the Fulton Fish Market to sell the scallops, *Cristeen* would be covered completely with thick ice."

THE TREACHEROUS AND THE DREADFUL

MILITARY VESSELS HAVE CONTRIBUTED more than their share of unwelcome gifts to the seas, including hazardous rubble. One fishing vessel captain, Kaare Ness, recalls handling one of these discoveries cautiously.

"In 1965 we were off of New York with the *Viking Queen*, and I was skipper. At about three-thirty one morning, my mate called and said we had a bomb in a drag. We left it in the drag and called the Coast Guard. They told us to steam toward Sandy Hook, New Jersey, and they would meet us. The guys came on the boat but said they didn't want to touch it. They took us into Sandy Hook. All of a sudden we had to get off the boat while they took the bomb out of the drag. It was a fourteen-inch shell out of a cannon. Only two Coast Guard boats had a cannon like that. They took it in and exploded it."

Another boat tried to avoid a confrontation with an explosive, as recalled by retired skipper Jack Jacobsen, now living in Florida: "I was on the *Solveig J.* after the war, and an unexploded torpedo got snarled in our propeller. We dropped it and steamed away fast in case it exploded when it hit bottom."

One crew handled a potentially explosive situation in a more casual way. "We was fishing in an area where we shouldn't have been (probably an off-limits military dumping area), and we picked up a big metal object in the scallop drag and brought it on board. We were bored and played with it like teenagers. We rolled it around the deck, had our photos taken with it and kicked it around until the captain saw us and made us stop. He told us to tie it up and so we did. It was tied up on the slippery deck for several days until we came in. Sometimes it slid out of the ropes, and we tied it up again. Then we had our photos taken with it when we got into New Bedford, and it was even in the newspaper the next day. The captain had called the Coast Guard, and they came down. They took one look, determined it was a live bomb, and closed the whole wharf and dock area. They loaded this bomb onto their cutter and took it out to sea where they exploded it. Can you believe—we were kicking it around the deck and it was live? The whole waterfront was closed, and everyone had to leave the area. I never will forget that."

THE *SNOOPY*

A MAINE CAPTAIN in the 1960s never got to see what he brought up in his net. The *Snoopy* was an American fishing boat out of Maine and well acquainted with the New Bedford fleet. *Snoopy* often sailed with the New Bedford fleet and sometimes had Norwegians on board as crew, one of whom was the now famous maritime entrepreneur Lauritz Eidesvik of Bomlo, Norway. He recalls that he had "just got home on my last trip from the *Snoopy* before it hit a mine."

"The *Snoopy* was sailing with the New Bedford fleet that fateful day off the coast of Virginia," recalled one fisherman, "and the shifts had just changed. *Snoopy*'s captain was talking with the captain of a New Bedford fishing boat, when he stopped his conversation to ask the skipper to hold on. He said the crew had just brought up something in the drag. It was large and made of metal, and he was going to see what it was. Those were his last words. There was a large noise and then nothing."

One retired fishermen related his experience with the *Snoopy* many years later in an interview in Norway: "Was down in Virginia—lots of things from the war in the water. There was a boat from Maine, *Snoopy*, and the crew knew everyone on the New Bedford boats. It picked up a mine, and there was nothing left of the boat. It exploded—nothing left—only small pieces. We were screaming at them and trying to find someone alive as we were very close to them."

One retired fishermen remembers: "I was in Fairhaven when the *Snoopy* went down. Heard about it on the radio. Seven or eight were lost and others really beaten up. Two men had been swept clear from the aft where they was sleeping, but they survived. These men had decided to go aft and take a nap. It was an especially warm time off the coast of Virginia as they dozed off, and next thing they knew they was far from the boat gasping for a breath of air They literally didn't know what had hit him. They survived—the others were not as lucky."

Another Norwegian, a native of Southern Norway, on a vessel farther out at sea, recalls: "We were fishing with another group of boats, and all of a sudden we saw and heard this terrible explosion in the distance. We knew some of our guys were over in that area, and we looked up and saw the fire. We couldn't figure out what had happened or whom it had happened to. We steamed over to find the spot where it happened, and I will never forget the smell of burning oil, wood and other stuff in the water. We didn't see any bodies. The sea was so calm that day—black—absolutely quiet and the awful smell from the fire. I can smell it today. There were little pieces of wood and debris floating on the surface where just a little time before there was the *Snoopy* and a crew."

CLOSE CALLS

ONE FISHERMAN REMEMBERS A CLOSE CALL: "On one trip we picked up those kinds of bombs that were meant to sink submarines and explode at a certain depth (depth charges). These, of course, hadn't exploded yet. They came up in the drag, and we dropped them back in and got away fast. They didn't explode. We were young and didn't think anything would happen. We were lucky that day."

A fishing boat can get into strange situations, and in the mid-sixties *Aloha* did what neither the American Navy nor the Russian Navy had been able to do. As John Isaksen recalls: "One guy on our boat picked up an unknown object in the drag. It looked like an American rocket. It was very new and had the whole guidance system with it. We called the Coast Guard, and the Navy came right away to get it. The Russians were around at that time and would have loved to have found it, as this was quite a big thing. The Navy arrived in thirty minutes. All the markings were there, so we handed it over. It must have been worth a fortune. Was in good shape. Never got thanked by the government, however."

NATURE'S CALLS COULD BE FINAL CALLS

MANY OF THE WOODEN BOATS in the first half of the twentieth century had no sanitary facilities on board. Although boats now have full bathrooms, in those days they had nothing. So bathroom duties were very public off the stern and sometimes in pails on deck. One fisherman related in an interview: "One day we were going out to Georges and there was several other scallopers to port and just ahead of us. I could see three or four bare behinds on the stern. That was the way we did it, but it sure was difficult on rough days."

Another retired fisherman related: "The real problem, though, was at night when nature called, because then it was very dangerous. Men disappeared during the night and were lost overboard. We all knew it, but didn't talk about it. It's an awful embarrassing way to die."

The late Jacob Ostensen sadly recalled his early days as a fisherman. "The men sat on the railings in the stern and did their business. There was nothing really to hold onto, and it was tricky and slippery. The sea came up and threw us onto the deck.

—AT photo of photo

Jacob Ostensen from the Haugesund area, in his youth. A serious, handsome and determined man.

Often there were men on the deck with their pants down, legs open, caught in the middle. Some were lost overboard in this manner. Some just disappeared, especially at night."

It only took one misstep to lose a life or sustain a serious injury. It was easy to be killed by being careless, so a fisherman had to watch himself every second. The deck was wet, cold and slippery. The fisherman was cold, wet and tired much of the time. He could be washed overboard at any second through a misstep, a collision with the scallop drag, or a tangled line. Actually, given the conditions under which the men worked, it is amazing that there weren't more accidents or loss of life.

"Many got caught in the winch. Others drowned. I knew a man who got married and after a few days went out on a trip and got caught in the winch and died," said Jacob Ostensen. "There were lots of accidents from handling the winches. It was very important to have reliable men operating the winches."

Men fell from riggings and masts. Some slipped overboard, others were caught in ropes and were carried overboard, and then there was machinery such as the capstan, a vertical spool-shaped cylinder that is rotated and around which a cable is wound, or the winch—which also caused serious injuries.

MAN OVERBOARD

ONE ELDERLY FISHERMAN described two potentially fatal incidents that ended fishing for him: "Me and the skipper were hauling in a net from a dragger. The seas were high and took me overboard. I went flying. Boy, was I lucky! I fell on top of the net and held onto the end. If I had fallen in the middle, I would have gone down. They hauled it up and I was OK. Another time in a storm, I slipped on the deck, went backwards and flipped over the railing. I was rescued, but two times was enough for me."

A retired fisherman, David Tollefsen, told his near-death story: "I was off Noman's Land at the tip of the Elizabeth Islands when I got pulled overboard by a snarl in the net of a dragger. I got my boots off, and someone saw me in the water.

—Alf Isaksen archives

Alf Isaksen shucking scallops on the *Aloha*. Circa early sixties.

They laid anchor and came and got me. I had lost three brothers to the sea, but it was not my time that day." David later lost his life to natural causes.

And then there were the young fishermen just over from Norway. Alf Isaksen remembers his date with fate: "I was thrown overboard once in an accident. Two were working on deck and we were fishing with one drag. I forgot the other was on deck. We were working on top of the drag and got flipped overboard. It took twenty minutes before the boat picked us up. They had to get the drag in, turn the boat around and pick us up. We were hanging on a life ring. Seagulls came out to investigate! They thought we were some kind of trash and eyed us for a meal. It was very cold. But it was more of a shock than anything."

"He reached down from on high and took hold of me;
He drew me out of deep waters."

—Psalm 18: 16

Accidents are not limited to the young or inexperienced. Kaare Ness, now a fleet owner out of Seattle, remembered his experience forty years later in an interview on Cape Cod: "I had some close calls myself. The winter sea took me overboard on Georges Bank one time. Can't remember when they picked me up. It was March 1958 and the wave came over me when we were on the way home. Was standing there opening scallops. Two guys on that side. I was furthest aft, before the boats had the shucking houses, and all of a sudden the boat took this big wave. I knew I was going to go over—like a brick wall hit me. I was ten to fifteen minutes in water. I had a knife in my hand and dropped that. I thought, 'Aren't they going to come around and pick me up?' The boat was going away from me full speed. Then I saw them turn around, and that is all I can remember. They threw out the ring and I didn't take it. The skipper jumped overboard to help me."

The skipper, Egil Ellingsen, a successful owner and captain now out of Seattle, still has nightmares about the incident: "One of the most frightening phrases a captain could ever hear is 'man overboard,' and those exact words startled me from my sleep in the early-morning hours one March day in 1958. The crew was busy on deck with a load of scallops, as we had finished our trip out on Georges Bank and were heading

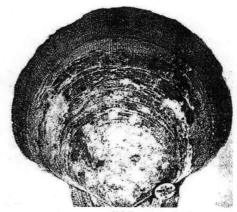

—U.S. Department of the Interior, 1957
North Atlantic sea scallop mid-century. This size is rare today.

218

—General fishing archives from Norwegian emigrants

Home from a trip, young fishermen relax with their friends at Fort Phoenix.

for home. I had been up all night keeping watch (midnight to 0600) and my mate was taking the next shift so I could get some rest. I had settled down in my bunk and fallen asleep. I was awakened by a crew member yelling, 'Egil—Kaare went overboard.'

"I jumped out of my bunk and rushed into the pilothouse. My mate was already in the process of turning the boat around. I took over the controls and gave instructions to the crew members to get the life rings and lines ready to rescue Kaare. My mind was racing, and my heart was pounding. I felt like the boat was moving in slow motion. I kept thinking to myself, 'How could I ever return to shore and tell Kaare's wife that he was lost at sea?' As we carefully approached him, the crew threw out the life rings and lines. They were easily within his grasp, but he did not react or reach after the lines or rings. It was obvious that he wasn't responding, but thankfully his oilers (weatherproof rain gear) kept him afloat.

"I realized quickly that something more needed to be done. I decided to go in after him. My mate tied a line around my waist, and I jumped as far as I could from the boat. I swam to him and put my arms around him so I had his back against my chest. The crew gently pulled us back toward the boat. As we approached the boat, I placed my legs against the side of the boat to prevent us from being hurt or sucked under. The crew quickly pulled Kaare aboard first, and then I followed. We carried him down to the fo'c'sle where it was warm. We removed his wet clothes, dried him off and covered him with blankets. We pushed on, full steam ahead, to shore. Thankfully, Kaare recovered and was back on the boat in a matter of weeks.

"I still have nightmares about this incident, and it will be with me for as long as I live. Fortunately, this was the most serious accident I ever encountered during my long career as a fishing captain."

FAITH AND THE FISHERMAN

FISHERMEN WHO LIVE WITH DANGER often have a deep faith. Organized religion and faith for the fisherman may or may not be related, but many fishermen are deeply committed Christians who both love and support their churches.

The faith of the fisherman may be both sincere and meaningful even when he is not part of an organized church. The fisherman whose life depends on the bounty of the sea, which he often believes to be a gift from God, often feels dependent upon God's power for his safety at sea. He has learned over the centuries that the sea can change at any moment. One moment it is peaceful, the next angry and vengeful. He has learned to put his trust in God for the safety of his boat, his crew and himself. This faith, plus skill and a sound crew and boat, is what brings him, many believe, back to port. The Vikings, the ancestors of these men, had a strong faith in their sea gods and depended upon them for their safety in much the same way so long ago.

The fisherman, when he is at sea, observes nature as no one else can. He sees the tumultuous waters of danger and death; he sees the peaceful waters of joy and contentment. He sees the rainbow of promise after the rains of despair. He is guided by the stars and given light by the moon. He enjoys beautiful sunsets and may enter or close his watch by sunrises whose colors have to be experienced to be believed.

One retired fisherman told me that the greatest joy in his life was to see the sunrise over Georges Bank. He had never seen anything to match that. There he felt God. This is the same Georges Bank where many good friends had lost their lives. It would be difficult for a fisherman to be at sea for a long time and not have some measure of faith.

"There were two of us in the wheelhouse, me and God."

—Jens Isaksen

And there are times at sea when supernatural strength and alertness must be maintained in order for the vessel and lives to be saved. One retired skipper and boat owner, the late Jens Isaksen, who was always an active church member, told of his extraordinary adventure with Hurricane Carol, one of the worst to hit New England in recorded history.

He recalled: "During Carol in 1954, I was fifty-two hours straight in the wheelhouse, laying out the storm and steering into the wind. I didn't trust anyone else at the wheel. The men trust the skipper. I prayed, and God helped me a lot in times like that. I thought of the wife. Didn't want to leave her. There were two of us in the wheelhouse, me and God."

According to Henry Pedersen, who was the son of a fisherman and who eventually entered the clergy, the belief of the fisherman is very strong. He wrote: "The fisherman's faith was not in the active participation in organized religion but the deep faith he had in God. My father is the best example of this, but I think also of others. My father didn't go to church very much when

—General fishing photo

Life aboard a New Bedford boat, mid-century. Men stow their gear.

—General fishing photo

Resting at sea. Some said the noise, motion, and cramped quarters had to be experienced to be believed.

I was young, but when I was with him, especially on the water; I sensed a deep reverence for the Almighty. There is something about being on a little boat in a big pond that causes one to have a deep respect for something beyond one's self. In modern-day parlance, my dad did not 'talk the talk' much but he 'walked the walk.' His love and respect for God did not show itself in church involvement but in his reverence for God's creation, especially other people and their needs. I believe that organized church was inconsistent for him and I feel others felt that way also."

Some fishermen mean well but get their theology confused a bit, as is related by this retired fishermen who now lives in Florida. "Once we were out to sea and it was one of those trips when everything went wrong. The net had problems, we lost nets, we had trouble with the engines, and one man got sick; another was injured. It just didn't stop. The skipper was frantic and called us all up on deck and told us we all had to pray together because it looked like that was the only way we would get home. So he looked up to heaven and said:

"God, hear us please! We need help. We need help to get back to our homes and we need your help now. Please hear us, God, and please help us personally yourself. Don't send your son . . . this is no time for kids."

HUMAN FACTORS

MEN LIVE IN CLOSE QUARTERS on fishing boats and often have to depend on each other as well as a higher being. Ike Isaksen remembers: "The boat took a large wave, which came in and broke the engine room door, and stopped the engine right away. My friend Gunnar (Haines) was coming through the door at the time, and I was in my bunk. I got out of the bunk, and got Gunnar, who had hit his head on the overhead and knocked himself out. I dragged him out of the room and pulled him to safety." Laughing, Ike said: "Heroes have to do it—have no choice."

Everything on a boat can be hazardous. Men at sea have to be neat, and store their gear safely. Safety demands that their environment be organized at all times; their lives often depend upon it. Fishermen are known for their neatness around their homes and personal environments. (I have often been taken to task by fishermen because I am generally not tidy and not even the Navy could correct this trait.)

FOOD

FOOD WAS AND IS VERY IMPORTANT to the crew and, as in the Navy, good food usually assures good morale. In the past, food was purchased from the ship store often known as the ship's chandler. The New Bedford Ship Supply, owned by Ray (Rasmus) and Sally (Sarah) Tonnessen, supplied Norwegian boats as did Karl's Ship Supply in Fairhaven, owned by Kjell and Johanna Risdal, and Babe's Ship Supply owned by my mother's cousin, Lillian Topham Oldham. There were other ship chandlers also, both in New Bedford and Fairhaven.

According to ship chandler Billy Kruger in an April 2001 interview in the Standard-Times, the chandler is "A middleman . . . he outfits a boat with everything it needs to go to sea—from food to cleaning supplies to nets and hooks." He went on to say, "Fishermen work hard and they eat good food. Some of the cooks are great chefs, but a fishing boat is not about food . . . the boats are about fishing. When the fish are running, the boat will stay until it's got a good catch, even if the food is gone. As long as you've got potatoes and fish in the hold, you don't go hungry. It was a bottom-line world in the old days."

One fisherman, Alf Isaksen, now living in Norway, still remembers the delicious food he had on his trips out of New Bedford. "We had lobster spaghetti that I will never forget and some of the best food I have ever had and lots of it."

—Alf Isaksen archives

Calm or storm-tossed seas, day or night, the shucking goes on and on.

THE COOKS

"Friends often fight with words when together at the table.
Feuds always follow when guests goad each other."

—"The Havamal"

There was a tried–and-true rule on the boats before microwaves took over: "You don't mess with the cook." The cook had very special status and special privileges and was needed for both the sustenance and morale of the crew. The cook was always right and he had to be kept happy while at sea. Ignoring that rule could mean a very bad trip indeed.

As one retired fisherman recalls: "The cook on my boat was a very small man, and one of the fishermen was bullying him. Finally the cook couldn't take it anymore, and he attacked the fisherman with his cleaver. Slashed his buttocks, and we had to sew the man up on the deck. Later he got thirty stitches in Seaman's Hospital."

And there were attempts at humor. One retired fisherman now living in Norway remembered: "One of the gang had just got married and then went out fishing. All he talked about was getting home. The cook got so tired of hearing it that he put saltpeter in his soup before we docked. The man didn't say much on the next trip."

THE CAPTAIN'S ROLE: A TIGHT SHIP

A SUCCESSFUL CAPTAIN was deemed by the crew to be the one who would find the fish, be fair, make money, and keep the gang working together productively. He had to know how to settle disputes. One skipper, the late Jens Isaaksen who had owned eight ships, was esteemed by his gang, and he believed, "If you are nice to the gang, they will be nice to you. No hollering, no screaming, no displays of temperament. I felt we should talk and help each other. When I saw a problem, I would say, 'Let's have a talk about that.'"

BEWARE THE SHARK!

FISH STORIES ARE NOT LIMITED to recreational fishing. Commercial fishing has its share, on perhaps a grander scale, and sharks often are the subjects of such stories.

One retired fisherman recalled one day when "the crew caught a shark and thought it was dead. They pushed it aside on the deck and forgot it. Days later one of the men was doing his 'business' in a bucket near the shark. The shark

—*General fishing archives*

Relaxing before their watch are, left to right: Steffen Vea, Leif Olsen, Johan Verne, John Johannesen, Jens Syre.

—*Old postcard*

Butler's Flat Lighthouse. A welcome view for returning fishermen.

raised its head and bit him on his behind. We had to go into port and he had, some say, twenty stitches. We loved to visit him at the hospital and tease him. After that everyone would ask him to show his scar!"

"We anchored at night," recalled a now-deceased fisherman, "and left one man on deck, usually the cook. He worked all night opening scallops. I had the watch one night and decided to catch a shark. I took a boatswain's hook and got one. Pulled him aboard and thought it was dead, but it came to life and woke up everyone on the boat. I could have been killed. One had to have respect for a shark."

And finally: Tale or Tail? Said one elderly fisherman, "I caught a shark and it played dead. I pushed it over (the side) days later after we cut off the tail and it swam away full of life."

THE BOOT AND THE SWORDFISH

THE LATE CAPTAIN JENS ISAKSEN was an experienced fisherman and sea captain, who had a brush with fate one lazy afternoon. He never looked at a pair of boots the same way again. They kept him alive that day.

He remembered: "We was on *Kathryn and Mary*, and we saw two big swordfish. I speared one and the other guy got another one. They swam away in different directions. I went after mine in the dory. The boat went after the other. I pulled mine in and then it disappeared. Its sword was very long, and

I couldn't figure out where it was. All of a sudden the sword came up right through my boat, and the boat started to leak fast. I took off my boot and began to bail with it; that was all I had there. The dory began to sink, and the fishing boat was way off in the distance. There was a few minutes there when I wondered what would happen. The swordfish luckily died, and they finally saw me from the *Kathryn and Mary*, and she picked me up just in time."

Most of these men loved the sea, loved their work, and lived their lives on the sea with daring, courage, bravery and sometimes humor. The deep held many secrets and still does. We can never know all that happened at sea when ships suddenly disappeared and men failed to return to their families. We can only speculate.

The sea is truly a "land of the lost."

Legacy & Folklore

THE FISHERMEN
AND THE COWBOYS

Men who work with danger and live a life of adventure have much in common. They risk their lives daily and develop patterns of living that are necessary for survival. These two distinct groups of men, cowboys and fishermen, who helped develop America had lifestyles that had provocative similarities, although the circumstances of their work were totally dissimilar.

Teddy Roosevelt, in "The Cattle Country of the Far West," called cowboys "quiet, rather self-contained men." Norwegian men are noted for their reserve and self-containment. They both delivered food to the marketplace from the natural habitat. One meat, the other fish! They had defined tools of trade and methods of transportation and they developed a unique folklore, tradition, and lifestyle associated with their work.

One worked on the sea and the other on the land. One rode in boats and the other rode horses. The boats needed constant care as did the horses. Without the boats or horses the work could not be done; much attention had to be paid to their care, and it took much of their time before, during and after a trip.

One had ropes and the other nets and ropes. The ropes and nets had to be kept in good repair. Skills were needed to ensure this, so in their free time the men worked on perfecting their knots, and the mending of their nets and their ropes.

Both groups were away from home much of the time doing dangerous work where they could not contact their families. Some just disappeared and were never heard from again; others lost their lives to circumstances beyond their control—the fishermen to the sea in bad weather; the cowboys through accidents with the horses, weather or violence.

The family men had to have courageous, independent wives who cared for the home and family while they were away and wives they could trust to raise their families well, and make do with whatever resources they had at hand. They had to trust their wives to be faithful to them and accept their lifestyle. This was true of both groups of men.

Both groups brought home large incomes based on their productivity and luck. The single men were apt to gamble, drink and carouse when they came back to their towns after a cattle drive or fishing. Some still saved some money, and others did not. There was some violence in the frontier towns as there was in towns with an active waterfront.

Both groups were acquainted with fighting. The cowboys had guns; the fishermen delivered a wild punch.

Cowboys tended to be religious and attended church with their families when home, as did the many fishermen. Both groups tended to be peripatetic and move to locations where there was a reliable supply side.

Both groups had to work closely together to do their work well, and they developed lasting relationships with their co-workers. The cowboys developed a reputation for telling tales, singing, cooking, working long hours in unsanitary conditions, risking their lives on a wild horse, getting little sleep and working with constant danger. So did the fishermen, but their horses were the boats. The fishermen loved country-western music; the cowboys originated this music.

Both were apt to learn the trade from their fathers. Sometimes they were known to be a bit on the rough side; however, the cowboys were more displaced than the fishermen. The fishermen had strong roots to return to and possessed highly developed social skills within a defined culture. The cowboys were apt to be loners. The fishermen were *pendlers*. The cowboys followed the cattle; the fishermen, the fish. Both groups had new support systems in their chosen towns.

The cowboys had nicknames for each other such as Pecos Bill, Tex, or Montana. The fishermen had names like Mickey Mouse, Romer Shoal or Balloon Bill.

They both had a high degree of trust in each other as their lives depended on each other's skills. They had to trust their leaders with their lives. One had a skipper to manage the trip; the other a foreman to manage the drive.

Cowboys had a distinctive walk, wore traditional hats, dressed in a prescribed manner and were generally young, energetic and in good health. So it was also with Norwegian fishermen. The cowboy loved his horse and the land; the fisherman loved his boat and the sea. They both spoke with distinctive but very different accents. They both wore protective clothing: boots, gloves, hats, jackets, ponchos or raingear. They both used knives in their work.

And last, but not least, both groups were filthy when they arrived home and were immediately given long baths, sometimes before they came into the house. And when they did come into the house, they assumed the role of provider, helper, father, husband, churchgoer, lover and helpmate "finest kind."

The Treacherous Shores

WATERFRONT LIFE

The New Bedford Waterfront as depicted by Arthur Moniz, showing some of the boats, stores, churches and streets where the fishermen ate, worked, drank, met their friends, bought their gear, picked up their checks, and found rooms to let.

"Wine makes a man better pleased with himself;
I do not say that it makes him more pleasing to others."

—Shakespeare

As a child, my earliest memories of Norwegian men were of a "funny scent"—a combination of fish and a kind of musky, heavy aroma. That and the suspenders they all seemed to wear, the scrubbed rough hands, the stained fingernails and the glassy, often reddish eyes, all were, I thought, characteristic of Norwegian men.

Did Norwegian men cry a lot? I wondered. When I was in a room with my mother, they would cry and talk about my dead father. Was that why they had glassy red eyes? My mother would visit her sister often, and they would sit and talk quietly in the front room. Two subjects mainly—their many operations and the evils of "drinking." We were told not to get in trouble and to be quiet and play in the back rooms while they had "grownup" talk.

One day I was standing in the little hallway near the living room and could hear them speaking clearly. "Did you read that in the paper? Oh, he drinks, you know. Ruined his whole life."

"They all drink, and it is terrible," my mother said to my aunt, and they commiserated with each other about this nameless person who drank too much and who was ruining everyone's lives. (My mother's family believed strongly in both the prohibition and the temperance movement.) I was puzzled about this, but couldn't ask because they would know I had listened, and I would really "get it" then.

That evening at supper, Momma asked me what I would like to drink. "Drink?" I responded. "Nothing." Because now I knew what happened to people who drank. But why was she asking me? In any event, I had no water, no milk until many meals later when I finally gave in. My little brother was drinking, and she smiled at him. So what was that conversation all about? I didn't find out until much later.

Things in life such as drinking, making money, sex, and other perceived sins were not discussed openly, ever, in my Yankee family and perhaps also not in Norwegian families. Perhaps this closed view of life was at the root of some of the problems.

When the emigrants came to America from Norway, and particularly those who lived in waterfront towns and cities, there were some predictable problems—problems that future generations might deem to be colorful. But they were not truly colorful then or now. Such problems wrecked families, individual lives and future generations. Many Norwegians remain reluctant to discuss this element of Norwegian life because they are too close to it, but it was and is a part of the community and ignoring it would not be honest or fair.

Seaports around the world have much in common with each other, and New Bedford was and is no exception. Today it is the greatest fishing port in America, but it had been a great whaling seaport for many years before the fishing industry was developed. The combination of a deep harbor, manpower, boats, trade and support systems is known collectively as a seaport or port and the waterfront is part of ths port—the geographical location of the boats and allied trades and the center of the seaman's life onshore. Peter Arnett describes his hometown in Bluff, New Zealand, and its waterfront in his book, "Live From the Battlefield":

"It was said that the early whalers drank their rum and drank it neat. The whaling era was long over, but my neighbors still put out to sea in ships working the dangerous waters, sometimes weeks at a time. Nature was demanding of those who would brave the deep, but was bountiful too."

THE NEW BEDFORD WATERFRONT: MID-CENTURY

THE NEW EMIGRANTS, especially the single men or the men with families in Norway, sought to live within walking distance of the waterfront. These rambling streets were their home away from home and contained their clubs, bars, friends, boats, union hall and the shops that supplied their gear. They were comfortable in this section of the city and were in their element below Purchase Street in New Bedford, an area where we as children were not allowed to venture. This area was the heart and soul of New Bedford for many a Norwegian fisherman and a source of despair as well.

New Bedford, below Purchase Street, was considered by many as adult territory only and had much in common with other port cities of the world where sailors ventured and lost their money. Many of the Norwegian men

—*Photo by McGee, circa 1950.*

New Bedford mid-century. The waterfront area near the New Bedford-Fairhaven bridge, where bars, rooming houses and commercial life existed together. Redevelopment wiped out almost all of this essence of old New Bedford.

were young, single, from small towns and villages—or they had wives in Norway and were alone in America. Most were handsome, had money to burn and had time on their hands with few places to go. They had very dangerous jobs and had to let off steam. We would sometimes see them as we looked through the bus window on our way home from school. Often they dressed in their beautiful Norwegian sweaters and their blond hair blew in the wind. Too often, however, these young boys were "three sheets to the wind." Thus they were "off limits" to most of us who were in high school and preparing for our future lives. We were about the same age—yet our lives were a world apart.

The fishermen wanted to be with their friends, relax, have fun and adventure and meet a pretty young woman—and if they were lucky, she would be Norwegian. Many of the older men who had been in New Bedford longer made sure their daughters got to meet single Norwegians who had not made their new bad habits an irreversible lifestyle. There were many weddings for Norwegian and Norwegian-American girls of marriageable age in our community.

In describing his hometown of Bluff, New Zealand, Peter Arnett might well have been describing the New Bedford waterfront: "I watched many of the seafaring men celebrating their return home, reeling in and out of the town's several pubs spaced half a block apart on Main Street, dissipating their considerable paychecks in formidable boozing exploits. I admired the tough men who braved the sea."

SOME MEMORIES

THE MID-CENTURY NEW BEDFORD and Fairhaven waterfronts had a rich, bustling daytime culture but there was very little activity at night. For it was in the daytime that the fishermen frequented the bars when they came in from their trips, and it was on these streets in the daytime that one fisherman, now in Norway, said: "Boy, we were really noisy in those days. But we had a good time. We'd shout and sing in the streets. We must have disturbed the people of New Bedford. Tell them I apologize. But we sure had fun."

A fisherman who now owns several boats explained: "When you came in (from fishing) you had to wait to get paid and you were in shreds. We would go to the bars with the gang and have a few drinks, and the longer you were with them, the more you drank. There were thousands of men who fished but just a small percentage drank heavily. You didn't see them at night, but you saw them in the day waiting for their money. So people said, 'They drink in the morning and afternoon,' not realizing it was part of their schedule and had to do with the boats. Hardly any men were around at night. They also got many business connections there, and the men going out to sea went in for a drink as well."

Gunleif Wilhelmsen remembers this time: "It was pretty hard when they come from Norway—don't know any families here and they are downtown so where do they go? The bars! One friend got in with the wrong people and spent all his money each trip. He was always broke and had to borrow money to buy cigarettes to go out. Another friend was supposed to take a percentage of his salary and send it to Norway for his wife and kids but he wouldn't do it unless my wife helped him."

One second-generation Norwegian describes the situation in this way: "The single fishermen were here all alone and in the bars, but when they were married they were often very religious, always in church. If they married a strong woman they were O.K. In Brooklyn, the Seaman's Church had the minister go right down to the docks. But they didn't do that here."

Norwegian fishermen also dated and married many proper and desirable New Bedford-area women who never saw the inside of a bar. But, as in any seaport, there were more than enough girls and women who hung around the bars ready to take advantage of this combination of free-flowing money, handsome men and alcohol. But far fewer Norwegians went this route than was perceived by the community. And if they did, they were often monitored and scolded by those fishermen already established in the community. Norwegians are apt to monitor each other's activities and to confront those who are breaking society's rules. Just the same, some women were picked up by Norwegian fishermen in the New Bedford area bars. A small percentage lived with women they met in this way, and a few were said to have children within this arrangement.

To many women who had few resources for survival, a fisherman with a pocket full of money ready to spend was considered a good catch. As one Norwegian-American man described an incident he saw when he was a boy: "I once was driving with my father when he saw a Norwegian man with a woman who was 'suspicious.' I had never seen my father upset, but he was that day. He stopped the car, jumped out, and really tore into this man, who he knew had a family in Norway. I was so shocked to see my father this angry. That was an eye-opener for me."

The central truth, however, is that the Norwegian fisherman most enjoyed socializing with his "gang," the men with whom he worked and upon whom he depended for his safety at sea. He worked with the gang, lived with the gang, socialized with the gang, drank with the gang and played with the gang. This was his extended family away from home.

And even when a respectable young woman had a date with one of the Norwegian men, she often would end up sitting at a table with the "gang" as they spoke and laughed in Norwegian. One woman remembered, "I dated a Norwegian fisherman in the late fifties who was very kind, handsome and gentle, and, well, just very special. I met him at a dance and liked him immediately. When he came in from a trip he would call and make a date with me for a movie, dinner or a little ride to Boston or some special thing. But we almost never went as we would have to drop by some local gathering place 'for *yust* a minute' to say hello, at wherever the 'gang' would be sitting, drinking or eating. And I would just sit there while they chatted and laughed in Norwegian. I remember 'finest kind' being said very often, and every few minutes my date, who held my hand the whole time, would ask me if I wanted more ginger ale. I liked him very much but he couldn't seem to separate himself from the 'gang.' I think he felt a bit shy about being alone with me too long, because his English was minimal, and I was a schoolteacher. But I did know that his friends from Norway meant a great deal to him."

There were no community agencies that took an interest in the social problems of the young fisherman—not the city and not as a rule, the Norwegian church, although at least one of the ministers, Pastor Johnnie Glad, tried to meet the boats and talk to the men on occasion. There were no Norwegian support clubs or Norwegian-managed places to eat or dance, homes to stay in (with one exception) or restaurants or other establishments. There were, however, the New Bedford restaurants and bars, such as the Hide-A-Way, Norway Café, Fore and Aft and Haskells where the New Bedford fishermen, mostly those without a family here, but sometimes those with a family, spent their days ashore, cashed their checks, ate, played, talked, relaxed, found jobs, shared letters, argued, met friends, heard the gossip from the boats and the news of Norway, and planned their evenings often gambling or nightclubbing before they went back out to fight the waters. And it was also here that many lives were set on perilous courses.

THE TONNESSENS

RASMUS (RAY) TONNESSEN and his New Bedford-born wife, Sarah (Sally) owned the New Bedford Ship Supply and acted as the local contact point, job finder, social worker, and often friend and counselor for these young men just over from the old country. They were a great help to them and sponsored many of them by putting up "the guarantee" to emigrate. They often acted as surrogate parents for the young boys, but there were simply too many men and too few Norwegians and local residents who were interested in their welfare. Sally Tonnessen often expressed concern about their lives to my mother as the boys were so young. She worried about their health and futures, and she also once expressed that she just got tired of "gathering them up and pouring them onto the boats."

Tove Ditlevsen, Danish author, expressed in her book "Early Spring" (*Det tidlige forar*), some Scandinavian attitudes toward drinking: "Either the men

.drank—and most of them did—or they harbored a violent hatred towards those who did"—an attitude which I have also heard from people I interviewed.

Some of the new emigrants were lucky enough to have relatives and friends who had already settled in and tried to watch over them, but far too many were alone, lonely, and had too much money too soon without the experience of knowing how to handle it. As the widow of a Norwegian fisherman said: "They had too much money, were too young to be here alone, just teens with too little sense and once they got drinking had no sense at all. The wealthier Norwegians and the church should have helped them more."

PERSONAL STORIES

MOST OF THE GANG DRANK when they came in from a trip while waiting for their pay, and some men drank before they went out on a trip—to reinforce themselves against the sea, as they would say. "One for the road." But it could result in a miserable trip out and working with a hangover the next day. One retired fisherman recalls, "Once I saw a crew that was drunk before they were to sail. They were loaded onto the boat like cargo, just as stiff as they could be, and the boat sailed with them."

Some hated their work, and they thought the liquor helped them to get going, but in one case it had the opposite effect. A retired fisherman remembers when he was young: "I went to look for a job my second day in New Bedford. I heard that one of the boats was about to go on a trip and needed a cook because the cook hadn't showed up. I found the cook drunk and still drinking in one of the barrooms, so I took my remaining money and told the bartender to give him two doubles, and then I went to the boat for the job. They hired me as a cook and off I went to the store for provisions, not even knowing how to open a can of food. When I got back, the captain realized I didn't know anything—I must have asked dumb questions—but he let me on anyway as a full hand. When I got out to sea, I knew this was not the job for me. I was sick the whole eight days. I continued to open scallops and continued to be sick all the time. I was aboard for about a year and never went to sea without being sick."

An Americanized second-generation Norwegian who grew up in New Bedford recalls: "When I was growing up, the fishermen liked to drink. When they were at sea, they were away from liquor many days at a time. They were dried out, and then they hit the bars when they came in. Once I saw some of the crew go into the Fore and Aft just after we came in and before we had cleaned up our boat. After our work was done, rather than stand around in the union hall, we went into the Fore and Aft to wait for our check. Before we could even get there, the others in our crew were blind drunk. They liked their liquor. I didn't get into that scene. Once I celebrated my birthday with them and went into Fore and Aft for a beer. I mentioned it was my birthday, and then the drinks came one after another. I made two guys take me home because I insisted they face my wife with me. I couldn't afford drinking and had a family. That was the big sin, spending the money like that. The scallopers used to hang around together. They were a clique among themselves—come in from the trips, go back to their rooms, shower, change, and go to bar so they could meet someone they could talk to. Once I saw a guy put a twenty dollar bill (worth about one hundred today) on the table, and the waitress left the change. He went to the men's room, and the money was gone when he came back. That kept happening, and he didn't even notice his money was gone. Young kids had nothing to do with their money, so they spent it."

Some would say they needed these few short days on shore to relax because on their next trip they would be working unendurable hours in strenuous labor under indescribable conditions, in great danger, in lousy weather, always dirty and smelly with almost no sleep. Said one retired fisherman: "How could you sleep? My bunk was in the bow and the waves would hit against that thin wood and knock me right out of the bunk. There was no sleep. Just trying to lie there was an effort."

Yet they had jobs that required them to have great endurance and caution or they could be severely injured or die at any moment. Accidents on fishing boats are quick, but not painless, and the results can last a lifetime. The same men who would endure pain rather than take medication such as aspirin would use alcohol on shore as a relaxant, a way to forget their work and troubles and as a reinforcement to go back out a few days later to fight the waters. They were often self-medicating and didn't realize it.

The New Bedford area communities perceived that Norwegians liked to drink and were critical of it. As with many Northern Europeans, drinking could quickly develop into alcoholism and that become a serious problem for the men and their families. These men did not come from drinking homes, as liquor in Norway was almost unavailable. Those from Karmøy could not buy it then and still cannot buy any alcoholic beverage other than beer on the island. Many in the New Bedford community perceived that the Norwegians were big drinkers as that was what they saw on the waterfront. They could not correct this perception as they had little contact with Norwegian families or Norwegian women, who tended to stay together and not integrate into the community.

"When men come to like a sea-life, they are not fit to live on land."

—Samuel Johnson, in "Life of Samuel Johnson" by James Boswell, 1791

I remember one Fairhaven woman who had been asked for a date by a Norwegian fisherman. She told me that her mother would have killed her if she had brought one of those "drunks" home. To her family, all Norwegians were "drunks," and this was often the perception in the community because of the daytime drinking and drunkenness on the waterfront. Other factors tended to reinforce this stereotype. The police would round up those who appeared to have drunk too much, or who had been in bar fights, and let them cool off overnight in the jail. The names of men held in jail were printed in the newspaper the next day. Norwegians weren't the only people on the list, but certainly there were many, and often they were very young. Such listings formed an indelible impression on the people of the community, and that impression exists to this day. It was an embarrassment to the Norwegian community and to the relatives of those whose names were listed. The men would simply pay a fine and go out to sea again. And it was not forgotten that they brought a lot of money into New Bedford.

A BLIND EYE

As young Norwegians who recently had been confirmed, or as older men who came from very religious backgrounds with no liquor at all, they would often rebel against their strict upbringing. New Bedford encouraged this behavior by turning the other way. The police didn't take much action until it was serious, and the bartenders did their bit to keep it going and to make as much money as they could. Everyone was there to share in the spoils. Said one bar owner: "I let them drink until they fell to the floor, and then I would call a taxi. I never tried to stop the drinking. I'm in business to make money. I started to serve inexpensive food also, to encourage them to come in more often. I could always trust the Norwegians to pay their bills, and I would always extend credit to them."

Many a man's reputation was made by his bar exploits in New Bedford, and there are still stories of the bar fighting and legends about fishermen who wrecked such and such a bar. But the Norwegians always paid, so the bar owners liked them and didn't make too great a fuss about the misbehavior. But it is also true though that some men were banned from certain bars in New Bedford.

Liquor purchases, even at age sixteen, didn't seem to be a problem for these big-spending fishermen, and the barkeepers and waitresses welcomed their business. They were heavy tippers as well as drinkers. And the taxi drivers loved them.

Those who drank heavily often didn't achieve their goals in life, and many died young. Of those still living, many have some very tight budgets today. There also are some who drank heavily but still succeeded in life. Many of

—Photo courtesy of a NBHS friend

Looking northeast from Purchase and William Streets to the "Five and Ten" on a cold winter night. (I can still smell the peanuts being roasted at the corner peanut store.) Just east of here, down a block, began the waterfront neighborhood of the fishermen.

these men had strong wives who enabled them to achieve some moderation and who made sure some money was put away before it was "all drunk up."

Said one fisherman, "The problem with some of them was that when they drank, even a little, they tended to want to fight—to work off the stress of the trip. I don't think anyone who hasn't been on one of those boats can realize how horrible it was and always the terrible danger present. These guys saw so much tragedy, and they were so young." One bar owner also remarked that he was surprised at the tendency to fight among the Norwegian fishermen and a Norwegian-American Merchant Marine officer once remarked to me that fighting was the one thing he connected with Norwegians in his travels to seaports around the world.

Some men would come in from a trip, spend every penny, and then go back out. Some became alcoholics and went back to Norway where they received help and lived out their old lives sober. Others were sent back by the captains who paid for their trip home. Among those to whom drinking had become a serious problem, some were encouraged by friends to go to AA and worked hard, sometimes throughout their lives, to contain this problem.

Some did nothing about it and lived lives of despair with continuing family tragedies. Even today in Norway there are groups who try to help these men who were introduced to drinking in America some forty years ago and are often successful even with the long-term drinker.

A boat owner who became extremely successful in life says, "It is so sad when you look at some of the people who had been fishing and they have nothing left and their health is gone too—they spent it all. They called those the 'good times,' when they spent money wildly."

Typical of the traditional Norwegian attitude towards drink was the testimony of a mother in the early 1900s who often told this story about her pregnancy with her last child: "I was quite weak and run down, and the doctor said I needed to drink a glass of beer each day to build me up so that my child would grow properly. So each day, I would take the Bible and read a chapter and then drink the glass of beer. Then I would pray to God to forgive me and remind him that it was doctor's orders. It was a sin to drink."

Among those who drank, there was great heartbreak for many of the families. Because of the pattern of heavy drinking established in youth, once a man married and tried to settle down with a family, he often could not totally change his lifestyle. Some tried very hard to change but often reverted to their old ways. Those who were not able to get effective help often lost their families or if there were no divorce, lived lives with poor communication and unhappy family members. Some divorced later in life, and others had tragic early deaths or, in some cases, did not get to know their children well.

Many a Norwegian wife in New Bedford took it for granted that her husband would be in the bar with the gang, and she would be able to find him there. These women had learned from previous generations how to handle the problem.

The adult daughter of a fishing captain remembered: "Many Norwegians drink too much and are too stubborn. Some of the men who got involved with friends other than fishermen seemed to handle alcohol well and the ones who went to church didn't drink so much. It was a compulsion for many, like eating pie. It's a national tragedy in northern countries and part of the overall culture. The Norwegian church was too strict. It looked at everything as a sin, and that didn't help the potential alcoholic. It built up too high expectations. That condition has modified a lot now.

"Usually the wives told people their husbands were 'angels on earth,' drinkers or not. Some ranted and raved about it. My father drank over the years, off and on, and once he came home drunk—so drunk my mother couldn't handle him. I was never that close to my father. I was happy when he drank. When I saw him drink, he was happy and gave me money and I felt loved. If I wanted to see him, I would go to the bar or I would bring a note there from my mother."

As one retired fisherman acknowledged: "I lost everything and everybody I loved in life because of drink. It looks like I loved that best! But I never thought of myself as an alcoholic. I always thought I could stop at any time."

Some Norwegian women also like to take more than one drink—but drinking problems among women are rarer and not often discussed. They too have to exert great care to avoid alcoholism.

THE STRONG MOTHER

A DAUGHTER OF A DRINKER tells her story: "In June of 1957, we left Karmøy to find my father. I was 12 years old and had never seen my father after he left for America. Rasmus Tonnessen put up a guarantee, which was five hundred dollars in the bank and a promise to take care of us. We went to Oslo by train to fly to Kennedy airport and arrived twenty-four hours later. The big buildings scared me a bit. I never saw so many cars and the big roads. We took a ride to the airport and was off to New Bedford.

"A friend had prepared a meeting with my father at three o'clock. When he came he had a big bouquet of roses and a big box of chocolates. He hugged us but I could smell alcohol, which scared me and made me not like him. I thought, '*How can I get rid of him?*' He sobered up after three or four kettles of coffee."

Her sister told how her mother tried to help others: "She would pull the men out of the bars and into the bank. After we all came to America, my mother would go down to the bars and find the men she knew had families on our island, pull them out of the bar and bring them to the bank to send money home to their families. She also went to the union hall or any other place where they got their checks. She remembered how hard it was for her when she got no money for so many years from my father."

Much has been written about Scandinavian attitudes toward liquor and the propensity to alcoholism there and in other Northern European populations. It is certain that alcohol often creates a conflicted life. The great Swedish filmmaker Ingmar Bergman, in "Fanny and Alexander," suggests that the Scandinavian walks with a mentor on each side; one is a party-loving father and the other the pious clergyman stepfather. The Scandinavian walks with two sets of instructions, two conflicting messages, throughout his lifetime.

Many Americans will drink at home and will have regular cocktail hours with their adult families and friends or wine with dinner. Norwegian men tend to drink in bars and drinking is not the casual thing as it is with Americans. Drinking has all kinds of religious and moral implications. One drinks heavily, or one does not drink at all. One drinks to get drunk.

It must be said, however, that even in America a great many Norwegian men resisted drink. Many were churchgoers and had loving, supportive families. They tended to stick with each other as friends and many became prosperous, some staying in America, some returning eventually to Norway as wealthy men. It is still widely believed in Norwegian communities, here and in Norway, that religion is the cure for alcoholism. Alcoholism is often seen as a moral or spiritual dilemma and not as a physical sickness.

COURAGE

"Life shrinks or expands in proportion to one's courage."

—Anais Nin, "The Diary of Anais Nin"

COURAGE COMES IN MANY FORMS. If it is to be measured by meeting insurmountable challenges or trying to solve problems while knowing that defeat is a strong possibility, then the men who battled alcohol and those who tried to help them, have a kind of courage that has to be admired and emulated. Some men fought alcohol all of their lives. Some won the battle, others continued to fight and never totally won, while others just stayed in denial.

The men and women who won these battles had great steadfastness and perseverance, but the ones who didn't win and still fought had an even greater courage, because they didn't give up even when they were not winning—they stayed the course and kept trying—sometimes throughout a whole lifetime.

So although courage in this book is often defined in terms of behavior at sea, these Norwegians had a kind of personal bravery revolving around alcohol—and still have—that is admirable and commendable. Their spouses, friends and supporters also had a special kind of tenacity as seen by the loving support they patiently gave through the years by encouragment, help, and forgiveness.

THOSE WHO HELPED

HELEN WILHELMSEN RECALLED: "Alcohol was a problem, especially among those who were here alone and just had a room downtown. Sometimes, someone would take them under their wing or send them back to Norway. Pa, Arnleif Veek, understood and used to take people home and helped them and nurtured them when they were drinking too much. He knew what they were going through as he had had the problem once himself. Some of the fishermen used to gather donations, and others bought clothing for the men and bought a plane ticket for them to go home.

—Photo courtesy of a NBHS friend.

Downtown New Bedford mid-century looking
north from Liggett's Drug Store

"Northern Europeans seem more susceptible to alcohol. My father was very active in AA. We went to Norway and saw some of the men he had helped, and they were not drinking and were gentlemen over there. One of them was a completely different person. He had left gifts, little fishing boats, for the boys when we got there. Mother was a teetotaler but very tolerant and was helpful to the alcoholics who came at Christmas and they were always at our house. Mother in her quiet way helped so many young men."

OTHER ACTIVITIES

OTHER ACTIVITIES IN THE NEW BEDFORD AREA for these young and "free" men included the racetracks, driving around in big cars, nightclubs, dancing at roadhouses, and late nights in twenty-four-hour restaurants where they most often ate beefsteaks, mashed potatoes, carrots and gravy. Said one former girlfriend of a Norwegian fisherman: "They would drive up to the racetracks in their new cars, often convertibles, smiling and laughing with their blond hair flying in the wind, as though they didn't have a care in the world. Some would go on the bus. When they got there, they would see their friends and almost compete with each other on who could gamble the most and the best. They ate and drank, enjoyed the warm summer evenings and thought they had really 'arrived.' They all felt they had the inside dope (on the horses) but I don't remember anyone ever winning."

Even today Norwegian-Americans like to visit Las Vegas or other gambling centers. They tend to love gambling, as do Norwegians in Norway. Even the religious gamble in Norway. It does not seem to be considered a sin, as it often is among Protestants in America. Many see betting as nothing more than a pleasant way to pass the time with friends. Others, often people with the same addictive personalities that lead to alcoholism, take it more seriously and it becomes a serious problem.

Waterfront life was by any standard of measurement a true subculture, and it brought much money into the city. Many in New Bedford were basically unaware of their city's waterfront life—were even unaware that many Norwegians were working there.

New Bedford has glorified the whaling industry and one day will glorify the fishing industry of the twentieth century. They tend to forget that the whalers in early days were even rougher, tougher and louder than the fishermen. It could be argued that the fishing industry—and, in particular, the Norwegian scallopers—has kept the New Bedford area viable though the twentieth century. What whaling did for nineteenth century New Bedford's prosperity, fishing did in the twentieth century and will hopefully continue into the twenty-first.

> *"Tell me, ye aged gray-haired heroes, who have come here to seek repose?*
> *Wherefore must I so many keep of such a set, who, one and all,*
> *right dearly love their souls to steep, from morn till night, in the mead-bowl?"*
>
> —Magnus Erlingson's Saga circa 1160

Today in Norway there are retired fishermen who still have some vestiges of the alcohol problem. Norwegians do what they can for people with this problem. There are societies set up to meet the spiritual needs of such men, and fund-raising efforts to provide for their more tangible needs. Norway shows zero tolerance for drivers with any alcohol in their system; the penalties are high, including loss of license and prison.

Many faces show the ravages of alcoholism, and the majority of problem drinkers there, as here, are dead before their time. But drinkers who have survived still talk about their youthful days working off New Bedford's coast, where life was one big amusement park onshore—and cold, wet, grueling, dangerous work while out to sea.

~

Discovering My Heritage

NORWAY

—*AT photo*

Follese, Norway, at Christmas time, 1960.

"For an occurrence to become an adventure, it is necessary and sufficient for one to recount it."

—Jean-Paul Sartre

YOUNG PEOPLE WERE COMING from Norway to America to work in the fifties and early sixties, but fewer Americans were going to Europe. Europe was still recovering from the war, and all over Germany, in particular, there were ruins of bombed-out buildings, demolition and reconstruction. London was still in a muddle from the bombings, as were parts of other countries. Travel to Europe was relatively rare in those days; the memory of the war was still too vivid for many and tourist services were not really viable. It was often considered an adventure to go "overseas," but it was one I wanted

~

to experience. So as Norwegians were coming to New Bedford to live, I was going to Europe to live, with the goal of visiting Norway. We passed on the crossing as "ships in the night."

Norway was an impossible dream during my youth, and even after I had graduated from college with a B.S. degree and worked as a teacher, it was still too great an expense. So I developed a plan that would take me there as part of my work—and give me the opportunity to practice my profession under rather delightful circumstances.

I learned that if I had two successful years of teaching experience in different geographical locations, I would have preferential selection for overseas teaching in the military dependent schools. So I did just that. I taught in Massachusetts and Florida and applied in 1960 for a teaching post in Germany because of its proximity to Norway. When I was informed by the Air Force that I had been selected to teach in Japan, my heart fell. Miraculously, a few days later, the Army informed me that I had been chosen to teach in Germany. In my mind's eye I could already see Norway, and I rejoiced that my plan was working.

As Norwegian emigrants were flying and sailing west to America, I was flying east to Europe in August of 1960. I can easily relive my first trip to Europe as it is stamped permanently in my mind as my first great lifetime adventure. I was beyond excitement as my dream was about to come true, and I can feel the same emotions today as I sit and write, some forty years later.

I left my weeping mother behind (as did the emigrants coming from Norway), as well as a young man I had dated all through college and who, finally, on my day of departure, decided to offer me his fraternity pin. I was free, and I was going to make the most of it and did not want to be committed to anyone while I was on my adventure to Europe. He was very special to me, but the timing was just bad and too late.

I was afraid to fly, but I wasn't afraid to meet people and open new horizons. The fear of flying didn't stop me from getting on the plane, and, clutching my Bible, I did. First we flew to New York and then were sandwiched into an Army charter, which headed to Gander, Newfoundland, to refuel. It was a noisy and very crowded four-engine propeller plane and flew quite low. Up to that point, the hundred or so teachers onboard were chatting and talking about their new teaching positions in Germany. But as we flew from Newfoundland to Ireland to stop at Shannon, more and more dozed off to sleep. I was much too excited to sleep, and I kept looking out the window, hoping to see something more than an occasional iceberg. I also felt it was my duty to guard the engines the whole way as they spouted flames through the dark night air. I did see some freighters and passenger liners, and I wonder now how many of them carried Norwegians headed to New Bedford.

We landed at Shannon Airport in Ireland, did some shopping, had some coffee, and watched many of the passengers make a run for the duty-free shop

Photograph of bearer

PARTMENT OF STATE
ASHINGTON

IMM. & NA.. SERVICE
NEW YORK, N. Y. 23
A D M I T T E D

AUG 24 1961

CLASS
ITO

—*Ray Whittaker photo*

My first passport photo in 1960. I
am tanned from a year in Florida.

and its liquor. I was surprised at that and couldn't understand why. We took off for Germany, and it was just after breakfast and we flew very low over Ireland and could see the farmers waving to us from the fields. Everything was so green. And then we flew over the Irish Sea to England and shortly after across the water again to France and then Germany.

I could see the rivers and towns, each town dominated by a cathedral or large church, and could now see from above the same scenes I dreamed over in my old French books. Europe was now real for me as I tried to identify each landmark I saw from the plane. I could hardly breathe, I was so excited. All my geography classes were coming alive at that moment. For me it was a vision come true.

I looked around and everyone was playing cards. Was I the only one who wanted to see everything? This was the trip of a lifetime. I was going to Germany. The war had ended only fifteen years before, and I could still see war damage through the window of the plane. The only German words I knew had been taught to me by a German girlfriend, Gerda Rosengart. I practiced, *"Mein auto ist ein Volkswagen"* (my car is a Volkswagen) again and again as I learned to make my tongue, jaw and lips respond to the hard consonants so typical of German words.

But more important to me was that this trip was the first step on my road to Norway. I wished the plane could have turned and headed north so I could get there right then. Finally, I would see my father's home and relatives. I felt as though I was really coming home as we flew over France and then into Germany. I spied the Rhine River and knew we were soon to land in Frankfurt. We landed and were taken to the communication room at Rhein-Main Air Base to send telegrams home.

AIRGRAM

"Dear Mom. Arrived safely.
Great trip.
Love Astrid."

When we got to the hotel, the others took a tour of the city. I went to a Volkswagen dealer and ordered a car so that in two weeks I would be driving around Europe to prepare for my trip to Norway. The next day we got loaded onto Army buses for our introduction to Mannheim, Germany, and BOQ (Bachelor Officer's Quarters) living. My year in Germany—that wonderful year—had begun!

I smile even today when I remember how I felt on that trip: excitement, fear, apprehension, anticipation—probably exactly how the Norwegian emigrants felt on their trip to Massachusetts. Such an adventure, such excitement—an impossible dream coming true. But be careful, I cautioned myself, this is a new world and a few more prayers might be needed. And they were!

Mannheim was very near historic Heidelberg, the home of the "student prince." I loved Europe immediately. There my name was not different; in fact it helped me to integrate quickly into the German community and learn the language. I had German friends and American teacher friends, and we shared some wonderful times. But the goal was Norway, and I never lost track of that.

As often as possible on weekends, I traveled through Europe with my new friends. What wonderful days those were! We were single young women professionals who lived together without rent in spacious private rooms with daily maid service. We enjoyed officer's club and post-exchange privileges, the use of military hotels in choice locations, an abundant supply of single, eligible college-educated American bachelors to date, wonderful colleagues, great skiing vacations in Bavaria and Switzerland, picnics at castles, tours in all of the famous cities of Europe, and enough money to travel modestly. We didn't appreciate then how truly lucky we were. We simply had a privileged life in Germany and the surrounding countries, and it could never be replicated.

THE AMERICAN *PENDLER*

I wrote to my aunt and uncle in Bergen and made plans to spend my two-week 1960 Christmas vacation there with my friend Greta, from California. Other teachers went to Egypt, Israel, Spain and exotic, warm locations, but Greta and I went to freezing Norway. But as she still says, "It was the best Christmas I ever had."

It started off peculiarly. My hair had been very sun-streaked from Florida and then strangely discolored from the water in Germany. I decided, foolishly, to have it colored for the trip, so my family would not think I had strange hair. That was the worst decision I have ever made. My German was not good enough to explain the correct color, so I had to go to Norway to be introduced in my father's home with jet-black hair. I felt I was wearing a wig and was so upset that I looked so different from the rest of the Norwegians and so different from me.

—*AT photo*

Weekends and vacations meant travel while we were teachers in Europe. I'm the photographer here on our Thanksgiving trip to Switzerland. In Interlaken after four days in Kleine Scheidig trying to ski are Mary Cockrell (Ehrendreich) from North Carolina, Greta Garten (Jelleson) from San Francisco, Barbara Ballard from Tennessee and former college classmate and fellow teacher, our driver on this trip, the late Richard Pleshaw of Framingham, Masssachusetts, who protected us as a big brother throughout the holiday. They all look casual here but I can personally guarantee each of us was in great pain from the four days of slips and falls on the mountain.

We drove from Mannheim to Copenhagen, Denmark, in a new but temperamental Volkswagen that periodically would break down on the Autobahn. At one point in Denmark we stopped at a gas station, and Greta asked for the restroom. They directed her out to the back. When she returned to the car, her eyes were double their normal size as she said, "You'll never guess what I just experienced. Can you believe—an outhouse with newspapers for toilet paper!" Greta was convinced at that point that all of Scandinavia was in the dark ages, compared to her city of San Francisco, and also nervous that Christmas in Norway would mean cold treks to outhouses in the snow.

She talked about that all the way to Copenhagen and was very worried when we left the car at an auto shop and rented a hotel room. She looked forward to the sights, sounds, and tastes of that bright happy city—but not to its bathrooms. Our misgivings were soon put to rest. In Copenhagen, we discovered the lovely but simple decorated Danish Christmas tree; modern and colorful furnishings, down bed covers (the love of which lasted a lifetime) and, of course, Danish pastry and open-faced sandwiches. And I discovered curry, of all things. We loved our days in Copenhagen, but were soon to board a sleeper-train for the long trip to Bergen via Sweden and Oslo.

It was my first extended train trip and one I would never forget. As the car began to fill up, I watched passengers come in and find their seats. I stared at them as I was startled to see that I was surrounded by people who looked like my family. I was also impressed with the handsome men, as was Greta. We smiled and nudged each other in our seats. Then, all of a sudden, I realized that for the first time in my life, I was with people who looked not only like my relatives, but like me. I saw my nose, the space between the two front teeth, my eye shape and hair color (of course not my "new" hair color). It was an eerie feeling, but I knew I was home at that moment. No one gave me a second look, and all addressed me in Norwegian—so I felt I had passed a test of sorts.

We had brought a bag of pastry, fruit and chocolate—in fact, "Princess Astrid" chocolates—and had cigarettes and other delights that twenty-three-year-old women should avoid, out of consideration for their skin and waistlines, both of which were important to us in those days. Greta was a beautiful, upbeat, athletic, very droll San Francisco woman of German ancestry with large blue eyes, and she easily passed for a Scandinavian. I, on the other hand, with my new black hair, had some apprehension about how I would be regarded.

We talked to people on the train and slept briefly in the narrow berths of the sleeping car. I would look out of the windows when the train slowed and would see the little town squares of Sweden with large Christmas trees decorated with Swedish flags beckoning to us to get off and enjoy a warm fireside, hot coffee and music.

We stopped over in Oslo where we briefly toured the city, and I attempted to get my hair re-colored. Unfortunately, it became blacker. (I did not speak Norwegian either.) I sought out the tall Oslo windjammer, the *Christian Radich*, a boat I had seen in a movie and a vessel that was to enter my life several times in the years ahead. After a delightful overnight, again with down covers, at the convenient Viking Hotel near the train station, we boarded the train to Bergen. This trip is often called the most beautiful train ride in the world, and I could see why, even in the dead of winter. How can one adequately describe the snug little villages overlooking the icy beauty of Norway's mountains and streams?

We wanted to talk with other passengers, at least I did, but most did not speak English. My basic German helped. We swapped cigarettes with the Norwegian soldiers going home for Christmas. Of course, we thought we were the young sophisticates from America, and that they were very interested in everything American and eager to talk to us, but in fact they were more eager to have our cigarettes. We were in our early twenties, they were eighteen or nineteen—we saw them as children. I remember seeing the strange look on their faces when they discovered the menthol taste of the cigarettes, something they had not previously experienced.

I decided to leave the compartment for a while and went out into the corridor. There I gazed in wonder as we passed by dark but dramatic snow-covered mountains and

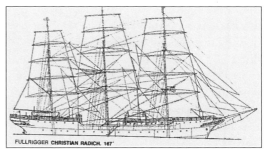

FULLRIGGER CHRISTIAN RADICH. 167'

—*Sven Ivar Langheller et al, SKIP.*

The windjammer *Christian Radich*. I first saw her in Oslo at Christmas 1960 after seeing the movie "Windjammer" in 1959.

—*Photo of unknown origin*

Trygve Lie (1896–1968), first secretary general of the United Nations.

frozen lakes and waterfalls, deep ravines and little villages, each with a huge Christmas tree decorated with white lights and Norwegian flags. At each village the train would slow down and stop briefly while some of its passengers would alight and immediately transform into friends or relatives being greeted enthusiastically by those who had waited for them, leaving us behind to feel a bit envious and to wonder what was in store for us.

At one village a lovely blonde woman, who had been in our compartment for a while, said good-bye, wished us a *God Jul*, and left the train. She put on her backpack, got onto her skis and simply slipped into the darkness. Norway is dark for more than twenty hours a day at that time of year. I watched her and wondered about her life and the home she would be going to that Christmas Eve, and what her life would be like in the future. The lonely beauty of a solitary figure skiing off into the night to celebrate Christmas at home was a very moving experience for me.

"My wish is for you to know your family, your heritage and your your father's country."

—Trygve Lie

The train started up again and I continued to watch the people and the scenery. There was a man standing nearby—an older man who seemed pensive but friendly—so I began to talk with him. He asked me where I lived in America, and I told him near Boston. He told me he had spent much time in that city. We talked on about Norway and my father, and I found him to be very interesting and knowledgeable. "Well," he said, "I have to get off here, but I wish you a very Merry Christmas and also that you will discover your father's country and learn to love it. My wish is for you to know your family, your heritage and Norway." And he left.

I went back into the compartment where several passengers stared at me and were strangely silent. Greta said, "They are shocked that you talked to him!" I wondered why. "That man was Trygve Lie, the first Secretary General of the UN," she replied. "He was," I responded, "very kind to me and gave me good advice, and we both, I hope, enjoyed our conversation." I think back now and wish I had talked to him longer about more diverse subjects.

BERGEN

WE CONTINUED ON AS THE TRAIN sped through the mountains and villages of Norway, depositing its passengers gently into stations where they would begin their trek home for Christmas. We traveled into the night and often made trips to the dining car or sleeping car by jumping over the treacherous icy couplings between the cars. We successfully navigated them but not without squeals of fright and sometimes nervous laughter. Greta's bathroom fears were not allayed much on this train trip either, as the toilets opened directly to the tracks—that was a cold experience, to say the least. I remember her coming out of the WC and saying, "Can you believe . . . " Now she was really apprehensive about Norwegian facilities.

Finally we came to the dimly lit station in Bergen. "How will I recognize my family?" I wondered. "Will they know me? Will they like me?" I started to get very nervous at this moment when I was about to fulfill a lifetime dream and mission. Greta and I got off the train and stood there together looking around.

Just then a distinguished-looking gentleman with a young boy came up to Greta and said, "Astrid?" I stepped forward. My black hair had confused them all. The man who had come to meet us was my Uncle Kristian. He told Greta that she looked like family, but he didn't think I did. I wanted to die at that moment because my dark hair misled him, but we all hugged and he welcomed me to Norway.

We went by ferry to the island of Askøy, where my aunt, my father's sister Marie, was waiting for us. She greeted us warmly and led us to a table laden with a variety of memorable treats. I couldn't recall ever before experiencing such warmth. Tante Marie was so loving, so dear and so kind to us. Tante and I somehow had the same mannerisms, and I could see myself in her expressions and hand movements. We seemed to understand each other despite the language barrier. She did speak a bit of German, (as I understand the story, before the war some German passengers were stranded in Bergen when their boat sunk, and she took several in and they continued to write to each other) and that is how we often communicated. I loved her immediately—her warmth,

—*Berg archives*

Gunnar Berg and his mother, my beloved "Tante Marie."

hospitality, generosity, laughter, and her sparkling, mischievous eyes. I could easily see why my father had loved her so much. I did too.

Uncle Kristian was very special. He had the dignity of a minister or judge and spoke English quite well. My cousin Ketil, who spoke some English, was lovable, happy and enthusiastic about his American "cousins," and Greta was adopted immediately into the family. Greta had another reason to be happy—they had a modern bathroom.

Ketil saw to it that our every wish was carried out, and he spent the whole vacation showing us his island and Bergen and watching us carefully to be sure we did not get lost as we went off in different directions in town. I remember looking for his red knitted cap bobbing up and down in the fish market, department stores and busy streets, and his calling, "Greta, Astri, come now!" He was wonderful.

My most vivid recollection of Bergen was the fish market. There the boats were tied up near the square, and the fisherman sold their fish, whole and fresh off the boats, with the Hanseatic buildings in the background. I remember one man flapping his arms in the air like a seal trying to keep his hands warm and Ketil's red hat bobbing up and down among the fish-stalls. It was so cold that day, but somehow very colorful and warm. Their home was on a hill overlooking Follese, on the island of Askøy, just outside Bergen where Uncle Kristian worked as a baker. In those days it was easy to walk to town; in later years the hill seemed much higher. The house was lovely, and the Christmas tree had candles on it—glowing in their light—simple but wonderful. We spent evenings listening to the radio, singing and taking photos. Uncle Kristian had a beautiful voice and he would sing, "Astri mi Astri" to me and I would cry. It was uncomplicated, warm and welcoming. We opened many gifts from them and also from their son Svein, who was in the Army stationed in Lapland at that time. We wished we had brought more, but we sent some things later from Germany—an electric mixer for Tante's waffles, chocolates and some personal things.

—*AT photo*

Greta Garten, right, in Bergen, Christmas 1960.

—*AT archives*

Author and Ketil Berg at the Bergen Christmas market near the fish pier.

Tante was amazed at the money we spent on things we wanted. I remember Greta and I buying Loden coats—designed in Austria, made in England, sold in Norway—and furry hats, as well as records. Greta loved clothes; no one in my lifetime has ever loved clothes as much as Greta, but she couldn't find clothing in Norway comparable to what she could find in San Francisco, her ideal. We still laugh about that. She has never changed.

On Christmas Eve we all went to church and also attended a Christmas play that the children of Follese presented. Ketil was very excited that evening, and while we watched the Christmas tableau, he leaned over and said, "Astri, see that angel. She is my girlfriend." I met a blushing angel after that Christmas play.

The Norwegian Christmas *Nisse*. The *Jul Neg*, the custom of putting out grains for the birds at Christmas, stems from ancient traditions.

Greta and I had seen a dried leg of something that had been sort of kicking around the kitchen all week, but we failed to appreciate that it was to be the *piéce de resistance* for Christmas dinner. Uncle Kristian thoughtfully told us that we might, perhaps, not like it and that it was OK if we didn't. We tried to like it, but our American throats resisted. Ketil beamed and asked if he could have our portions, which we happily gave him. He still remembers that Christmas when he got three portions of his favorite salted lamb.

Tante came out with five bowls of rice pudding, one of which contained an almond that signified good luck for the next year. She carefully put a bowl in front of me with an elfish smile and a *Vær så god* (here it is, enjoy). My bowl contained the almond, and I could have my wish come true. But it was too late—my wish had already come true.

Perhaps the traditional Christmas lamb was not to our taste, but that was of no consequence compared to the wonders of Tante's "magic table"(the table that just sort of appears laden with delicious foods) which each day had unlimited waffles, cakes, meats, preserves,

—AT photo

Uncle Kristian and Ketil Berg on Christmas Eve in Follese, 1960.

cheeses and coffee—now treasured in our memories for all our days like a beautiful photograph—and with a delightful fragrance and unexpected new and delicious tastes. This was coupled with Tante's loving eyes smiling down at us and enjoying our pleasure.

We made another trip into Bergen by ferry to have dinner with a woman named Gerda, a friend of Tante's, who had been my father's friend, perhaps his girlfriend, when he was young. She had had several husbands and now lived high above Bergen in a wonderful view home with a huge fireplace. I remember that we hardly saw her. She spent all of her time in the kitchen and would come out once in awhile, pat my black hair, give me a hug and say, *Oh, ja,*" and disappear again.

She had a handsome, somewhat younger husband, and an absolutely beautiful daughter with flaming red hair who was preparing to work in London at the Norway House. Dinner was memorable, but what I remember most was the luxury of the surroundings. She had gold and onyx place settings, beautiful old burnished silver, crystal and exquisite linens. Her table that night was to be one of the most beautiful in my lifetime and the food was wonderful. I never could forget that evening with Gerda and her family high on a hill above Bergen with the old beautiful Hanseatic city set beneath us, sparkling and glowing with twinkling lights against the snow, and the harbor beyond. The room glowed in a sort of soft rose candlelight from both the candles and light of the hearth. It made the china and silver almost come to life as it mirrored the warm glow of the people. Even today I feel warm and happy when I think of this wonderful evening with the beauty of family, friends and food in this lovely setting filled with love and fond memories of my father. My aunt looked so lovely and content that evening.

SKUDENESHAVN

THROUGHOUT THE TRIP I kept washing my hair hoping to get the awful black out, and I think Tante and Uncle Kristian thought their niece was a bit strange and went through life with rollers and wet hair. After the holiday we were to return to Germany, but first we went to my father's home in Skudenes on the island of Karmøy by overnight ferry. My Tante had arranged this by telephone, which was very complicated as one had to find a phone, then leave a message at the post office in Skudenes and then be at home at a prearranged time for the caller to find the person who made the call. It took several days.

We went by overnight ferry to Kopervik and then by bus to Skudeneshavn. We were able to spend only a half-day there with my Great Uncle Kristoffer Hansen, and he walked us around the town. He also showed me my father's home across the little harbor and I was breathless with excitement to see it for the first time. I also met a man in 1960 who had been with my father when he died, and he told me the story of that fateful day. He told me of my father's last minutes with him in a Brooklyn-New Bedford-Norwegian accent.

I remember the very old white houses in the Søregate, the historic section of town on a hill, set right up into the rock. We walked the narrow lanes and people would come outside dressed in their beautiful sweaters and greet us. My uncle seemed to know everyone, and many had known my father. I saw children playing in the narrow lanes with their sweaters and colorful hats, pink cheeks, the bluest eyes, and smiles that would cheer Scrooge himself. They were as beautiful as today's children in Norway still are. The only negative I could see among these uniformly attractive people was the general bad condition of their teeth, perhaps from deprivation during the war years. Today the teeth are fine because of better food and care.

On that day I promised myself I would come back and live in that wonderful village in one of those white houses in the Søregate—and I did, almost thirty-eight years later. It did not disappoint me and was worth the wait. I was to live in one of those antique houses for several months while I interviewed people for this book and experienced and researched Norwegian culture. My little house was in the back of one of the oft-photographed white antique great houses and set into the rock. It was very old and still had all of the original wood and charm and had been thoughtfully furnished with Norwegian antiques and memorabilia by the delightful owner, Randi Wareberg. It even has a pot-bellied stove. My son and other family members have since stayed there on nostalgic trips home to Norway. There was and is magic in that town.

RETURNING TO GERMANY

GRETA AND I WENT ON TO KRISTIANSAND to take the ferry to Denmark and stayed overnight in a hotel near the ferry. The hotel had a sign in the room that said Nelson Rockefeller had stayed there when his son married a young woman from Kristiansand. Getting back to Copenhagen to pick up the car became a problem as the sea was too rough for us to cross over on the ferry, so we elected to go by train back to Oslo and then on to Copenhagen, which was devastating to our budget. We dined in a very old restaurant near the palace and stayed again at the Viking Hotel near the train station. Then it was on to Copenhagen where we picked up the car and drove to Odense to see the home of Hans Christian Andersen—where we bought too much Danish pastry.

In those days in Europe it was rare for women to drive, but we got used to people staring at us or sometimes honking their horns at us, as well as truck drivers looking at us in fearful amazement. We stayed overnight in Bremerhaven, Germany, at a military guesthouse where we were entitled to stay because of our officer status as teachers. We dined alone on "C rations"—which we always carried in the car—for New Year's Eve, as we were just about out of money. There were no credit cards in those days.

We watched the fireworks from our window as the Germans welcomed the New Year of 1961 and we felt quite lonely after this memorable trip. We had to get back to Mannheim, but with gas at ten cents a gallon on military bases and with two jerry cans filled with gas in the car, we would make it fine. And we did. Once back at the BOQ, we began a regimen of canned diet drinks to counteract our days of eating while celebrating a Norwegian Christmas. "That was our best Christmas ever," says Greta, all these years later remembering the family no longer there. I echo that.

That Christmas I started to learn what it meant to be a Norwegian, and I felt close to my father and his roots. I learned about family love, caring, and my heritage. I felt it was a gift from my father and that he had somehow reached out to me to help me achieve my lifelong desire. I really went home that Christmas of 1960. It was a feeling that has lived with me throughout my life. I made a return trip in 2001, but as the bus entered Bergen my eyes were too filled with tears to really appreciate the city. My aunt and uncle were gone now. Bergen without them was just another lovely city.

And while I was experiencing "home in Norway" in 1960, many Norwegians were settling in my old hometown and experiencing . . . New Bedford, *Amerika*!

Legacy & Folklore

THE *BUNAD*

NORWEGIAN PAPER DOLLS
WITH VARIOUS *BUNAD*

THE *BUNAD*, a beautiful ethnic dress designed in many colors, textures and styles, designates the wearer's birthplace and is worn exclusively by Norwegians on special occasions. A woman may have a *bunad* from her town, kommune and district. They are very different and could almost be from different countries yet come from within a small area.

Norwegian women and a growing number of men often have a *bunad* that is inherited. They can also buy a *bunad* or make one if they follow the set rules accordingly. The *bunad* is worn with national pride and was part of a new national identity when Norway was finally free from Sweden and Denmark and had her own King. This time, also known as the "Romantic period," gave birth to many new *bunads* designed and created by local folk.

The name is based on the word *"kleddebunad,"* meaning local dress. According to Leif Meling, Norwegian journalist, *"Bunad* comes from

257

bu, and *bu* is the place where you live or where your home is. So when you wear the *bunad* today, you mean to tell people where you come from. The word *bunad* can be traced all the way back to the Vikings and the Snorre Saga. Sometimes a community wants to create a new *bunad* as Karmøy did in the 1980s. They had to apply to the board of *bunad* to be allowed to use a certain pattern and call it *bunad*."

Many *bunad* were based on designs of earlier centuries. *Bunad* materials must be local to be authentic and there are different versions of the costume for Sundays and religious holidays and everyday use. It is important to be careful to wear the right type of *bunad* or use the right accessories for each occasion. A *bunad* based on everyday clothes should not be worn for a formal occasion, or vice versa. Sample occasions to wear a *bunad* are: confirmations, baptisms, weddings, Christmas Eve, the 17th of May, audiences with the king, special events such as birthdays and anniversaries, and formal dinners. Headwear was an important part of this traditional folk costume and in many districts indicated whether the wearer was married or not. Silver jewelry is not as traditional and used more on today's *bunad*.

Some people have several *bunad*, not because they collect them but because they grew and their *bunad* didn't. It is a mark of pride for a woman to wear the same *bunad* for many years but there are many of us who have not worn it since our youth. The men's *bunad* is masculine, handsome and closely related in color and design throughout Norway. The shirt is especially attractive. I personally would like to see more men wear their *bunad*. Wearing of the *bunad* makes any occasion more festive and lovely. It is a beautiful tradition well worth preserving.

Norwegian dolls in *bunad*.

Totally different Norwegian *bunad*.

12

~

The Language Whirlpool

—New Bedford Standard-Times staff photo,
courtesy of the John F. Kennedy Museum, Boston

Congressman John F. Kennedy, campaigning for the U.S. Senate, visits a New Bedford fishing boat in 1952. He learned first-hand, as did many emigrants, that words do not always mean what the speaker intends. As president in his *"Ich Bin Ein Berliner"* speech, *"Berliner"* was meant to refer to the people of Berlin, but to many German ears it meant a local form of doughnut.

~

Language was an obstacle for the Norwegian emigrant but an endearing quality to those who heard them speak. Americans generally found the Norwegian accent to be charming and melodious, but the Norwegian trying to communicate and be "American" found it to be a barrier, and for succeeding generations it often was an embarrassment. A fisherman's daughter in Fairhaven, Barbara Simonsen Medhaug, spoke of her childhood days when she would come home from school, and her mother would speak to her in Norwegian. She would answer, "Speak English. Speak regular. I don't want to hear that!"

EARLY MEMORIES

I remember as a child sitting in overly warm rooms with many relatives making sounds I couldn't understand. Occasionally they would come over to me, give me a hug or a kiss and say, "I don't understand why you don't speak Norwegian," and then continue speaking Norwegian and shaking their heads.

They had this special way of inhaling a short breath and letting it out with a "*Ja*," which seemed to show compassion or understanding. That sound displayed feeling, empathy and emotion. It was a warm, friendly and loving sound. I loved it.

No one volunteered to teach my brother or me this language with its many musical sounds. We learned to say the Norwegian equivalent of "I love you," "Merry Christmas," and "Thank you," but that was about all, and Momma taught us that. She also taught us to count in the Norwegian she had learned from my father. In fact, any Norwegian she knew, which was minimal and mostly mispronounced, she taught us. She would sing Norwegian songs while playing the piano and I remember her tears because they were songs she had sung with my father while he played his accordion.

THE EMIGRANT DILEMMA

It seemed not to matter how many years Norwegians lived in America; they retained their accents and would seamlessly go from one language into another or mix the words together. That is still heard in Norway today—Norwegian mixed with American words, especially slang words. I remember that Norwegians loved to sing and would memorize the songs as they heard them in English. A Norwegian friend in my adult years would sing "Old Cape Cod," with Norwegian-accented English and words he thought were English. It was delightful.

Henry Pedersen, formerly of New Bedford, says he really didn't notice his Norwegian father's and Swedish mother's accents until one day when he brought home his fiancée, who was of Norwegian heritage. She mentioned that his parents had such charming accents. "What accents?" he wondered. "They don't have accents." Then for the first time in his life he really heard their accents. He also recalls that they always pronounced his name as if it had a "d" in the middle—"Hendri," rather than "Henry."

AN AMERICAN IN NORWAY

THE NORWEGIAN LANGUAGE is difficult to pronounce, and Norwegians, like the French, can be very fussy about pronunciation. I learned German very quickly in Germany, as I sought out people who did not speak English, so I had to speak German. Because the people there were so good about letting foreigners try to speak their language, we were permitted to make mistakes. They encouraged us to try and didn't correct every word. As long as they understood, they were satisfied and eventually our German improved. Not so in Norway. Norwegians are not as accustomed to hearing people try to speak their language, as are the Germans or the Americans.

There are Norwegian sounds that are almost impossible for the American tongue—three distinct "eu" sounds that originate somewhere behind the bridge of the nose—and, in addition, there is a cadence and singsong, lilting quality that must be maintained. To make these problems even more difficult, there are two distinct "official" languages in Norway—*Bokmål* and *Nynorsk*. There is also one more rarely used called *Riksmål*, the kingdom's language. According to Ellen Piatowski, an active Sons of Norway leader in Massachusetts, "*Bokmål* is 'book talk'; that is, educated or city talk. *Nynorsk*— new Norwegian—is more like the rural dialects or *Landsmål*, the country talk. *Nynorsk* is being heavily promoted as the 'true' Norwegian language and the least Danish. Both languages are still used. The debates on this issue have heatedly gone on for years. Many of the TV shows that are in *Nynorsk* have *Bokmal* subtitles. I won't even get in to *Riksmål*, the kingdom's language, because it is rarely used anymore, although most people would understand it."

Each town, island, and city is likely to have a dialect or variation in pronunciation and usage. I bought a Norwegian language book one day, and a man from the south of Norway decided to help me learn the language. But he got frustrated, saying the book had the wrong pronunciation, and we gave up. He spoke with his own regional accent, and the book guide was the standard TV Norwegian as spoken in Oslo.

Returning from Norway a few years ago, after hearing Karmøy-Norwegian for several months and beginning to really understand it, I was on a train traveling into London from the airport when I heard a group talking in a language I had never heard. Curious, I asked the woman next to me if she knew what language they were speaking. "Norwegian," she replied, "from the Telemark region." It was totally different than any Norwegian I had ever heard, especially the Norwegian on Karmøy, which is considered very thick by those not from that area.

Southern Norwegian is more akin to the flat Danish, compared to the melodious and "easy on the ear" language of Southwest Norway, or the harder Oslo dialect, which is more akin to Swedish. So which language, which inflection, which pronunciation, which of the "eu" sounds is appropriate? That depends on whom you ask and where you are asking. I am resigned to the fact, after visiting Norway for long periods over the past four years, that I am now too old to learn the language. I can understand it and read some, but I cannot speak it. My tongue simply will not make some of the sounds that are necessary for understanding. I believe my problem has more to do with my limited short-term memory than with a lack of affinity for the language.

One cannot just attempt the language in Norway, as one will not be understood. One must say it perfectly and that is not likely after a certain age. When I see a short word that looks easy and then hear it and it becomes a long word with strange sounds, learning seems impossible. I said to a Norwegian friend one day that it is not that the language is hard; it's that Norwegians didn't spell words properly in the first place. You can imagine how popular that statement was!

Regrettably, I have given up on my quest to speak Norwegian and will be content with understanding a conversation and reading it a bit.

NORWEGIANS IN AMERICA

MANY NEW NORWEGIAN EMIGRANTS frequently found themselves in difficulty when speaking English. They would use the wrong word and when it had some sort of sexual innuendo, they were very embarrassed. Norwegians do not joke about sex as Americans so often do; there is no double entendre in Norway, so when they mispronounced a word and found themselves in that quagmire, as most of us have experienced in other countries when we mistook one word for another, they were mortified.

One such story comes from a retired fisherman, now in Norway, when he recalled an embarrassing afternoon many years ago with his mother.

"When we lived in New Jersey we would sometimes go out to dinner with the family. One day we were to go into a restaurant and my mother, who was a 'take charge' kind of person, went into the restaurant with me first, while the others parked the car. She planned to make all the arrangements with the headwaiter before the others came in. Now my mother spoke both English and Norwegian, but she would often speak a little of both and sometimes would mix it all up together and didn't realize she was doing it. The head-waiter welcomed her and asked if he could help. She answered: 'Yes, I would like to have a big table in the corner for *Sechs*." (*Sechs* means six and is pronounced sex.) He remembers that the headwaiter was a bit startled.

It is difficult for the Norwegian emigrant to pronounce some of our sounds, and their alphabet has more letters than ours. Our "th" is very diffi-cult for them and other Europeans. They, for instance, pronounce the "j" as "y" and have trouble with a double-l. As Henry Pedersen loves to tell audi-ences about his parents, "My father said it took twenty years to learn to say 'yelly,' and now they call it 'yam.'"

It is my prejudice, however, that a Norwegian accent is simply beautiful and I am not alone in this. One day I was coming out of a restaurant with a male Norwegian friend, and a woman came up and asked if he were Norwegian. He replied, "Yes, but I've been here for forty years." She replied, "Never lose that wonderful accent—it is so good to hear it." And it's doubtful that he ever will.

My son speaks fluent Swedish, having lived there for more than seven years. When he is in Norway, he speaks Swedish and is answered in Norwegian. Most of the languages of Scandinavia are much allied with the exception of Finnish, which is totally different and with a different root base. We might compare the languages of Scandinavia, outside of Finland, to an Australian speaking to someone from Mississippi, in the most difficult case, or a Bostonian speaking to someone from North Carolina in the simplest.

But if you are going to Norway, don't worry. English is taught in the schools and has become almost a second language there, virtually accent-free, perhaps slightly British and grammatically correct, except, to be sure, for the "j" and "y," and the American "r" and "th." Norwegian English often is more correct than the English spoken by many first-generation emigrant Americans. It is charming and pleasant to hear.

TOBIAS, TOM, THOMAS

"What's in a name?"

—William Shakespeare

SOME NORWEGIAN NAMES can be especially difficult to pronounce. Names such as Gunnbjorg, Ragnhild, Ingvild. Bjørn, Torleiv, Trygve, Gunleif and Hallvard are a great challenge for the American tongue. Often when Norwegians passed through Ellis Island, their names were changed inadvertently by the officials and some parts of the names were dropped alto-gether—sometimes because the official couldn't pronounce it.

Many emigrants gave their children names that sounded more American. One fisherman brought over two children who had Norwegian names, but his next two children were born in America and therefore were given American names. That was commonplace among Norwegians. Or they might give their children names that were common in both countries, such as Marie, John, Ellen or Alexander.

My brother was named after his Uncle Tobias, an old family name. Tobias was often called "Tom" in America, so my brother was named Thomas. His middle name was after his grandfather Sivert, who spelled it Severt in America for better pronunciation; so my brother became Thomas Severt, rather than the correct Norwegian, Tobias Sivert.

My father named me after Princess Astrid, who is the sister of the present king, and I was born within a few hours of King Harald. Astrid is a very old Norwegian name from the Viking years as well as a royal name. King Olaf II, the patron saint of Norway, was the son of Astrid of Upland and husband of Astrid, Princess of Sweden.

When pronounced "Ah'stree" (the "d" ending is often not pronounced in Norwegian and the "r" has a trill to it), it sounds very light and lovely. Pronounced "Ehh'-strid" in America, it is far less lovely. My mother and her family insisted on calling me "Ehh'-strid." I always loved to hear my name spoken by my Norwegian relatives as it felt like a caress and evoked memories of my father, but to my American friends it was often a source of ill humor. I was called asteroid, aspirin, ostrich and other unpleasant names, and then, of course, it was shortened as a nickname and that was even worse. People still ask me what kind of name it is. In fact, it wasn't until I lived in Germany that my name was at all recognized and taken for granted.

NORWEGIAN NAMING TRADITIONS AND CHANGES

I DIDN'T KNOW A LOT about Norwegian naming traditions, but I did know that my mother was concerned that she might not be legally married because so many in her husband's family had different family names. She could not understand that at all and hoped that Tollefsen was the correct one.

I knew that last names ending in "sen" were Norwegian, but also could be Danish. I knew that most Swedish names ended in "son." I also knew that in our family, my grandfather and his two brothers had different surnames. This custom did not pass down to my father's brothers, and I did not know why when I was a child, but now I realize it is because they lived in America. I also knew that some of my relatives gave two first names to their children and they called them by both just as though it were one long name, such as Tor Arne. My cousin Gunnar Wilhelm Berg was called "Gunnar Willie" by my father.

I also learned later that where Norwegians began their names with a "K," as in Kristian, Swedes and Danes used a "Ch." (Norwegians changed from a Ch when they became independent and wished to distinquish themselves as Norwegian. They took out the "Ch" in words and put in a "k.")

This all seemed very confusing, and later when I read Sigrid Undset's *"Kristin Lavransdatter"* in college, I learned that women, at least in the older days, used "datter" after their names to identify themselves, in this case, Kristin, the daughter of Lavrans. And I knew that some Norwegian names did not sound Norwegian at all and did not have a "sen" at the end. This name was often the farm name or the section of the town he/she came from.

I once asked a Norwegian friend about a man's last name, and he said to me: "Well, I don't know which name he is using." That totally confused me until I learned there were just traditions and no hard-and-fixed rules for Norwegian names until 1923 when a law stated that families had to have one last name, and it should be hereditary. This resulted in too many Olsens and Pedersens, so many chose other names.

Norwegian women once lost their last name upon marriage but today most keep it. The exception to all of these changing rules are those families who are very distinguished or traditionally wealthy. They have kept the same name through the centuries.

Names further changed when Norwegians emigrated because so many mistakes were made by the staff on Ellis Island. That is where many Norwegians got "son" in their name rather than "sen." The officials made them Swedes. Many misspellings occurred here also. Some of the names do not look like the names in Norway. Berta was now Bertha, and Pederssen became Peterson. Second and third names often disappeared from the immigration documents altogether.

What is the most important name? Most believe that the name given the infant at baptism is the real name of the person. During some of the early years it was one to three names, then one, and now, most recently, hyphenated names, such as Hannah-Amelia. I was born during the period of one name.

My great-grandfather's children followed the tradition of his last name for one boy, son of his first name for another boy, and the farm name for the other. My great-grandfather's name was Tobias Tolleivsen and he was born in the Høynes part of Skudeneshavn on Karmøy. He married Elen Gurine Sjursdatter. One of his sons, my grandfather, was named Sivert Tollefsen Høynes. Later he was called Severt Tollefsen in America and naturalized as such. He married Henriette Emilie Hanssen and they had ten children. My father was one of their ten children.

My grandfather had many siblings. One of them, Karl, took his father's first name for his last and was called Karl Tobiassen—Karl, son of Tobias.

Another brother took the name Høynes, the farm name, for his last name. In some emigrant families, Høynes was Americanized and spelled Hoynes, Hoines or Haines.

Others might do it a different way in Norway. We might have a man named Nils Davidsen Moe. He is Nils, son of David living on the farm Moe. If he moved from Moe he could use another farm name.

Hyphenating two first names is a newer custom, and old Norse names are also becoming popular again. These were discouraged prior to 1900 because of their heathen heritage.

Old Norse: Astrid = Ast (a god) + fridr (fair)

Is this all confusing enough? If you don't understand it, don't worry, as it is likely to change again in the next few years.

IN AMERICA

"Must a name mean something?" Alice asked doubtfully. "Of course it must," Humpty Dumpty said with a short laugh: "My name means the shape I am—and a good handsome shape it is, too. With a name like yours, you might be in any shape, almost."

—Lewis Carroll, "Through the Looking Glass"

WHEN WE THINK OF NEW BEDFORD'S waterfront during the whaling days, we recall names such as Moby Dick, Captain Ahab and other such characters created by Herman Melville. They are made-up names that seem real. But New Bedford has a group of twentieth-century seafaring men who are real but carry made-up names.

Historians will probably never point to the Norwegian men of New Bedford's "finest kind" and write about them using their real names, because most of them used names that not even their mothers would recognize. Although born Nils, Gunnar, Ole or Jon, they were not known by these names. These men who worked the fishing boats out of New Bedford with skills learned on their native shores of Norway were known by names created in Norway or New Bedford or in some cases inherited from their fathers.

New names often were chosen just to sound more American. Rasmus might become Ray, a Jens—Jimmy, or Magnus—Mike. Others followed in the tradition of the early Vikings with descriptive names that the Vikings had, such as Erik the Red, Harald the Fair-Haired, or Svein the Fork-Bearded. According to a July 11, 2003, New York Times article entitled, "Islands of Rocks and Mystery," the Orkney Islands, off the coast of Scotland and once inhabited by Vikings, have "a list of the present Queen's Norse ancestors.

Elizabeth II's dead relatives include Olaf the Quiet, Magnus Barelegs, Sigurd the Stout and even Thorfinn Skull-Splitter."

Naming patterns followed in this Viking tradition, and these nicknames added to the colorful folklore of the New Bedford waterfront from the mid-twenties through recent times. Although some men from all sections of Norway may have had nicknames, it was with the men (and sometimes women) from Karmøy that this Viking practice was most popular. And it was also in this area where the Vikings once dominated and the last Viking king died.

The fisherman's nickname might suggest an event in the man's life (an event he would most likely wish to forget) or the place he was from or had visited, or a personal characteristic he had. The names were not always kind, and teased in a way to serve as a reminder to the men of their foibles or characteristics.

FOLKLORE

ONE NAME STANDS OUT from the others: Sadie Ben. Many people have some memories or stories about Sadie Ben, who was a colorful character in the twenties and thirties and who frequented the waterfronts both of New York and New Bedford. He is most remembered for the origin of his name.

He was known as Ben and there was a woman named Sadie whom he knew in New York and trusted. One time when he was out to sea, she left with all his money and possessions—therefore the name. He had the reputation for not spending money, so for this event to happen was something the other fishermen would never let him forget. One of his relatives tells how he was so "cheap" that he refused to pay a cabby fifty cents for a ride to the dock, and another tells how vocal he was at the fish auction. People found him very humorous and likable.

But most stories about him are about his old clothes and his scallop bags. He was a wealthy man, but lived as though he had not a dime. He picked up his money from a trip and would put it in scallop bags and carry the bags on the bus to New York. He did not trust banks or people as a result of his earlier experience, so he carried his wealth with him. Sadie Ben belongs to history and family stories, but he is just one of the countless fishermen who had a colorful life and name.

According to an old Howard Roy column, "The Off Beat," in the Standard-Times, there was " 'Pontiac John' who loved Pontiacs and shipped them to Norway, or 'Mickey Mouse,' who it is said was called that because his voice was squeaky." It is also related by a relative that Mickey Mouse never seemed to sleep in the same bunk on board the boat more than once. Others confirm he was constantly moving from one place to another.

—*Simonsen-Medhaug archives*

"Scarface Jack" and his wife Pauline Simonsen in their senior years.

Roy wrote further about "'Scarface Jack' who had just that, and 'Burn-em-up-Olsen' who was a cook with the reputation of ruining the food he cooked. There was one Norwegian called 'Moon Man' who pedaled his bike at a mean pace to the harbor. When he arrived with a screaming stop at the boat, he threw the bike into the water. He was known to sit on the bow of the boat and stare at the moon."

Former New Bedford fisherman Aastein Aase, now a teacher in Norway, remembers: "The skipper on the *Dartmouth* was named 'Hurricane Axel,' but his real name was Aksel Naerland, a son of a farmer from Jaeren who ran away from home as a young boy, became a sailor, a farmhand in the Midwest and later a fisherman in New Bedford. He was named Hurricane Axel because he went out to fish whenever there was a hurricane warning, hoping to get top price for his scallops if he survived the trip. I met him quite casually several years later in Jaeren, where he had returned to live in a small cabin near the farm where he was born. He died shortly afterwards."

Aastein wrote about one of his relatives: "'Mickey Mouse' was my cousin. His name was Torger Tonnesen, owner and skipper of the *Brant*. He helped me start out as a fisherman, and I lived in his house in Fairhaven at the beginning of my stay from August 1958."

My uncle Magnus Thompsen was widowed and later married my Tante Ellen Gurie. He had a daughter, Margie, from his first marriage. Margie was a very candid and disarming person who loved a good joke, and she asked me to put this one in the book as she thought it was a great story about her father and his crew. Uncle Mike was called "Big-Ear Mike," because he had very obvious large ears and it is said he also had excellent hearing. He was the captain of one of the highliners, the *Edgartown*. He was well respected and known to be the man who found the biggest scallops.

—*AT photo*

Aastein Aase, a teacher at Sandnes High School, on a trip to New Bedford in the late nineties.

A crewmember told me that it had been a long hard trip on the *Edgartown*, and they were about to return home. The men were very tired but the skipper decided to save fuel and extend the trip a bit by sailing in the good breeze. So he went over to two crewmen, who were totally exhausted and resting, and told them to climb the mast and hoist the sail. That was the last thing they wanted to hear, so one of them looked at him and his ears and said: "We don't need to do that. There is a good breeze today. Just turn sideways. That will get us home "finest kind.""

THE WOMAN IN THE HAT

THERE IS ONE MORE NICKNAME that must be mentioned although it neither belongs to a Norwegian nor a man. However, this woman has been mentioned by many fisherman who held her in high esteem for her hard work, and because she was such a colorful person on the waterfront. It would be improper to leave "Fish Mary" out of this book.

I believe she was of Portuguese descent and lived in the North Fairhaven area. Most of us had heard of her because she walked in the parades and wore very decorative, albeit outlandish, hats. But the Norwegian community remembers her because of her hard work as a "lumper"—traditionally a man's job—on the boats.

One fishing captain mentioned that he always liked to have her as a lumper because she was dependable, really cleaned up the boat and worked very hard. She also would give him a Christmas tree from her back yard during the holidays. Lise Medhaug, a fisherman's daughter, remembers her as always talking to the girls and being very friendly. "Fish Mary" will be remembered for a long time on the New Bedford waterfront.

Many of the names have lost their meaning over the years or have been so modified that the true

—Lise Medhaug archives
"Fish Mary" in a photo taken in the early sixties by Lise Stol Medhaug.

origins have become obscured. Some cannot be printed, and other names have a different meaning according to who remembers the person concerned. It might be fun to guess the meanings.

"At present our only true names are nicknames."

—Henry David Thoreau, "Walking"

—*AT photo*

Typical Norwegian design over front
door of a Skudeneshavn house.

SOME NICKNAMES OF NORWEGIAN-NEW BEDFORD FISHERMEN IN MID-CENTURY, AS REMEMBERED FONDLY BY THEIR FRIENDS:

Balloon Bill: Karmøy man who had gained weight.

Big Andy: A large man from Southern Norway.

Big John: Father of Gunnar Gundersen and a large man.

Big-Ear Mike: Yes, he had them. It is also said that he had the best hearing of anyone anywhere. He was a dear uncle.

Brooklyn Bill: Lived in Brookyn. Was Dutch and a very good friend of Norwegians.

Bullassen: Entire family called by this name.

Bullxxxx Mike: Big talker from Haugesund.

Chicago, or Johnny the Gangster: He had traveled to Chicago.

Crazy Andy: Norwegian from Kristiansand.

Crazy Pete: From Karmøy.

Eddie Faen, Eddie the Devil (may care): A very nice man and a friend of my father. His own father had that name also.

Flat-nosed Mike: as named.

Hard-to-Port, also called Skakke Leo: He walked crookedly.

Hop-a-long: Henry Simonsen, because he moved quickly.

Hound Dog: unknown.

Kisteman (Norwegian for coffin maker): Johannes Wilhelmsen, who made coffins in Skudeneshavn.

Kopervik: Skipper born in Kopervik, Karmøy.

Kris Pase: Nickname same as his father. Would cry *"passere"* (pass by), from the rigging.

Little Jesus: Unknown derivation. (Lived at Mrs. Stone's boarding house.)

Liste Sam: Liste is an area in Norway fifty miles south of Stavanger.

Lola Jacob: Mother's name was Lola, so he was Jacob, son of Lola.

Long John: Was very tall.

Melke Skvetten: Cook who took all the cream off of the top of the milk (*melke*).

Mickey Mouse: Had a squeaky voice and changed bunks daily. Some say he changed his seat often at home and in the theater as well.

One-eye Lars: Yes, he did.

One-tooth Einer: (called *Einer med tanner* in Norwegian) From Hardanger, a popular man.

Portland Pete: Had visited Portland.

Red Tom: Had red hair and was from Kristiansand.

Reno: Taxi driver, a *Sørlending* (southerner) from Kristiansand.

Romer Shoal: He ran the boat aground on Romer Shoal.

Sadie Ben: A long story, as previously noted.

Scarface Jack: Yes, he had a bad scar on his face.

Silver Fox: Silver hair and a smooth fellow.

Sjokoladen: His mother had a sweet shop in Skudenes and sold chocolate.

The Acrobat: (Also called "The Jockey") He was in the circus when young and it is said he was also a Norwegian Laplander (Sami).

The Terrible Swede: Both father and son were called this. Swedish. Good men.

The Twins: Identical twin brothers from Kvinesdal, Norway.

The Viking: A handsome man who resembled a Norwegian magazine cover.

Wildwest: Unknown

Yokohama Louie: He fondly remembered his special visit to Yokohama.

13

In Homeport

Rosemaling designs.

Hardanger fiddle.

Traditional waffle maker.

Solje traditional brooch.

—*AT photo*

Part of the dining room of a second-generation Norwegian-American family.

*"The best is when the man tells you you've got a trip in the hold,
and you can hang the doors and go home."*

—*"Oil and Water,"* William MacLeish,
quoting a fisherman identified as "Oley" on the *Valkyrie*

I HAVE ASKED MYSELF MANY TIMES: What is the central core of Norwegian life and values? Is it still influenced by the Viking legacy? Is it a combination of rigorous church training from youth, pride in honesty, the accumulation of money, the *Janteloven, pendling,* the hundreds of years of control by a foreign power, the national search for an identity separate from other Scandinavians? Or is it all of these factors combined?

The more I got to know and experience Norwegians, the more I realized that the need to preserve their identity is more than love for their homeland. It is tied to belonging to a tradition of *pendling.* They live as Norwegians and carry on their own traditions because historically they have often returned and do not wish to have an interruption of lifestyle and values. That, I now believe, is the key to the preservation of cultural traditions, language, food and lifestyles. They subconsciously want and need to keep their intrinsic Norwegian identity as they may need it in Norway tomorrow if they go home. And "home" is the word many use to describe Norway.

One consistent trait about the Norwegian spirit is the willingness to work hard. The seafaring men and their families who came to Massachusetts brought this cultural trait with them as they sought wealth from the North Atlantic waters—wealth that had been there to be discovered. Money and security was the goal; money was the motivator. Many who saved their money became rich beyond their dreams; many who made no effort to save ended up impoverished, with memories of youth gone astray. All had adventure, all had great risk and loss, and none totally escaped the tragedy of losing friends, family and members of their gangs.

The great majority wanted families with wives, children and well-kept homes in which they could have pride. They wanted wives they could love, respect and trust—partners they knew would take care of the home and children when they were out to sea, which was often. They wanted women who could make decisions, who could act alone. They wanted attractive women who did not drink to excess and who would make their time at home very pleasant.

The great Norwegian playwright Henrik Ibsen describes the role of Norwegian women through Hjalmar's words in Act Three of "The Wild Duck":

"As a rule, I leave the everyday details of the household to her; for then I can take refuge in the parlor and give my mind to more important things."

Consequently the men married strong women who took in stride the risks and pains of a seaman's life. They did not want their women to complain, to worry or to whine. They looked for women who went on with their lives from day to day, tending to their children and their homes, and to them when they came home. They wanted wives whose social lives, like theirs, would revolve around their church, their friends and their Norwegian culture. They preferred to marry Norwegian women, or women who could adapt to their lifestyles. But they sometimes married women who were the daughters of emigrants from other northern lands who understood the adjustments of emigration, such as those from Sweden, Germany or Ireland.

The men who married into established American families participated more in the traditional American culture. But in the early years it was frowned upon to marry women other than Norwegian, as my mother quickly learned from my father's family. The men needed to be surrounded by people who understood them—and Norwegians understand the traits of their own people, including, sometimes, the stubbornness that has achieved some fame over the years.

> *"An emigration is possibly the loneliest experience a man can suffer. In a way it is not a country he has lost, but a home, or even just a part of a home, a room perhaps, or something in that room he has to leave behind."*
>
> —Paul Scott, "Jewel in the Crown"

Increasingly after the war, the men went back to Norway to search for brides and bring them back to America. The brides often came to America on the Norwegian American liner *Stavangerfjord*, with stars in their eyes as they passed the Karmøy-coppered Statue of Liberty. Often the new husband had prepared the way for her, with a newly furnished apartment complete with all that she needed. And all too often, the bride had little or no time to settle into her new home before her husband went out to sea. Not all women could adjust to living in this new country.

Ole Rolvaag addressed this issue in his novel about Norwegian emigrants, "Giants in the Earth," when he put this dilemma into seaman's terms: "You remember how it was in the Nordland (Norway). We had boats that we sailed to Lofoton in, big crafts that could stand all kinds of rough weather, if properly handled; and then there were the small boats that we used to use for home fishing. The last were just as fine and just as good for their own purposes as the other kind for others, but you couldn't exchange them; you couldn't sail to Lofoton with the small boats, nor fish at home with the larger ones. For you and me, life out here is nothing, but there may be others so constructed that they didn't fit into this life at all . . . She (your wife) has never felt at home here in America. There are some people, I know now, who never should emigrate, because you see, they can't take pleasure in that which is to come— they simply can't see it!"

ADJUSTMENT

SOME WOMEN DID NOT ADJUST to America and returned to Norway. Some had a difficult adjustment. Some may have felt the experience more exilic. One man who brought his wife over had planned all the living arrangements and was altogether proud of his accomplishment. He went out on his first trip after his wife was settled in, only to find her, upon his return, waiting for him with her bags packed for Norway. He persuaded her to give it another chance, and they eventually worked out a life together in New Bedford. Now living in Norway, she speaks of the Elim Baptist Church as being very important in her life at that time, and of how kind her American neighbors were to her when her husband was out to sea. Together they built a life in both America and Norway. Some simply went home to Norway. Others divorced.

One fisherman's fiancée came to New Bedford where she had an apartment and a car, but left her broken-hearted fisherman when she suddenly went back to Norway and eventually married another there. America apparently did not have what she wanted in life. Some wives returned to Norway because of family responsibilities there, but the majority stayed with their husbands and were by their sides as they followed the waters.

Norwegians as a group were not generally interested in the greater community activities in America unless the activities had something to do with fishing, and politics was of no interest unless it influenced their trade. If the government wanted something of them, they gave it willingly, no questions asked, no arguing about taxes. They simply did as they were told in the community and often at home. Even today many do not read the local newspaper. Their source of news is likely to be the church newsletter, a Norwegian newspaper printed here or in Norway, or perhaps an Internet site that carries Norwegian news and views.

They are not generally philanthropic except to their church and really are not interested in the social needs of the greater community except for groups that help with alcoholism. Their basic feeling was—and often still is—that everyone should take care of himself.

At home, although the men tended to be reserved and a bit impersonal with strangers, to their friends they may have resembled their famous Viking King Håkon, as described in "The Saga of Harald Hårfagre," as: "cheerful and friendly in conversation, playful and youthful in his ways, and much liked by the people."

Many men did help with the work around the house, and shopped with their wives and families when they came in from a trip. They liked quality, long-wearing goods, and big, comfortable cars, and would pay for what they wanted—no haggling. Most were uncomfortable discussing money. New Bedford car salesmen and other merchants who "saw them coming" would have no difficulty taking advantage of Norwegian fishermen who had not been here long.

Money was something to be earned and saved in the bank and often in minimal-interest savings accounts. Most resisted investing in anything beyond boats and houses. They did not like to take risks with money and certainly not in the stock market. On the other hand, paradoxically, some lost great amounts of money by gambling or by losing an uninsured vessel. They did not like to buy insurance in the early days—again, the idea of unearned money. They were loath to bargain about anything and they could be easily taken advantage of in business transactions. Money was to be earned, and there was something a bit uncomfortable about investment dividends. Cash was paid for goods, and credit was distrusted. Many, however, partnered with other fishermen, and trusted friends and relatives to buy boats with them. Sometimes such partnerships that were particularly successful were, surprisingly, with non-Norwegians.

THE FAMILY

"Father has promised to read with me; but he has never had time yet."

—Henrik Ibsen, "The Wild Duck"

MOST OF THE MEN INTERVIEWED expressed regret they were not close to their children because of their work at sea. When home, they often were too exhausted to spend much time with them. Some have related that they didn't know their children well and are glad that they now have the luxury of time for their grandchildren. Almost all said they could rely upon their wives to take good care of the family.

"The thing that holds the members of an emigration together is only their recollection of a mutually shared past."

—Paul Scott, "Jewel in the Crown"

In the sixties, the young Norwegian emigrants socialized with other fishermen and their families when they were home from a trip. They might meet on a Saturday night or Sunday afternoon at another family's home for a small

—*AT photo*

Mrs. Ivar Olsen shows Ann Arthur of Jaffrey, New Hampshire, how to set a Norwegian table for coffee.

party or an afternoon meal. While they were home, they generally spoke Norwegian, ate Norwegian-style foods, drank a lot of coffee, went to the Norwegian church and socialized with Norwegian friends. They lived generally in small Norwegian clusters throughout New Bedford, Fairhaven, Dartmouth, Acushnet and later Mattapoisett and South Dartmouth. One fisherman and his family might find a home in a neighborhood they liked, and others would look for similar places nearby.

A cluster of new houses in New Bedford's North End was known as "Piney Acres" and was very Norwegian, as was "Hamlet Homes," a subdivision in East Fairhaven, where many bought houses before they moved on to more expensive areas. Streets in the West End of New Bedford such as Union and Arnold had numerous Norwegian occupants clustered near the schools and around Buttonwood Park. These were nice middle-class neighborhoods from the thirties through the fifties. But the Norwegian affluence did not extend as far as Hawthorne Street, one of New Bedford's most elegant streets. The Norwegians favored safe, comfortable, tidy neighborhoods, near the sea if possible—no nonsense and practical.

Many Norwegians were scattered throughout Fairhaven, and some neighborhoods became largely Norwegian. There they had easy access to the piers and docks, Fort Phoenix for good walks, harbor views and swimming, tree-lined streets, good schools, parks, safety and comfort. That's where they built their churches and where they preferred their children to attend school. Fairhaven was smaller than New Bedford, and this made the transition easier for them. Generally the Karmøy people settled in Fairhaven, with other Norwegian emigrants moving into New Bedford and Dartmouth, but this was not a hard-and-fast rule. Often interviewees related that there was feeling among some Southern and Northern Norway emigrants that they were left out of the mainstream of settlement and activities, which were dominated by people from the island of Karmøy. There was some resentment on the part of both men and women concerning this issue, but the Karmøy people, who were in the majority, seemed unaware of their clannishness. One Norwegian skipper related that it was the opposite in Seattle where people from Karmøy

—AT photo

Liv Haines shares family memories from her
home in Fairhaven, Massachusetts.
Her Norwegian husband was owner and skipper
of a New Bedford dragger for many years and part
of the Norwegian resistance during the war.

were the new guys in town and felt a bit left out in the beginning. Norwegians simply were friendlier with those from their hometowns who spoke their dialect.

Generally the men from other parts of Norway were draggers, and the Karmøy men scallopers. But again, there were many exceptions. A number of boats were equipped to do both kinds of fishing. While the men were home from a trip, much of their time was spent on the boat—painting, repairing, and getting ready for the next trip. Life on the boat did not stop when they came in, especially for the skippers and the owners. There was the never-ending race to repair, supply and man the boats, and that race needed to be won before each trip.

Much of their decision-making at home was based on their experiences at sea. Typically a fisherman might say, "I only went to school until I was fourteen and have spent my life on the sea, but I know fishing and when there is water in the boat, I know we have a leak. So when the politicians in this town see a problem, why don't they know the cause? We do." Or, "I only know fishing, but I know my trade, and when there is a strong wind, I know we are in for a storm. So when a doctor sees all the signs for a disease, how come he doesn't know there is a bad time coming? Doesn't he know his trade? He is better educated than I am." And so forth.

I have found that the wisdom learned through this trade generally is sound, practical and astute. The more one talks to a fisherman, the more one sees that his life is guided by his occupation, both at sea and ashore.

PASSING DOWN THE TRADE

THE WIVES OFTEN SAID they had too little time with their husbands because of the men's total commitment to the boats. And as the sons began growing into manhood, the fathers could be counted on to suggest they might start thinking about going to sea. The Norwegian father tried to cultivate his son in the ways of the sea, but as the years went by in America, he did not press the issue as much. While some sons wanted nothing but a life on the sea and their own boat, many who were educated in America had higher educational goals. This was difficult for some of the fathers, as it was the tradition in Norway to undertake the father's profession. But the fishermen fathers adjusted to the new ways and were proud of their children—especially if their male offspring would at least try fishing. And many stayed with it, particularly the boat owners' sons who would inherit the business.

One father introduced his young son to fishing off New York at a young age. The son, Arnleif Jensen, recalls: "In 1929, when I was ten years old, Papa was captain of the fishing vessel *Mosquito*. He would go out to the Grand Banks, and other favorite spots of the commercial fishermen, and stay for about two weeks, or at least until he had filled the hold of the vessel. It was not a big vessel, probably about eighty feet in length—diesel but it also had sail. Mamma was apprehensive, but he convinced her there was no real danger. I remember him bringing me aboard and taking me down to the galley to meet the cook. The cook, wanting to make points with the captain, gave me a banana. I went up on deck to look around and eat the banana. Pretty soon the first mate comes to me with another banana. A bit later, the engineer comes and gives me a banana. By the end of the morning I had eaten seven bananas. I didn't care about bananas for many years after that.

"We left Fulton Street dockage, and proceeded down into lower New York Harbor, turned left around Brooklyn and headed for the Grand Banks. It wasn't until we passed the end of Manhattan that Papa had the sails raised. We used the sails if the wind was good, to conserve fuel. We were after bluefish. 'Blues' ran in huge schools in the Gulf Stream in those years, and by the summer they would have passed Cape Hatteras and New Jersey, and would be in the neighborhood of the Grand Banks. It took two days to get there.

"One time, I felt the tug on my line so I knew I had a fish, and started to pull it in. It was a big one and it was hard to pull, and there was a lot of line out. Pretty soon a crewman noticed and came to help pull it on board. It must have been over two feet long, and was flapping on the deck like mad. Boy, was I proud, and that night the cook made a special dish with it. About ten days out, our hold was full, the *Mosquito*'s railing was barely out of water, and it was time to head back to the Fulton Street fish market. It was a good trip for Papa and the crew. They were on shares—they got a percentage of the price of the bluefish that were sold at the market. For me, it was a great adventure, and I was anxious to get back home to tell Mamma and friends all about it. When my brother Alek went, instead of bananas, it was pears and I seem to remember that he wasn't very fond of pears after that."

The proud son of a fisherman, Ike Isaksen tells a story about his first time on board a fishing boat: "First trip, as I was leaving the harbor, I felt wonderful. My father had been promising to take me to sea for two years. We had fair winds, wind on stern—a great day. Then it got rough. I would have given anybody anything to throw me overboard. The first time I started to pick scallops, I had to shovel the shells and mess overboard. I started to shovel but had to throw up because it stunk. I was hoping for pity, but my father just said, 'Do the other side.' And now I think that was good."

"I'm on the sea! I'm on the sea! I am where I would ever be."

—Bryan Procter

Ike's cousin John remembers his own time being trained by his father: "After graduating from high school, I went fishing. Had it in my mind that I would go fishing all along. I felt that was what I wanted to do. It didn't go over too well with the teachers in the vocational school. They thought it was a waste of time. But I didn't know anything else. All the family was fishing. All my relatives were fishing here and in Norway. Everything was involved with boats. I love the sea. It's my life. I relax on it. When it is an angry sea—well, that comes with the territory. When there are really nice days you have to pay for it with the bad days. As long as you have a good boat and pay attention to it, you are OK.

"Father was training me to learn the engine, learn the running of the boat before I got to go into the pilothouse. One time we broke down, and I had to take the pump apart. It was a double-acting pump, and the check valves had worn out. I had to figure out how to get it to work. It took a flare-type fitting. The diameter was same as the bolt. So I cut the end off and it fit right inside and I almost had a new piece, spring-loaded. Told my father I had got it together. He said, 'That was a good job.' Boy, oh boy. It was like he had given me a million dollars—that was the ultimate for me! It was more than the star for me. We pass on our trade from generation to generation."

Another man who entered a totally different profession and whose father had owned several boats, said later in life, "I don't believe I realized it consciously at the time, but unconsciously, I knew that my father and I could never work together. We were too much alike, and both of us were too bull-headed. I believe that it would have been a disaster as I look back on it."

My mother as a widow, who had lost her Norwegian husband when his boat went down off Georges Bank, did everything she could to keep her only son, Tom Tollefsen, away from the docks and away from the influence of Norwegian men. Although he was raised a died-in-the-wool Yankee, he still made his living from the sea as a Merchant Marine and Naval officer and in many ways lived a Norwegian lifestyle without being aware if it. His father's influence, however remote, still somehow, perhaps genetically, influenced his way of life.

As a teen, Henry Pedersen, whose family came from Northern Norway and who became a minister, worked for his boat-owner father during his high school years. "I used to take some fish and scallops from the boat after it was

—*Ådland archives*

Magne Ådland with his boat in late fifties.

unloaded and sell them to make some money like other fishermen's sons. I would paint and scrape and help with the boat. Once when the fishermen went on strike, I helped unload the boats. One guy was so strong he could take the scallop dredge by the end and heave it up on the boat. They would easily catch the heavy cases of Coca Cola they were loading for a trip."

A very successful fishing entrepreneur, Roy Enoksen, whose father also came from Northern Norway, remembers when he began to learn the business at a young age. "I would get extra scallops from my father's boat and then sell them in the neighborhood." He went on to become one of the largest fleet owners in New Bedford.

It was understood in the greater community, sometimes erroneously, that New Bedford fishermen's sons were apt to become fishermen. So much so that when one Norwegian fishing family decided to adopt a child, the social worker was concerned that the child might not have freedom of choice as to his chosen profession. The family had to promise that the boy would be able to make his own decisions about his future and would not be pressured to become a fisherman. As it turned out, he became an executive in a maritime museum.

THE GIRLS

EVELYN OLDEN, daughter of a captain, remembers her time as a youth when she waited with her mother for her father's boat to come into port. That was always a special occasion for her. "I recall going down to the docks and jumping on the boat into my Dad's arms. It was great fun to go onboard and later get a Norwegian Longren candy bar at the Tonnessens' store near the docks, which was always a treat."

Even at a young age, the girls would welcome the men, and the boys would take a job with the boats. Both early roles prepared the children for their duties later in married life. The girls up to mid-century were prepared to be mothers, homemakers and good housewives for the future fishermen. Piety, motherhood and homemaking were taught as the three most important elements of life.

—*Tollefsen-Hoaglund archives*

First-generation Norwegian-American Carol-Anne Tollefsen weds Don Hoaglund in March, 1967. Proud father David and mother Marie Dahl Tollefsen stand to her right.

THE MARRIAGES

"Absence extinguishes small passions and increases great ones, as the wind will blow out a candle and blow in a fire."

—Duc de Francois LaRochefoucauld, 17th Century French writer

ONE COMMON DENOMINATOR in all of the interviews conducted with the fishermen and their wives was that men and women never discussed their personal lives and, unlike Americans, never referred to sex. One would almost assume that it was nonexistent, but the truth is quite the reverse. It is simply a subject that was and is not discussed. I think it is fair to say that the majority of men were loving and affectionate to their wives in private. They showed no affection in public, as was and is their way. But at home they were known to be adoring husbands who treasured their wives and made up for their long time away with physical passion and ardor. Every return was a reunion for many, and their marriages tended to remain strong because of this.

One Norwegian emigrant who fished in his youth in New Bedford, but went on to university degrees and management, worked in a distant state for many years and flew home several times a month to be with his wife and children in Massachusetts. He looks back on it now as quite natural and states, "It really kept my marriage alive. I was fortunate to marry a self-sufficient woman who could handle all the problems at home and her work. Coming home was always a honeymoon for us."

*"Viking gods, like the individuals who created them, were . . .
ardent and passionate. They displayed the qualities the Vikings
valued in themselves—anger, lust, humor, courage, strength, and
guile."*

—Yves Cohat, "The Vikings, Lords of the Seas"

Many wives would wait at the docks or out at Fort Phoenix for their men
coming back to port. They would meet the boats and pick up the men, their
checks and bring them both home. Sometimes the men would stop in a bar
for a good-bye drink with their gang and then come home. Sometimes that
was too long a wait for the wife, so she would then go out and bring him home
herself. Sometimes a caring friend would bring him home. If there was a
problem, it was most often related to drinking. Many Norwegian wives simply
took it for granted that if her husband was not home, he would be in the bar
with the gang and she would be able to find him there.

Some in the community found it strange that Norwegian wives would
meet the boat and take the check home with them. They did not know that
these wives often had to do this in order to pay their bills, because some
husbands drank up the check before they got home. Norwegian women had
learned from many generations of experience to handle this problem, and they
did. But, of course, many Norwegian wives met the boat simply because they
wanted to see their husbands and welcome them home.

"How much the wife is dearer than the bride."

—Lord Littleton

THE BATH

THESE VERY TIRED MEN had been at sea for many days without a bath, as
the boats had no such sanitary facilities until the latter part of the century.
They wore the clothes they had on when they left home. They were filthy
from the fish, wet decks, weather, and rubble brought up from the bottom of
the sea. My mother used to say that my father's clothes stood up alone when
he came home. The men hadn't shaved, washed or even taken their boots off
during this time. Today's fishermen have much better facilities, and cleanliness is not a problem any longer, but prior to 1975 or so, it was.

One Norwegian boat owner and skipper, Jens Isaksen, tells the tale of a
new crewmember in the fifties: "One day a young Norwegian who had been
a steward on a Norwegian ship came aboard with a white sheet, pillow and
pajamas. The crew couldn't believe what they were seeing! They slept on old,

—From: Martin Gjersvik estate, *"De som dro fra Karmøy til Amerika."* With permission.
A boat launching with Jens and Malene Isaksen, their daughter Jane, son Arne, Rasmus (Ray) Tonnessen, my Tante Ellen Thompsen and her husband Magnus (Mike) Thompsen.

dirty blankets, lived in crowded quarters and never washed. I had to let him know the ropes real fast."

The men were so filthy that some wives put showers just inside the cellar so their husbands could strip and take an initial shower there before coming upstairs for their long tub bath. The wives in the first half of the century would often say that the stink was unbearable and that their first job was to clean them up, throw the stiff, smelly clothes into the wash or trash and get the man into a tub.

The scallopers had a particular problem with their hands, even though they wore gloves. They had very rough hands from the knives, the scallop juices and sometimes the allergy to it, and the rocks and shells brought up from the bottom. No matter how many times a scalloper bathed or scrubbed his hands, he always looked out of place when he donned a suit. His hands and fingernails inevitably looked unclean.

In the tub, the husbands were often scrubbed by their wives and then left to soak off the dirt, along with the stress and fatigue of the trip. Then they would dress and perhaps eat or at least drink some coffee, and catch up on the activities and news of the week. This was often the personal time for the husband and wife, and the children might be cared for elsewhere, so that the parents could be alone together for a while before they had their family activities. Some husbands were said to sleep for twenty-four hours before they ventured out of the house. One wife said that sometimes the boat would come in late at night or very early in the morning, and she would get up and greet her husband, cook for him and get him cleaned up, even at three a.m.

ENJOYING NEW BEDFORD

Plans were made for their short days together and would always include a trip to the bank and some shopping and entertainment, and, of course, church for most. They would often eat at each other's homes, maybe have a party now and then or dine out at a restaurant. The entertainment might be a trip to Lincoln Park for the amusements, or in the summer, a picnic at the beach. Some would go to the races and others might drive to Brooklyn to visit friends and relatives.

Alf Isaksen, a retired former fisherman now in Norway, recalled his life in New Bedford. "I spent the whole five days with the family. Sometimes we took trips to New Hampshire or New Jersey or down to the Cape. We went to Mary's Pond, beaches, or to visit other people we knew—families with families, single with single. We had about five Norwegian families where we lived, plus all of my cousins, aunts and uncles. Always had something to do at the house." Norwegians sometimes brought the "Norwegian coffee table" with them from Norway, providing a favored place to sit, have coffee and talk. Such tables are about five inches higher than the American coffee table and very convenient for serving coffee and food or reading magazines. They are virtually impossible to find in America, but Norwegians find them highly desirable for comfort and family togetherness. Often they were laden with waffles, breads, cheeses and meats, but most of all coffee, for visits between husbands, wives and friends.

—*AT photo*

Typical New Bedford architecture in a neighborhood that once housed Norwegian fishermen.

The hours at home were precious, and for most fishing families these were the times to store and treasure for the days and years to come. The men listened to their wives and their tales of home life, but usually did not intrude into this territory. This realm belonged by common consent to the woman, and the men did not interfere; neither did the woman interfere with the activ-

—AT photo

The late Jakob Ostensen, a leader in the Masons and in the Fisherman's Union, with his wife at home in Dartmouth, 1996.

ities of the vessel, and if she did, she was subject to criticism from the community.

There were clearly defined roles and relationships, and one could easily get the impression that Norwegian men were very quiet and gentle, obedient and agreeable in manner. They acted this role at home, but it was not the whole picture. At sea, the opposite was true. There they acted with courage, steadfastness, speed, skill, stubbornness and daring.

Some men became Masons, as they would have been in Norway, and their wives gave time to the Salvation Army, as they would have done in Norway. A few participated in the events at school, but some parents were even shy about that because of their accents. Later generations were more active, because they came to America with better English skills taught to them in the Norwegian schools.

THE CLUB

AT TIMES IN THE HISTORY of the Norwegian-American community, the women formed social groups which gave them welcome opportunities to meet for coffee and share their experiences. Once a year they might plan a dinner party at an impressive restaurant, often out of town, so that they and their husbands might have a "dressy night out" with their friends. These parties were special to the community in the sixties, in particular, and the men and women still talk about those happy days.

The women also, at times, formed small private clubs, both in America and Norway, to give themselves a social outlet while their husbands were at sea. One still hears, "I have to go to club tonight." These clubs seem to be ad hoc clubs of uncertain tenure but with some lasting a lifetime. Norwegian women over many hundreds of years have had to learn to entertain themselves.

A variety of Norwegian ethnic groups, such as the Nordlyset Society of New Bedford and the Sons of Norway, have been formed in the New Bedford area. The Nordlyset Society was founded before the war years and was very active. The Sons of Norway, North Star Lodge, has been active for a number of years and emphasizes traditional Norwegian culture and holidays such as the Midsummer Night festival—also known as Saint Han's Night—which is a particularly memorable holiday, and a 17th of May program for children. On Saint Han's night, Norwegians meet together at a local beach, eat Norwegian foods and enjoy the large traditional bonfire in the sand. Throughout Norway, bonfires are blazing and people dancing by the shores on this beloved holiday.

The group that has survived the longest is Sons of Norway, in existence since 1971. Several members of my own family have served as president of this group, but in recent years the Sons of Norway has had problems finding leaders. The leadership problem became so difficult that for one term they elected a non-Norwegian president, but the last few years they been ably led by a Norwegian-American woman, Kirsten Bendiksen, whose Norwegian husband Reidar was once a fisherman but now has a marine-related manufacturing firm where they both work in Fairhaven.

Sometimes they had programs open to SON groups from other communities and therefore expanded their relationships and horizons. Their activities, which gave the at-home women in the mid-twentieth century a chance to build some leadership skills, were very important to the emigrants. Gunner Berg, formerly of Bergen, a retired newspaper compositor, my favorite cousin, and the inaugural president of SON, was to govern this group for five years and another cousin led it for several more years. He feels that it was and is "important for the Norwegian culture to have Norwegian-Americans get together on a social basis to talk and discuss mutual issues as well as have social programs and work for a common goal such as providing scholarships to local youth."

CHRISTMAS PARTIES

IN THE 1940S, the Nordlyset Society of New Bedford was responsible for the Christmas parties so fondly remembered today by youth of that day. They also sponsored banquets and dances for the adults. They assisted needy fishermen's families on occasion as well.

The large Christmas party for the Norwegian children of the community became a special memory for everyone who was lucky enough to attend. One man remembers the table groaning with food. I remember being asked to sing a song for which I would be given a doll, but I was too shy to sing in front of the group and my mother was quite upset with me.

Some remember dancing around the Christmas tree and others the Norwegian costumes. One Norwegian woman, the former Evelyn (Evie) Olden, recalls, "The Norwegian community hosted a Christmas fest where there was singing around the Christmas tree, followed by many Norwegian specialty dishes and cookies and cakes. This Christmas party helped to give

—*AT photo*

Sonja Sovik and Eli Syre with Norwegian artifacts at Euro Ship Store in 1996.

us children a Norwegian-American identity and helped keep some traditions alive."

This was often the only opportunity to meet people who were part of the general Norwegian community beyond the local church. Evie Olden says, "It was the only time that I remember meeting Norwegians in a social setting when I was young."

Christmas traditions from Norway were usually observed in America and included church services, special foods and the unwrapping of gifts on Christmas Eve. Christmas tended to be much more of a religious event for the Norwegian family, as well as a continuance of their ethnic traditions. Single or married men with families in Norway went back to Norway when possible to spend Christmas with the family. They traveled to New York to board a Norwegian liner termed the *Julebåt*, or Christmas boat, for this occasion and were laden with gifts from America for their waiting families and friends. This was a very special time in Norway—awaiting the return of their men on the *Julebåt*. Simon Vea, now living in Norway, spent his whole career in America without his family, and he returned to Norway each winter on the *Julebåt*.

MUSIC

NO ONE CAN OVERESTIMATE the power of music in the life of the Norwegian. In Norway, one sees choirs traveling from one town to another to sing or be part of music competitions—choirs of youth, adults and seniors; small and large singing groups traveling from one place to another to share their talents. When one is invited to dinner at a home in Norway, there is likely to be the after-dinner treat of wonderful family music. Beautiful songs sung either solo or in close harmony are often accompanied by piano, accordion or violin.

My Uncle Kristian in Norway, who was part of a choir that traveled to foreign countries, sang *"Astri mi Astri"* to me when I visited his home. It was my namesake song, and always it made me feel welcome and loved, and brought me to tears. I have two cousins, Svein and Ketil Berg in Norway, who are part of a men's singing group that wins national competitions each year. New Bedford is especially blessed with the beautiful voice of tenor Thomas Helgeland, who has brought the soul of Norway through serious music to Norwegian gatherings for many years. And on today's music scene in both Norway and America, there is Aleksander Hauge, who continues to bring the emigrants memories of their native land through his special folk music and resonant baritone voice.

Norway has been blessed with classical composers such as Edvard Grieg, and also with talented young musicians who sing in the folk, country, rock and jazz modes. Summer music festivals are held throughout the country. So it was quite natural for Norwegians to bring some of their music with them and to also adopt American music. Some came from Norway with fiddles, accordions, harmonicas and other instruments tucked into their trunks. Many took a special liking to what was known in the fifties as hillbilly music and that now, modified a bit, is called "country." Music of the fifties and early sixties is still popular among the men who returned to Norway. Some particularly like the music of Jim Reeves and others of his genre. When there was time, there were moments aboard the fishing boats that were filled with singing and, at times, with accordion and harmonica music. Norwegians have more than their share of good voices, and they often use their voices to express their love of their homeland.

THE LANGUAGE

THEIR LANGUAGE IN AMERICA was Norwegian in its many forms and dialects. English generally was learned from other Norwegians, especially in the earlier days. Their English was flavored with some Brooklynese, a bit of the New Bedford slang and pronunciation, and their Norwegian hometown

—*AT photo*

Norwegian-American women chat after the "Two Flags" concert at the Trinity Lutheran Church.

dialect. They spoke and speak in a lilting manner, which can be very pleasing to the American ear, but sometimes difficult to understand. It was very difficult for the emigrants to learn American spelling, and often, even forty or fifty years later, many cannot write and spell accurately. The accents, delightful as they were and are, often do not diminish with time and age when Norwegians marry Norwegians. Those who marry Americans speak more clearly and with the American rhythm. Some have been in America for seventy-five years or more and still have a lovely accent, even though they speak English all the time. In fact, the Norwegian who learns English in the schools in Norway is easier to understand and has little or no accent.

Spelling can be a real problem even today and can affect communication adversely. It is sad that the people of New Bedford missed an opportunity to weave these people into the fabric of the community when they arrived initially. It could have been easily accomplished by providing English workshops and instruction, and it would have made the wives more aware of the community and provided opportunities to meet people from diverse groups.

I had one fisherman friend whose English made people feel he was here on a vacation for the first time. When they asked him how long he had been in America, he would blush and say forty-three years. This being said, however, my prejudice is that English spoken by Norwegians is the most delightful and melodious accent I have ever heard, and I enjoy every moment listening to it.

THE HOMES

ONE OF THE TASKS that the husband often felt was his exclusive domain was the selection of a house. The man felt that job belonged to him and many a wife had a home totally furnished when she arrived in New Bedford. One

—David Tollefsen archives

Three generations of the Tollefsen family celebrate Pappa'sma's birthday in the fifties. Left to right are daughters-in-law Marie and Ragnhild, Pappa'sma (Emilie), grandson Gunnar Berg, sons and fishermen David and Hans, granddaughter Diane, and daughter Helene Tollefsen. The children are David's daughters.

fisherman, Karl Berg, kept his wife alone in Norway for more than five years without visiting her until he could accomplish this task. Another purchased a house in a neighborhood that was too distant from the core of Norwegian activity, and although his wife, more than sixty years later, still lives there, she persists in referring to the house as something she hated, but stayed in.

Norwegians are apt to live in the same neighborhood as their families, and they tend not to move very often. They live that way in Norway because of the family farm and the inherited land, but they do it also in America. More often than not in Norway there may be a grandmother, mother and father and children all within calling distance of each other.

More than one Norwegian fisherman has saved his money by living on his boat, so he could buy a house to set up as a home for his wife before she came over from Norway. When a husband decides he wishes his wife to leave Norway, he may well tell her to pack, sell the house, and come. In following the waters, there can be currents that prevent an easy course.

THE HOUSEHOLD

AS A RULE, furniture was bought in complete suites from the furniture store. Rarely were things bought from auctions, antique houses or in other less traditional ways. Unless the man had a wife from America, most homes would be furnished with matching suites of new furniture and artwork. The taste was more allied to that of other European immigrant groups than to more traditional American homes that were influenced by English taste. The more money a family had, the more "fancy" the house might become. This is also true in Norway. It is rare to see traditional Norwegian-styled furniture, antique or contemporary, in a Norwegian home. American furniture was highly prized.

There was a tendency to keep the same furniture over the years and sometimes the first pieces can still be seen today, lovingly cared for, dusted, scrubbed, vacuumed, maybe refurbished but still there. When a woman describes a sister Norwegian as a "woman who had three sets of furniture during her marriage," it sounds like a criticism rather than a compliment. Americans like more frequent change; Norwegians buy for life.

Dinnerware and linens are another matter. Generally much care goes into the kitchen of the Norwegian-American home because this is the most important room in the house to the woman. Women prize their Norwegian Porsgrund dishes, silver and linens, and many still sleep under their down comforters as they did in Norway. If they didn't have the money to bring these things with them when they came over, they would often return to Norway to select, purchase and bring them back when they had the money.

FOOD AND MORE FOOD

ALTHOUGH MUCH CARE is given to dishes, silver and linens, when there is a party, one rarely sees the hostess. She stays in the kitchen most of the time because food preparation is of paramount importance. At Norwegian dinner parties, the guest often entertains himself while the hostess works in the kitchen.

Another idiosyncrasy I experienced was at a party when the Norwegian guest couldn't understand why the hired housekeeper didn't eat with the guests. In fact he invited her to sit and eat although she was being paid to serve at the party.

The most popular ethnic dishes in Norway are just as popular in Norwegian-American homes in this country. The meat cakes, meatballs, stews, heavy potato dumplings, salted cured lamb and *lutefisk* are still highly prized. Fish balls, fishcakes and fish pudding are also treasured. In fact, each family feels it has the best recipe for these treasures as well as for waffles. Norwegian waffles are often heart-shaped and sweeter than American waffles. They are served hot, warm or cold with butter and lingonberries, which are similar to cranberries in taste. Other popular preserves are made from gooseberries and currants, strawberries and cherries. Lingonberries also are eaten with meat and are an especially delicious accompaniment to reindeer meat. Whale is eaten in Norway, but not, obviously, in Norwegian-American communities. There is also a pancake, very thin and large, called *pannekake*, that is a variety of a crepe. There are potato breads and other thin breads, known as *lefse*, as well as delicious round crackers and soft cheese with shrimp and ham. In Norway, one can buy *pannekake* filled with bacon at the local delicatessen. (Warning: This dish may lead you to think you have died and gone to *pannekake* heaven—it is that delicious!) *Krumkake*, which looks and tastes like an American ice cream sugar cone and is made on a special iron, is enjoyed frequently. Cheeses include Gjetost, Jarlsberg and others with high fat content and strong flavors. Gjetost tastes to the American like butterscotch. Most Norwegian foods are acquired tastes. The American generally loves the desserts, waffles and the grainy breads but has difficulties with some of the other foods. Cakes are filled with cream—heavy cream. Delicious, yes, but Norwegian food is a cholesterol nightmare. Norwegians today may eat more American-style food than Norwegian-Americans. But they dislike peanut butter almost universally and prefer not to eat anything sweet in the morning.

I once heard that each Norwegian woman is proud of her own recipe for meatballs. At one formal dinner in America, a woman gave out her recipe, so that everyone would cook in her style. Because she had been born in America, those born in Norway were quite insulted. Cooking is an opportunity for competition and pride. The *Janteloven* goes up in smoke, so to speak, on these occasions.

LATER GENERATIONS

THE LOVE OF NORWEGIAN FOOD often extends into the second and sometimes the third generation. Young Norwegian women were recently featured in the New Bedford Standard-Times, in a March 26, 2003, article entitled: "Setting a Norwegian Table."

One woman, Ann Nerbonne, expressed that her emigrant mother knew how to cook Norwegian foods only and that is what they ate throughout her years at home. She told Tyra Pacheco, the Standard-Times correspondent, that she now cooks American foods for her own children but intersperses them with Norwegian foods weekly. She pointed out: "I like the (Norwegian) food and I want to keep my heritage alive."

Grethe Berg explained in the same article that: "I like to bake. I would say my husband cooks more Norwegian food than I do. He likes to make waffles and *lefse*." She went on to explain that Norwegian food preparation is very labor-intensive. "You just don't whip up Norwegian food. It's time-consuming and just to make fish cakes is an all-day affair." The article explained that "she prepares fish several times a month, and she and her family visit her mother's house for traditional Norwegian fare pretty regularly."

Another first-generation Norwegian woman, Linda Olsen, explained that her mother "added more seasonings" to traditional foods (as did my own aunt) as "she discovered other ethnic foods and decided to borrow from other lands."

Norwegians and other groups in New Bedford were treated for many years to the celebrated Norwegian bakery, Midttun's. It was the finest bakery in the area, and a place where Norwegians could meet and talk. Everyone was saddened when the owner, a Norwegian, died. Midttun's was a place to get the wonderful rye breads, cream cakes, rolls, and other bakery products beloved by the Norwegian and baked to their style. It was never replaced, and after it closed the Norwegians did not have the bread they loved so much.

THE HUSBAND ONSHORE:
A FISH OUT OF WATER

"Those who live by the sea can hardly form a single thought of which the sea would not be part."

—Hermann Broch, "The Spell"

A NORWEGIAN HUSBAND ashore during the mid-twentieth century sometimes appeared as an awkward visitor when in his own house. He would almost always wear suspenders and suits, not sports clothes, and sometimes would wear an undershirt, suspenders and dress pants with dress shoes. His face was reddish and his hair often resistant to the comb. His hands were very rough and never, so it seemed to a child, clean.

Many a fisherman would do all he could to hide his hands when he went out. The hands were very strong from the constant use of the knife opening the scallops, and the fingers looked rather stubby and wide. It is always interesting to see a retired scalloper with his clean hands and fingers that look long and graceful.

He was generally a quiet man, who said little and seemed always to be drinking coffee and smoking a cigarette. He listed a bit, which was typical of a "seaman's walk." And when out of doors he almost always wore a hat that was tilted at an angle. The aroma of aftershave and fish surrounded him. I remember my uncles coming in and giving me a hug—their necks always had the smell of the boat. I remember that they had money in their pockets, and my eyes would pop when they would peel off the bills.

They would often end a conversation by saying, "Well, I'd better go to the boat, now." When they talked, it was often about the weather, and they listened to the radio to get the weather report. Even in retirement, the men take an extraordinary interest in weather reports and make most of their decisions based upon them.

When asked about their happy times, they showed their single attention to the boat by responding individually, but collectively:

> *"My happiest day was the day I bought the boat and the day I sold the boat."*
>
> —Saying of numerous fishermen.

They would welcome the cousins, but they preferred the children, it seemed, to play together outside, and they were not a big part of their lives. Often they would hand some money to the kids to buy something for themselves at the corner store. They were always a source of pennies and nickels for the kids, and the kids knew it. But in the later part of the century, they were more at home in sports clothes and showed more American influence in their hairstyle and general appearance.

Many men did not want to wear their Norwegian sweaters ashore because they felt it identified them too quickly. It would be difficult, however, for the New Bedford native not to recognize a Norwegian in a predominantly Portuguese community, so they might as well have worn their sweaters. They tried to blend in, but their hair, eyes and walk gave them away.

They may be compared to their famous King Håkon of Viking times as described in "The Saga of Harald Harfagre"—"a handsome man in appearance, well grown, tall and thin; but rather broad-shouldered."

THE WOMEN

THIS DESCRIPTION COULD ALSO APPLY to Norwegian women who were noted for their beauty, lovely skin and hair. Many Norwegians claim that the Viking men selected the loveliest women in whatever country they had invaded and brought them home to Norway. Some say that is why there are so many beautiful women in Norway today.

> *"Scandinavian women were universally respected; to them fell the domestic responsibilities and the management of the holding during the frequent absences of their husbands."*
>
> —Yves Cohat, "The Vikings, Lords of the Sea"

The women paid great attention to their husbands when they were home from a trip. My aunts were always dressed up finely and were made up beautifully with their hair especially pretty at that time. I recall that the wives were very protective and took care to give their men all the privacy they wanted. I also remember that their conversations did not often include their children. It seemed to this child that they lived in a very grown-up and different world.

To me, who lived with a widowed mother with no father or male figure around, it represented the world of men, and that was a world with which I was unfamiliar. So I would watch and note everything in my mind so that I would be more knowledgeable about these strange people. I was very shy around them and a bit afraid—to be honest, very afraid. It was fear of the unknown. It didn't help that they spoke in another language most of the time and that I didn't understand it. The images are very clear to me because they were the only images I had in those days of men and their lives at home. I never saw any affection between husbands and wives displayed at those homes, but I noticed how the men were the center of attention for their wives. The wives doted on them and did everything they could to make their time spent at home

—Marie Dahl Tollefsen archives

The lovely Marie Dahl, daughter of a fisherman, on Gerritsen Beach in Brooklyn in the early fifties. She was to marry fisherman David Tollefsen and raise four daughters in Fairhaven, MA.

pleasurable. That perplexed my young mind. I also remember clearly that my uncles would try to give me a big bear hug each time I visited and that scared me so much that I would stand on one side of the room and not go any further. They could not understand why I was so afraid and thought I was a bit hostile to them. They were very strange for me, living as I did in a woman-centered world, and also a curiosity. It took many years, too many years, to overcome this fear.

The late Margie (Margot) Gustafson, daughter of a Norwegian fishing captain, described the Norwegian woman as " . . . difficult to know. It's not that they are cold but they are very self-sufficient. They are not quick to accept someone into their family. Norwegian women are born with strength. The men lean very much on their wives. Women have the authority in the family. They had to carry on when the men were not there."

> "The Viking family was a remarkably tight unit. Everyone jealously guarded the family honor. Injury done to one family member would bear on all of it . . . Family ties gave security to an individual, not only to his or her siblings but also to that person's uncles, aunts and cousins—whole series of close and distant blood relatives. The family was a very strong nucleus, the most robust part of society."
>
> —Yves Cohat, "The Vikings, Lords of the Sea"

The wives are very much take-charge, decision-making women who are both independent and submissive at the same time. It has been said that the ideal Norwegian woman is very attractive to her husband, a good homemaker, cook, mother, wife and daughter. She trains the children to fear God and to go to church and she is also industrious, gracious and even-tempered. That is quite a lot to ask of anyone. But today's Norwegian woman has gone from the kitchen cabinet to the prime minister's cabinet and indeed the office of prime minister itself. The Norwegian woman both in Norway and in America often was put in charge of the family's finances. You will often hear in conversations with men that "I gave the check to the wife." Money is power, and many husbands gave them this power.

One skipper's daughter, now deceased, told this story which indeed gives an insight into the thoughts and role of Norwegian emigrant women: "One day I was sitting and talking with some Norwegian women at the dining room table, and one woman said she couldn't understand these American women and all this "woman's lib" nonsense. Every Norwegian woman knew it was a woman's duty to wait on her husband and to do everything for him and she just couldn't understand that type of American women's thinking and was dismayed by it. Then her husband walked in, a skipper just coming home from a trip, and she said: "Be nice, go into the kitchen, bring the coffee in and pour it for us and don't forget the cream, sugar and rolls."

One Norwegian-American woman views female expectations in this way: "Women did everything with their families. It was understood that a Norwegian woman would be attractive, a good mother and cook, a church-goer, good housekeeper and also be a bit sexy to her husband. Although it was not discussed, these were the givens about a Norwegian woman. Mother was a strong person. Her job was to take care of the home while her husband was away. She didn't worry: The sea was their life. We actually competed with each other on housewife skills in this community."

FINDING A BRIDE

MARRIAGES OF NORWEGIAN men and American women had mixed results. Marriages to women of other Northern European countries with similar traditions and religion were likely to be more successful. The men sometimes found a bride among the Norwegian daughters of fisherman in America or married in Norway. It was considered particularly desirable for the fisherman to marry a boat owner's daughter, and the daughters of "high-liners" (boats that consistently made money) were courted extensively.

It had been a tradition in Norway for seafaring men to scour the coast for brides. In fact, there was a belief that women from the South Coast of Norway near the Flekkefjord were the most beautiful. Seafarers liked to put into port there to meet these women, perhaps marry them and then bring them home. This is one of the ways people migrated to different areas of Norway, through marriage to a seafaring man. Most Norwegians can point to ancestors from other parts of Norway, and they are almost always women.

This also happened in the emigration to America. One Fairhaven Norwegian-American woman, Karin Hansen, whose father was Norwegian and whose mother was of Scandinavian descent, fell in love with a Norwegian fisherman who had emigrated to America. They married and decided to live in Norway. Her sister then married a Norwegian and did the same thing. Their father died in America, leaving the mother alone. So although she had no roots in Norway, she decided also to emigrate to Norway to be close to her daughters and grandchildren. Then the first daughter divorced and was left in somewhat of a quandary: "Where do I go now? My sister is here, my mother is here, but I am an American and my friends and home are in Fairhaven."

I posed the question to her mother: How did this happen? She answered with a dismayed look: "It all began with a Norwegian fishermen!" This situation will probably never be totally resolved to the satisfaction of everyone concerned, but is partially relieved by long trips to America and visits from Norwegian-American friends to Norway.

Some refer to these groups of people who live in one country and often return to another—or people who love both countries and go back and forth—as "transnational." This term partially applies to the Norwegian but it should be noted that their feelings for both countries are conflicted. They feel a part of both countries and have deep feelings for both flags. *"Pendlers"* is a better term for their situation. In many families, Norway is spoken of as "home."

DIVORCE

IN THE EARLIER DAYS, divorce happened only rarely and by mid-century it happened occasionally. Today, both in America and in Norway, it happens frequently. But these days it is different in that emigration is not the main factor, and the marriages are often between Norwegians and non-Norwegians.

Divorce did happen in the earlier years of migration to New Bedford, and the reasons were many. Adjustment to America and the problems of *pendling* were among the causes. And emigration issues made some of the divorces more complicated, particularly when children were involved.

A divorced Norwegian spouse might decide to return to Norway for a lengthy stay, and if the other spouse remarried and remained in America, the emigrant might find that upon his return he had lost the legal right to help raise his children.

One can only imagine the many complications emigrants faced when there was divorce. Children returning to Norway, or remarriage with more children in the new marriage—the possibilities are many.

And then there is "child-stealing," which is always a possibility and a fear according to one wife who said: "Every fisherman who had a Norwegian emigrant wife hoped and believed that she would still be there when he returned from the sea."

In one family there was a bitter divorce, with the American mother receiving custody of the three children. The father had made threats and then one day acted on them and took off with his eldest daughter—bringing her to Norway. The mother, after a period of time, was able to find the address of the house where her young daughter was living and secretly went there and brought the girl back to America. The mother did not press charges against the parties involved.

Doubtless there were many similar stories and complications for the emigrants, but most knew it was in their best interest to come to some kind of an understanding to keep their marriages intact. Most marriages did survive, and some flourished under difficult circumstances. Many marriages were able to overcome homesickness, the pull of the motherland, adjustment to a new country, long periods alone, a spouse's dangerous life at sea, drinking, and cultural clashes. The great majority were nurtured by their heritage and their church and thrived where they were planted.

A few did not, and perhaps would not have succeeded under optimal conditions. The parents most often went on to new lives. And among the children, I found many successful adults who had not let such traumatic events reshape their lives.

—*AT photo*

Norwegian and Norwegian-American women wear their *bunads* at a Norwegian music concert, "Two Flags," in 1999. Left to right: Karen Hansen, Sonja Sovik and Aaslaug Larsen.

THE STATUS OF NORWEGIAN WOMEN

"In 1965, nine out of ten mothers did not work. Today, nine out of ten mothers have jobs outside of the home.

In 1978, Norway enacted "Act no. 45 on Gender Equality." The act stated: "differential treatment of women and men is not permitted." Among other things, the act stipulated that women must be given equal pay, equal access to education, and established that forty percent of the members of all public bodies with more than four individuals must be women. The act is strictly enforced.

In the 1993 elections, both candidates for prime minister were women.

Between fifty-two and fifty-five percent of the students in Norway's universities are women."

—Gro Harlem Brundtland, former prime minister, Norway
Former director general, World Health Organization

THE 17TH OF MAY

NORWEGIANS CELEBRATE THEIR national holidays in America, even after being here for many generations. Norwegian Constitution Day, May 17, is the most important holiday for the Norwegian. In Norway, Brooklyn and Seattle, and in parts of the Midwest, it is celebrated with parades, flag-waving and much enthusiasm. New Bedford celebrated it very colorfully in 2001 with a waterfront ceremony, a children's parade, women and children in bunad, recognition from the local government of New Bedford as well as the governor and state legislature, a flag raising and reception by the city and later in the evening, a beautiful reception, concert, and Norwegian delicacies at the city's whaling museum. Often in the New Bedford area it is celebrated by a children's party at the Lutheran church.

One other artifact associated with the Norwegian is the family silver. Most of us who are from emigrant families have lovely silver. It is intricately wrought, beautifully crafted and very ornate. There are pieces of all descriptions for all dining occasions, and particularly for desserts and coffee, the national passion.

> *Have you ever attended a May 17th celebration held in this country by a group of Norwegian men and women? Have you watched their graceful dancing of the "hambo" with its quick steps and whirls, and then been amazed at the heavy stamping in perfect time as they danced the "Oslo-Rheinlaender"? Have you listened to their booming voices as they sang in their native tongue, their national anthem, — and then noticed big, stalwart fishermen taking their handkerchiefs surreptitiously from their pockets and wiping away tears?*

—Berg archives

Aletha Berg describes the 17th of May in a note.

300

HANDICRAFTS

In the New Bedford area, the women would meet at each other's homes for coffee and talk while their husbands were away, and while there they often knitted and crocheted beautiful and intricate hats, sweaters and gloves. There was much competition among the women related to their household skills, their handicraft ability, and the achievements of their husbands. The women often went to the Trinity Lutheran Church on a selected morning each week and chatted with the larger Norwegian community of women while they knitted, sewed and crocheted.

The Norwegian woman almost always has a knitting basket nearby filled with yarn and sewing to work on while she talks and drinks coffee. In Norway there are women in the malls who knit all day and take orders for their work. It is a national treasure to have this never-ending source of handiwork, and one can see the raw materials for such handicrafts offered for sale in shops in every town, no matter how small.

—AT photo

Norwegian hand-knits sell well at "Phoenix," a local Fairhaven store.

THE CHURCH

NORWEGIANS GROW UP IN A COUNTRY with a state religion, meaning that religion, school, and family values were most often totally integrated. It is a difficult concept for Americans to understand. The Lutheran faith was taught in the schools, and confirmation often coincided with graduation. Other religions were officially viewed as dissenters. The state supported the Lutheran faith through taxation, and consequently everyone supported the church through their money, although that has been modified to some degree today. The Lutheran Church, therefore, is the official church and its teachings to many shaped what being a Norwegian was all about. The emigrants who came to America longed for their church, because it gave them the comfort of familiarity, a chance to express their faith and also to meet others from their home country and make friends and associations. Consequently, as soon as enough people could afford to have their own congregation, a group formed a church.

Earliest services for the Norwegian community prior to 1943 were held at St. John's Lutheran Church, a German Lutheran Church. on Sunday afternoons and were organized for Swedish and Norwegians in the area by Swedish Lutheran pastors. In 1943, services were held in Norwegian and English at the Oxford Street Chapel, which was rented for services and meetings.

The Norwegians wanted their own church but an adequate and affordable design seemed to be a problem. The Standard-Times related that parishioner Ingolf Isaksen hit upon the idea of an L-shaped church, in which a curtain could separate the church services from the Sunday School and other activities. And so with this design, the Trinity Evangelical Lutheran Church was built and the first service with the Reverend Tor Aanestad from Norway was held on Christmas Day 1951. It was dedicated on New Year's Day, and three hundred parishioners could now be seated for worship. One fishing captain expressed his feelings for the new church by saying that he felt the same way as he did when he tied up his ship for the first time. The church members built a parsonage with their own hands next door to the church. The new church had both a Men's Club and a Ladies Aid Society, the latter founded in 1943.

There are many fond memories of the first Fairhaven church that was in essence Norwegian. The former organist, Gunnar Gundersen, remembers that, "the church first started in a small building called the Oxford Street Chapel and people remember the pot-bellied stove there. We built the Park Street Church in 1950, an L-shaped church and Pastor Johnnie Glad, a Lutheran minister from Norway, was our pastor after Pastor Aanestad.

—From a church note card

The Trinity Lutheran Church, built in large part by the Norwegian fishing families of the Greater New Bedford area.

Pastor Glad remembers: "As a member of the Lutheran Church that now is called Evangelical Lutheran Church in America, ELCA, I was serving a parish in Wisconsin, USA. While serving this parish I received the call to become pastor of Trinity Lutheran Church in Fairhaven."

Some feel, both clergy and members, that the style of worship in the early days of the church was more evangelical in nature and somewhat reflective of the *bedehus* (prayer house) in Norway. Over the years it became more liturgical and in keeping with the overall Lutheran Church world-wide.

Egil Ellingsen remembers the church in a personal way: "Family time together when I was in port was valuable and centered around our children. We were actively involved in Trinity Lutheran Church with Pastor Tor Aanestad and later Pastor Johnnie Glad. Sunday school, church services and daily vacation Bible schools were integral as we wanted our children to know the Savior, Jesus Christ."

And Janna Isaksen, who taught Sunday school for many years, remembers the church as a place where she could meet people and feel less lonely. Many women in particular remember the sewing circle as a lifesaver to them and a cure for their isolation when their husbands were at sea.

In the earlier days of the church, Norwegian was spoken predominantly but as the years passed and the church became more ethnically inclusive, this practice was modified. The Trinity Lutheran Church of today was built in the early sixties to accommodate the growing emigrant population and was funded with money from the parishioners led by the boat owners. This church building might be considered more formal by some and was designed in a mid-century "New England colonial-modern" style.

Today the church is composed of many ethnic groups, some former Catholics, and is inclusive in race and welcoming to those from other denominations in that it allows communion to all believers, according to one former minister. The Norwegian influence and atmosphere has become less, due to deaths and moves to other areas.

In the beginning, when the emigration was in full swing, this church was the acknowledged glue that kept the people together and helped them in their accommodation to living in America. The sacraments of baptism, communion, confirmation, marriage and death remain extremely important rites for the Norwegian and a time when they still come together as one body.

Confirmation is a very important rite of passage for the Norwegian youth and the family also. Lutheran confirmation is more than a ritual and has much deeper meaning than it would appear on the surface. It means that a young man or girl has accepted the principles of the church belief system and is now ready and able to participate in its life as a full member, such as taking the sacraments including communion, eventual marriage and the right to be buried in the church yard (Norway). The name of this new member is

—Lise Stol Medhaug archives

The Trinity Lutheran Church confirmation class, 1960. Front row:
Carol Anne Tollefsen, Ingrid Frostad, Bonnie Wilhelmsen, (unidentified),
Pastor Aanestad, Linda Risdal, Lise Stol, Mayfrid Bendiksen,
Mabel Bendiksen. Back row: David Tonnessen, Terje Tonnessen,
Kenneth Shervo, Dennis Jacobsen, Per Flem, Johan Gundersen,
(unidentified), (unidentified), Geir Tonnessen, Karl Thompsen, and
Severin Haines. The pastor must have stressed the "Golden Rule" for many in
this class were particularly helpful to me with this book. They included,
Carol Ann Tollefsen, Bonnie Wilhelmsen, Lise Stol, Linda Risdal,
Johan Gundersen and Severin Haines. Mabel Bendiksen went on to become
Miss Massachusetts later in the sixties.

inscribed in the permanent records of the church for posterity and genealogical research.

It also once meant on a practical basis that the boys and girls were ready to be self-supporting at ages fourteen or fifteen. Its meaning now has changed to a more social connotation. The rituals are still observed but the emphasis now, at least for the young people, is on the party and the gifts. However, it still means a relinquishing of childhood and an acceptance of a Christian life with more responsibility. It is the end of formal religious teaching and for too many the end of a church life altogether. It could be compared to the Jewish Bar Mitzvah in its symbolism. In Norway there is also a civil confirmation for non-believers where the young people can have a party but do not make a statement of faith.

Up until mid-century, confirmation also meant a gift of new clothes from the parents. This was often the final set of clothing given by the parents as the son and daughter were now considered adults. It was a rite of passage met with great expectations, and the "confirmation class" often became a source of identity and friendship over the years. Many people interviewed spoke of others as being a "member of my confirmation class" here and in Norway, young and old.

Some people in Norway still have confirmation class reunions and almost always there is a confirmation photo sitting proudly on the mantle with a daughter in a lovely white dress or the son in a new suit, a suit often brought on the passage to America.

The Sabbath has a special meaning in the life of most Norwegians. It is considered a day of rest and to most Norwegians in this emigration a day not to work in any way. Even among Norwegians who do not attend church, this tradition is very meaningful. Fishing boats always tried to be in port by Sunday, and Sunday was considered a family day to worship together, to have a special meal with the family or to invite members of the extended family or friends to dinner. This tradition is still usually kept, even in the face of the American more casual approach to Sunday.

THE MINISTER

WHEN THE BOATS WENT DOWN and men were lost, the skills of the minister as pastor and the community of friends cannot be overestimated. It happened too often to this group, and the minister especially in the earlier two churches had to be in touch with the waterfront, the families, and the ebb and tides of the seafaring life. His pastoring skills were sorely tested—often under unique conditions. Many parishioners speak lovingly of their former ministers, while others are happy that the newer modern way of looking at Christian life allows them, as some put it, to participate more in the world at large and not feel guilty about it. Some point to the wearing of lipstick, jewelry, dancing, smoking and drinking as the formally forbidden but now permitted practices.

One member, Barbara Simonsen Medhaug, described her love of the Trinity Lutheran Church with these words: "Our church is not a building. Our church is the people. It is our second family. I feel embraced by the church each Sunday and feel the love of the people there."

The membership of the church was also a lifesaver for those who came to the New Bedford area from other parts of Norway and didn't have connections here. It saved marriages, provided an outlet for the women, and most of all gave them an opportunity to meet and make new friends. Older women have said again and again how important this social group has been to their lives over the years.

The ministry of the Trinity Lutheran Church had been directed by their hierarchy to make the church more ethnically inclusive and indeed that was done with success. But to many it is still known as the Norwegian Church, and it is certainly a fact that the Norwegian community founded it, financed it and worked hard to keep it viable, as many in the community still do.

The Elim Baptist Church was predominantly Scandinavian in membership (Danish, Swedish, Norwegian and Finnish) and a member of the Baptist General Conference, founded by Swedish–Americans. It suffered because of a lack of understanding about the importance of socializing with friends. One new minister ordered the sewing group to disband, as such a gathering was not a "Christian activity." He never understood how painful that was for the women of his church, but he might have wondered later why so many families left and went to the Lutheran church where the women had a vital sewing group as a central activity.

COMPETITION

MOST WOMEN EXPECTED their husbands to become skippers and boat owners, and when the husband did not strive toward this goal, the wives could be disappointed. That sometimes was a factor in disputes, divorce or separation. Although divorce was rare even in the sixties and seventies, it happened occasionally and was generally related to alcohol, homesickness, an inability to adjust to a fisherman's life, or his lack of achievement. Onshore the wives were as competitive as husbands were offshore. To the American it is interesting that, although these emigrants lived very much by the laws of the *Janteloven*, they also were competitive. "Keeping up with the Johansens" was a reality in everyday life.

WHICH CULTURE?

SOME WERE ADAMANT in wishing their children to be Norwegian rather than American—wanting them to observe their traditional cultural values and beliefs. Consequently the relationships became most complicated. Husbands, wives, mothers and fathers lived in both America and Norway. Some siblings were here and others there; some had Norwegian citizenship; others had American papers. The children had mixed citizenship within one family depending on where they were born. There were Americans of American and Norwegian descent living in Norway, as well as Norwegians living in America. Children went back and forth, some staying, some returning. Some of the children were American citizens and returned to America as adults.

Some were American citizens and as adults lived in Norway. The family situations were convoluted but quite normal within the community.

On the island of Karmøy, it is said that just about every family had at least one relative in America and that in the early sixties some towns were without men. They were all-woman towns, and the post office became the lifeline to their husbands. One daughter, Marit Synnove Vea, now the public relations director for the island of Karmøy, and whose mother and siblings stayed in Norway, shared her memories: "We would go down to the post office and hope to see one of those red, white and blue envelopes in our box. Then we knew our father was alive, as of a week ago at least. We would bring that precious envelope home where mother would read the letter and share it with us all. Those were the most treasured moments, when we heard from our father. Those envelopes in the post office (and the enclosed checks) made our lives bearable."

My Norwegian cousins Tove and Alf Isaksen and their children lived in America until it was time for the children to go to school. They decided that they wanted to raise their family in the Norwegian culture and took them back to Norway. Today the mother and family are retired in Norway, and their two sons live in the Texas with advanced degrees from American and Norwegian universities. They feel they did "the right thing"—but they have to travel a long distance to see their boys and their grandchildren.

"LITTLE NORGE"

A NORWEGIAN EMIGRANT, Lise Stol Medhaug, who came to these shores when she was twelve and now lives in Norway, describes her teen years in New Bedford: "Little by little when I went to high school I started dating Norwegian boys. They were coming more and more to the city dreaming of big cars. Some of the boys I knew in Norway found their way over. I got a job

A welcome sign as seen throughout Norway.

at the drugstore, and I made more money because the Norwegians came in and ate there. I earned money and got over one hundred dollars a week in tips from the fishermen. I also got my driver's license, and Dad bought a Buick, which I drove. In my free time I went to Cape Cod to the beaches with friends—all Norske, of course. There were about a thousand Norwegian people in the area. They were all over. We called it 'Little Norge.' There were many weddings celebrated at New Bedford Hotel where our Vikings married some from here and some from Norway, and there were showers and baby showers a year later."

HUSBAND AND WIFE—AND MOTHER-IN-LAW

"I couldn't bring myself to go into the house because I knew how things would go. One thing was clear to me: My mother-in-law was in charge—she didn't have to ask anyone."

—Gro Holm, "Life on the Løstøl Farm"

THE MOTHER-IN-LAW in Norway often has a different and much stronger role in the family as an adviser and helper as well as grandparent, compared to the traditional American family. It is very common in Norway for the mother-in-law to actively help to raise her grandchildren. One can still see it today. When I call or visit friends, they are almost always with their grandchildren and even in my own family, I saw this several times among my cousins. The mother-in-law, the grandmother, has a strong role in imparting values, lifestyle and often childcare. Although this is understood among Norwegian women, American women found it to be a problem—an intrusion upon their role. A mother-in-law might feel in cases when her son married an American that she had to protect her son from American lifestyles, or must make his American bride into an ideal Norwegian wife.

Norway is a country of strong, well-meaning women, but that can backfire on American women who are also determined and feel, justifiably, that if one emigrates here and marries, one should try to understand, embrace or at least tolerate American ways.

Sometimes a blending of cultures just didn't happen—as was the experience of one American wife. She described her mother-in-law as basically one who would not let her live her own life with her husband and who was determined that they live a more Norwegian life with all of its cultural mores and sentiments. She described her married life as destined for failure because of the constant criticism, cultural misunderstandings and personal problems. Both were determined strong women who were deeply rooted in their respective cultures which they both held in high esteem. The marriage failed for many reasons and in the end there was deep sadness on many levels.

The mother-in-law experience was not unpleasant for all families, especially if the American woman accommodated herself to the ways of her Norwegian mother-in-law—as in this account, related by a now deceased Irish-American widow: "I loved my mother-in-law very much, and even went to live in Norway for a few years. She was good to us. I had no complaints."

The Norwegian mother-in-law was most often accepted as just doing her job when the husband and wife were both Norwegian.

On balance I feel that the brides of recent European ancestry had an easier time with the Norwegian mother-in-law than established American women, who are more independent and set the American tradition as their template.

I have also noticed that when a Norwegian daughter marries an American from a different ethnic background that often this man is encouraged to live in a Norwegian style, encouraged also by the mother-in-law. They, in some cases, also work in a Norwegian profession. The Norwegian lifestyle often perseveres even when the non-Norwegian spouse is a husband.

CULTURE FROZEN IN TIME

LATER IN THE CENTURY the role of women began to change in Norway, and more quickly there than for Norwegians living in America. Here women's lives remained insulated by the choices they had made regarding friends and church. Many of the emigrant's ways became frozen in time, even out-of-step with those in their home country. In their mind's eye they saw a pre-war Norway or a Norway of the first post-war years, or a Norway of their parents' memories. Norway changed dramatically in the 1970s and was quite a shock to some who returned after a long absence. They never found "my Norway" again.

This is not a condition exclusive to Norwegian emigrants but perhaps a bit more puzzling because of the dramatic changes in Norway. I took my dear stepfather, Joseph Boffoli, to visit his hometown in Italy in the 1990s, and he could not find anything that reminded him of the Italy he knew in his youth. He remembered colorful costumes, dancing, music, primitive farmhouses and horse-drawn transportation. On our trip together, he saw up-to-date housing and lifestyles, and that was bewildering to him at first. The only things in Italy that reminded him of his early years were the vineyards, figs and the olive trees.

Many emigrants to America lived in all-Norwegian environments virtually untainted by American lifestyles and with few, if any, non-Norwegian-American friends. This is true even today, after several generations. The great majority number only Norwegians or Norwegian-Americans as friends, unless their children have married into another culture.

—Johansen archives.

Stanley Johansen in the Air Force in the fifties. He followed his family into the fishing world for his whole career.

In many cases they have lived several generations in a pluralistic society while adhering to values dating back to the time they emigrated. Norway has changed; many of them haven't. Few Norwegian women took any courses other than English or household arts and simply did not mingle very much with those outside their own culture.

Although the Norwegian lifestyle is the choice of the majority of Norwegian-Americans in the New Bedford area, not every family lived that way. One successful emigrant family forged a lifestyle accommodating what they regard as the best of Norwegian and American values and qualities. They have as many American as Norwegian friends, and would like to think they opened new cultural horizons when they became involved with their children's school activities, particularly sports. Although they kept a Norwegian home and taught the language to their children, they also integrated into the greater community and in later years moved away from the area's Norwegian enclaves. The wife, who is married to a fishing captain but works outside the home, says, "I liked the Norwegians, and we have Norway and its customs in common, but not always the same interests. Therefore we were drawn to Americans."

This fishing captain's wife says she was "curious" and wanted to learn more about the people of her adopted country. As a result of her outreach, her English skills and those of her husband are highly developed, and virtually accent-free. This is the natural outcome of intellectually curious people who have daily English practice with American friends. Highly developed English skills are also common among Norwegian men who married into American families.

Sports and American pastimes lured them out of the exclusively Norwegian lifestyle and into a blending of cultures without sacrificing their Norwegian identity. Both summer and winter sports are very important to the Norwegian, in America as well as in Norway. Sports and music are often favorite pastimes.

MORE ABOUT WOMEN

KARMØY HISTORIAN PEDER ELIASEN points out: "Women (in Norway) came into their own in the seventies and eighties and before then were not as well educated as they are today. When conditions improved they got into the picture and participated. Our prime minister was a woman (Gro Harlem

—Ådland archives

Emma and Nils Ådland back in
Norway after many years in America.

Brundtland). The women participated in
building up the country. Women's
equality and rise to power in Norway
came quickly without mishap or much
debate."

Norwegian women were ideally
suited to this role by independence and
experience over the centuries. As one
Norwegian man stated: "I was not
surprised to see a Norwegian woman
become prime minister; the women have
always run this country."

Most of today's young Norwegian
women in Norway, unlike their grandmothers, graduate from high school and
then attend college. Many go on to earn
advanced degrees. They take strong leadership roles in the private and public
sector, and there seems to be no area in
which they do not achieve. Women in
Norway have fewer problems than do
American women in terms of equal
opportunities. In the year 2000, women college and university students
outnumbered men for the first time.

Gro Harlem Brundtland, former prime minister of Norway for several
non-consecutive terms and former president of the World Heath
Organization, stated in a 2004 interview with Denise Logeland which was
published in the "Viking Magazine," an arm of the Sons of Norway, that:
"Norwegians, more than any other country, I think, owned their own land.
They were peasants (Middle Ages), but they were independent. Now, in that
context, women worked on the small farms while the men were out warring
or fishing. So women had a strong role in Norwegian society. Maybe in the
last hundred years, that has helped us look upon things this way—in more
egalitarian terms."

It is also the case that many Norwegian-American emigrant women and
second-generation Norwegian-Americans worked outside the home before
their children arrived and after they were grown. Some worked as beauticians,
cooks, clerks in Norwegian-owned stores; others assisted their husbands in
Norwegian-owned businesses, and worked in the travel and real estate industries. Several attended college and became teachers. Many volunteered in
church-related work.

Emigration to America also had its victims. One man, now living in the
New Bedford area, had been forced by his family to emigrate to America with

them when he was young. He didn't want to leave Norway. He went back to Norway off and on to live at the family farm with other relatives, but eventually the family died out. He was not able to find in America what others found to be fulfilling, and to this day he regrets his family's decision. In some ways he is a man without a real home. Home for him is still a dream of the Norwegian farm of his youth. His "absolute faith in the Bible," he says, has seen him through many difficult times in his life.

But this homesick man is an exception to the rule. Today, most Norwegian-Americans are a part of the fabric of their chosen American communities, and many have prospered. In Fairhaven one can see well-kept lawns, tidy and solid homes, large estates, and many blonde women and children still walking to the store or the beach or to each other's homes. As my old friend Evva Meyer Larson commented on her first view of Fairhaven, "I can see the European influence in this town. It is neat and clean with beautiful gardens like Germany and England."

Walking is still a pastime for many men and women and very long walks of several miles the norm. They usually have a considerable amount of money but it does fluctuate with the quantity and price of fish to some extent. Many own several boats; some own both small and large companies and others have small empires. They are Norwegians; they are Americans. Most are citizens but some are not.

Visiting Norway is always the high point of the year for them—calling on old friends and reliving memories. Many are buying or building second homes there, and some say that when they are in Norway all they do is talk about how great it is in America—just as they get nostalgic about Norway when they are in America. One man, Karl Johan Melkovik, now living on Karmøy, told me, "When I see the Fairhaven water tower, I know I am back home and it feels wonderful."

They have loyalty to two flags, two countries, two cultures on two continents. Increasingly, their lives are culturally rich and diverse as their children marry people from the ethnic mix in their communities. This is also true in Seattle. *Pendlers*, Norwegian-Americans, sometimes citizens of both countries but almost always with relatives living on two continents and with emotional tugs felt here and there, they have brought much to their new country and have left their communities richer and better places to live for their having been there.

"The legacy we leave for future generations, the struggles, the victories, the joys and the sorrows weave the story of our lives but the most significant of all is the fact that ordinary men and women with vision and courage stepped forward to change the future."

—Egil and Kitty Ellingsen, Seattle

Legacy & folklore

NORSE WISDOM
FROM THE ELDER EDDA (CIRCA 1300)

—Edith Hamilton, "Mythology"

"The fierceness of men rules the fate of women.

Tell one of your thoughts, but beware of two,
All know what is known to three.

A paltry man and poor of mind
Is he who mocks at all things.

A silly man lies awake all night, thinking of many things.
When the morning comes he is worn with care,
And his trouble is just as it was.

Brave men can live anywhere.
A coward dreads all things.

I once was young and traveled alone.
I met another and thought myself rich.

Be a friend to your friend.
Give him laughter for laughter.

To a good friend's house the path is straight
Though he is far way.

In a maiden's words
Let no man put faith,
Nor in what a woman says.
But I know man and women both, men's minds are unstable
toward women.

None so good that he has no faults, none so wicked that he is
worth naught.

The mind knows only what lies near the heart.

Modestly wise each one should be, not overwise,
For a wise man's heart is seldom glad."

The Perilous Waters

THE *F/V MIDNIGHT SUN*

—Risdal family archives

Here she is . . . The *Midnight Sun* . . . New Bedford's
newest fishing vessel and the pride of the Risdal family.

"The pilot cannot mitigate the billows or calm the winds."

—Plutarch

~

WHEN IS THE BIRTH OF A BOAT?

Dozs the life of a vessel begin when it is launched or when its plans are first drawn up? Or does it begin as an idea, a dream in the soul of a captain who is ready for a new and larger boat to ply his trade?

Dreams of new vessels, new adventures and better lives have been in the hearts of Norwegian seamen throughout the ages, and Captain Magne Risdal of Fairhaven was no different. A well-respected skipper noted for his great care and skill, he commissioned a new boat to be built and, in the words of Alexander Pope, "his native home deep imag'd in his soul," named it after one of the great characteristics of his Norwegian heritage—the "Midnight Sun," the summer sun that lights his native Norway twenty-four hours a day. This fishing boat *Midnight Sun* was to be a new light in his life and a crowning achievement in his career as a skipper and boat owner.

THE *MIDNIGHT SUN*

His excitement and pride was intense on April 9, 1960, as his daughter Linda christened the 73-foot, $75,000 *Midnight Sun*, built at the Gamache Shipyard in South Bristol, Maine. It slid proudly down the ways into Maine's

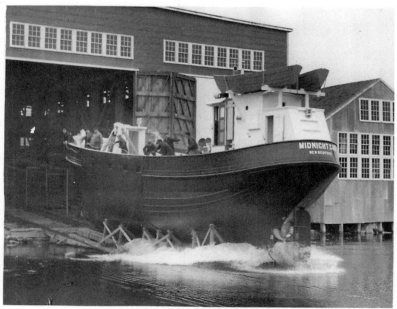

—Risdal family archives

The *Midnight Sun* is launched with memories of his homeland "deep imaged in his soul."

—*Risdal family archives*

The day the *Midnight Sun* was christened. Karry, Linda and Magne Risdal. A happy day for all.

Damariscotta River and this green-and-white wooden craft was to arrive in her new home-port of New Bedford in about a week. Although designed as a dragger, she was to be outfitted as a scalloper so that she could take full seasonal advantage of the fishing harvests. Masts and riggings were to be installed before she made her maiden voyage to New Bedford, where Captain Risdal would skipper her and carry a crew of ten when scalloping and five or six when fishing. There was great excitement and pride that day for the Risdal family.

Captain Risdal was his wife's second husband. Her first husband was lost to the sea in the legendary "Hurricane of '38," and she had fair knowledge of the wrath of the sea. She knew the risks and the dangers, yet most likely had confidence that this boat was the best and safest that could be built for them. Together, she and Magne Risdal planned to have successful, happy, productive years with this new light in their life, the *Midnight Sun*.

Being a Norwegian skipper, it was expected that he would follow in the accepted tradition and hire Norwegian seaman. The crew would eat Norwegian food, observe Norwegian traditions and customs, and speak Norwegian. Norwegian-owned boats were admired because of their cleanliness and pride of ownership. The New Bedford Standard-Times featured a photo of the *Midnight Sun* as she moved up New Bedford's Acushnet River ten days after her launching in South Bristol, Maine. It was described as the second new vessel to join the New Bedford fleet in 1960. It could be said that it was built to be a vessel that in the words of Thomas Moore, 1779–1852, "stood the storm when waves were rough."

She was a proud boat that day when she entered confidently into New Bedford Harbor with her name prominently emblazoned on the stern as well as the port and starboard sides of the bow. Flags were waving from the rigging, and the American flag was flying off-stern. Her home was in Fairhaven at Kelly's Shipyard, and her arrival was a large step in demonstrating the port's growth and influence in the scallop and fishing industry.

The year 1960 was also the year that Norwegian emigration to New Bedford was reaching new heights. Daily, young men, some with their families, sought out Rasmus Tonnessen's ship store to learn of available work on the Norwegian-skippered boats out of New Bedford and Fairhaven. Many of these young men were just in their late teens but still had several years of Merchant Marine training and fishing experience and "knew the ropes." They were eager, healthy, strong and knowledgeable and were hired quickly after their arrival in New Bedford.

As another captain from Karmøy once said, "We hired the men from Karmøy first because we knew them or their families, and we could trust them. We hired men from other areas in Norway after we hired the Karmøy crew." Risdal was from Skudenes on Karmøy; he hired Karmøy men first. And so Captain Risdal had no problems manning his pride and joy. There was available talent and experience, and with this expertise and a new boat, life looked very promising to him and his crew.

"The Ballad of the Midnight Sun," Aleksander Hauge, Verses 1 & 2

*From the West Coast of Norway
to America's eastern shore
He crossed the North Atlantic just after the Second World War.
When he sailed in New York Harbor after seven rolling days,
he was met by Miss Liberty who wished him "welcome in."
The skyline of Manhattan was a strange sight to see
for a man from a little island who met his childhood dream.*

THE SKIPPER

CAPTAIN RISDAL WAS IN HIS FIFTIES, and he had at least twenty-five years experience working on the seas where he had established a "reputation for caution and skill," according to an interview with his stepson in 1995. He is described by his niece as "a true gentleman, who was very kind to his whole family and who, in turn, was adored by them." He is further categorized as a conservative, churchgoing, hard-working, very private Norwegian man, honest to a fault who was very respected among his peers for his discerning life as well as his seamanship skills.

The vessel was known in the community as "the boat" to be on. It was new, it was well-skippered, and it was productive. It sailed an even course in its first year until it was disabled with engine trouble 165 miles east of Pollock Rip Lighthouse in late July of 1961. The Coast Guard cutter *General Greene* raced to render aid successfully.

Within a few days, on August 6 of that year, the *Midnight Sun* was open for public inspection at the popular Third Annual Scallop Festival in New Bedford, where locals boarded the boat and learned a bit about scalloping

—*Risdal family archives*

Magne Risdal during WWII in the American Army, circa 1942.

—*Risdal family archives*

Magne and Karry Risdal on their wedding day.

before going to the large outside tents on Pope's Island Park for fried scallops and potatoes. The same men who manned the boats often cooked the delicate, delicious scallops and it was one of those special New Bedford events, which also featured a "scallop queen" selected from the community. It was at this festival that the Greater New Bedford community got a view of the Norwegian fishing fleet, as well as a taste of its harvest. It seemed as though every Norwegian turned out, but the event also attracted a great many New Bedford area residents who up to then had not been aware of the extent of this Norwegian community among them.

—*Risdal archives*

Magne Risdal as he looked after fishing for many days.

While the *Midnight Sun* had a prominent role in the 1961 festival, all was not perfect with her, as was related in an interview with a former crewmember, a Norwegian-American who worked in the *Midnight Sun*'s engine room for several trips: "She rolled so bad. When she was rolling you had to pin the bushel basket of scallops between your legs, otherwise it would be all over you. I thought she didn't have the right ballast and was light as a cork on the water."

"The Ballad of the Midnight Sun," Verses 2–3

—Aleksander Hauge

The autumn-colored maples he looked at from the road.
On the turnpike and Route Six they drove,
five hours or so. And then they met New Bedford,
this town would be his home. His friends met him there
and the year was '61.
He got a job on a dragger and fished off Georges Bank.
and quickly made money for a new flat and a car.
But this story that I tell you has not a happy end.
This story I have heard from his best friend.

THE STORM

IT WAS A NOVEMBER STORM, considered by fishermen to be one of the worst of the century. The fishing fleet headed home as soon as the skippers realized that this was not just an ordinary gale—this was a big one. As reported by Brad Hathaway, the Standard-Times writer who covered the waterfront: "The two-day storm packed winds of more than 90 miles an hour and whipped seas into 50-foot waves as it ripped across Georges Bank. The *Monte Carlo* and the *Moonlight* were badly damaged as they limped into port while other vessels straggled in."

It was a great relief and answer to prayer for the families of the men on those boats.

"And do not stay on the sea in the autumn if you can help it."

—"The King's Mirror," a book of advice from a Norwegian father to son.

EXCERPTS FROM THE NEW BEDFORD STANDARD-TIMES

"THE CREWS WERE CRITICAL of the lack of warning given by the weather bureau when the hurricane-force winds bore down on them on Wednesday, November 14, 1962. By Saturday, the vessel *Midnight Sun*, which had failed to return to port along with her sister vessels, was listed as 'overdue,' the precursor to tragedy at sea. A Coast Guard plane was dispatched to look for the missing scalloper, but adverse weather conditions hampered its search. Two planes were sent aloft the next day as the Coast Guard prepared to send ships into the area where the craft was last reported. John Isaksen, then a mate on the *Aloha*, told the press that he had spoken with the skipper (of the *Midnight Sun*) on the Wednesday of the storm and that Captain Risdal said he was on his way home. 'He didn't say where he was, but from talking with him, I figured he had started out five to six hours before. So, he had already traveled 60–70 miles west of us. He gave no indication of anything wrong." The Standard-Times continues: "Other ships in the area were *Aloha*, *Fleetwing*, *Florence B.* and the *Edgartown*, which were a bit to the southeast. We were then about 90 miles east-southeast of Nantucket. In normal weather, the trip back to New Bedford would take 18–20 hours." That trip took Isaksen and the *Aloha* 60 hours.

The exhausted skipper of the *Florence B.*, Skipper Hans Davidsen, finally sailed his vessel into port, but was so distraught from the trauma of this horrendous storm that he never wished to "follow the waters" again. At one point, his boat was totally submerged and that was to be, by choice, his final trip. The storm was one of the worst ever experienced and as one fisherman in port at that time said, "I put my head out a window and said to the other men, "Thank God, I am not out fishing on a day like this. It is the worst I have ever seen. I feel sorry for anyone out there at a time like this."

The Standard-Times of November 21, 1962, wrote of those anxious days: "Offshore, crisscrossing a 120-square-mile area southeast of Nantucket, planes and ships are searching for the scalloper *Midnight Sun* and her 11-man crew, missing since last Thursday's blow struck the fleet. Waiting is the hardest thing in the world for those who must wait for whatever word there is. Only the men and women whose kin and colleagues go down to the sea in ships understand fully the nature and loneliness of this vigil. Yet, of all the demands made of the ocean upon those persons who live next to it and rely upon it for their livelihood, probably none is more traditional than waiting for ships to come home after a storm. This makes it no easier, but it has endured through all the ages of the coaster, the line trawler, the whaler, the handliner, and now the dragger. If there is comfort in it, those who wait in this instance must know that virtually all of the seaport community joins with them in hoping, and that literally hundreds of 'neighbors,' nameless to them, yet sharing their anxiety, would assume a portion of the burden if they could."

THE FAMILY

ONE FISHERMAN DESCRIBES Mrs. Risdal as: "standing on the hill at Fort Phoenix, an observation point near her home, waiting hour after hour for a glimpse of her husband's boat"—waiting and wondering, looking and hoping as so many wives of seamen had done before her on this very spot. What was Mrs. Risdal thinking on those days? *Surely this cannot happen to my family again—surely not to this new boat, surely not to these young men who worked for my husband?* She thought and prayed as she sat, smoked, and waited in her kitchen. According to a relative, she could be seen there years later: sitting, thinking, remembering, and grieving.

How does a wife cope with losing two husbands in similar tragedies in one lifetime? The church and faith are very important, but on a practical level, it is a disaster and has a long-lasting effect on lives, especially for the children. As her son said to me, "I felt so bad for my mother. It was the second time for her . . . so hard for her."

Her daughter remembers those days and years well: "Yes, my father was a very special person—as was my mother, Karry. I lost my dad when I was 16. When my mother and I sat at Fort Phoenix and Pier 3 and waited and prayed for the *Midnight Sun* to return, I thought no, this couldn't really be happening. My mother had lost her first husband and many from his family in the Hurricane of '38. It couldn't possibly happen to her again. And my dear cousin Gordon was with my dad for his last trip before he was going to go back to Norway. And all the other men! It still brings tears to my eyes whenever I think about it."

THE SEARCH

BY NOVEMBER 20, the vessel and its crew were feared lost, and the Coast Guard had four planes and the seagoing tug *Acushnet*, from Portland, Maine, crisscrossing the 120-square-mile area southeast of Nantucket. Many Norwegian-American relatives were calling the Coast Guard from New Bedford and Norway for any bits of information about the boat.

Ralph Brown, former Coast Guardsman, experienced many such scenes as he recalled in 2001: "When I was in the Coast Guard with the Public Information Office, my district included New Bedford. It was very traumatic for me when a boat was missing. I had grown up with Norwegians as they had boarded at my grandmother's home, and they were like fathers to me. Families would call in, and I could feel their pain, but I would have to withhold information until it became official. That was awful for me personally! I remember once we had spied men clinging to wreckage out to sea, and I knew we would not get to them in time and that they were dead, but I couldn't tell the families that until it became official. Those phone conversations with the families are something I shall never forget. It was so painful as I knew them quite well."

*"The Nordic hero cherished existence and knew how to enjoy life,
but he could also face death with a calm mind and a smile. No
matter what happened, a hero could choose to behave with honor."*

—Douglas "Dag" Rossman, "Ancient Nordic Spirituality:
Quest for Wisdom and Balance," Scandinavian Press,
Vancouver, B.C., fall 1996

HOPE?

SOME OF THE FISHERMEN were still hoping that the *Midnight Sun* might
have run out of fuel, as she had a low capacity, and that she might be adrift at
sea. One said, "She does not have much of a fuel capacity and she left port a
week ago Wednesday." Another spoke of the *Midnight Sun's* prior trip when
"she had run out of fuel and had to get fuel from another scalloper at sea." The
scalloper *Fleetwing* had sighted the *Midnight Sun* as late as early Wednesday
afternoon on radar and both vessels had started home at the same time,
according to the *Fleetwing's* skipper, Captain Gundersen. Captain Risdal's
brother Nils, owner of the scalloper *Neptune*, said his brother would have
made contact with shore before this time, unless the scalloper was badly
damaged and adrift without working communications. All tried to find plau-
sible explanations for the disappearance and lived in hope that somehow the
boat and the crew would be found safe and sound. They recalled when the
dragger *Palmers Island* returned to port after being given up for lost in 1940.
She drifted south, plummeted by gale-force winds, but was luckily sighted by
a British steamer 200 miles away from the area where she had been disabled.
The Coast Guard brought her back to New Bedford. There was dwindling
hope that *Midnight Sun* might share this miraculous fate.

November 21, The Standard-Times: "The search for the scalloper
Midnight Sun moved into its fifth day today as three Coast Guard cutters and
two aircraft searched the area 200 miles southeast of Nantucket where an oil
slick and wreckage was spotted yesterday. No word has yet been heard from
the *Amelia*, which left port on November 14, the day before the storm struck.
The dragger *Sea Gold* arrived safely to port today with a catch. Participating
in the search are cutters *Acushnet*, *Mendota*, *Mackinaw* and two planes operating out of Bermuda. The five planes searching yesterday reported back
without a sighting. The cutters and other surface craft continue their search
around the clock, and the search area has been extended 450 miles southeast
of Nantucket."

November 23, The Standard-Times: "Hope waned today for the eleven-
man crew of the missing New Bedford scalloper *Midnight Sun* as three Coast
Guard planes entered the seventh day of an air-and-sea crisscross pattern

search for the vessel. The *Amelia* returned to port today with her crew of 11. After riding out the blow, the vessel continued to fish, although they could not restore radio contact. And they came home a day earlier than planned. The skipper was unaware there was a search out for them. Captain Risdal of the *Midnight Sun* was last heard from last Wednesday when he expected to arrive in New Bedford, Saturday or Sunday, but was unheard-from after the storm. The 90-mile-an-hour wind reported at Provincetown caused heavy damage to the New Bedford fishing fleet. Several vessels were unreported, having lost communications and receiving heavy damage from heavy running seas but all have been accounted for except the *Midnight Sun*."

November 25, The Standard-Times: "The search was called off today after nine days of extensive hunting by the Coast Guard. Boats and merchant ships have been asked to keep a lookout for . . . any sign of the vessel. Coast Guard officials said the search had turned up some debris and it will be brought to New Bedford this week for identification."

November 30, The Standard-Times: "Howard Nickerson, secretary/treasurer of the New Bedford Fishermen's Union, requested an examination of the debris picked up by the Coast Guard in its *Midnight Sun* search. The debris consisted of a plywood table top with some linoleum or plastic attached to it, a torn life jacket, and a 55-gallon drum. Also, several pieces of wood were picked up. The request was made that it be sent to New Bedford for identification." According to the daughter of Captain Risdal, Linda Risdal Knott, "The debris that was found was not from the *Midnight Sun*. I know that my Uncle Nils was one of those who examined the debris."

THE MEMORIAL SERVICE
AND THE COMMUNITY

THE NORWEGIAN COMMUNITIES of New Bedford and Karmøy were numbed by this great loss. Many of the men were young and eight of the eleven had recently come over from Karmøy to make their way in New Bedford. Ten of the men had Norwegian roots. Their deaths seemed to touch everyone on the island.

The families in Norway would never see their sons, nephews, brothers, fathers, husbands, sweethearts or friends again. They had left Norway to make their fortunes in America and to live the American dream. They left home with the optimism of youth and promise and were never to return to the arms of their loved ones. Those on the island of Karmøy suffered as a whole because each of them knew or had someone in America. And they now understood, only too well, that this fate could easily await any of their loved ones in America.

Who can understand why some survive and others are lost? Who could possibly understand the grief of Mrs. Risdal who twice had lost a husband to the sea? One New Bedford fisherman had just left the *Midnight Sun* to sign onto another boat. He knew the men well and was very grieved, but still felt he had had a bit of luck in that he was not on this boat when it was lost. Another fisherman had had his brother substitute for him at the last minute. Who could understand what he was feeling that day? Norwegians met in churches here and in Norway to seek answers, to try to find some understanding and to pray for their men, each other, and themselves.

Those who gathered at the Trinity Lutheran Church in Fairhaven that day remembered other days when they had met on similar occasions. Very few had not been touched by death in their family or among friends. Some had lost many friends and relatives over the years and so they met to grieve and pray together and somehow find an answer to this tragedy.

But in the congregation that day was one family whose grief was deep but who also felt personally blessed and grateful that they had been spared. They had the bitter experience of telling the Karmøy Norwegian families about the deaths of their sons. Their father from Karmøy was the cook on the *Midnight Sun*, and he never took a trip off. But this time, his daughter remembers: "While he was preparing to go out to sea as usual, he and his wife had a slight disagreement. That last trip he decided to stay home because he had a bad cold. He came home and told my mother he wanted to stay home because 'I don't feel good.' She told him he was not that sick and could go out, but he wanted to stay home. He didn't go out, and he survived because of this decision. I was very sad for all of us as we all had someone we knew on the *Midnight Sun*. Two brothers were from the same place that we came from, and one was in Brooklyn working and had come up to visit his brother and died. It was an awful time for all of us. My mother had to call some of the families in Norway to tell them. It was the hardest thing to do."

A PASTOR'S MESSAGE

Pastor Johnnie Glad, the Norwegian-born minister of the Trinity Lutheran Church, well understood the feelings of the congregation. He had performed many memorial services for this population over the years and had counseled with them as they sought to reconstruct their lives. New Bedford Standard-Times of December 3, 1962 describes the service: "Eighty percent of the male church membership earned their living on the sea. Many ages and nationalities were present at the memorial service and many lives had been touched by this tragedy. More women than men attended because the men were at out to sea once more. In a deep, resonant voice, Pastor Glad read the

Pastor Johnnie Glad in 2001 at the Karmøy Fisherman's
Memorial dedication. Now living in Norway, he ministered in
Fairhaven to the fishing families for many years.

—Dr. Hans-Eirik Aarek photo

names of the men lost on the *Midnight Sun* to the friends, families, girlfriends,
relatives and fellow church members."

> CAPTAIN MAGNE RISDAL
> GORDON KALLESTEIN
> OLAV FERKINGSTAD
> JENS FERKINGSTAD
> ARNE LINDANGER
> JOHN W. WAGNER
> JON NILSEN
> AUGUST LARSEN
> TORGILS HOLMEN
> SAM LUND
> ASBJORN PEDERSEN

Pastor Glad reminded the congregation, "As we embark on life's voyage,
remember that it also must have an end." And he delivered the Christian
message that, "One must have Jesus as the pilot on the ship of life." During
the service one fishing captain, who had been a close friend of Captain Risdal
and who had had a narrow escape himself from the storm, left the service early
with his wife. He was too distraught to continue to sit and mourn with the rest
of the community. It was too traumatic, too painful, and too personal for him
to bear.

THE CAPTAIN AND HIS CREW

CAPTAIN RISDAL HAD A YOUNG DAUGHTER, a wife, a stepson, a father,
three brothers from Norway living in Fairhaven, and two sisters, one in
Florida and one in Norway. He was born in Skudenes, Norway, and came to
America in 1926. He lived in the Midwest and New York before moving to
Fairhaven in 1942. He was a World War II veteran and took part in the invasions of North Africa and Italy. His life was fraught with high danger in the
military and on the sea, yet he is best remembered for his gentleness to
everyone and his kind manner.

The men who were lost to the waters

Magne Risdal, skipper

Gordon Kallestein

Arne Lindanger

Torgils Holman

Jens Ferkingstad

Olav Ferkingstad

Sam Lund

No photos of John W. Wagner, Jon Nilsen, August Larsen, Asbjorn Pedersen

THE CREW

GORDON KALLESTEIN, almost twenty-three, was Captain Risdal's nephew and his goal was to save enough money to return to Skudenes to purchase a tractor for the family farm. He left behind his parents, Andreas and Ragnhild, three brothers, three sisters and his grandfather Nickolai Risdal.

Olav Ferkingstad, mate and chief engineer, lived with his brother Jens in New Bedford. They were from Karmøy.

Jens Ferkingstad was also a World War II veteran who had a young son in New Bedford. Almost as if he had had a premonition before this trip, he purchased some new clothing for his son and asked a friend, the regular cook's wife, to give it to him in case he didn't come back, and if he didn't return to look after him. His son eventually moved with other family members to Norway, where he lives today.

Arne Lindanger, 53, lived in New Bedford for eight years, and had a wife in Norway and several unmarried children there.

Jon Nilsen was 18 and had just arrived in America two months before. He was living with his brother just before the tragedy. He was on his third fishing trip and had three brothers in the area and his mother in Norway.

August Larsen, 33, of Brooklyn was the substitute cook for that trip. He worked mostly out of New York and was unmarried. His father lived in Norway.

Asbjorn Pedersen, 44, was born in Norway but lived in New Bedford.

Sam Lund was a last-minute replacement for his brother on this trip and lived in Brooklyn.

Torgils Holman was from Åkre on Karmøy. He had one son living in Norway as well as sisters and brothers.

John Wagner, an American fisherman from Gloucester, was making his third trip with the *Midnight Sun*.

Mrs. Karry Risdal, the grieving widow, gave the flowers from the memorial service to Captain Charles Leach of the *Bright Star*. At dawn on December 4, in the area where the *Midnight Sun* had reported a full catch, the crew of the scalloper cast the flowers upon the chilly waters.

Why did the other ships survive and this one surrender to the wrath of the sea? The balladeer Aleksander Hauge of Karmøy poses that question in

"The Ballad of the Midnight Sun," Verse 4:

In 1962 he entered his new boat, Midnight Sun,
And sailed from New Bedford across Nantucket Sound.
Then came a northeaster with waves mountain high
Eleven lost their lives. What happened that black night?

WHY?

A FORMER CREWMEMBER, who had worked in the engine room, has his own perspective: "I was on *Midnight Sun* before it went down. It came from Maine and was the first boat in New Bedford with the scallop boxes enclosed at the shipyard. They were completely enclosed for winter. It is my opinion that they made the enclosed boxes wrong because they just covered the whole area over and didn't redesign it. There was swinging doors between the enclosed area and the mid-section of the boat and no place for the empty shells to go if the wind blew at you. You had to keep the door open to throw out the shells. The wind would blow them right back so you were constantly ducking scallop shells coming back to the boat. Eventually they put in a chute and then you pulled a handle to dump them. Now they have a trough for the empty shells . . . you throw in the scallop shells and the running water takes it out to sea.

"I think the reason the boat went down was because of those boxes as they could put the boat off balance. If we took a wave, the water would come into the enclosed area and go aft and there was no place for it to run out except into the engine room. There was only a half-door to the engine room. If she took a real bad shot at the side, I figure the water went into the engine room, and once the water hit the hot engines, that was the end."

This view is reinforced in part by the Coast Guard report as stated in the New Bedford Standard-Times, February 15, 1963, headline: "Scallop Boxes Suspect in *Midnight Sun* Loss: Shelter, or Hazard?"

"Enclosed shucking boxes on the *Midnight Sun* may have been a contributing factor in her floundering at sea last November, the Coast Guard reported in its report on the tragedy. It listed the cause of the sinking of the 11-man, 73-foot vessel, *Midnight Sun*, as the stress of weather. The report said that the plywood-enclosed shucking area was essentially secure against wind, rain and spray only. It formed an enclosure capable of temporarily trapping in appreciable quantities of sea water, with attendant complications including the establishment of a head of water against the deck house doors, particularly the after doors. About one-third of the 50 scallopers in the New Bedford fishing fleet are equipped with these comparatively new boxes installed to protect scallop shuckers from the weather. In March 1962, eight months before this mishap, the deck passages on both sides of the aft deck were enclosed by the plywood shelter to the height and length of the deckhouse. Sliding plywood across doors was fitted in the shelter at the forward end. Hinged wooden ports were provided at the sides above the bulwarks for disposing of the scallop shells. A small-hinged door in the after end facilitated handling of the mooring lines. Two after-deckhouse doors, port and starboard, were for access to the engine room. They were made with upper and lower halves separately hinged. They opened only six inches above the deck. The report indicated that the closure could interfere with the shedding of water and that the after doors leading to the pilothouse were two feet above deck. In the absence of surviving witnesses, it must be concluded that the *Midnight Sun* foundered on or about November 15 in the vicinity of Little Georges Bank and that her entire crew of 11 men is presumably dead, the report concluded. It said the storm was extensive in scope and violent enough in nature to have taxed the seaworthiness of any craft of comparable size.

"Continuing, the report stated the *Midnight Sun* was of conventional and proven design, in good physical condition, and known to have embodied the normal features. The investigating officer has not overlooked the important part in the security of a vessel played by her machinery, the closing appliances fitted in way of openings in hull and deck, the seamanship of her crew and the possibility of deficiencies in one or more of these elements contributing to the cause of the disaster. Any specific conclusions must be speculative under the circumstances. A recommendation that the case be closed without further hearing by the Coast Guard was accepted."

Others in the fishing industry and boat owners say that these same shucking boxes were used for years on other vessels without a problem.

THE AFTERMATH

AFTER A TRAGEDY SUCH AS THIS, time is needed to rebuild and repair lives, but unfortunately further pain would be inflicted on all of the survivors. Victims' families wished to be compensated for their losses, and they sought legal recourse. The result was they had to relive the pain and the tragedy over and over again.

Norwegians have had to face this type of tragedy since their country existed—as Egil Skalla-Grimsson wrote in the thirteenth century:

Egil's Lament: The Irreparable Loss of Sons

Our family shield-wall is torn wide open.
Cruel waves broke my father's firm line.
How vast is the breach, how empty the place
where the sea entered and snatched away my son.
Ran the fierce sea-god has
ravaged all my land.
All those I loved he seized as his spoils.
Broken are his bonds that held us together,
the links I held firmly between my hands
The pillaging sea has robbed me of my riches.
Hard it is to speak of the loss of my kin,
he who was our shield has left us defenseless,
lost to our sight on the distant roads of death.
What can make amends for the loss of a son?
What compensation pays for such a death?
How could I beget another such boy?
Who should be held the equal of his brother?

Lawsuits seeking more than one million dollars were brought against the vessel's owners and were documented in the Standard-Times under these headlines:

"*Midnight Sun* Case Petition Answered," May 25, 1963

"Suits Filed for 5 Lost Fishermen," October 29, 1963

"Lost Vessel Firm Files Case Objection," February 7, 1964

"*Midnight Sun* Hearing Opens in U.S. Court," December 15, 1965

"Risdal Blamed by U.S. Judge in Boat Sinking," January 8, 1966

"Charges Heard in Boat Sinking," January 27, 1967

"*Midnight Sun* Claim Petitions Under Study," January 28, 1967

"*Midnight Sun* Crew's Kin Get Awards," October 24, 1968

THE VERDICT

THE STANDARD-TIMES: "On January 8, 1966, the U.S. District Court judge blamed the skipper of the *Midnight Sun* for the 1962 sinking. The vessel's owners, Risdal and Anderson Inc. of New Bedford, petitioned for exoneration or limitation of liability in connection with the sinking, but their petition was denied by the judge. He ordered that the case stand for a hearing on assessment of damages. Suits totaling more than $1 million were filed against the corporation. In the end, the judge declared, "Captain Risdal's attempt to return to port was negligent and this negligence was the proximate cause of the loss of the *Midnight Sun*." He ruled that the shucking boxes had caused the vessel to become unseaworthy. He also noted that Captain Risdal had used bad judgment in deciding to head back for New Bedford rather than 'lay to' and ride out the storm."

This decision was heartbreaking to those who knew the captain, and many felt it reflected upon the judge's lack of maritime knowledge. Coupled with the witnesses feeling they had not been listened to appropriately, the ruling made for negative feelings that persist until this day. One of the men who testified at the trial is still upset and angered when he discusses those days of testimony. A witness who was the last to speak to Captain Risdal felt then and now that the judge neither listened to him nor took him seriously.

The financial settlements were very late and comparably small. The families of the dead seamen were awarded a total of $72,760, which was essentially the cost of the vessel. The lowest award was $1,860 and the highest $24,000. The average was $8,084. One wonders what criteria was used to value one man's life at $1,860 and another at $24,000. The awards appear to be in direct relationship to the number of dependents left behind.

THE TRIAL, THE JUDGE, AND THE WITNESSES

IT IS DIFFICULT TO BE AN EMIGRANT and handle the English language effectively and efficiently. Norwegians tend to hold onto their native accents after many years of living in America. Sometimes, one can even hear an accent in the next generation through inflection and pronunciation. In the *Midnight Sun* trial, many of the Norwegians who testified had strong accents and used nautical jargon that may have mystified the judge.

The judge mentioned, according to one witness, that he "knew nothing about fishing or the ocean," and therefore may have had some problems with terminology and understanding. When one witness spoke of "queer water" or a "rogue" wave, the judge, according to him remarked that waves were all the same height as far as he could see by looking at them from Horseneck Beach in Westport.

Although one might conclude that Coast Guard witnesses ably stated their case regarding the enclosed scallop boxes as the probable cause of the loss of the vessel, this apparently did not have a great bearing on the case. With the problems of communication between the judge and witnesses whose language skills were taxed by the trauma of the day, plus the concept that this great loss demanded some compensation to the victims, there had to be someone to blame.

ACT OF GOD

A FINE MAN'S REPUTATION was at stake, and it is a sad indictment against our insurance system that families cannot be well-compensated without destroying a captain's image in the community. They deserved to be very well compensated, deserved far more than they received, but not at the cost of the captain's good name. Our insurance and justice system demands a person somewhere down the line has to be proven negligent in order for damages to be awarded. It is therefore taken out of the "Act of God" classification, which is usually a specific exclusion to most insurance policies. People's lives and reputations are sacrificed every day in our courtrooms to this legal principle. And it is in the maritime tradition that the captain always has the ultimate responsibility for his boat.

TODAY

CAPTAIN RISDAL'S DAUGHTER wrote, "I was blessed with parents who genuinely loved one another. I am so thankful for the richness of time, even though short, that I had with them. My mother died before I was thirty. The

—*Risdal family archives.*

Magne Risdal and daughter Linda in their
early happy days together.

—*Knott archives*

Linda Risdal Knott today.

official cause was cancer, but I think it was brought on by her sense of loss.
When she was dying, I thanked God that my father wasn't alive to witness it."

WHEN IS THE DEATH OF A BOAT?

IS IT WHEN IT FIRST STARTS to sink below the waves, or when the
skipper knows in his heart that it can't be saved or is it when the last piece of
wood disintegrates in the sand? Is there a death at all, if it still lives in the
memories of those who knew it, worked on it, loved it or had loved ones who
were lost with it? Does a vessel ever die if its memory is kept alive and life-
sustaining lessons are learned from its disappearance?

"Ballad of the Midnight Sun"

—Lyrics, Verse 6: Astrid Tollefsen
Melody: Aleksander Hauge

They followed the waters
And came to this sad end.
That trip brought their loved ones
Pain that will not mend.

And there may be stories
Of dark and stormy nights,
When wind and the high waves
Frame a strange sight.

When echoes are heard
Through the fog and the mist,
The sounds of the gangs,
We have all missed.

Saying, Gud velsigne våre brødre,
Your safety we keep.
God bless you, our brothers;
Your safety we keep!

—AT photo

Aleksander Hauge sings "Ballad of the Midnight Sun" in front of the Seamen's Bethel cenotaph after dedicating his music to the men who were lost on that fateful day in 1962.

—AT photo

The Seamen's Bethel, which was mentioned in Melville's "Moby Dick," is where lost seamen are memorialized, and where my grandparents sang in the choir. My mother's memorial service was held here.

Legacy *&* Folklore

THE MEN AND THEIR BOATS

Fisherman's Statue, Åkrehamn, Karmøy, Norway

Then God said, "Let us make man in our image, in our likeness, and let them rule over the fish of the sea..."

—Genesis 1:26

They that go down to the sea in ships, that do business in great waters, these see the works of the Lord and his wonders in the deep.

—Psalms 107: 23-24

FISHING VESSELS OF THE TWENTIETH CENTURY evolved from mostly-sail schooners in the early part of the century to sail-engine wooden boats in mid-century to the modern large no-sail steel, heavily electronically equipped, sleek and sophisticated vessels of the late twentieth century.

Many owners made fortunes from fishing over the past century but, also, many lives were lost and many men injured. Those who are successful today can look back with appreciation and see the changes in vessel design and safeguards that helped them achieve their success.

After each loss or accident, the United States Coast Guard conducted investigations and made recommendations. These recommendations would often initiate changes in vessel design, safety equipment, and navigational or weather aides. In addition to the Coast Guard, fishermen themselves often had new and innovative ideas to add to the process of modernization. (see Appendix)

As the years went by, vessels become safer and more efficient, better equipped and more productive. Theoretically crews would be better paid, investors would make more profit and fish could be in the marketplace more abundantly and at lower cost.

In reality, unfortunately, today's fishing world is a very different one. With federal laws limiting days of fishing, poundage and size of fish caught, many fishermen are giving up the trade after years of frustration. The future is uncertain.

In any event, the heady days of twentieth century fishing out of New Bedford and Seattle/Alaska will never be replicated. And there will forever be a debt owed to those who gave their lives to the sea.

THEY CAME FROM THIS LAND

Norway on left with neighbors Sweden, Finland and Estonia to the east. Denmark is to the south and the United Kingdom to the west. Iceland is to the northwest. Notice how Norway curves in the north passing over both Sweden and Finland and touching Russia. This was a strategic factor in her history, especially during wartime. This area is also the home to the Sami, formerly called Laplanders. Also, note the irregular coastline with its thousands of islands as well as some of the dark lines which look like rivers, but are actually fjords. Fjords, extremely deep salt water fingers, extend into the mountainous land and flow inland from the sea for many miles. This is another unique factor in Norway's geography that affects her history and life. One can easily see that driving in Western Norway also means taking many ferries.

The oil wells are located in the North Sea and surround Norway to her south and west—one after the other, mile after mile.

ON THESE SHIPS

The *NAL Stavangerfjord, 1918-1964,* shown here in Stavanger, was 12,977 tons gross. She was built in 1917 by Cammell Laird & Co., Birkenhead, England, for the Norwegian American Line. She initially accommodated 88-1st, 318-2nd and 820-3rd class passengers. She sailed from Birkenhead on her maiden voyage to New York in April, 1918. In October, 1918, she made her first Christiania–Christiansand–Stavanger–Bergen–New York crossing. After the German invasion of Norway, she became a depot ship until after the war when she was used as a troopship between Norway and New York. In 1946 she was refitted, but in December, 1953, she had severe rudder problems during rough weather while in the mid-Atlantic, and was escorted to Bergen. In 1956 she was again refitted and her tonnage increased to 14,015 tons. Her last voyage was in November, 1963. In 1964 she was scrapped at Hong Kong after 45 years on the sea. During this time, she crossed the Atlantic 768 times, 2,800,000 miles and had carried 403,618 passengers.   —*Adapted in part from The Solem, Swiggum & Austheim emigration ship index, courtesy of Børge Solem.*

The *NAL Bergensfjord, 1913-1946.* Liner (2f/2m). *L/B/D*: 512.1 × 61.2 (161.5m × 18.7m). *Tons*: 10,666 grt. *Hull*: steel. *Comp.*: 1st 100, 2nd 250, 3rd 850. *Mach.*: quadruple expansion, 2 screws; 15 kts. *Built*: Cammell, Laird & Co., Ltd., Birkenhead, England, 1913. She was the second ship built for Norwegian American Line and entered service in September 1913. She carried passengers between Christiania (now

Oslo), Kristiansand, Stavanger, Bergen, and New York until 1940 when she served as a troop ship for the duration of World War II. In 1946, the Norwegian American Line sold her to Home Lines and she was renamed *Argentina*. In 1953 *Argentina* was sold to the Zim Israel Navigation Company. She was scrapped at La Spezia in 1959. The second *Bergensfjord*, 1956–1971, was sold to French Line and renamed *De Grasse*. —*Adapted from Bonsor, North Atlantic Seaway. Braynard & Miller, Fifty Famous Liners 2.and The Ships List*

The NAL Oslofjord was ship #44 of the NAL. Tonnage: 16,844 gross, 9,306 net. Dimensions: 545,4 × 72,3 × 25,1 feet. Machinery: Two 7 cylinders 2S.C.DA oil engines by Gebr. Stork & Co.N.V., Hengelo, driving twin screws. Passengers: 266 first class, 359 Tourist Class. 2nd. April-1949: Launched by N.V. Nederlandsche Dok en Scheepsbouw, Maatscappij, Amsterdam (Yard no.410) for NAL. Delivered: November 1949. Renamed *Fulvia*, under the Italian flag. An explosion in the engine room set her on fire off Tenerife in July 1970, but the passengers and crew escaped in the lifeboats. The burning ship was taken in tow for Tenerife, but sank in position 29.57 N, 16.30 W.

1st. *Oslofjord*, 1938–1940 Mined and beached at South Shields, total loss.

2nd *Oslofjord* #44, 1949-1970 chartered to Costa Line, renamed *Fulvia*, 1970 burned and sank near Canary Islands.

3rd *Oslofjord* #72 1977–81. Sold to Karana Lines in 1981.

"That's the sad story of ship # 44, the second NAL *Oslofjord*.. She was the first large ship I ever saw when I was eight years old, and I was impressed," writes Harald Koksa of Oslo who wrote about the *NAL Oslofjord* (and its several incarnations) and how he became the last Norwegian onboard. "I signed on #72 *M/V Oslofjord*, (1977–1981) as a Chief Engineer, and was the person(s) responsible for selling her to Karana Line in August 1981. I am sad to say I was the last crewmember, officer and chief engineer aboard this ship with the proud history of bringing Norwegian emigrants from Norway to the USA to find a better life." —*Courtesy of Harald Koksa and the Norwegian American Line Museum of Oslo.*

TO THESE WATERS

—*National Park Service Photo*

The emigrants came first to New York City and passed Bay Ridge, Brooklyn, where many would live, were welcomed by the Statue of Liberty and then were processed at Ellis Island. Many fished out of the Fulton Fish Market in Lower Manhattan (by the East River.)

Southeastern New England showing New Bedford, Cape Cod and the Islands. Georges Bank is located east of Cape Cod and the trip there and back could often be perilous in bad weather.

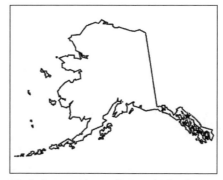

Alaska's rugged coastline and islands from where many emigrants fished in the frigid waters for crab and scallops. Many lives were lost but many fortunes were made.

340

TO WORK

—*Fishermen archives*

A good catch for a New Bedford boat. Circa mid-century

—*Fishermen archives*

Unidentified fishermen in the mid-thirties.

—*Fishermen archives, courtesy Aleksander Hauge*

Jörgen Knutsen with Berdines Ferking bag up scallops. Circa mid-century.

—*Fishermen archives, courtesy Aleksander Hauge*

Karsten Nes sets dredge on rail of scalloper. Circa 1960.

—*Fishermen archives*

On a fishing boat in mid-century.

—*Simon Vea archives*

Simon Vea (right) and John Bø, surrounded by scallops on the *Mary Hayes* in 1952.

—*Fishermen archives*

Working in port after the last trip to prepare for the next one. Circa 1960.

—*Courtesy Aleksander Hauge*

Walter Tangen and Magne Berg with unidentified man take a break between shifts. Circa mid-century.

—*Simon Vea archives*

Gabriel Skaar catches a lobster onboard the *Mary Hayes* in 1952. Simon Vea in background.

—*Courtesy Aleksander Hauge*

Selmer Fagerland takes a break during a rough sea on a scalloper, mid-century.

—*Simon Vea archives*

Fishermen play a hand of cards in their cramped living space, mid-century.

—*Courtesy Aleksander Hauge*

Fishermen gather to talk near their boats at the dock in New Bedford. Circa mid-century.

—*AT photo*

Work on a boat is ongoing, even when it is in port. Here a Norwegian-American-owned boat gets a bit more "ship shape" before her next trip.

—*AT photo 1996*

Skipper Malvin Kvilhaug with some crewmembers finish their work after a trip.

—*Dahl-Tollefsen archives*

Captain Martin Dahl of the *Stars and Stripes*, Point Judith, Rhode Island, with a codfish mid-century. He is the son of Norway's famous painter Hans Andreas Dahl.

—*General fishing archives*

Nets, nets and more nets—to repair, mend, organize, or replace. For the dragger fisherman, it the core of his work.

—*Tollefsen archives: New Bedford Fisherman's Union newspaper.*

David Tollefsen straddles the 135-pound prize codfish that won first place for the *F/V Stanley Butler* in 1954.

—*Marie Dahl Tollefsen archives*

A good catch of codfish in the forties.

ON BOATS
SUCH AS THESE . . .

—*The late Otto Olsen archives, Skudeneshavn, Norway*

The F/V *Norma* owned by Martin Dahl out of Gerritsen Beach, Brooklyn, New York, in the twenties.

—*Marie Dahl Tollefsen archives*

A painting of an early fishing schooner out of New York City, circa 1930, with Otto Olsen and Sadie Ben onboard.

—The late Otto Olsen archives

The same schooner was also seen in New Bedford harbor. Otto Olsen and Sadie Ben were on board when this photo was taken. These beautiful schooners, originally all sail, were a sight to behold around New York and New England.

—Stanley Johansen archives

The Western Rig, F/V *Edith*, a scalloper in the forties, was sailed by members of the Johansen family.

—Wilhelmsen archives

The F/V *Sunapee*, Eastern Rig. Built before 1920, she was owned by Arnleif Veek, beloved by Gunleif Wilhelmsen—who termed it a "great little vessel"—and eventually fished in Alaska in the later part of the century. Shown here in New Bedford.

—Isaksen Archives

The F/V *Ursula Norton*, Eastern Rig wooden boat, built in the forties and worked til the eighties. She sailed to Texas and became a seafood restaurant.

Trial Run For Kim

The recently built Kim, an autumn addition to the New Bedford fishing fleet, is shown here on her trial run in Maine. The boat, named for the granddaughter of Captain Softus Mortensen, is 73 feet long and is valued at about $90,000.

—Tollefsen-Hoaglund archives

EASTERN RIG SCALLOPER

—With permission from Arthur Moniz Galleries, New Bedford

Formerly the F/V *Jane and Ursula*, this wooden Eastern Rig scalloper was built for Jens Isaksen in 1964. He worked it for many years until it was sold and renamed.

—Ivan Flye photo, Maine

The F/V *Sippican*, Eastern Rig, wooden scalloper, little sail, 1956. Once skippered by the late Soren Hendriksen.

—John Isaksen archives

The *Hustler*, Western Rig, part-owned by John Isaksen, out of New Bedford.

—Marie Dahl Tollefsen archives

Stars and Stripes, Point Judith, Rhode Island, was owned and skippered by Captain Martin Dahl.

—Isaksen Archives

Three of Jens Isaksen's scallopers docked together. The inboard boat is Western Rigged and other two are Eastern Rigged. Jens Isaksen prided himself on keeping his boats in prime condition at all times.

—© Steve Kennedy with permission, Sovik-Jacobsen archives

A steel dragger, the F/V *Valkyrie*, built in late sixties; 98 feet long. She fished for about forty years and was owned by one family.

—AT photo

A modern New Bedford scalloper, F/V *Nordic Pride*, owned by Roy Enoksen, 1997.

Late-century scalloper, *F/V Warrior*
Exterior and Interiors

Fishing gear awaits its owners.

Topside on the *Warrior*.

Up-to-date, do-it-yourself galley replaces the role of ship's cook.

New and modern bunks with some privacy.

A staple on board a fishing boat and also a hazard: the winch.

Navigational evolution: From a wheel and a compass to a wheelhouse with every imaginable communication/ navigational aid available—all in one lifetime.

The scallop drag. The rings change size with each government decision, but the rest remains about the same.

—All Warrior photos were taken by author on a tour of the boat with Harriet J. Didriksen and Sigurd Johannessen.

The *F/V Northern Aurora*, Seattle

—Photos and description courtesy of Berit and Magne Nes

Example of a scalloper in the later twentieth century, Seattle, WA
Scalloper: 156′ × 30′ × 15′, built in 1975. Complete shelter deck from bow to stern.
Owners: Magne Nes, Tor Tollessen, Charles Knutsen and more. These three men
also fished out of New Bedford.

To make this kind of income

Sample settlement in 1996. Solveig's Boat Settlements, Fairhaven, Massachusetts,
showing income and expenses.
Courtesy Solveig's Boat Settlements
Names of personnel deleted.

```
7/15/96   SETTLE                      Solveig's Boat Settlments              Page   1

BOAT NO. .                    _  TRIP  7      FR 6/21/96 TO 7/15/96   NO. OF DAYS  24   NO. OF MEN  6

          GROSS STOCK                                        LBS. @      .00    70,859.50
          OTHER STOCK   _____         LBS. @      .00         .00
DED       TOTAL STOCK                                                          $70,859.50

005       Captain's per       .045                                 3,188.67
020       Engineer's Per      .002                                   141.71
025       Cook's per          .002                                   141.71
030       Mate's Per          .002                                   141.71
040       Solveig's                                                  300.00
060       Bags             RED DOT                                   171.80
          TOTAL DEDUCTIONS                                                       4,084.80
          NET STOCK     .                                                       66,774.70

          BOAT SHARE          .40                                              26,709.88
          BOAT EXPENSES                                                 .00
          NET BOAT SHARE                                          26,709.88

310       Capt to Mate        .070                                   150.00

          CREW SHARE                                                           40,064.82
510       Fuel                                                     6,899.42
520       Ice                                                      1,302.00
540       Icing                                                       43.20
550       Water                                                       50.00
580       Food                                                     1,286.60
600       Shacker                                                    286.00
610       Food             CREW CREDIT                               512.00-
          CREW EXPENSES                                                          9,355.22
          CREW SPLIT  6.000  MEN @  $5,118.26                                   30,709.60

EMP  NAME                      SPLIT %   $ SHARE DED     BONUS     FICA   FED   STATE    NET PAY
                             CAPT 1.000  5118.26 310    3038.67                          8156.93
                             MATE 1.000  5118.26 310  30 291.71                          5409.97
                             ENG  1.000  5118.26  25  20 283.42                          5401.68
                                  1.000  5118.26                                         5118.26
                                  1.000  5118.26                                         5118.26
                                  1.000  5118.26                                         5118.26

          CREW TOTALS                    34323.36                                       34323.36

                                                       BOAT SHARE              26709.88
                                                       FICA
                                                       EMP TAX        8.10     2780.19
                                                       NET SHARE               23929.69
```

SOME NAMES OF SCANDINAVIAN-ASSOCIATED FISHING VESSELS OUT OF NEW BEDFORD HARBOR IN THE TWENTIETHTH CENTURY —AS REMEMBERED BY THEIR FRIENDS*

Scallopers

F/V Abraham H.
F/V Aloha
F/V Alpar
F/V Ambassador
F/V Antonia
F/V Bagatelle
F/V Baltic
F/V Barbara
F/V Barbara and Gail
F/V Barbara H.
F/V Barnacle Bill
F/V Beatrice and Ida
F/V Blue Sea
F/V Brant
F/V Brighton
F/V Camden
F/V Charles Ashley
F/V Chivas Regal
F/V Commodore
F/V Concordia
F/V Contender
F/V Crown Royal
F/V Dartmouth
F/V Debbie Joann
F/V Delehence
F/V Diligence
F/V Dolphin
F/V Dorothy and Mary
F/V Edgartown

F/V Explorer
F/V Fairhaven
F/V Felicia
F/V Florence B.
F/V Hunter
F/V Ike and Jens
F/V Jane and Ursula
F/V Janet and Jeanne
F/V Jerry and Jimmy
F/V John Michael
F/V Josephine Mary
F/V Katherine and Mary
F/V Killegrew
F/V Laure H.
F/V Lauren Fay
F/V Liberty
F/V Lillian B.
F/V Linus Eldridge
F/V Louise
F/V Lynn
F/V Mariner
F/V Mary
F/V Mary and Julia
F/V Mary J. Hayes
F/V Midnight Sun
F/V Moby Dick
F/V Moonlight

F/V Narrangansett
F/V Navigator
F/V Neptune
F/V New Bedford
F/V North Sea
F/V North Star
F/V Patriots
F/V Pelican
F/V Raider
F/V Rush
F/V Sandra Jane
F/V Sea Breeze
F/V Settler
F/V Silvester
F/V Sippican
F/V Sylvia Mae
F/V The Baltic
F/V Ursula Norton
F/V Venture
F/V Victor
F/V Vivian Fay
F/V Wamsutta
F/V Whaling City
F/V William Eldridge
F/V William H.

Draggers

F/V Endurance
F/V Gannet
F/V Hazel S.
F/V Invader

F/V Krilica
F/V Nautilus
F/V Odin
F/V Pauline H.
F/V Pocahontas
F/V Rosie II
F/V Shannon
F/V Sheelegelee
F/V Smilyn
F/V Sunapee
F/V Tor
F/V Valkyrie

Scalloper-Dragger Convertibles

F/V Bell
F/V Christina J.
F/V Dagny
F/V Eunice Lillia
F/V Fleet Wing
F/V Huntress
F/V John Michael
F/V King Fisher
F/V Michigan
F/V Ocean Gem
F/V Pat San Marie
F/V Poseidon
F/V Sippican
F/V Smaragd
F/V Solvieg J.
F/V Tempest
F/V Valencia
F/V Venture

*spelling as remembered by the fishermen

15

~

Working the Waters

LIVES OF THE FISHERMEN

—Photo courtesy of James Nachtwey /VII

Gunleif Wilhelmsen, 1975.

"They're terrific," I said, and meant it, for there is no better company anywhere than men who love the sea.

—John Le Carre, "The Secret Pilgrim"

~

354

THE EXTRAORDINARY WATERS

HOW MANY FAMILIES can tell about the time they caught a nuclear submarine in their nets? Or can credit themselves with the legend of the Bermuda Triangle? This family can!

Many of the Norwegian emigrants to Southeast Massachusetts led somewhat predictable lives within their unique set of circumstances while others had lives fraught with the dangers and complications of the sea and *pendling*. Some had lives rearranged by the risks of their adopted lifestyle while others led lives that were touched by the unexpected—that were ennobled by responsibility.

This extended Norwegian family with their extraordinary lives was not a typical fishing family. Amazing incidents at sea or at home seemed to follow them and the family included fascinating people, historic events and a positive outreach to the community.

I interviewed part of this family at the home of Gunleif Wilhelmsen along with his wife Helen and her brother, Arnold, who died recently. Gunleif also had a brother, Alf, who lived on the same street and was married to Helen's sister Doris. In addition, both Helen and Gunleif had fathers and mothers who had been very active in the fishing community and whose lives were frequently discussed in the conversation. During the interview everyone seemed to be talking at once. And to add to my confusion, two of the family members discussed also had nicknames.

I left this interview warmed by these very special people I had just met, and also by their hospitality which included coffee and sweets, but was confused about who was who and who did what. Gunleif has since assured me that I have it right. I saw him at a concert I had planned a year later and he came up to me

—AT photo

The Veeks and the Wilhelmsens discuss their lives with me in 1997.

and gave me a big hug and told me how much the music had meant to him. His wife Helen died, and he recently passed away himself.

I will never forget this enthusiastic family who so proudly and without reservation told me their stories. I instantly liked and respected them and will always remember them. This is their courageous and unpredictable family story.

THE VEEKS AND THE WILHELMSENS

ARNLEIF VEEK, BEFORE COMING TO AMERICA, lived in Skudeneshavn on the Island of Karmøy where his mother ran a chocolate shop. Arnleif Veek was therefore called *Sjokolade* (chocolate) throughout his life because of that. Johannes (John) Wilhelmsen, father of Gunleif, was also from Skudeneshavn where he worked as a carpenter and coffin maker, *kisteman*, and was called that throughout his life. Both men were quite well known on the island. They both emigrated to America and eventually came to the New Bedford area. *Sjokolade's* daughter, Helen, married Gunleif, the son of *kisteman*. Her sister Doris married his brother Alf.

—*Courtesy, Ellen Isaksen*

Arnleif Veek shortly before his death.

Gunleif Wilhelmsen's dad came over in 1923. He scalloped and clammed in Brooklyn and New York as well as hired out boats for rentals. Gunleif and his brother Alf came over later and went up to New Bedford with him in 1946. Gunleif remembers: "I came to New Bedford where I fished on my father's boat. They had gone bankrupt in Norway and had exhausted everything, and my sister was crippled from tetanus and had lockjaw and her legs were a problem. We heard about what the doctors could do here, and in 1930 we came and a doctor helped my sister. Her right leg was four inches too short.

"I was on many kinds of boats scalloping or dragging. In 1941 I went into the service until 1945." Gunleif was in the Navy and on the small Naval vessels used in the D-Day invasion of Normandy—vessels that brought both men and equipment into the battle through the perilous seas—but he modestly kept that to himself.

"My dad and mother bought a house in New Bedford, and we used to take the steamer from New Bedford to Fall River to New York. It was an overnight steamer to New York City.

"I was on a tugboat for a while, went to Puerto Rico, Nassau, New York and before that I was a captain for Sandy Hook Marine Laboratory at Fort

With France and the Germans in the background, Gunleif Wilhelmsen rests on his boat after the harrowing D-Day invasion in 1944. He never mentioned this fact in his interview—it was just another life challenge for him that he took in stride.

—*Wilhelmsen archives*

John Hancock. I skippered their research vessel, had three vessels to operate and then was the port captain. I was the engineer on the tanker *Tidewater*. When I was just out of the Navy and was at the shipyard waiting for a position on a tanker, I was a licensed diesel engineer."

THE BERMUDA TRIANGLE MYSTERY—SOLVED!

GUNLEIF REMEMBERS, "My father, John, was fishing off Virginia in the early thirties when he was on the *John and Mary*. They were out in a storm that just wouldn't go away. It lasted and lasted and they were running out of fuel and food—everything that was needed for the boat and men. They were in trouble! A merchant ship stopped to see if they could help and stood by, but finally the captain told them he could wait no longer and had to go on to South America. So the captain of the *John and Mary* decided that they should abandon ship, and everyone would go with the tanker because they had no radio or phone and were in danger. So they abandoned ship and went with the tanker to South America and then came back with the same ship. My dad with his cabinet-making skills made deck chairs for everyone aboard.

"Later we heard stories of the Bermuda Triangle and all the mystery and strange happenings that surrounded it. They had originally found an empty boat—no sign of crew, no sign of what happened to them—just a boat alone in that area. It was the *John and Mary*. No one could figure out why this boat was alone without a crew, and so the legend began."

THE BIG CATCH

"I BROUGHT UP PIECES of wreckage on trips sometimes, and once I found a large anchor which is now on the grounds across the street from Sally Tonnessen's house, but that was nothing at all compared to my father-in-law, when he got the biggest catch of all time.

Gunleif's wife, Helen Veek Wilhelmsen, recounts the story about her father, Arnleif Veek. "When he was on the *Red Tom*, in the late fifties or early sixties, his boat was running along just fine and the fish were plentiful that day.

USS Nautilus superstructure. Not many fisherman can claim an encounter of this kind.

Then all of a sudden he started to go backwards. He couldn't understand what was happening, but he knew something very, very large was dragging them backwards. They finally got the boat untangled and had to come in. They were all caught up in wire and all kinds of things. The Navy denied any involvement, but when the atomic submarine *Nautilus* came in, they saw the damage on her and finally recognized the problem. The *Red Tom* had caught the *Nautilus* in its nets. The Navy compensated the fishing boat— more than the loss—but we had to go through Congress to get the money. My father was on 'I've Got a Secret,' and his secret was that he caught the atomic submarine, *Nautilus*."

OUR FAMILY,
THE WIFE'S STORY.

HELEN REMEMBERS HER FATHER'S colorful life fondly: "The Veeks had a ship supply store here and in Brooklyn. My family would have the store and if times were not so good, my dad went back to sea. Father was well known on the waterfront.

"Arnleif Veek had his eighty-year birthday party at the Wamsutta Club. Everyone was there and enjoyed the party. As described by a friend, "He went to bed as usual after the party, and next morning he didn't come up for breakfast. So I finally went in, and he was dead. All of the people who came for the party from far away were now there for the funeral. He was a colorful personality who exited in style."

TO RUSSIA WITH (OUR) FISH

GUNLEIF REMEMBERED, "When we were scalloping during the Cold War, there was Russians fishing nearby, and we were up alongside talking to them. We gave them some scallops that we exchanged with cigarettes. They gave us herring. We all spoke the universal hand language. But one other man was a military type, and he came up and said something—so that was the end of it. Can't criticize them for doing their jobs. Of course, we did get mad at them but the government didn't do anything until it was too late. There was so much fish out there before they came that we could lose our nets from the weight. Codfish by the millions of pounds—used to be. But after the Russians took all the herring, there was no feed for the fish."

THE FISHING LIFE

GUNLEIF CONTINUES: "I worked in many different places because I wanted work where I could get home more often. Never had enough time with the family. Two days ashore and five days at sea was wonderful. I liked the sea but couldn't be with the family. Two-thirds of your life was dead—gone. Two-thirds of life spent out at sea was just a waste out there. We had to get along with all of the crew, but there is not that much to talk about.

"We had four children, two and two. My children didn't become fishermen except one, Gary, who became a captain. We called him Captain Kid. The women had responsibility for the families when we were at sea. It was a colorful life and an interesting life for those who can handle it. When you are younger, you are so busy you don't have time to worry; you don't imagine what it is like until you are older and find out how bad it is out there. Now that I know more, I would be very worried. Used to go out with very little knowledge of the weather, unlike today. Some guys just can't do it. Some men get very sick, and others sit in the pilot house and cry because they are so sick."

ADVENTURES, ADVENTURES AND
MORE ADVENTURES

GUNLEIF RECALLS SOME OF THE TIMES when the sea was a bit too rough. "There was that storm in 1962 when the *Midnight Sun* went down. My sister called me to tell me that our boat, the *Sunapee*, which was owned by my father-in-law Arnleif Veek, was reported as missing. My sister used to worry so much. We just happened to be out in a storm and the guys didn't want to go in—wanted to wait till it was over. We had decided to ride it out, but the storm got to be a lot worse than we had anticipated. We expected thirty-five-mile-per-hour winds but got winds over seventy. Listening to the news, we heard *Snoopy* was presumed lost. We had a small radio-telephone and tried to call the Coast Guard and finally got through to Castle Hill near Newport. He made out the name and I said, 'Tell the owner, the boat will be in as soon as we can.' That was the *Sunapee*—great little vessel—a wooden boat built in 1918 and still floating today on the West Coast. It scalloped out of Alaska, and it went through the Panama Canal to the West Coast."

He continued, "We was on the *Janet and Jeanne* in the '54 hurricane. The *Redstart* was lost then. Knew we couldn't make it, so I set a course for just offshore where there was a more even bottom without bad rocks. We were offshore to get away from the shoals. We survived very well, but I sure missed my brother who didn't make this trip because he had hurt his finger. I was up and down, in the pilothouse, engine room, back and forth. Didn't realize how much I missed him until he was not there, but had a terrific mate who had been a captain for many years called Whaling Bay. His real name was David and his brother was named Thor. They knew what to do and how to handle the boat into the sea, and I would handle the throttle, slow down and stop, or go ahead and line up the seas right.

"The seas were angry and the biggest worry was with that. With a small sixty-five-foot fishing boat, if the seas broke, it could have gone 'right-over-keel.' I was leaning on the bulkhead. I was surprised a few boats survived that I didn't think would survive.

"The *Sea Hawk* was in trouble in that storm. Jens Isaksen saw the vessel was in trouble, so he went in with his boat, steamed in and got a line on them and towed them away from Noman'sland. (Many fishermen have remarked that this feat done by Jens Isaksen was selfless and extraordinary.)

NIXON AND REAGAN YEARS: FOE & WOE TO THE FISHERMEN

"IN THE NIXON YEARS they did away with the money for the fisheries bureau, and I lost my job. Reagan came and stopped the medical services for the fishermen. So I got a tug-boating license. But I was low man on the unions when I went fishing again. I worked also as experimental machinist for the Connecticut Atomic Nuclear Engine Laboratory, operated by Pratt and Whitney experimental engines in Connecticut. My dad said, 'Come back and we will buy a boat together.'

"My brother and I bought a tugboat and took it scalloping and dragging. Never did both at the same time. We had to change all the equipment and it took a week to do it.

"There is general talk that Norwegians are cold, but they are warmer on the islands. I think of the warmth and love of my family—we had a very close family and still do. I was sixty-five when I retired, and I was lucky to be in good health. There were all kinds of accidents aboard the boats. I was lucky!"

I remember looking at Gunleif Wilhelmsen during this interview and thinking of my father. Somehow he made me feel close to him and I think, perhaps, my father was like him in many ways. They were from the same town, with the same attitudes and there was something else about him that I couldn't quite perceive, but I felt a special closeness to this man and I was so happy to have met him. For me he symbolized the Norwegian fisherman. Gunleif Wilhelmsen died in 2002, several years after the death of his wife, Helen, and his brother Alf. Her brother Arnold died in 2004.

LIFE AS AN AMERICAN-NORWEGIAN FISHERMAN IN NEW BEDFORD

CAN ANY GIRL FORGET her first youthful "crush"—the first time she realized there was a boy in the world who was different, who had a bit of magic, who glowed—someone she wanted to know better or at least speak to just once in her life? I was about eleven years old in the seventh grade at the Rodman School in New Bedford when a blond, handsome, eighth-grader walked into the room with a message for the teacher. I looked at him from behind my geography book and felt myself blushing. He looked like a young Viking god: blond, blue-eyed and wearing a beautiful Norwegian sweater. He had rosy cheeks, a mischievous smile, and walked with confidence while exuding friendliness and also a bit of sophistication. Even the teacher smiled at him differently.

That day marked the beginning of many months of looking over heads in a crowd to see him, blushing when he entered a room and being embarrassed if we passed on the stairwell. I never spoke to him, I never had the nerve, but once I remember smiling, just a little, when we passed on the stairs. He looked startled and ignored it. I had thought that since I had a Norwegian name, we had a connection of sorts and that he might smile. I had a knot in my heart as I rushed to my classroom. We never spoke and eventually he left for high school. I remember where he sat in his classroom, in chorus, in the auditorium and my notebooks were covered with his name. I missed him when I was in the eighth grade and he was in another school. I never saw him again.

When I decided to write this book, fifty or so years later, I was looking into my past for names and relatives and thought of him. Could I, should I, try to find him again after fifty years? I looked in the phone book, and saw his name. I decided to call, and felt all the embarrassment of the eleven-year-old who used to watch for him in the corridors. We made an appointment, and I went to interview him. I cannot ever remember being as nervous as I was that day. I almost did not ring the doorbell, but did and asked the mature man who answered if I could see Karl (a pseudonym, as he asked to not have his name printed). The man then told me that he, indeed, was Karl.

Had I really expected to find a thirteen-year-old blond boy in a Norwegian sweater? I did not recognize him at all and since he had never known me or who I was, he had no recollection of me. In my girlhood dreams and fantasies he had always been at the center of my life. In a way I am glad he didn't remember me or how I had made a fool of myself. It would have been horrid, if he had said to me, "Oh, I remember you, that girl who was always staring at me."

His interview proved to be one of the most candid interviews I'd had. He was relaxed, open, honest and forthright. His was an interesting life—not a conventional Norwegian-American life in some ways, but very traditional in others. I decided to put it in this chapter because it is typical of many different Norwegian lives all in one.

This was not a man who had become a captain or wealthy. He doesn't take long, expensive vacations or visit Norway. He has financial constraints and has worked hard all of his life. He has a family, and his wife stayed home to raise the family. He is proud of his work, and he sees his chosen profession objectively. He is a thoroughly nice person, open, honest and not complex. He is not the boy I had dreamed about as a young girl, but he is a man who deserves respect for a life well-lived. I am so happy that I finally got to say "hello."

AN AMERICAN-NORWEGIAN LIFE

HE NARRATES HIS LIFE by beginning at the beginning.

"I was born in Brooklyn where my father was a carpenter before he came up to New Bedford to fish. I went to New Bedford schools, Rodman and Voke, and always considered myself an American. I didn't speak Norwegian or attend Norwegian church or activities and had few Norwegian friends. Father was very American also. Mother and father didn't participate in the Norwegian community. Even in New York we didn't have Norwegian friends and didn't live in the Norwegian section. Mother came over when she was fifteen from Kopervik on Karmøy, and her mother insisted that they all speak English so that she could learn it also. My father was from Åkrehamn on Karmøy.

"Growing up in New Bedford we were assigned jobs scrubbing the floors every Saturday morning while my mother worked downtown in a department store. My grandmother would cook Norwegian bread—but not Mother. At Christmas, we celebrated Christmas Eve, but it didn't register as Norwegian.

362

We never wanted to learn Norwegian. I went to St Paul's Methodist Church, and Father belonged to the Moose Club. We had Polish friends through relatives. We were Americans!

"Mother went back to Norway five or six times recently. Before Father died, they made about three trips, once we were grown and out of the house. I never went but my brother did.

"My grandfather was named Johan. According to my parents, when he became a citizen he actually had a choice of names, the farm name, father's name, etc. My grandfather fished out of New York. My father worked for a construction company and did metal ceilings and also had his own business. In 1940 my uncle told him to come up to New Bedford to fish as my uncle was here. In those days, New York and New Bedford had to take the catch to Fulton Fish Market in New York City and make the circuit—no buyers in New Bedford at that time. When the buyers came to New Bedford, then the boats came here directly to get the fish to port a day fresher.

NEW BEDFORD

"FATHER CAME UP BEFORE WE DID, and we came up to New Bedford in '44. Mother's family all lived on Long Island. Mother and Father spoke Norwegian all the time. In the beginning we had Norwegian food but later not. Once a skipper asked me why I never learned to speak Norwegian, and I said, ' I've heard it all my life and don't care. It sounds like gibberish to me.' I can catch a word here and there. On the boat, I was the only American and I would go down and eat, and then grab a book while everyone sat at the table talking. I was there for seven months, and the only time they talked to me was when they had a question about something. My cousin learned, writes and speaks it.

"I tried carpentry after graduation from Voke (New Bedford Vocational High School), building boats, ship-to-shore whale boats (traditionally boats which would take Naval personnel to shore) for the Navy. A hurricane wiped out the plant and I then worked on roofs and went into the service. Went into the Air Force and married.

"I came back to New Bedford in 1958 and went on the *Edgartown* as a shacker. Made one trip and pulled a muscle in both hands from opening scallops. My wrist was as big as my forearm. 'Big-ear Mike,' the skipper, said, 'Not again.' I got a job as shacker on the *Ruth Moses* and then went out as a man on the *Debbie and Joanne* for about seven years. A guy usually shacked a long time before you became a man. We averaged a dollar a bag take home, $280 per five days. It was steady work.

"Years ago all the boats did both—scalloping in the summer and dragging in the winter. Grandfather's boat, *The Edith*, was an old boat and double duty with western rig. Mother lost her whole family on a boat in a hurricane in New Jersey.

SCALLOPING AND DRAGGING . . .
THE BIG DIFFERENCE

"I WENT TO TWINE (rope) school in New Bedford and got out of scalloping when the price went down. Then I went on a few draggers. What a difference—so much work! We have to know so much about the nets. Scalloping is by rote. Anyone could stand and close his eyes and shuck a scallop. Much more to dragging. A scalloper doesn't even know how to tie a knot. I have done both, and I could see the difference. There were more men on a scalloper. On a dragger, everyone has a job to do and it had to be done. Scalloping was more dangerous, though. A ton of steel comes over the rail swinging with heavy rocks—not too much control.

F/V MIDNIGHT SUN

"I WAS ON *Midnight Sun* before it went down. It came from Maine and was the first boat in New Bedford with the scallop boxes enclosed at the shipyard, and they were completely enclosed for winter. I made three trips with *Midnight Sun*.

"Tried to tuna with Japanese long line. We lost gear overnight and when we found it and hauled it back, it was loaded with swordfish. So it clicked—swordfish were feeding at night. So when the contract was up, we made big swordfish trips. It took two days to take it out and the gang made five thousand per man. Unheard-of at that time—1965. The fishing boat *Rush*'s owner rigged his boat for swordfishing and lost all the gear. He ended up with washtubs only and a line hauler. Guy from *Debbie and Joanne* bought what was left from him and rigged it up, and we went out swordfishing. One shot—you made money or didn't. I put a hook through the hand once. Later the swordfishing price went down to nothing again.

"I quit the *Debbie and Joanne* and went on *Catherine C.* scalloping. Went with Tommy Larsen on *Venus*, *Debbie and Joanne* and *Catherine C.* as an engineer. I heard they were making good money swordfishing in Newfoundland. They asked me to rig up the *Catherine C.* for swordfishing. First time we set the gear we started hauling the next morning with six hundred hooks in the water.

"The first three hooks had swordfish on it. The cook asked for three tubs of gear and we said, 'No, we got three hooks in.' He said, 'Oh, no, we have six hundred hooks out there.' 'Don't count on that,' I said,' but we caught fifty-two swordfish that day on Georges Bank. Hauled again the next day and then had total of a hundred fish. The cook tried to straddle one of the fish so we could gut it, but it was so big he couldn't get his legs around it, and it dressed out at five hundred pounds (meaning without head, tail, sword fins and guts).

HURRICANE

"WAS IN A HURRICANE with *Catherine C.* We were coming home and the hurricane changed direction. We were way out to the east—were as far as you could go on Georges Bank. As we came west, the hurricane came west and caught us . . . We made it, though.

"Last boat I was on was the *Ocean Spray*—lobstering. Was there for eleven years. Almost sunk on the *Ocean Spray.* They put a brand-new engine in it and the owner was out with us to try out the engine, and I was running the engine. Was too rough to fish and they decided to let it lay. I told him the engine technicians said not to let the engine sit in idle because it was brand new. But it was six hours in idle. Stopped the listers—small auxiliary engines for electricity and hoses on deck. So I shut them off, closed the door and went off. The lister blew a hose and water started going into the engine room. Over time the boat rolled and I got wet. Water was splashing on the flywheel on other side so I got up to look and it was all water just one step down. Water was halfway up the main engine. Got it all shut off and took the water out in buckets. I was up to waist in water. The Coast Guard sent a helicopter out. *Pauline H.* laid alongside us in case we went down. The Coast Guard brought pumps and drained it all. We started it up and went back.

"I liked fishing. Some got drunk. Before they went out they drank because they hated fishing so much. Some threw up when they knew they were going out. It never bothered me. I just went out. Got into a rhythm—nine hours on and three off.

LOOKING BACK

"I GOT OUT AT SIXTY-TWO. I have a pension and Social Security. I fished for thirty-eight years. When you are in your sixties with an extra hundred pounds of weight, it was difficult. I enjoy eating and like meat, potatoes and gravy. Can't afford to travel. I was a skipper once but didn't like it. Was a mate also, but it was too much on the nerves.

I had four children and was never home. My wife had to raise them all alone. I never saw my children grow up until now that I am retired and can spend time with my granddaughter. I was an engineer, and when I came home I was down at the boat every day taking care of the stuff that needed work so hardly saw my children.

"I love to work with wood now and remember those old days."

A NORWEGIAN-AMERICAN FISHERMAN
FROM KARMØY: SVERRE MANNES

*"I am Norwegian, but in my heart I feel just as much for the
United States.
If it hadn't been for the U.S. where would we be? If it wasn't for
them we would be speaking German or Russian. It's a good
country!"*

—Sverre Mannes

OFTEN A YOUNG MAN FOLLOWED his father to America after a few years
of testing the waters. Sverre Mannes was such a man. He followed Oskar
Mannes' emigration to New Bedford as an eighteen-year-old boy in 1961.
Later he brought over his wife and child. He stayed until 1970 when he and
his family returned to Norway, and then he made periodic visits to America
until 1980. He and his wife were divorced, and Sverre raised his daughter who
was about twelve years old at that time.

He loves America, loves Norway and cherishes his life in the New Bedford
area when he followed the waters to earn money for his family. His is a
Norwegian-American story that again is "everyman's" story as it encompasses
many elements of the lives of many emigrants.

A very personable and articulate man, he was especially candid and open
in my interview with him in Norway, and I respected his honesty and responsibility for his life experiences.

—*Sverre Mannes Archives*

Sverre Mannes with father Oskar in
the early sixties.

—*Mannes archives*

The family of Sverre Mannes: Aud, Arild and
Jacob with their new car and home at Piney Acres
in 1965.

KARMØY TO AMERICA

"I WAS 18 WHEN I CAME TO USA. Many had come from Karmøy and all were doing all right. In 1961 we made much more money than we could make in Norway at that time—up to $10,000 a year for a man's share. The *Sandra Jane* paid us that much when Kopervik was skipper. The fishermen made more than college-educated professionals. (Schoolteachers were beginning at $3,800 in that year.)

"I got married three days before I left Norway and had a son when I came back home. When my wife came over with my son, we lived in an apartment on County Street in a house owned by a man from Skudeneshavn. After a year we built a house in Piney Acres outside of New Bedford at 31 Green Briar Court.

"Our lives revolved around the waterfront, fishing and our community of family and friends. I would meet my Norwegian friends at the waterfront, and we would all have our new shiny cars—nice!

—*Sverre Mannes archives*

Sverre Mannes shucking scallops in the Alaskan fishery 1983.

"We really didn't like fishing, especially in the winter. We would look at those ten days—all that dirt on the deck, mud, gravel, and anything else we scraped up from the bottom when we got the scallops—and wasn't too happy. We loved it when they called a trip off during winter's frigid days. We felt like a million dollars.

"Once we got up and out to sea and got started, after a few days it was good, everyone was cheerful and looked forward to the five days at home. We came in, got the check—good money—put some in the bank—wife picked you up at the dock—nice car—went shopping—filled up refrigerator. When it was nice weather we went for a ride. It was good!

"The five days at home was a good family life. We socialized with other fishermen and families. But I just hated the fishing!"

THESE WERE THE BEST DAYS OF MY LIFE!

"WHEN I THINK BACK, I had my family there for seven years. We had plenty to do. We would drive around and sometimes drove to New Hampshire. Those five days we did what we wanted Some invested in boats

—*General fishing archives*

Karl Johan Melkevik cleaning up scallop shells to make room for the next dredge in the sixties.

and worked hard and deserved good—they deserved every penny they got. I was married young, and I went out with single guys when I was alone. We went for rides to Cape Cod, and I liked to drive around.

"The single men and married men with families at home in Norway often met each other in the bars. Where else could we go except the bars when we were alone. Family was in Norway, and we got lonely.

"But as much as we hated offshore, we loved the shore. I really missed New Bedford.

"There is nothing more enticing, disenchanting, and enslaving than the life at sea."

—Joseph Conrad, "Lord Jim," 1900

THE SEA

"WE WAS OUT THERE on the water when there was sometimes forty- to fifty-foot waves off the coast of Virginia, in particular, or when fishing off of Cape May, New Jersey. The currents are bad there. I had a close call on Jacob Jacobsen's boat. My father was on boat with me. Closest call I ever had! I was cutting scallops on the starboard side—no shucking houses in those days—on the port side the deck was full. We were going quite fast and the boat rolled and the sea took me. My father grabbed me by the shoulder by instinct. I was hanging halfway over the rail 'til I got my other hand on the rail of the pilot-house. A half load of scallops on deck went overboard. Jacob came down to the galley, and said he had to have a cigarette—and he didn't smoke! He was all shook.

"It takes both luck and skill when men survive at sea. Boats didn't look good in New Bedford, but they were very seaworthy.

"I really didn't like fishing. It was the worst job—hard, but good money. There was lots of competition. The more you did, the more money you made.

After 1961 we could fish as much as you wanted. We made more money when fish was scarce. The Union was there the whole time. It was better in them days than now. Seven days out in winter and eight in summer . . . making good money and steady, good reliable men didn't waste time.

—*AT photo*

Sverre Mannes in Norway, 1998.

"I will retire in America. My son is an American citizen and has dual citizenship. Everybody on Karmøy has somebody that has been over there in the states. I was in Alaska for a year and was working also on platforms on North Sea.

"I hope that Norwegians will be remembered for being good workers and taking care of their family and doing their best. I only regret that I never took out American citizen papers."

Sverre retired in 2003 and moved to America for part of the year. So in the end he got both wishes: to live in Norway and to live in America. He earned it. He has spent his most of his life—forty-two years—working the waters. Skoal to your retirement, Sverre !

HANS HARAM, THE OLD-TIMER

HANS HARAM was one of the first Norwegian fishermen to come to New Bedford from Norway, via New York, to fish and raise his family. He was from Haramsøy in Northern Norway.

According to his grandson Stephen Small, of Maine: "My grandfather was already middle-aged by the time he left for the U.S. He had an older brother who inherited the family farm. I know that my grandfather struggled to make a living in Norway, spending much of his time at sea. He wished to be more successful, and that is why he came to the United States, and that is why he stayed.

"He came to America around 1920–24. He wanted to come, but

—*AT photo 1999*

Stephen Small in Maine recalls memories of his grandfather Hans Haram.

my grandmother, who came over later, was very unhappy and didn't want to leave home. She and their three daughters came over four or five years later. My mother was thirteen years old at the time. He prepared for their arrival for those four to five years, working construction in New York City and living in Bay Ridge, enticed by an older cousin from Haramsøy who preceded him.

"He was quite successful in his trade, and although he loved living in America, his wife did not. After a stay in New York City, he came to New Bedford where he lobstered and worked very hard and eventually bought a boat, a dragger where he dragged from both sides. He had two boats, *Viking* the *Arnold*. He was resourceful and always tried to get the best price.

THE RESCUE

"WHEN HE WAS A CAPTAIN in 1941 he rescued some shipwrecked mariners off the M/S *Oregon*. Nothing was stated that they had sunk because of a German submarine. It was kept very hush-hush because people would have been upset if they knew it was a German sub so close. But the family knew it was and he received a letter from Benjamin Small of the *Oregon* on behalf of its crew.

"December 14, 1941 Sunday

Capt Hans Haram,

My dear friend,

Hope you're well—also the rest of the boys on the Viking. We're all getting along fine.

I would appreciate it very much your sending me one of the life preservers that was brought aboard when we were rescued. I want it badly for a remembrance. The camera I left aboard any of the boys who wants it, is more than welcome to it.

Please send me the preserver express collect—I insist on paying all the freight expenses.

Hoping you will grant me this one last request.

Thank you. Your humble and grateful friend,
Benjamin Small, M/S Oregon

Regards to all the boys from myself and the crew of the Oregon.
1130—6th Ave.
Des Moines, Iowa"

A MAN OF FEW WORDS

"No other home was like his home. His was a 1930s house and had a big wooden door with oval glass, grandfather clock in hall, and much woodwork, stained and varnished. He lived at 1063 Rockdale Avenue in New Bedford, and a farm bordered their backyard when I was young. It was a nice house they built. He put a goldfish pond in back and planted grapes and in winter kept goldfish in the basement in oil drums. He also made *lutefisk* in the basement. He spoke Norwegian in the home, and the silver was Norwegian, and probably the china too. We ate Norwegian food that I remember to be white with lots of potatoes, codfish and carrots.

"Grandfather followed the form at home and church. He did what he was required to do and that was that. He was a man of a few words, very quiet. He was one of first Norwegians in New Bedford and the first successful one.

"At the time of the *Viking*'s heyday, it was considered to be a large boat and was for several years the highliner (the biggest money-maker) out of New Bedford. I remember the builder and owner of the stern trawler *Valkyrie*, from the next generation of successful Norwegian boat owners, Leif Jacobsen, speaking about my grandfather with respect as one who 'paved the way for him and others.'

—General fishing archives

A good cod catch, mid-century. Such a catch would be rare in the late century.

"I didn't feel love from my grandparents—more of an indifference. My father, who was not Norwegian, was not enthusiastic about his inlaws. My cousins spent more time with them and I felt a distinction from the other cousins, who were all Norwegian. I was shy and afraid of them as my cousins were more open. My mother didn't make any effort to speak Norwegian and spoke English all the time.

"When my grandfather was dying, he gave Mother some money and said to give it to me, and she bought me a bank in the shape of a Norwegian woman. You put a coin in her mouth and she turned her head. He treated my mother with kindness, but he was always out fishing. She used to sit on his knee when she was young, and he would tell her stories. When she was a teenager she had riding lessons and tennis lessons—middle-class hobbies.

THE DANGER

"Fishing was a dangerous trade, and my mother worried about her father going out fishing. They had dangerous jobs so that children could have good lives without danger. Grandfather didn't care too much about American or Norwegian cultures. Grandmother really cared. He had to take her back once a year to visit the family.

"The *Viking* sunk after his death. It was getting old when it sunk—no one killed, all rescued. Grandfather was very meticulous about his boat when he owned it. He watched them at shipyard, and there was an explosion in the yard once. He worried that it might have loosened some of the stays on his boat, and we thought about that when the boat eventually sunk.

"He was not really happy in his marriage because grandmother was so unhappy in the states. She died before him, and then he went fishing a lot for pleasure. He took expensive vacations to Canada or to Key West for big-game fish. He met a woman in Key West, twenty years younger, and married her."

Hans Haram was a man who worked very hard, lived his life as best he could in his very reserved way with his homesick wife. After her death he spent the rest of his life doing exactly as he pleased. His grandson remembers him with fondness and admiration.

16

Finest Kind

—Olden family archives

Andrew Olden with crewmember in classic fishing portrait of the fisherman and his catch. Cod are rarely seen this size any longer.

SOME MEN WHO MADE A DIFFERENCE

- *Mathias Bendiksen: A leader among men*
- *Harald Mannes: A man who cares about people*
- *Andrew Olden: Innovations in the scallop industry*
- *Kaare Ness: New frontiers*

THE *Janteloven* is thought by some to prevent innovative thinking and creative decision-making among countless potentially ingenious Norwegians because its essence is "not to be different." It encourages doing things in the same "old" way and those who have clever ideas for improvement, advancement or enhancement or who are imaginative, especially talented or gifted, or who may be potential shakers or movers, decision-makers or specialists, often do not have their ideas realized. They would have to have extraordinary conviction to override reproach by the family or community or have very high self-esteem, a thick skin and independence.

Family and community social censure—being termed "special"—meaning something akin to defiant, weird or different, is an obstacle that is not easy to overcome. Whereas Americans generally (but not all) tend to embrace the new, innovative, different or creative, many (but not all) Norwegians and other Scandinavians often do not. Fitting in and not making waves is more important than standing tall for change and innovation. Group consensus is the norm, and generally one is not taught to "stand up and be heard," as Americans historically (but not as much in recent years, I feel) have been taught. When Norwegian men and women, whether in America or Norway speak out, act creatively, take risks, embrace or create the new, one must appreciate that in many cases it is a brave act, indeed.

MATHIAS (MATT) BENDIKSEN:
A LEADER AMONG MEN

"To ask well, to answer rightly are the marks of a wise man.
Men must speak of men's deeds. What happens may not be hidden."

—#28 Hávamál

IN A NORWEGIAN-AMERICAN community where men concentrated on their boats and women on their homes, leaders outside the traditional sea captain's role were and are all too rare. Little attention was or is given to the greater community and almost none (with a few exceptions) to the nonprofit service community.

Mathias Bendiksen did not fit that mold. He was a man who chose to enter new waters in his home country as well as internationally. He also invested his time in his local community. His leadership benefited the fishing industry in both American and international waters.

He assumed many leadership roles in his life and pioneered concepts, programs and ideas. He was a member of a family who also took leadership roles in Norway, such as serving as mayor of Karmøy itself. It is a family known for its drive, intellectual leadership and commitment to furthering their local communities.

His son, Robert, called "Bob," holds a Ph.D. in sociology. He remembers viewing a film of a helicopter flight over Utsira, his father's home island in Southwest Norway—"where I saw the school, church, and the harbor from where he sailed for New York in 1928 at the age of sixteen.

"Mathias Bendiksen, like many others, went to Brooklyn where he joined other family members. Family members remaining in Norway eventually went to Karmøy and Stavanger to live. Times were hard in Norway, with little money and no electricity, and were especially difficult on cold winter nights visiting the outhouse. He enjoyed school and he had fun with friends—but there was no money to pay for further schooling, and he had the 'America fever.' He borrowed money from his older brothers so he could join them and his father pole-fishing out of Brooklyn and Islip, Long Island.

—New Bedford Standard-Times staff photo

Mathias Bendiksen from Utsira, Norway. A leader of men and a man whose work and perseverance helped to improve the world's fishing industry.

"Matt worked as a carpenter with his father and later took work as a cook aboard a fishing boat. He quickly learned that he needed an engineer's license to make it in the fishing business. He went to night school where his English improved, and he earned his license. The Depression was not a hardship for Matt, Mike and John, because they shared a room and always had work on the boats. Their simple lifestyle was comfortable compared to harder times at home in Norway. *Bestefar* (Grandfather) and *Onkel* John sent money home to their wives whenever possible.

"The Brooklyn-Norwegian fishermen heard that fishing was better in New Bedford, so in the mid–1930s many of them headed north to the Whaling City for jobs on scallopers and draggers on Georges Bank. Matt and Mike lived in the same room in New Bedford and they dated and married American women who were friends. My mother, Doris Gustafson from Worcester, spoke Swedish which she had learned from her immigrant parents."

Doris remembers those special days when she first met Matt. "My girl-friend had a boyfriend named Mike Bendiksen. I told her that he was so nice that if he had a brother, I would like to meet him. Matt, the brother, came to visit in New Bedford, and I met him. Because fishing was good up here, he decided to come and stay."

Her son Bob writes: "They were married in a simple ceremony in 1938 and I was born in 1940. When war broke out, we moved to Staten Island, so that Matt could work on the oil boats in New York harbor, a job that exempted him from the draft because of its importance to the nation.

The Bendiksen family attended the Elim Baptist Church before Trinity Lutheran Church was built. I remember them very well and particularly Doris. I would see her each Sunday, and she was always beautifully dressed and very friendly. She seemed so interested in young people, and she would make a point of coming over and saying hello to me after church. My mother always described her as "that lovely, friendly and sincere Swedish woman." It was very special for me many years later at a Norwegian event, when a woman came over to me and asked me if I were Astrid. Indeed it was Doris Bendiksen, still lovely, still interested and still with her warm smile and beautifully dressed.

THE FISHING YEARS

"AFTER THE WAR," recalls Doris, "we moved back to New Bedford and Matt got a site as an engineer on the F/V *Growler*. My husband scalloped, came in, sold his scallops, and went out the next day. His hands were very swollen as they used table knives in those days to open scallops. Their hands were short, strong and all cut up.

"The new boats have toilets, TV, fridge, microwaves and rooms. In the old days, everything was all in one room."

"My husband was in some bad storms when the pilothouse windows crashed in (the usual sign the boat will be lost). He had the *Growler* and the *Challenge* built in Maine. Fishing was very hard in the old days. Gone ten or eleven days and sometimes went into other ports including Newport."

Matt's son relates: "He was soon offered the chance to buy into the boat and become skipper. When the owner died, my father remained half-owner and captain."

Says Doris: "My husband took a course in navigation in New York and stayed with a relative and she spoke with a dialect—lots of 'K' words—and I had a hard time understanding. Swedish and Oslo Norwegian are similar but not on Karmøy, where there is a dialect.

"After the war, my husband went to Norway and he felt so bad for them there, that he got his brother Johan to come over. He was a carpenter, but he fished anyway and he brought his wife and two little children, a son and a daughter, and they had American names. I taught his wife English. My husband associated with Americans and spoke good English."

Bob remembers: "*Onkel* Johan, a skilled carpenter and net man, became a valuable deckhand on Matt's boats for the rest of his fishing career. *Tante* Thala also moved to New Bedford in 1950 with her daughter, Liv, and husband, Tor Aanestad, who was called to be pastor to the Norwegians in the Trinity Lutheran Church in Fairhaven, and in 1954 was my confirmation pastor. The Aanestads returned to Norway in 1960.

A BURGEONING LOCAL LEADER

"Matt became very active in the fishing industry in New Bedford and beyond. He and other industry leaders formed the New Bedford Boat Owner's Association, an insurance plan for fishing boats, and the Seafood Co-operative. Matt often commented on how he could 'not understand why other skippers didn't think about the greater good of the industry, rather than only catching as many yellowtail flounders or scallops as possible.' Of course, those were the good years in catches.

"He also joined the Exchange Club, a service organization that organized annual scallop festivals to raise funds for community projects, and he was a thirty-second-degree Mason and Shriner. His brother, Johan, recalled how Matt had negotiated a compromise during a fisherman's union strike. He found a settlement that was equitable and fair, and that got the fishing boats out on Georges Bank again. Matt and several other captains were also instrumental in installing memorial stone tablets in the New Bedford Seaman's Bethel, which commemorated the fishermen and fishing boats that had been lost at sea. He remained a life member of the prestigious Port Society of New Bedford until his death in 1979.

"Commercial fishing was so good in the 1950s," continues Bob, "that Matt and his partner sold the F/V *Growler* and bought the F/V *Cap'n Bill II*. During the summers of my college years, 1958–62, when I was a deckhand working for my father on the *Cap'n Bill II*, we had catches of seventy to ninety thousand pounds fish, mostly yellowtails. Naturally, prices were low because of the high supply. Matt wanted to keep prices at a reasonable level, which was possible because of the Seafood Co-operative buyer at the daily fish auction on Pier 3.

"In the early 1960s, he decided to build a new wooden-hull fishing boat in Maine, a boat he and his new partner, Captain Bill Beaumont, named the F/V *Challenge* in acknowledgment of the difficult times in the fishing industry."

SAILING INTO INTERNATIONAL WATERS

BOB REMEMBERS: "During the late 1960s and 1970s, larger issues affected the fishing industry. The 'Law of the Sea' international negotiations began because the traditional twelve-mile ocean borders were not sufficient to limit access to the fishing grounds by larger fishing vessels from other nations, such as the USSR with their mother ships that processed fish caught by smaller boats. Matt and other leader-skippers in the industry became technical advisers to the American negotiators at the International Council of Northern Atlantic Fisheries, ICNAF, meetings in North America and Europe."

As remembered by Doris: "He belonged to International Northern Atlantic Fisheries and they had meetings all over the world and the wives 'went with.' We met in Copenhagen, Italy, Canary Islands and Scotland. I loved the travel."

> *He who has seen and suffered much, and knows the ways of the world, who has traveled, can tell what spirit governs the men he meets.*
>
> —Hávamál

Doris recalls: "Matt became frustrated with these political discussions as the negotiations dragged on year after year. However, he and the others remained supportive, and finally the 'Law of Sea Treaty' was passed, and it created a new hundred-mile offshore protected zone."

And Bob remembers: "The major problem that affected the Massachusetts fishermen, however, was that the line bisected Canadian and American fishing grounds, cut through Georges Bank and limited the American boats to only part of their traditional grounds. In recent years, some skippers have been arrested by the U.S. Coast Guard for fishing across this international line in a desperate search for scallops or groundfish.

"In the 1970s, Matt and other industry-minded captains found there was a shortage of deckhands on fishing boats (partially due to many Norwegian fishermen returning to Norway). They convinced the New Bedford Vocational High School to offer a high school major in commercial fishing. This program included not only academic classes and shop skills needed onboard, but also on-the-job training on fishing boats. This program was initially successful, but the demands of being at sea for seven to twelve days each trip were more than these graduates could manage, especially when jobs ashore were available and the young men were not raised in fishing families. Unfortunately, the program closed after a few years.

"By the age of sixty, Matt became a shore-skipper, managing not only the *F/V Cap'n Bill II*, but also the *F/V Challenge* which he co-owned. As he approached sixty-five, his heart began to fail. During one conversation we had, he said how proud he was when I graduated from Concordia College with an undergraduate degree, and the University of Maine with a master's degree, and finally a Ph.D. from the University of Minnesota. At that time I was thirty-four and was told by him in no uncertain terms that I was 'too old to consider taking over one of his boats.' It was clear to me that he deeply valued education for his son, but that he had personally hoped that his only son might go back to sea and fishing.

"In the last few years of his life, it became evident that fishing was going to get harder, with diminishing catches. At that point, he was very pleased that I had found my own career in university teaching, as well as my wife, Marlie, whom Matt felt was exactly who I needed."

THE END

CAPTAIN MATHIAS BENDIKSEN died on July 21, 1978, and was buried in the Riverside Cemetery in Fairhaven where many other Norwegian fishermen were laid to rest if their remains were not sent back to Norway.

His wife Doris remembers the days before his death well. "During his retirement he still had the boat and was involved in all the problems with the shipyard people. It was hard to argue with all the shipyard people and that was a strain on his heart. He held office in the co-op between worker and boat owner—with more arguments. The last time he went to one of those meetings, he had to open up his shirt to breathe and could hardly get upstairs. After that episode, he gave it up. He had a heart attack at a meeting in Montreal, and we had to go out in the street and get a cab. We were up there for a week in the hospital.

"His partner took the boat over after he died. My husband loved the fishing industry and was very good with advice. He was very smart and should have been a lawyer. He was that smart. All the children have been educated. My husband loved the sea."

Bob remembers his 1990 trip to Norway when he visited John and Helga Rullestad from Skudenes and his cousins Jostein and Marit Espeset from Torvastad. "We had second-row seats at the Karmøy cabaret performance, in the Åkre Cultural Center, of 'Those Who Have Gone to America!' These original musicals, skits, and 8-mm film of a scallop trip portrayed the fisherman, their work on Georges Bank and the Bay of Alaska, as well as their return visits to Karmøy bearing gifts.

"Jostein Espeset, my cousin, was *ordfører* (mayor) that year, and he asked me to present flowers to the performers during his thank-you speech on behalf of the people of Karmøy.

"I had found my roots in Norway!"

HARALD MANNES: THE LIFESAVER

HARALD MANNES was not roughened by decades spent in the perilous waters but rather his experiences at sea inspired him to pursue a second career as an inventor—work that both enhanced the fishing process and saved lives at sea.

His inventions, which greatly improved standard operating procedures, are the result of experience and vision as well as the willingness to take chances. And he did not let the *Janteloven* stop his progress. His inventions were designed to save countless mariners' lives both at sea and on the oil rigs and, also, to increase the productivity of the industry.

THE CAREER

HARALD MANNES, whose formal education ended at the traditional age of fourteen in Skudeneshavn, began his career at sea in 1955 as a cook on the Norwegian ship *Flaggholm* and worked until 1963 on many other Norwegian ships until his last job as an able-bodied seaman on the Norwegian vessel *Janette*. He then came to America to fish out of New Bedford.

He liked New Bedford and lived the typical fisherman's life there, but after a year or so he got Alaska fever, as so many men did at that time, and went off to Seattle to begin a career in crab fishing out of Alaska.

He fished for crabs for twenty-five years and it brought many changes to his life. During this time he commuted once a year to Skudenes in the *pendling* tradition to visit his growing family. Early in his career in Alaska he made a technical innovation to crab fishing. He believed that the crab boats' cargo holds were far too small, so he rigged a canvas tarp on deck to store the extra crabs. This was the beginning of many innovative ideas and inventions for a man who did not just dream but made his dreams come true.

In 1972 he got his first skipping job, and fished for shrimp, salmon and crab.

—Harald Mannes archives

"Phantom," the underwater camera Harald Mannes developed, allows skippers to see crabs on the bottom of the sea.

He became an owner and part-owner of boats and for many years was to spend seven to eight months a year working in an isolated environment where he and his crew were cramped in small vessels in dangerous, frigid waters— work that demanded the utmost instinct, wisdom and seamanship.

Some call the Alaskan crab fishery the toughest and most dangerous job in the world with countless lives lost to the storms and sub-freezing temperatures of the Bering Sea. There is no other fishery like it and it is difficult to imagine any work more cold, rough or dangerous. But, it is also extremely lucrative.

THE INVENTOR

ON ONE TRIP HOME to Norway, he saw a video clip about the Solstad Shipping Company on Karmøy describing their technique of using underwater cameras to conduct pipeline inspections in the North Sea. According to the Western Viking, a Seattle newspaper for Norwegians, when Mannes saw the clip he remembers he "saw a crab perched on the pipe," and immediately rethought an idea he had had several years earlier for locating fish with a camera. At that time he thought it might be a risky venture, but the Solstad film persuaded him that it could work if done properly.

When he returned to America, he sought out an engineering company in California and they made the equipment for him. He brought it to Alaska and refitted his boat with the new equipment for the fishing season.

The Western Viking continued, "It is actually (says Mannes) a family of remotely operated vehicles (ROVs) that carry a video camera and other accessories, including manipulators. They are used for a wide range of underwater exploration, survey and salvage work. Photographers taking photos of the *Titanic* used a similar device." This system had many inherent possibilities for the dangerous crab fishing work he did in the Bering Sea.

Mannes said, according to the *Fiskaren* newspaper for Coastal Norway, "It was important that no one discovered what he had purchased. Competition among fishermen in the Bering Sea is fierce." He named the system Phantom and after several minor adjustments, he was able to see sharp, detailed pictures of the ocean bottom from his screen in the pilot-house. The *Fiskaren* went on to say that, "The razor-sharp pictures even showed the sex of the crabs. For an Alaskan fisherman that is vital, as it is illegal to fish female crabs. The remote-controlled camera also revealed if crabs were young or old."

He found when he used Phantom, "that his catch was larger and that fishing time is used more efficiently." There are no quotas for the very short ten-day season in September, so time and expertise are critical to success— getting the most in the least time.

In the Western Viking, he described the ocean floor: "Like a potato patch down there in some places, balls of crabs piled one on top of the other." Using the Phantom, "Mannes' take was at least forty percent higher than another fisherman who was working in the same area at the same time. Phantom could also be used to recover lost traps and to determine bottom terrain before the traps are dropped."

He introduced the technique to several boat owners in Seattle, along with videos showing the process. He also saw the possibilities of using the process in Norway with shrimp, flounder and other bottom fish. Other uses include searching for lost fishing equipment, sea rescue operations and fighting oil spills. But first and foremost his technique represented a modern-day revolution in standard crabbing methods.

A HAND UP

DROWNING AT SEA is the ultimate fear all fishermen must live with in their trade. Toward the end of the twentieth century, Harald Mannes developed a new system to rescue men from the sea. Many die yearly as a result of accidents, storms, mishaps, malfunctions, bad weather and carelessness. In Alaska particularly, there is a very high death rate, and death comes very quickly in the frigid waters in places like the Bering Sea.

In an October 15, 2003, Seattle Post-Intelligencer story, "Crabbing industry faces a sea change," Mike Lewis describes the loading of crab pots as "stacking them like Legos 15 feet high. Each pot can weigh at least 650 pounds empty. For the 250-mile trip out to sea, the pots are lashed together and chained to the deck so they don't shift and capsize the boat. . . . Coast Guard officials say it is the trip out to the crab fishing grounds on Bristol Bay northeast of Dutch Harbor that often is the most dangerous portion of the trip. 'The boats are fully loaded with pots,' said LCDR James Robertson, who spent the pre-season week making safety inspections on the 254 boats registered to fish for crab this year. When the weather is bad there isn't much room for error.'"

Harald Mannes was very concerned about this problem as he saw many of his colleagues become victims of the unforgiving sea. Consequently he developed a new system for rescuing men from the sea and called this life-saver, "Hand Up." "I did this," he said in a phone conversation from Norway, "for the men. I wanted to do something that would save lives. That means a lot to me. It makes me feel so good to know that I have helped to save a life."

According to an October 1997 article in the *Norsk Maskin Tidende* (Norwegian Machine News), Mannes said: "When I was in Alaska tragedy struck many of my colleagues and their families. Loss of life at sea affected me greatly." He realized the need for an adequate rescue system that could be used under all conditions. Safety and survival courses offered through his employment in the North Sea convinced him that the present systems were inadequate and even dangerous under some conditions."

The standard operating procedure had been to pick up victims of the sea with a basket or a rescue net. But even with safety courses and survival training knowledge, it was not enough to save the many who fell into the water and died because of the extreme low temperatures, storms and condition of the water's surface. After being at sea for almost thirty years, Mannes knew well what the problems were, but up to this time he had no real solutions for an effective rescue system.

An effective rescue system had to have the ability to work under all weather conditions and also to rescue one crewmember or a large group of people at the same time. One day while he was fishing in Alaska, Mannes got an idea that would revolutionize safety at sea. It could be used in all weather, and it could be used to rescue one or many.

A trawl boom on a shrimp boat he saw that day inspired his idea. He developed a series of lines which, when assembled onto any ship's crane, could

HAND UP

Step 1. The rescue equipment is swung into place ready for men-overboard to catch it.

Step 2. The men in the water attach themselves to it.

Step 3. Harald shows how a man is brought onboard to safety.

Step 4. Safe onboard, Harald Mannes shows how a rescued man is attached to the equipment.

—Photos courtesy of Harald Mannes, Skudeneshavn, Norway

rescue those floating in the sea safely and effectively. The lines were equipped with a hook and a hard rubber seat on the end. They hung from the ship's crane and a floating person could grab a line, straddle over the seat and attach his survival suit to the hook. Then the crane lifted the survivors and swung them over the deck to safety. It could rescue up to forty people at one time and had a range up to fifteen meters, therefore reducing the need for ship maneuvers.

It is said that most great inventions are basically simple. Mannes' idea was both simple and effective. The *Haugesunds Avis* newspaper recounted the story of Captain Arve Sandnes, who tried it in the North Sea, praised the system as "rational, simple, ingenious, and one hundred percent operative in all weather," saying, "It is the best we have tried."

Leif Nordbro, captain of the F/V *Scandies Rose*, also tried the system at sea and reported that: "Here we are out to sea, testing the Hand Up system that Harald Mannes brought over from Norway. And it worked *excellent* as they say in English. . . . By the second time they knew what to do, and it was like putting on your boots. I think it took thirty-one seconds to get the men on board. . . . If there are people who don't believe that this system works, then they haven't seen it or don't want to see it."

Harald Mannes is often deemed a "Peter Smart," a fictional Norwegian who can do all things and can be best compared to the American term, "Handy Andy." He has taken out an international patent on the system and has hopes that it will be used worldwide in the future. Hand Up had the potential for making Harald Mannes a wealthy man, but he says, "Saving lives is my best reward."

> *"To know even one life has breathed easier because you have lived. This is the meaning of success."*
>
> —Ralph Waldo Emerson

ANDREW OLDEN: SCALLOPING PIONEER

MANY MEN CAME FROM NORWAY to fish the waters off New England, and many accumulated great wealth and success. But one man, the late Andrew Olden of Haramsøy, Norway, stood out as a pioneer in the advancement and improvement of the scallop industry due to his innovative ideas and inventive skills.

His story was well-told by his son William (Billy) Olden of Seattle in a letter to the author:

"Andrew Olden was born in Haramsøy, Norway, in 1903. He grew up in an area where farming and fishing were the mainstays. He told me that when he was in his late teens, he made some trips on whaling boats to Iceland. He came to America in the early 1920s and lived in Brooklyn. There were some friends who came from Haramsøy there, and he found work as an ironworker. He worked on projects such as the George Washington Bridge and other large installations. It was in Brooklyn where he met my mother, who had come from Oslo. They were married on Christmas day in 1927, as that was the only day he could get off from work.

"Sometime after that he fell and had to give up iron working. Dad had an uncle named Hans Haram, my grandfather's brother, who was in the fishing industry in New Bedford at that time. Dad contacted Hans and he asked him to come to New Bedford to go fishing on his boat. Dad worked there until 1941 when we moved to Staten Island, New York. The fishing industry was pretty depressed during that time. Dad found a job with an oil company working on a barge as an engineer as he had gone to school and received his marine engineer's license. We lived there until the summer of 1944.

—*Olden archives*

Andrew Olden, left, with Martin Helgeland the morning after Hurricane Carol 1954 on the *Amelia* in New Bedford. They both look happy that they had survived the storm.

"Because of the war, the fishing industry flourished and Uncle Hans persuaded my father to return to New Bedford again. Dad then became the skipper of Uncle Hans' smaller boat, the *Arnold*. After two years he was offered a job as skipper of the *Amelia*. The *Amelia* was based in New Bedford and Dad skippered that boat until he had a stroke in 1958. That ended his fishing career. But he had a large impact on the fishing industry while he was in New Bedford.

"Through letters, information from friends and from what I know personally, I learned he was a very active and progressive factor in the scallop industry. The Fisherman's Union and the boat owners' association were at odds over the limit of pounds of scallops per trip that could be harvested. He wrote a letter to the boat owners suggesting an 11,000-pound limit per trip, saying this was a good two weeks' work by the men. As far as I know, the owner's association went with this and it worked out well.

THE SKIPPER BECOMES AN INVENTOR

"IN THE EARLY FIFTIES Dad designed a modification for the drags used to harvest the scallops from the ocean floor. It made the whole dredging process more efficient and Dad received a patent for this (modification) in 1954 after filing for it in 1951."

Newspapers, including the New Bedford Standard-Times and the Boston Globe, announced the new patent in articles describing the scallop drag, explaining that Andrew Olden of 323 Reed Street, New Bedford, had received a patent that was filed on May 14, 1951. "This scallop drag," it was written, "allows the net to be free to closely follow the contours of the sea bottom, increasing the yield into the net. It also prevents large stones from entering the net. The device is comprised of a frame which is supported by properly positioned shoes so that it rests three to four inches above the bottom. The net is secured to the frame. Mounted in front of the latter are one or more downwardly inclining plates, which not only assist in holding the mechanism against the sea bottom but also are designed so that a suction is created by the passing water to stir the scallops and allow the shellfish to pass more readily through the net. The agitating action is aided by a chain located in front of the net, which assists in keeping out large rocks. When the drag is full of scallops, it can be lifted to the boat deck and emptied by manipulating a back-positioned dump chain.

—Olden archives

The scallop drag as designed and patented in 1954 by Andrew Olden.

"Dad was a highly respected skipper and the *Amelia* was always among the top boats as far as the yearly tonnage of scallops was concerned. I went out a few times with him during summers while I was in college, so I had first-hand experience in seeing the operation. Many of our family friends were fishermen who came from Norway and helped contribute to the fishing industry in New Bedford. He had very loyal crewmembers who were with us over the years. I think that pioneers like Dad's Uncle Hans Haram really did a great job during the years before World War II making the scallop industry very strong for the years following. My father was typical of the young men who came from a fishing background in Norway and really contributed to the industry.

"Because the men were out to sea a lot, I really didn't get to know or appreciate what they went through until I did it myself in my college years. The work was hard and sometimes very dangerous. Friends and boats were lost over the years, but those men worked together for the benefit of all.

PERILS AT SEA

"THERE WAS ALWAYS THE UNCERTAINTY on whether or not Dad would be lost at sea. Fortunately there was only one situation like this that occurred before the war ended. During the war, the Coast Guard had taken the radios off the boats and, if there were a problem, there was no way to communicate. It was summertime and the rudder of my father's boat malfunctioned, so they were drifting around. The boat was a few days overdue and, of course we suspected the worst. However the Coast Guard planes found the boat, and they reached home safely. Dad was out in a couple of hurricanes also, and they managed to ride them out. Some boats tried to make it to port, but the cross tides in shallower water sank the boats.

"The families always lived with uncertainty in the fishing life, but they supported each other and were always there to help.

"I couldn't finish my thoughts without remembering my mother, who virtually raised me while Dad was gone. She and other wives raised the children, handled chores at the home and really were very strong in many ways. Growing up, I was not really aware of the good things that my Dad (and my Mom for that matter) did to contribute to the legacy of the fishing industry in New Bedford. It was only in later years I knew of his influence, which makes me very proud. I guess the Viking heritage of 'roaming the seas' was very much alive in my Dad."

KAARE NESS: NEW VENTURES, NEW RICHES

"Do not go where the path may lead,
Go instead where there is no path and leave a trail."

—Ralph Waldo Emerson

THIS IS THE STORY of a man who endured the arduous war years as a youth in Norway while his family struggled to make a living. He immigrated

387

to the United States after the war with one goal: to find a better life. But he had no idea just how good a life he would have or the enormous success he would achieve in his adopted land. Kaare Ness could see possibilities and took the necessary risks to achieve them—and in so doing he helped build an industry and also became a leader as he established a strong role within both his field of work and the Norwegian community.

I first met Kaare when he came to my home to be interviewed. He struck me as one of the most perceptive men I had ever met and as a man who could get along well with people and could size up a situation quickly. I felt he had extraordinary intelligence and could see value in things that others may not see.

This is his saga, in his own words, of his achievements and of the excitement, adventure, risk and success he found along the way.

"FISHING WAS WHAT I KNEW"

"I WAS A KARMØY MAN, and Karmøy men fished because that was what they knew. They went into the Merchant Marine or fishing. They had no choices—no choices. Everyone was very, very poor. As soon as we were fourteen or fifteen, we had to work. I went in the Merchant Marine and shipped out to London after the war ended in 1945. Came home in 1949, married and then started fishing. Some still go into the Merchant Marine, but now they have a better education and have more choices. No parents thought to send kids to school after age fourteen. Financially they were not able to.

"I left for New Bedford because I couldn't see any future in Norway. It was impossible to make a decent living there or to get a decent job. My wife and son came the same year. I became a boat owner after nine years in New Bedford. We always saved money—many didn't save money. To be successful you took care—didn't drink, and put money in the bank. We lived on Sconticut Neck and were friendly with all the others from Karmøy—lots of them around Fairhaven.

"I didn't consider fishing dangerous, but of course it is. I just thought it wasn't. Was never scared of it. When I think of all the men who died, I know now how dangerous it is. My father-in-law drowned off a fishing boat in Norway, and his widow had eight kids.

"I always thought being a fishermen was a very nice life. Those of us who grew up with fishing were used to it. Always like a honeymoon when we came home. Our wives didn't worry much, or at least never said anything about it—it was our way of life. It didn't do harm to marriages. We were away a lot and were gone for two to three months when we fished in Alaska. But we came home for longer stretches. The women who came from our area were used to being independent. They were alone for long periods of times.

"Some men went home to Norway every winter and took the Christmas boat back. They went fishing in Norway and then came back to America, forth and back every spring.

A DIFFERENT WORLD

"When I said goodbye at the dock and took the boat through the harbor, I didn't think much about going out (to sea). I wondered about weather. If the weather was bad, that was like a blessing, and then I didn't go. I didn't really like to go out. Once I stepped onto my boat—then a different world started.

"I was with the same guys (crew) for seven years. On the way out, the crew read and played lots of poker on some of the boats. They played all night and some lost a lot of money. They played poker all the way out and all the way in. They just put a blanket on the table and played. We were good buddies, and there were no big arguments. But we were very surprised when we came from Norway to New Bedford to see the crummy living conditions on the boats—no refrigerator, no running water. Everyone lived in the fo'c's'le, where they did the cooking. The captain and engineer lived in the stateroom aft. The living conditions were very poor. Didn't bathe, didn't undress—just rolled into bed with dirty clothes day after day. Can't remember I even took my pants off, and we never put water on our faces until the day we went home, and then we shaved. We must have been stinking very bad. The boats didn't even carry that much water for washing. We worked around the clock—six hours on and six hours off and six on.

"I had gone out west to visit one of my brothers (in the late sixties) and wanted to see the king crab fishery out there. He asked me to come to the West Coast and see it because fishing was so much better there. I said, 'You must be crazy. I just bought a boat, the *Viking Queen*—$200,000 with a mortgage.' But I decided to make a trip out there anyway. It was harder to get going as a boat owner in New Bedford and easier in Seattle. The bankers were friendlier in Seattle, and the banks in New Bedford were very conservative unless you knew someone to get a loan.

THANKS TO NORWEGIAN REPUTATION

"On the West Coast I needed a contact, and I went to Rainier Bank and spoke to a banker. He liked me, and the first day I was there he took me home and brought me back to the ferry. I had a very good relationship with the banker very quickly. Norwegians in the area had developed good reputations with bankers. They went by a person's character rather than his pocketbook.

"My brother was building a boat. It was delayed three months in the ship-yard, and it was getting to be early December. I told him that if there is nothing going on, I might as well go back to New Bedford, but he told me I can go up to Adak, Alaska, way out on the Aleutian chain as the skipper (of a boat there) wanted to go home for Christmas. I had never seen a king crab, but he showed me what to do. The crab pots were seven by seven feet, and they weighed six hundred pounds. I fished for the holidays there.

"I stopped in Kodiak on the way back to look at a boat that had tried to fish scallops. I thought I could do it successfully, so I got in contact with the fish buyers there, and they got in contact with the National Marine Fisheries. They decided to put up an experimental charter for someone who was experienced in scalloping. I went back to New Bedford and stayed in contact. They also stayed in contact and called me and said that if I wanted it they could help me get that charter.

THE UNEXPLORED WATERS: GREAT ADVENTURE AND NEW DISCOVERIES

"THE FISH BUYERS, government and state put money up for the charter in March of 1968. We (my crew and I) were ready and, we decided to go to Alaska the long way. I figured if I got there and it didn't work out, I could always do something else. The family stayed in New Bedford, and we went out to do the charter. I wanted to get into king crab because that was where the money was. I wanted to get further ahead money-wise.

"During the spring of 1968, I got all the paperwork done. Lots of guys wanted to get away from New Bedford (the scalloping prices were low), so the crew was easy to get.

40-40-40

"THE TRIP FROM NEW BEDFORD to Juneau with the *Viking Queen* took forty days. Forty more days for the charter and the contract was for $40,000. Spent half of money just to get there. We were five guys on this adventure. In my mind, I thought life was going to be better. It was a very interesting adventure.

"It took thirty-two days to reach Seattle in our ninety-one-foot-long fishing boat. We didn't carry much fuel . . . seven—eight days of running. We planned on where to stop to get fuel. When we went through the dike in New

Bedford, there were people there to cheer us off, but some thought we were crazy. The New Bedford fleet was lying off of New York, and they knew we were going. Talked to Henry Simonsen there. First stop we made was in Miami after five days. Took on fuel and then went to Panama in about four days. We went through the Panama Canal and then to Acapulco for fuel.

—*Simon Vea archives*

Onboard the *Viking Queen* in 1968.

"We came there early one morning, and I knew we needed a pilot. I knew exactly where the pilot station was, but he didn't come out to us. We asked many times, finally went on our own and tied up. As soon as we tied up, the pilot came and said, 'You can't tie up there—you need a pilot boat to bring you in. So you have to go back out again.' He took us out and then back into the dock. We were greenhorns and didn't know what to do. The health inspectors had to come on, for instance. We took on fuel and stayed overnight and went around the town, and the guys enjoyed it.

We left the next morning to go to San Diego for one day, and then we went to Seattle before going to Juneau. We painted the boat and we looked pretty nice when we sailed into Seattle.

SEATTLE

"We had to make contacts in Seattle. The Rainier banker had done a lot of business with the Norwegians out there, and the president's wife was Norwegian. We stayed four to five days in Seattle and then another five days to Juneau where we got the National Fisheries people onboard. Then we always had three officials on the boat to tell us where to fish and how many days we would be there. Our contract was with the government, Alaska and Fisheries. After the contract was over in forty days with good results, we were on our own."

Kaare continued, "We got more people from New Bedford to come onto our boat. I hired men from Karmøy, and when we needed more they got their friends. The boat owners always hired someone they knew.

"The rumors got back to New Bedford that the *Viking Queen* had found a lot of scallops. Before the year was over, sixteen or seventeen scallop boats, much of the fleet, left New Bedford for Alaska and New Bedford was nervous that they would lose most of the scallop fleet." A century earlier, New Bedford suffered the loss of much of its whaling fleet when it went to California during the gold rush, and some thought history might be repeating itself.

—Simon Vea archives

Simon Vea has a bit of fun when the *Viking Queen* docked in Acapulco in 1968.

THE MOVE

"I GOT ANOTHER SKIPPER for relief on the *Viking Queen* and began my move. My son was studying at Pacific Lutheran University in Tacoma, and I went to New Bedford to pack up. I was forty years old and drove back across the U.S. My wife had packed before I came, as I had said to her, 'You better be ready when I get there.' We drove across the country and stopped in Seattle for a few days but then decided we would live in Alaska. So we drove to Seward, one hundred thirty miles south of Anchorage.

"We leased a plant to pack our own scallops under the 'Bountiful' label. We were selling so many scallops. Now I was an entrepreneur and ran the refrigeration plant rather than fished. I could be with my family as I had not been able to be with them much over the years. We leased a house, as did other families that came from New Bedford. We lived there for only one year. Winters are terrible there.

"I wanted to get out of scalloping and into king crabbing and couldn't use my boat for that. My other younger brother was building a boat and told me that if I wanted to get into king crabbing, I could use the boat and try it. I went to Seattle, left the family in Seward, and fished all summer. Then we all moved back to Seattle. Again my wife Sigrun packed up, and I met her in Seward, got a sea/land van and shipped everything. I stopped by and she was ready to go.

"We rented an apartment there, and my daughter said, 'Buy a house because I don't want to change schools again.' So we bought in Richmond Beach. My wife didn't want me to buy into the boat with my brother because business and family isn't a good idea, and her advice was good.

FISHING IN ALASKA

"The weather in the Bering Sea was awful—nothing to compare to in New Bedford—so much worse. Every winter we had wind over a hundred miles an hour. Sometimes we rode it out, and other times we ran for the beach. The waves were averaging twenty feet in a typical storm. Fishermen were always wet and often developed arthritis.

"I wanted to build a boat on my own and wanted to get rid of the scallop boat. A man I met in Kodiak in 1968 was from Tennessee. He had sold his boat and was working for a fish company, and I had delivered fish to that company. My partner in the scallop boat bought me out. I told the guy from Kodiak, 'I'm going to build a boat, but I need a partner as I don't have enough money on my own.' We contracted in the spring of 1972, and the boat was ready on August 4. We called it the *Royal Viking*—one hundred eight feet, $443,000.

"We then went fishing—came home after the season and my partner wanted to build a different boat, with processing onboard at sea. We fished, cracked and cooked on the boat. It was one of a kind—almost $1,000,000—one hundred thirty-five feet, really a big boat, the biggest in Seattle. We named it the *Billiken*. My partner was its skipper, and I was skipper on *Royal Viking*. I fished for three or four more years. At that time, 1973, our company was called the Royal Viking Company, Inc. We built more boats with the Royal Viking: *Pacific Viking*, *Viking Explorer* and *Colombia*. That was just five years after we had arrived to the West Coast.

EXPANSION, EXPANSION, EXPANSION

"In 1975, Trident Seafood bought a floating processor and moved it to Alaska to Akutan in the Aleutian Islands with ninety native Alaskans living on it. The land belonged to someone in Seattle. We built a pier for the processor and put a building on the beach. Boats came in with king crab, and we processed it and also opened an office. We hired an old guy in Seattle to do the sales and we produced crabs for the market. In 1977 we built a processing plant on the beach. We had our own boats and also bought from other boats.

"There was nothing there except the ninety natives. We put up housing for the people and generated our own power. The plant burned down two years later from faulty electricity, but the housing was still there, so we built the factory up again—bigger than it was the first time. All of the people and material had to come up from Seattle. Lots of Filipinos worked for us. Now we have seven hundred people at the plant. We started to buy salmon in Bristol Bay. In the eighties we started processing whitefish because the king

—Trident Internet photo

The Trident Seafood compound in Alaska where it operates a large processing facility approximately one-half mile from the village. The facility has a plant, large cold storage, docks, and state-of-the-art processing equipment.

crab started to disappear. We diversified and had to modify our boats for other fisheries.

"Credit was very important. My partner was aggressive. We had a lot of luck, lots of work, met the right people, and didn't waste money.

ON LEADERSHIP

"Wealth didn't change my values and didn't change my life at all. I bought my home for $35,000 in 1971 and have just recently moved to a new one-level home. Have a home also in Norway, where we live part of the year.

"I was active in the fisheries management on the West Coast—we didn't have that in New Bedford. I was also a member of the boat owners' association in Seattle and then a director for several years and president for four years. Fisheries management was the purpose of the group.

FAMILY

"I feel that leadership has to do with background. Many people are followers and not leaders. It had to do

—AT photo

Kaare and Sigrun Ness at Haugesund airport in 2000.

394

with the upbringing. There were a couple of generations that didn't speak out. None of us wanted to be too visible in anything. Men were quiet at home, and the women ran it all at home. It had to do with life in Norway. When the husband came home, he was like a visitor and was on the sidelines. That passes on to generations. Norwegians have been here for two to three generations, and no one is active in politics. Norwegians do not participate, as do other nationality groups. It will take a long time before that changes.

"I didn't get too involved with the kids because I was always working. I do more with the grandchildren in one week than I did in six months with my own children. We were out fishing and came home for two or three days. And when we were home, we were working on those darn boats.

"My heart is here in the states—this is where I made it. I came here because I wanted to make something out of myself. I could never move back to Norway. Here we have so many friends, kids and grandkids. I achieved all I wanted to achieve in the states."

And the states can thank these men also, because the fishing industry on two coasts is better, safer and more productive because of their vision, courage, lives and work.

—Courtesy ©Steve Kennedy photo, Wellfleet, MA

The F/V *Viking Queen* in a poignant photo taken by Steve Kennedy just before she was scuttled. She was back in her homeport of New Bedford after a brilliant career. She pioneered the scallop industry on the West Coast by bringing the men who had the know-how from New Bedford to Alaska via the Panama Canal. Instead of this image at the end of her life, I prefer to think of her as she sailed for the first time into Seattle Harbor with an enthusiastic and triumphant captain and crew—newly painted and shining from stem to stern to begin a new exciting and successful life on the Pacific Ocean. Unfortunately no such photo was available to me.

17

~

Discovering My Heritage

THE NAVY YEARS

—Circa early 1960s

My view of Manhattan from Fort Jay, Governors Island. I watched ships from many countries come into this harbor carrying goods or emigrants. I crossed by ferry at this point every day to lower Manhattan in rain, sunshine or snow—-and loved it. I viewed more than one damaged ship limping or being towed in from a collision at sea including the *Queen Mary.*

NEW YORK

IN THE EARLY-1960S, I decided I wanted more adventure in life; so, in the tradition of my Norwegian ancestors, I joined the Navy, as the recruiting posters used to say, to see the world.

I was accepted into the U.S. Navy Officer's School for Women in Newport, Rhode Island. One morning while getting ready for classes there, I heard on the radio that a New Bedford fishing boat was missing and presumed lost. I listened intently as I put on my hat and then heard the skipper's name—my uncle, Arnleif Tollefsen.

~

Not again, I thought. *Not again.* Already my father and three uncles had lost their lives to the sea. This was to be my fourth uncle who died at sea and here I was preparing for a life in the Navy. It was a soul-searching moment for me and my heart went out to my family and, in particular, my grandmother. The Navy did not allow time off for a niece to attend a funeral, however, so I had to continue with my studies and not participate in the grieving at home. This was the first time in my Navy service that my Norwegian background would surface, but it was not to be the last.

After graduating from officer's school and with my ensign's bars on my collar and single stripe and line-officer star glowing from my sleeves, my new orders were to report to work in lower Manhattan's Federal Office Building at 90 Church Street, then known as the FBI Building. I was to be the educational services officer there as well as the sea power officer and would be replacing a lieutenant commander and an ensign.

—Tollefsen archives,
Carleton La Porte Studio, Worcester MA

Newly commissioned Astrid Tollefsen, Ensign, USNR, after eight challenging weeks at the U.S. Navy Women's Officer School in Newport, Rhode Island. This brief respite was followed by another eight weeks of training. Christmas vacation, 1963.

Although I was a Navy line officer, commissioned women in those years were still casually but incorrectly referred to as WAVE officers—WAVES being the World War II acronym for "Women Accepted for Volunteer Emergency Service."

I was able to live at the beautifully situated and historic U.S. Army's Fort Jay, on Governors Island in New York Harbor. From my bachelor officer quarters room on Governors Island, I had an unobstructed and very dramatic view of New York Harbor, the Statue of Liberty, Ellis Island and lower Manhattan.

In fact, Miss Liberty became quite a good friend as I greeted her each morning upon rising, watched her as I rode the Army's ferry to work in lower Manhattan, and spent the whole day with a view of her from my fifteenth-floor office window at 90 Church Street. I saw her from many angles and she was my companion for more than two years. I didn't know at that time that her copper skin came for the island of Karmøy, my father's birthplace, but there seemed a spiritual connection. I was to have many Norwegian connections in New York City—this close relative was one that was unknown at that time. I also viewed many ships sailing past her in New York Harbor with Norwegian emigrants who were to live and work in my hometown, New Bedford.

In 1963 Ellis Island just sat there in relative ruin and I wondered if some day something might be done about it. There were many rumors about new housing being located there and other expansive plans, but eventually, I am pleased to note, the former emigration center was made into a museum for all to visit and to learn about their ancestors. Every time I looked over to Ellis Island I was reminded of those who had come to this country from so many lands via ship, many of whom were my relatives.

My Norwegian heritage opened many doors for me and proved helpful on my job because of the Commandant of the Third Naval District, Rear Admiral Redfield Mason. Through his generosity, I was privileged to participate in many special events in 1964 and 1965 and, although my primary work was in education, the commandant saw to it that I was invited to numerous receptions and he also gave me the opportunity to take a leadership role in several international events, sometimes to the dismay of other women officers senior to me.

—U S Navy photo, 1964

I was onboard the classic aircraft carrier *Essex* this day in 1964 when we approached the bridge at low tide. The *Essex* had been under extensive repairs at the Brooklyn Navy Yard and was sailing to New Jersey.

—*AT photo*

A lovely smile from my helpful Tante Ellen Tollefsen Thompsen, circa 1997, on Cape Cod. I never let her forget the story about the fish balls and the admiral.

In the spring of 1964, when all of New York was preparing for the World's Fair and "Operation Sail," the first time that the international tall ships sailed into New York Harbor, I was summoned to the admiral's office where he handed me an envelope concerning the upcoming events. "What does this mean?" he asked as he pointed to the official seal of the sender printed in Norwegian. I didn't know many words in Norwegian and felt some discomfort, but replied, "I'll find out, sir," words every young ensign knows to be the only appropriate response. I was slightly nervous as I walked to my office wondering how I could translate these few words.

So I telephoned my *tante* in Fairhaven, who, surprised to hear from me, asked where I was. I told her I was in my office in New York and she advised me that it wasn't a good time to talk because she was "in the middle of making *fiskekake* (fishcakes) and her hands were "all covered with fish." "Could you call back later? My husband is coming in tomorrow and I have to get ready for him," she exclaimed. I explained that I had to have this translation immediately and she agreed to help. "Spell it out," she said impatiently, and I did. "Oh, that's easy—he's the big cheese." I asked her what she meant. "Well, he's the head man—Astri, he runs the Norwegian Navy." Then she told me she had to get back to her fish and we said our goodbyes.

The admiral's aide escorted me back into the admiral's impressive office with a corner, twin-river view of New York Harbor, and he asked me for the translation. "Sir," I said, "Admiral Sorensen is Norway's Chief of Naval Operations." "Good," said the admiral. "Thank you. I knew I could trust you to get me the answer. Now, Miss Tollefsen, I was just about to have some coffee. Would you like some?"

After that he always saw to it that when any Scandinavian ship or officers came into town, I would greet them and welcome them to New York. So I found myself lunching with Swedish captains—one the skipper of an Ethiopian-flag ship—and other Scandinavian senior officers. I became known as *Valkyrie* among my officer friends.

At a reception for some French officers in the admiral's residence, I met Mayor Wagner's administrative assistant, and the admiral told him I was

Norwegian. Next thing I knew, there was a call from the mayor's office asking me to represent the mayor in leading Brooklyn's annual 17th of May Parade, commemorating Constitution Day in Norway. The admiral called me in and told me that was a great honor. But I respectfully declined because I did not speak Norwegian and was "only half" Norwegian. I somehow felt I would not be acceptable to the Norwegians of Brooklyn, even though my mother and father had lived there. And because I had led the Navy contingent of the long Armed Forces Day Parade down Fifth Avenue the week before, my legs still ached. But to this day I regret that decision. Being half-Norwegian didn't entitle me to a Norwegian identity, I thought at the time—because that was what I had been taught by family experiences when I was young. I didn't truly appreciate the significance of the holiday, and it was unfortunate that I knew so little about my heritage in those days.

—Photo taken with AT's camera by fellow officer

Adlai Stevenson, former governor, presidential hopeful and then U.S. ambassador to the UN, makes a friendly point about Operation Sail, 1964, to Ensign Astrid Tollefsen while a Navy nurse looks on. She and I were the only two women onboard that day. I was so captivated with Ambassador Stevenson that I forgot to salute the incoming boats. He was extremely pleasant and friendly. He seemed to be on excellent terms with the president of the Norwegian Shipping Lines, who was also very outgoing. I enjoyed my time with both of them on the flight deck of the *USS Wasp* as we watched sailing vessels from all over the world come into New York Harbor. Our ship welcomed them to the USA that summer of the World's Fair. Ambassador Stevenson died in 1965.

That summer when the first "Operation Sail" was in full swing, I had orders on the day the tall ships entered New York Harbor to escort Lady Bird Johnson and her daughters Luci Baines and Lynda Bird, while they were aboard the official greeting ship, the *USS Wasp*. I rode out to the carrier in a small boat and then had to hop onto the carrier in dress uniform, which was a feat unto itself. This was the ship that took the salutes from each of the tall ships as they entered the harbor. After the salute, the crews who were perched on the masts and riggings of the ships unfurled their sails and sailed into the harbor—a spectacular sight. We had to continue saluting as each national anthem was played, and I remember that my right arm was quite tired after several hours.

Because President Johnson's family decided at the last minute not to come, I had the freedom to meet and talk with anyone I pleased—all dignitaries from one country or another. It was a thrill to enjoy this event as one of two women aboard. I talked a bit with the president of the Norwegian American Lines and with Adlai Stevenson, then the American ambassador to the United Nations—both very friendly and interesting men.

The admiral, of course, was there and introduced me to the Norwegian captains who were representing their country. Senior Norwegian naval officers surrounded me, and together we watched the *Christian Radich*, my favorite Norwegian windjammer, come into the harbor with all of the other tall ships from around the world. I was proud as a Norwegian-American to be able to be part of the official salute to that wonderful vessel, as well as to two other Norwegian tall ships, the *Sorlandet* and the *Statsraad Lehmkuhl*. It was very exciting to me to see the *Radich* in her full glory. I had enjoyed the movie, "Windjammer" featuring her and had seen her once in Oslo harbor one Christmas.

As a result of meeting the senior Norwegian officers, I was invited to a reception on the *Radich* as well as on many other foreign ships, and to the formal grand ball on a pier, compliments of a Norwegian captain. The pier had been beautifully decorated for this international event. Because of my Norwegian name and interests, the admiral saw

—Tollefsen archives

LTJG Astrid Tollefsen (with a slight view of Admiral Mason) while on the admiral's naval reserve inspection trip, in 1964. U.S. Navy photo framed with hat insignia and ensign and lieutenant junior grade bars.

to it that I had the best week of my life. (Many years later I was invited to a reception on the *Radich* when she made a trip to Boston—because of my relationship to her during Operation Sail.)

A few weeks later, Admiral Sorensen, Norway's Chief of Naval Operations, returned to New York and Admiral Mason arranged a personal introduction. I went to his hotel and met both him and his wife in the lobby. We chatted a bit about the Navy and women's roles. At that time, most of the navies of the world were all-male, and officers from other countries were very interested in our work. Mrs. Sorensen was particularly friendly to me, and she told me she also had roots in the Karmøy area.

Having a Norwegian name, roots, demeanor, a Viking spirit and an interest in navies and ships in general opened many doors for me in New York during those wonderful two years. I began to feel more Norwegian and to appreciate the importance of my roots. It has been a long, delightful process that continues to this day.

18

~

The Beckoning Waters

SEATTLE, NORWAY OR NEW BEDFORD?

—Photo, Lise Stol Medhaug

Norwegian children dressed in *bunad* enjoy the 17th of May and the culture of their homeland.

"I have been a stranger in a strange land."

—Exodus 11: 22.

"The golden opportunity you are seeking is in yourself. It is not in the environment; it is not luck or chance, or the help of others; it is in yourself alone."

—Orison Swett Marden

~

THE SIXTIES

THE SIXTIES after the 1963 assassination of President Kennedy were tumultuous years in the lives of Americans—1968 being the most traumatic. In view of the escalating Vietnam War and the subsequent rioting at colleges and universities, the brutal murders of Martin Luther King and Robert Kennedy and the Democratic Convention madness in Chicago, Americans were beginning to question their own futures. If Americans themselves were posing such questions, what was happening in the minds of young emigrants?

Despite new wealth and productive lives, many began to wonder what they had got themselves into in this land of milk and honey. They began to face head-on the less lovely side of America. Although they cared for America and what they believed it stood for, they were unused to the conflicts, the dangers and the escalating hysteria. Did they really want their children to grow up in this culture or did they prefer the calm, comforting and stable Norwegian homeland? Even the former American First Lady had fled to Greece. What should they do?

Some originally came to stay for a lifetime and become Americans; others had come with the idea of giving it a try for a few years to make enough money to build a home in Norway. Still others came only for money and adventure. And a few more came to be near family and friends.

Even in this new hometown of New Bedford, there were to be racial riots, fires and bedlam in the streets. One can imagine that the new emigrant living in the West End of New Bedford would become rather phobic. The long-time residents were very afraid. But for the woman who didn't speak the language well and whose husband was out to sea, the justified fears might often have limited her life to her own home or that of other Norwegian friends. Those were very frightening days for everyone. The Norwegians came to America to survive and to make a better living for themselves and their children, but what price would they have to pay for this?

NORWAY

THE EMIGRANTS REPEATEDLY heard that things were changing swiftly in Norway and that many good jobs were becoming available there. A large aluminum processing plant was being built on the island of Karmøy and there was the exciting and promising news about great oil discoveries off Norway's ragged coast. What were the implications now for them and their families in this rapidly changing situation? Would Norway for the first time in history become self-sufficient?

America had all of the comforts of life: the electronic kitchens, telephones, nice cars, reliable income, entertainment, affordable food and clothing as well as great variety and low prices for everything they needed. It had all of the things their Norway didn't have including better weather. Norway, when they were growing up, had war, cold outhouses, simple kitchens, sometimes without running water, often one telephone per town, few cars and no chance to get a good job. As one man remarked in Skudeneshavn, "People forget that prior to 1960, Norway was a third-world country. We had so little and no conveniences at all. Many had no indoor plumbing. It's almost inconceivable now when we remember what it was like then."

And some Norwegian-Americans were visiting Norway and finding it had indeed changed. Could they, should they, would they return? Would they be happy and have productive lives there? They had known nothing but poverty and war in Norway—what would Norway be like if it had wealth? Did they now have to decide between possessions and Norwegian values or could they have both?

As America became more untenable in the late 1960s and Norway became more desirable, the emigrants were increasingly conflicted about the decisions that must be made in the near future for them and their families. Some husbands and wives did not see eye to eye on this pending decision, and many of their children had ideas of their own. Over the years many emigrants or children of emigrants went back to Norway. Norway was a mother figure to many a Norwegian through many generations. As noted by Peder Eliasen in Skudeneshavn, "The ties to the home country are very strong—even for those who have never been here. They would come back and get soil and bring it back to America. They would say: 'This is where my great-grandfather and great-grandmother lived and this is a memory.' Ties are over a hundred years old but they would still say, 'This is my homeland.' When there are depressed times in Norway, there is emigration to the states—good times here, no emigration."

For those from Karmøy or contemplating living in Karmøy, the new aluminum plant would employ up to sixteen hundred people and who knows how far they could go if they got in on the ground level? Furthermore they could be home with their families and not have to undergo the rigors of the sea. Now they would be

—*Photo, Lise Stol Medhaug*

17th of May on Karmøy.

able to have steady jobs, security, nice homes, be close to their extended families and friends and live essentially Norwegian. They would be home again, but Americanized to the point that they would be a bit more sophisticated than those who had stayed. They could achieve, they could assert themselves, and they knew it.

Peder Eliasen described the situation then in Norway: "We trained people at the aluminum plant (to recruit emigrants) and they spoke English and told others to come back to work in Norway. Then, in the sixties, there was a search for oil and gas. We became rich and things changed a lot. Good jobs and incomes rose immensely. In a welfare state, we are safe when we get sick or old. Some felt that they might not earn as much in Norway but felt safer here because of the welfare state—social democratic ideology. People like it this way."

THE DECISIONS

RUMORS AND QUIET KITCHEN conversations concerning these changes became more and more frequent. It became the one subject when two or more Norwegians visited together. It was discussed on the boats, in the bars, in the homes, on the beaches and over coffee after church. They had to look at America as it was in the late sixties and weigh that against what Norway might become if all the rumors were true. They then had to weigh all of this against the possible implications of the cold war and Norway's geographical proximity to the Soviet Union. And to add another ingredient to this already complicated mix, the scallop prices were very low and therefore money was not as plentiful in New Bedford. In fact, those who owned boats had great difficulty even paying the loans on them.

> *"When you come back to Norway you see how narrow the roads are here."*
>
> —A returned emigrant

One family with an American-born wife returned to Norway with all their possessions and as the husband said, "I knew right away that it wouldn't work out." Then they had to make enough money to ship themselves back to America with all their worldly goods, which meant that the husband was to travel back and forth many times to earn enough money in America to afford the return trip. This frenetic living was not an unusual situation as many over the years went back and forth. But it was under a different set of circumstances that the return emigration took place in the late sixties.

One returned emigrant now living on Karmøy explained his return: "I wouldn't have gone home (to Norway) but she wanted to because of the parents. But when we got home, she was more homesick than me. I went over to make a good start for the marriage and to make some money. Like an adventure—very excited. Our boy who came back to Norway was baseball-crazy. But over the years he lost interest and went to England to play soccer. He would like to go back now to the states. Something about the roots. He was a kid there and now loves it again."

Most men had come over single and then married. Now after a few years, there were children to consider. Did they want their children to be raised as Americans? The children would always be American citizens because of their birthplace, but they could also hold dual citizenship.

A PATRIOTIC BEGINNING

Alf Isaksen of Skudeneshavn described his family story and dilemma. "My father was in the U.S. military while I was stranded in Norway with mother during the war. I came to America on the Fourth of July in 1946 and lived in Atlantic City. I went to third grade and finished high school in 1956. I had two sisters born in America. I started to fish in Atlantic City and in New Bedford. I visited Norway and got engaged to a local girl there who also had many relatives in America and I came back to America in 1960 and stayed till 1969. My parents stayed in Atlantic City and my mother is still there. (In Atlantic City and its suburbs, there was a settlement of Norwegian fisherman and their families throughout the century. Alf's Tante Serine was the wife of my Great Uncle Karl Tobiassen there.)

—AT photo

Tove and Alf Isaksen with their aunts (my father's cousins): the late Gunvald and Kristine (Høines). They were very gracious ladies.

"My wife and I bought a house in 1965 in New Bedford as I had uncles and cousins in New Bedford. New Bedford was the biggest fishing port and the money there was in scallops.

"In 1969 our boys were eight and four years old and one was in second grade. Norway had discovered oil and the aluminum plant had been built, and we felt if we were to go back, we should go before the boys got too old. So we decided to go back and five or six others went back to Norway, and others left for Seattle from New Bedford. Fishing varied—prices up and down. I was tired of fishing and being at sea so many days at a time—not much family life. Now I work eight to five at the aluminum plant and am home each day and weekends free. I liked New Bedford but missed the family. We have everything here we need. I miss sports fishing in America and also miss the ethnic restaurants you can't get in Norway. We had more vegetables in America too.

"But we wanted our boys to grow up in a smaller place. Better place to raise the children in Norway. We have good schools here, lots of sports and it's easier and better for young people here. But in the end, our boys went back to America and now live and work in Texas and have their own families there. Now we go and visit them in Texas whenever we can."

"The best had emigrated, we wanted them back."

—Peder Eliasen

Peder Eliasen says of his work: "I was the personnel man at the new aluminum plant and I went to the states two times to recruit emigrants to come back home. Many recruited were the people who went to America after the Second World War and who wished to return if they knew they could make a good living in Norway. Also those who came after the war had children who were school age, and they wanted them to be educated in Norway. If they went through school in America, they would be Americans forever, and they didn't like to leave children in one country and live in another."

In looking back at those days in the lives of the Norwegian emigrants, it is interesting to note that many of these young married Norwegians were basically living in two new subdivisions where they had built homes. One was in Fairhaven and the other in the extreme North End of New Bedford. Gossip and experiences were shared among their neighborhood groups, and decisions were made accordingly. It was easy to get wrapped up into the almost-community-wide decision. The Fairhaven group more or less stayed and the New Bedford group generally left.

An Åkrehamn man living in Northern New Bedford described his family situation at the time: "In the late sixties many went back home and we thought we should do it too. We decided to sell the house and go back to Norway. Some single men were getting draft notices. They didn't even open them.

They left right away during the Vietnam War for Norway. We had money and thought everything would be fine when we got to Norway, but found that the prices there were so high we had to change our lifestyle, and had a lower standard of living."

"One left, the next left and one by one we left Piney Acres."

—a returned emigrant

According to historian Peder Eliasen: "When they left Norway after the Second World War, it was another Norway. It was poor, it was destroyed, had been occupied by Germans. Those who left earlier had remembered the pure

—Courtesy Aleksander Hauge

Road to home through a rocky path.

Norway. They couldn't imagine what it is like today. The roots are stronger among the older people. It was a pure Norway consisting of farms, fishermen and sailors. Low income—big families on a small amount of land—difficult. Some American emigrants returned to Norway hoping to get a job. Telephones were installed in Karmøy and from the 1980s on, everyone had one. Before that there was just one in each village, in the post office. Norway became modern in a few years. In thirty years was the big jump from homes with no refrigerators to taxis with computers and satellite positioning. It's a big, big jump. The washing machine came in 1952," he remembered. "Before that they just boiled water on wood stoves. The refrigerator and stove became common in late sixties and early seventies.

"You might not become a millionaire here but it will feel safer for you and your family. I also once thought of emigrating to the States in 1954 but I prefer Norway. You have to work hard in the USA by yourself. If you go down, nothing. We have possibilities to be cared for here. It is more regulated in Norway."

ANOTHER CHOICE ADDED TO THE MIX

ONE MORE IMPORTANT INGREDIENT was added to further complicate the decision-making process. Through the ingenuity of New Bedford

Norwegian-American fishermen, who joined together in the Alaskan Scallop Fleet Partnership, the waters around Alaska were opened to the scallop industry and now there was a chance to go to Seattle and Alaska with friends and family and have the opportunity to make big money there. But again the inherent danger of the sea and the famous storms and frigid waters of the Bering Sea tempered some of those decisions.

So now they had three choices:

—*AT photo*

- To stay in New Bedford
- To go back to Norway
- To go west to Seattle and Alaska

And some never made the decision and held their options open, as told by successful skipper and boat owner Malvin Kvilhaug, who came over in the early '60s. "I was in Merchant Marine and was going to Persian Gulf and USA. I came back to Norway two years later. Fishing was not great in Norway and many Norwegians went over to States for spring and summer season. I thought I would try it for a year or two. I was engaged and got married and then my wife came over, and we decided to stay for a couple of years. We came to New Bedford and then got the kids and stayed year after year. Got an uncle who was fishing, so I could get a green card. I have been here for almost forty years and we still haven't decided to stay and may still go back—have the options. I can always go back to Norway as a Norwegian citizen."

Berit and Malvin Kvilhaug in New Bedford, 1996. They now have homes both in America and Norway.

> "*What lies behind us and what lies before us are tiny matters compared to what lies within us.*"
>
> —Ralph Waldo Emerson

Another man, Magne Ådland, explained his situation to my son, Kristian Simsarian, in a 1996 Karmøy interview: "My father fished out of New Bedford and I lived in New Bedford for thirty-three years and also lived in Florida. Wife came after five years. My kids were born in New Bedford but came to Norway on vacations. I built a house in Norway for my daughter, and then my daughter went to Seattle. So she stayed in Seattle, and we moved into the house. We had two sisters in Norway and had land here. We've got no problems here. We waited too long so we couldn't get our children back here though. Children are American citizens and married American citizens."

Lise Medhaug told her story in Norway: "I met the man I married in 1963. He was from Karmøy and living in New Bedford. In 1964 about fifty

—Lise Stol Medhaug family photos

Two lovely Norwegian children prepare for the 17th of May festivities in Norway.

families moved back to Karmøy. There were new working places: aluminum and the oil business. They could make money here then. Some came home to retire here, because we had health insurance and the nursing homes.

"The people in America from Karmøy those years were as close as relatives—not many in America now—only a few families that we know now. They are always welcome to come visiting, and we fight about having them stay with us. The memories of Fort Phoenix where we danced—those times are now past—but I had a beautiful time until I was twenty and got married.

"We arrived back in Norway in Christmas 1964 and my husband had to take over the farm, and I was longing to go back to New Bedford. I cried a lot. Imagine going to an old farm and living in the same house as my mother-in-law instead of driving around in my car, shopping and visiting all my friends in the States! I was twenty years old then and had four beautiful children by the time I was twenty-eight."

"The years teach much which the days never knew."

—Ralph Waldo Emerson

"I FOLLOWED THE WATERS"

MERY VILHELMSEN, an emigrant to America who returned to Norway, recalls her emigration experience during her youth. Elements of her story are common to many other emigrants' experiences.

"In the early spring of 1959 my brother and I went on a plane to the USA. When we came to New York, I couldn't believe it. And when I came to New Bedford my mother was at the airport with her girlfriend, and my sister and some of the girls from New Bedford with her—they had Norwegian parents but were born in New Bedford. They wanted to see what the new Norwegian girls looked like and also some Norwegian boys came who I knew in Norway and had come to New Bedford to fish scallops.

"I couldn't believe it was me who was in America. The sun came up, and everything was just a dream. We drove through the city, and I saw the big streets and nice cars. So this was America, and I was just like in heaven. And we came to my mother's home—she had a big apartment on second floor, three big bedroom, kitchen, living room and bathroom with big bathtub. They had a TV and telephone and nice rugs on the floor. It was just like the movies. We were so happy, but I had to pinch myself.

"My father was out fishing, so I didn't meet him right away. Then he came for four days, and it was very strange. I was going to see my father and I had not seen him for twelve years. I could hardly remember what he looked like, and my mother said I had to give him a hug when he came.

"So I gave him a kiss on the cheek, and I felt a little strange because he had stayed away for so long. I was angry and felt he had forgotten us for a while. He did his best and was very kind and was always doing what was best for us and buying us things and good food. He was cooking on the boats. After a while we got used to him and that he was our father. So many years had gone by, and we had to pick up a lot.

"The girls I met at the airport called right away and wanted me to be their friend and picked me up in their nice cars. I was surprised that they could drive those big cars in all of the traffic. Was so strange to me. This was a totally different world than I was used to. They bought me the biggest ice cream I had even seen . . . a banana split. It was so big I could hardly eat it, and was the best ice cream I had ever tasted.

"On Sundays we went to Lincoln Park with the Norwegian boys who picked us up in their cars. We went on all of the rides and had a marvelous time. We were about twelve (in all). We always met someplace and joined up together—a big Karmøy gang. One from Akraham became my very best friend. She was staying with her sister for about a year. We had a lot in common, and we were out almost every day. When the girls came home they called me or picked me up, and we went shopping downtown or went to Fort Phoenix where we went swimming a lot as soon as summer started. We met at Fort Phoenix every day—all of the Norwegian young people went there and sat as a big group every day.

"When the boys went out fishing, they let the girls borrow their cars. Soon I had to start driving too, of course. I picked it up. I had a few jobs at the donut house and housecleaning. I had no high school education and I could only do housekeeping. I took care of a boy for a while and I fed him, gave him a bath, dressed him and took him to my mother's house. I worked in a few places. Everyone started to get her own boyfriend. I met my husband on the street as he was from Karmøy too.

"We got engaged. Three of us couples got married in the spring of 1961. My husband and I planned to go to Norway for our honeymoon and went on the *Stavangerfjord*. It was the longest honeymoon anyone could have because we stayed on for a whole year in Karmøy with his parents. They were very nice to me and I couldn't complain, but he wanted to stay in Norway, so he could finish his fishing boat. I was very happy and he had a fancy American car, so when I came home to see my old girlfriends they were staring at me when they saw me driving my fancy pink Ford Crown Victoria. I felt like a queen just doing what I wanted to do, and I had nice clothes and money and could go where I wanted to go.

"I took my girlfriends with me to ride, and we went shopping and visited my relatives So much had happened in those two years, it was incredible. Things had changed also

—Vilhelmsen archives

Mery and the late Tønnes Vilhelmsen with their first baby as they return to Norway after several years of living in New Bedford which for Mery would always hold a special place in her heart.

on Karmøy for the better. They had started to get their TVs and new houses and had better jobs. Some of my relatives had cars. Things had exploded in two years—such a big difference. I went to see my grandmother who was over eighty, and she was so happy to see me. She was sitting in the bed all day waiting for me, and she had heard I was coming home. So good to see her again! When you are young, two years is a long time.

"But the days got longer and nothing to do, so we headed back after a year to New Bedford. Bought ourselves some furniture and got an apartment, and we made a little home for ourselves. This was my home now, and I felt Norway was more old-fashioned. I was used to the comforts of New Bedford. In America, I was used to doing things that people never did in Norway. In America we could go out and buy dinner and no one would look at you, but in Norway if you went out to buy dinner, people would think you were lazy or had an awful lot of money. People made their own food.

"One of my girlfriends had a baby boy, and I started to work for a lady doing cleaning. After two years I was expecting my first baby. I was so thrilled and two other girls were expecting at the same time. Myself and two other girls were in the hospital the same day. Two had babies on the same day, and one the day after. We are still close and friendly after all these years. We had a good time together with the small ones. Took them to the beach and had a great time. Had a club with about eight of us who met every two weeks. We had just what we wanted.

—*Photo, Lise Stol Medhaug*

The new generation on the 17th of May in Norway, 1999.

"My husband started to talk about Norway again and wanted to move back and fish there. It was hard for me to move, but I decided to go back anyway. My parents and younger sister also planned to go back. We left New Bedford in 1964 and went home by ship, all of us. Made big cases with furniture and moved everything we had to Norway. Came back in time for Christmas and it was good to see old friends and family. Got an apartment and made new friends and joined old friends.

"After a while my husband took a boat to Seattle to fish in Alaska and make some quick money for a house we wanted to build. He left, and I had to manage the house and family alone. I got the house built, and he came home after nine months and I had already moved into the new house. Everything was fine and I got to choose everything. I now had two girls.

"Years went by. My husband went to Alaska many trips to fish crab and salmon. He would stay there two or three months and come to Norway where he would fish shrimp as he still had his boat. We had a good life together. Once I visited him in Seattle with the two girls. We also had a boy. The family was completed. I stayed in Norway and went to America to visit. Sometimes I wonder why we didn't stay in America as he went back and forth so often. But it was safer in Norway. The kids could play outside and not be afraid of kidnapping day or night.

"In 1984 my husband died suddenly. He was walking to the boat and didn't come home. I heard the sound of the boat and wondered why it hadn't gone out and his friend found him on the deck, dead. I was forty-three and the oldest had married but the youngest was only five. I had to think of survival again. We had to sell the boat. When I think about it and look back, I have had a good life in Norway and you are well taken care of here. If you get sick there is nothing to worry about as you have free doctors and hospitals. If you are out of work you have the same as anyone else. You get the same treatment, rich or poor. When we get old, everyone who needs it gets a nursing home place. That is a good thing here. We may have high taxes like the gas is four times more expensive and that is funny because Norway is such a big oil nation. But that is why we have it so good. Norway is the second richest country in the world.

COMMUNITY

"HERE ON KARMØY we know each other, and know if anyone needs us and try to help. We all help each other. People care for themselves in the big cities. Norway and America are about equal now—things you buy, food, clothes, and technical things. If you have the money, you can buy it here or there. The weather is nicer in America and we have a lot of wind and rain here. I miss the good weather in America—especially the long, nice beautiful summers with warm weather. I miss going to the nice stores, seeing different things. Sometimes we went to Brooklyn to see the 17th of May parade and it was so nice to see all of the Norwegians down there. I feel that I have been very privileged to live in America and have had a very interesting life."

It is interesting to note that many emigrants interviewed pointed to socialized medicine and free education as a major reason to live in Norway. But in longer conversations they also admitted that the medical help is difficult to obtain there because of long waits and that specialists are almost impossible to see. They had concerns about the sick and the old and many felt they did not have first-rate care. And also many were critical of the schools and lack of supplies. So although the anticipated government benefits of living in one of the world's wealthiest countries was a strong enticement, it also could become a source of conflict and frustration.

SEATTLE AND THE ALASKAN FISHERY

SEATTLE ALREADY HAD a large Norwegian settlement by the late sixties centered in Ballard, and many Norwegians there, mostly from Northern Norway, owned boats. There were a few cultural differences to overcome, but the support systems such as ethnic stores and churches, clubs, neighborhoods and potential friends were already in place, even though the dialect might be a bit different. One Norwegian emigrant described it as "just like going home." Also to the Norwegian man, the lore of Alaska meant new challenges and opportunities for courage, daring and adventure. That appealed to him as he had also heard that the riches there could be had for the taking.

The decisions in New Bedford were made approximately in even numbers. About one third stayed, one third went back to Norway and one third went to Seattle and Alaska. So many boats left New Bedford to make the long trek around the Panama Canal to Alaska that New Bedford was alarmed that they would lose their entire fishing fleet. Others took planes home to Norway and shipped all of their goods home.

The Egil Ellingsen family from Skudenes and Haugesund fished out of New Bedford and then followed the waters to Seattle. He recalls, "Adventure began at an early age and has continued throughout my life. While in New Bedford, I had been studying the downward trend in the scallop fishing industry in our area, knowing I would need to look into other fishery possibilities. Little did I realize that our journey would eventually lead us to 'The Last Frontier.'

—*AT photo*

Gunnar Fagerland and Harald Mannes: home again in Norway, 1998.

"In the fall of 1967, I traveled to Seattle and met with National Marine Fisheries regarding the possibility of scallop beds in Alaska. Their information was extremely limited, so we met with Alaska Fish and Game in Juneau to look at their data. We then traveled to Kodiak where we observed a Kodiak vessel equipped with East Coast scallop-dredging equipment prospecting for scallops. We estimated that with modifications in equipment, we could be successful in offshore scallop fishing.

"The Alaskan Scallop Fleet Partnership was organized with the owners of the fishing vessels *Bountiful*, *Viking Queen* and *Smaragd* in early spring of 1968. The *Viking Queen* went ahead to fulfill a charter agreement with the State of Alaska. The other three vessels left the Fairhaven/New Bedford harbor for Alaska on May 15, 1968, under my direction. It was my responsibility to get the vessels safely from Massachusetts to Alaska.

"The journey was filled with anticipation as we ventured into new territory. I will never forget that as we passed through the Panama Canal I received news that the *Viking Queen*'s charter was a success and that it had a substantial load of scallops. We were thrilled as we navigated north to San Diego and then to Seattle to refuel. In Seattle we met with the crew from the *Bountiful* that had flown in from New Bedford. As planned, we sent the *Bountiful* on ahead to the fishing grounds while we continued north to Seward with all the processing equipment for Alaska scallop processors.

"My wife Kitty and the children remained in Fairhaven until our home sold. The decision to uproot and move the family five thousand miles away had been an extremely difficult one. We had to leave our New England home we had loved so much, as well as the schools, church and many dear friends. We struggled for months with our decision. The big question, 'Are we doing the right thing?' would remain unanswered for a long time.

"Kitty and our three children, Evelyn, Kenneth and Erin-Joy, flew to Seattle on July 9, 1968, and we were reunited in Seattle and then flew together to Anchorage. We drove to Seward, one hundred twenty-eight miles south-east of Anchorage on the Seward Highway. What a surprise the landscape was to the family as they saw it for the first time. Steep, rugged snow-covered shale mountains, tall trees with few branches, the beautiful wildflowers, fireweed, tundra, creeks and waterfalls for miles and miles with no sign of civilization anywhere!

"The Alaskan scallop fleet and the owners and families were welcomed with open arms to Seward. All of the original owners of the Alaskan Scallop Fleet relocated their families to Seward and enrolled their children in the local schools. Crews for our fishing vessels flew from New Bedford to Alaska to begin this new adventure. With the success of our company and the lucrative scallop beds, many other boats from the East Coast followed.

THE BEAUTY OF ALASKA

"ALASKA, ALSO, is the 'Land of the Midnight Sun.' It never got dark during those beautiful summer nights. During the short summer months we drove to Anchorage to do our shopping, and we always stopped on the top of Turnagain Pass. We enjoyed a delicious picnic lunch that Kitty prepared for us and spent time walking around on the tundra enjoying the maze of beautiful small wildflowers of all colors and sizes. On that same route was Portage Glacier, where we often stopped to watch the amazing ten-story-high chunks of cobalt-blue ice floes. We had good times along the Kenai River with picnics, berry gathering and occasionally seeing moose in the woods or even crossing the main highway. Black bears were aggressive and sometimes would topple over garbage cans for something to eat. They knew all the tricks, even when the cans were on stands about four feet off the ground. Summer passed too quickly!

"Soon fall arrived, and by October we had our first snowfall. Severe snowstorms and the biting cold did not affect community activities. Even with ten feet of snow on the ground, the children never missed a day of school. Believe it or not, the 17th of May—'*Sytende Mai*', was our last big snowfall. What a contrast to the beautiful New England springs we had grown to love. It was a tough year on everyone and we missed our friends terribly. Yet, the ruggedness of Alaska was captivating, and each of us grew to appreciate and love Alaska for what it was.

"The Alaskan scallop fleet continued to bring in large amounts of scallops and the news quickly reached the East Coast. Our plant, The Alaskan Scallop Processors, processed the scallops under our "Bountiful" label and packed them in five-pound bags for shipment to a large freezer warehouse in Seattle. The lucrative profits attracted many East Coast boats and as a result the scallop fleet grew to seventeen vessels besides our own four vessels. We were buying and processing all scallops through our company. That many boats had a negative effect on the scallop beds, so by the fall of 1970 many of these vessels decided to return to New Bedford.

"In the meantime, the Alaskan Scallop Processors sat with an inventory of over a million pounds of frozen scallops in Seattle. Our broker in Seattle did not develop the West Coast scallop market successfully, and that put us in a very difficult position. With an inventory worth millions of dollars unable to move, our situation was bleak. Two of our partners left, and the rest of us hired a new Seattle broker who distributed the scallops effectively. As a result, we bought out the other two partners. This was the turning point for Alaskan Scallop Company (revised name) as the broker continued to move vast quantities of scallops. The fishing grounds improved and production and sales went very well. The Alaskan Scallop Company became a very successful business.

"In 1973 one of the major fish companies in Seattle approached us with interest in acquiring our boats, the processing line and our scallop brand name, 'Bountiful.' Their offer was one we could not refuse! As part of the sale my partner and I agreed to manage the business for three years in Seward. Relocating to Seattle in 1976, I was asked to serve as the manager of fisheries development and marine technology in the corporate office downtown for the same company. This position involved providing technical expertise in all phases of vessel design and operation within the company as well as to prospective suppliers. More specifically, I was a specialist in the areas of vessel design and construction, gear and equipment and in more general areas of fishery development. I also coordinated with their U.S. mariner division on strategic planning for the development of the entry into new catcher/processor vessel activities related to bottom fish. This was an invigorating three years with many new opportunities and experiences.

"During this time, Kitty and I offered a young Norwegian man a partial partnership in a new vessel I was hoping to build. In 1978 I contracted to build a hundred-twenty-five-foot vessel capable of crab fishing and/or trawling in Alaska. This state-of-the-art steel vessel was equipped with the latest and most reliable equipment. The process went smoothly with *Flying Cloud* being completed in September, christened in Seattle, and shortly thereafter left for Dutch Harbor, Alaska.

—*AT photo*

Former fisherman Johannes Johannessen with Karin and Eleanor Hansen in Norway in 2000.

"Fisheries naturally have their peaks and lows over the years, which is what occurred with crabbing in Alaska. Fortunately, experience and vision provided direction for us and as crabbing waned, the *Flying Cloud* was equipped for bottom fishing, another highly successful fishery to this day. During the years I had the *Flying Cloud* I rarely skippered the vessel, but I did several charters with National Marine Fisheries and took care of all the accounting needs of the *Flying Cloud.*

"I sold the *Flying Cloud* in the early 1990s but in the meantime had ventured into another type of fishery—summer salmon fishing in Bristol Bay, Alaska. My son Kenneth was a businessman in Wisconsin when I was contemplating the purchase of the salmon boat, *Little Dipper.* He loved the ocean and wanted to be a part of this venture. We purchased the *Little Dipper,* and I enjoyed the challenge of being in the right place at the right time for salmon fishing, as well as the camaraderie of many fine men from all walks of life who became close friends. These few weeks each summer were like a vacation for me and I thoroughly enjoyed each memory of those times. I sold the *Little Dipper* in 1994."

THE END OF THE EMIGRATION

THOSE EMIGRANTS WHO RETURNED to Norway also live very well with an exceptionally high standard of living. Only those in both countries who lost their battle with alcohol or lost their spouses to the sea or divorce have to struggle a bit today.

Those who survived the terror of the sea made it! Many became wealthy beyond their wildest dreams fishing the waters in Massachusetts and Alaska. It is said that at least one man a week loses his life fishing in Alaska during the crab season—a job many consider the most dangerous job in the world. Some feel the money is worth the risk. Some may be multi-millionaires, many are millionaires, and others very well off. The emigration has essentially ended, although some Norwegians still go to Alaska for short periods to make quick money.

But there is a post-emigration scenario, which includes many visits back and forth between Norway and America. The Norwegian-Americans visit often and some have second homes in Norway. The Norwegian emigrants who returned to Norway also like to take their vacations in America where they visit again the communities, old friends and places they loved, as well as explore new neighborhoods and changes. They sometimes have homes here also. Some of their children decided to move back to America.

And so the *pendling* continues in a different way and may always continue in some fashion because of the shared loved for—and roots in—these two beloved countries.

Legacy & Folklore

HEXES

Fishermen's superstitions about foiling bad luck at sea.

No whistling on board.
Turn clock-wise when leaving dock.
No talk ever about a pig or its parts.
No talk about horses.
Go out the same door as you came in.
Shave on incoming tide.
Don't go out to sea on a Friday.
Don't go out to sea on the 13th.
Bad luck comes by:
  – Women on board vessel,
  – A hawk, owl or crow in the rigging,
  – Breaking a mirror,
  – Dropping a hatch in the hold,
  – Turning a hatch bottom up,
  – Driving nails on a Sunday,
  – Letting the splices of a cable stop in the hawse-pipe
    when the vessel is anchoring on the fishing ground.
A horseshoe prevents bad luck.
But a bee or small bird landing on board brings good
fortune.

19

The Following Waters

LATER GENERATIONS

—*Courtesy, Haugesunds Avis*

Hollywood times two. Academy Award winner Brian Helgeland relaxes in
Haugesund, Norway, in1998 while Marilyn Monroe appears to look over
his shoulder from her statue-perch. Her father is known to be a
Haugesund native. Brian's family had roots in the Haugesund and
Karmøy areas.

*"But the seafaring man who
follows the waters, follows the stars.
And if you choose them for your guides,
you can reach your destiny."*

—Carl Schurz

SUCCESSIVE GENERATIONS OF EMIGRANTS' FAMILIES, especially the men, were often influenced by their seafarer's heritage. Until recently, women, through conditioning or choice, carried on the traditional roles of Norwegian women. Today there are some very successful women in professional fields.

Women thoroughout Norwegian history cared for the home, organized the family and managed the "estate" as they did back to the Viking days, while their husbands were out to sea. There was little time or inclination to go on to college. In truth, many emigrant parents, who had left school in Norway at age fourteen, thought that getting a high school diploma alone was quite an achievement. A few did let their daughters go on to professions such as nursing or teaching, beauty culture or secretarial work before they married. Others got degrees as adults after they had raised their families.

And as strange as it sounds now, in the fifties women basically had four choices: secretary, beautician, nurse or teacher. Roles were very defined and opportunities rare for women up to the mid-1970s. The majority stayed at home and performed those needed tasks of caring for and raising families, managing the households, finances and overseeing their children's church training.

Norwegian or Norwegian-American women were apt to marry Norwegian men who were several years older than the traditional two-year-difference American standard. It was normal for a woman in her teens or late teens to marry a man well into his twenties or even into his thirties.

Some women later branched into areas related to their husband's trades— areas that enhanced or supported their lives at sea or the fishing industry. Some work in Norwegian-related businesses and others are in real estate or the travel industry. They have the reputation for doing well at whatever they chose. Their homes were the best kept, their children well-disciplined, neat, clean and well-dressed, their tables groaned with food and they were always well-groomed. Their husbands were well-cared-for and it was an achievement for many men to have "a good Norwegian woman" as a wife.

Many of the sons went to high school, often the vocational school, as it prepared them with traditional carpentry and mechanical skills. Others went on to college, often Lutheran colleges. There was a tendency for Norwegian-Americans to do very well academically. Although many became fishermen—and often to great success—others did not and went quite natually into unrelated professions.

The next generation of men and women, those born after 1960 or so, if they did not marry early, often did go on to college and universities. The men who did not choose the fishing industry sometimes went on to earn advanced degrees, and many professions were represented within this population. Many of those who went on to school were both of Norwegian and American stock.

Professions for first- and second-generation men and women include engineer, businessman, lawyer, artist and professor, landscape designer, nurse, dentist, accountant, military officer, stockbroker, government worker, airline employee, teacher, museum manager and other professions. There are at least three Ph.D's among the succeeding generations in petroleum engineering, sociology and computer science. Those who chose the fishing industry chose to do it more on an ownership/management level and used book-learned business skills to advance in their professions. And, of course, some inherited the whole business from their fathers and managed it very successfully when they had acquired the additonal skills.

I had to make choices when I wrote this chapter about who I would profile. I chose people who in some way were representative of the community and who have led challenging lives. I also wanted to show a different side. While many Norwegian-Americans achieved great riches from fishing, others found success in other areas—areas that demonstrate the tendency of Norwegians, even those with only a bit of Norwegian blood, to possess courage, independence and follow in the *pendling* tradition.

Representing the achievements of many Norwegian-Americans are:

- Two women who succeeded in very different ways. One broke all the barriers for women in uniform and the other achieved success from highly developed entrepreneurial skills.
- Three generations of a hard-working emigrant family who produced a grandson, once a fisherman, who brought fame to the Norwegian community when he won an Academy Award in Hollywood as best screenwriter.
- A man from a Swedish-Norwegian family who, in his life as a clergyman, made choices that reflected his unselfish nature rather than his need to be front and center. He cared for the forgotten people.
- My son, because I am proud of him and his accomplishments as a Ph.D., and also because he chose for eight years to live, work and study in Scandinavia and get to know his Norwegian roots in depth. He is a modern-day *pendler* and had enough patience to encourage me throughout the writing of this book.

These people represent later generations with a Norwegian-American heritage. They are all, I believe, a credit to their families and culture both here and in Norway.

INTRODUCTION

When I was an officer in the United States Navy, I tried to seize opportunities to go out on ships. Except for an occasional day trip, I did not succeed. Once I did take the helm of a destroyer escort, the U.S.S. *Coates*, as we steamed through Long Island Sound, but only because the captain was a close friend. I remember the tugboat captains doing a double-take when they saw me, a woman, sitting in the captain's chair at the helm of a naval vessel in New York Harbor in 1964.

Women were not permitted to serve aboard Navy ships at that time. I did greet U.S. Navy vessels and foreign ships coming into New York and was often invited for dinner on board. That was the extent of my shipboard experience.

When I was stationed in lower Manhattan, female officers were not even permitted to have rooms at the Naval Bachelor Officers Quarters and had to find housing on their own. If we married, we could not qualify for dependent allowances or family housing. According to regulations at the time, we were full line officers, but we did not have many of the privileges.

Within a few years after I left the Navy, things were to change—everything opened up for women in all of the services. But it took years of endurance by female officers to achieve these goals. Years later, one of my male superior officers happened to see my brother at an officers club and told him, "Your sister was ahead of her time. I didn't realize then what she meant, but I do now."

With that experience in tow, I very much appreciated the achievements of another New Bedford area woman, with a similar Norwegian-American background, who had opportunities that had been denied women officers in earlier years. As far as I can ascertain, we were the only two Norwegian-American women from the New Bedford area who chose this Norwegian way of life and became commissioned officers.

LINDA JOHANSEN, COMMAND AT SEA: THE WOMAN VIKING

"When a goal matters enough to a person, that person will find a way to accomplish what at first seemed impossible."

—Nido Qubein

In 1976, Linda Johansen was a sixteen-year-old Norwegian-American girl in Dartmouth, Massachusetts—part of the greater New Bedford area where many Norwegians had settled. Her father was a fisherman, as were most of her male Norwegian relatives who came from Akraham and Kopervik on Karmøy. She, like them, had a deep passion for all the elements of the seas: the peace, the tumult, the adventure, the beauty, the danger and most of all, the boats.

"Whenever she could, which was often, she would go down to the docks with her father or grandfather to her grandfather's boat," said her grandmother, Mrs. Simon Johansen of Acushnet. "She would be up at the top of the mast before he could turn around." While other girls were wheeling doll carriages or giggling together, Linda was at the dock or on the boat, learning everything she could about life on the sea.

But she was a woman, and women in 1976 were not allowed to work at sea in any meaningful capacity. Most of the armed services had kept their female personnel on land. Linda was, nonetheless, drawn to the sea and to that disciplined and challenging life, so she sought to find a career solution to her aspirations and goals. She was particularly impressed with the traditions of the United States Coast Guard, as her family and their friends had had close and frequent contact with this branch of service, especially in times of emergency. It was dangerous work and she had some knowledge of it. She knew it was essential for commerce, it was humane and it had a good image. In all, this prospect was very enticing to her.

When she heard that the service academies were finally looking at women candidates for admission, she thought she might like to attend the Coast Guard Academy in New London, Connecticut. The Coast Guard had been involved in the rescue of many Norwegian-American boats over the years, working hand-in-hand with her many relatives and ancestors at sea. They had learned to trust the skills of the Coast Guardsmen. She perhaps did not know that her ancient ancestors, the Vikings, often had women on their voyages and that they had to do their share of the dangerous work along with the men.

She passed all the requirements for the Coast Guard Academy, including a stringent physical examination as well as meeting the strong emotional, mental, moral and academic standards. Then she waited. She was good in math and knew that this was essential for Coast Guard officers, so she had high hopes.

THAT SPECIAL NEWS

ONE MOMENTOUS DAY, she received the letter announcing her acceptance to the academy. The news was an occasion for great joy and excitement, but to her friends and family there were concerns along with their good wishes. She was a woman pioneering in a man's field. She was part of the first class that accepted women and this would be just the beginning of many "firsts" in her life. Although several women were accepted, there was no guarantee that they would graduate and it certainly would not be an easy time for any of them. But Linda was determined that she would be among the graduates four years later.

She took to her training and discipline as a fish to water and rose immediately through the leadership ranks. In her junior year, she became the first female battalion commander in the academy's history and in her last year she was named regimental commander. This was the highest accomplishment a cadet could achieve and, to the astonishment of men and the joy of women, she did a superb job. She was, according to the New Bedford Standard-Times, "the first woman ever to command an entire cadet corps at any of the nation's four military academies." She had been chosen to lead eight hundred and seventeen cadets, of whom thirty-eight were women. The previous year she received the honor of being the first female cadet in the academy's history to be chosen a battalion commander."

—Courtesy of the New Bedford Standard-Times

Cadet Linda Johansen at the United States Coast Guard Academy, New London, CT.

According to the no-nonsense Johansen, "As regimental commander during my first class year, I was in charge of the entire corps of cadets, a responsibility ranging from training to the daily routine of leading the corps in military reviews (parades) for visiting dignitaries. There were fourteen women in my graduating class of about one hundred fifty-five. The class started with three hundred and fifty cadets of which thirty-eight were women.

After graduating fifth in her class from the Coast Guard Academy and being commissioned an ensign, she was assigned as operations officer on the USCGC *Bittersweet*, a one hundred-eighty-foot buoy tender home-ported in Woods Hole, on Cape Cod. This ship was responsible for all buoys from Cape Ann to Block Island and all the waters in between. Her next challenging assignment was as executive officer on the USCGC *Red Oak*, a hundred-fifty-seven-foot buoy tender home ported in Gloucester City, New Jersey. It was responsible for buoys and range lights on the Delaware River, as well as lighthouse refueling.

Progressively given more responsibility, she became the first woman to be named company officer and admiral's aide at the Coast Guard Academy in New London, where she was, in her words, "responsible for one-eighth of

—AT photo

Linda's counterpart, a female Norwegian cadet midshipman on the training vessel *Christian Radich*, during her visit to Boston in the early nineties.

The first two ships Linda Johansen served on as an officer. Her last ship, the *Redwood*, which she commanded, was similar to the *Red Oak* in size and line.

George E. Bieda, Windjammer Arts, 9092 Washington Avenue, Studio 7, Silverdale WA www.windjammer-arts.com donated the use of these two detailed prints.

the Corps of Cadets in a 'guidance officer' capacity." She was also responsible for all ceremonies conducted at the academy.

It was rare in those days for an admiral to have a woman as his aide. My Navy classmate, Lieutenant Evva Meyer (Larson), had been an admiral's aide stationed in London and traveled all over Europe in this capacity. This position in the services was often saved for well-connected male officers. Evva and Linda were significant exceptions.

After completion of this duty, Linda was awarded a command of her own. A woman having a command at sea is extremely rare and a highly desired assignment. As commanding officer of USCGC *Redwood*, a hundred-fifty-seven-foot buoy tender home-ported in New London, she was responsible for buoys from Watch Hill, Rhode Island, to Execution Rocks in New York Harbor, and all waters in between, including the Connecticut River. She was also responsible for lighthouse refueling and renovation—an impressive area of responsibility critical to the safety of shipping all along the heavily traveled waters of the East Coast and certainly waters that included much of the New Bedford fishing fleet.

Tending to buoys means that the boat has to be in close, but safe, proximity to the buoy, and that requires very sophisticated boat-handling skills on a normal day. But in rough weather, it requires outstanding boat-handling skills. To keep the personnel safe while they are doing this dangerous work and to also keep the boat stable is a feat of excellent seamanship. Linda was particularly good at the helm and established this reputation very quickly.

"My entire career," she has said, "was a nontraditional adventure at sea. Mostly what I did was heavy construction work at sea—not too glamorous, but interesting, nonetheless."

She later married a retired Coast Guard officer and decided she had done all she wanted to do in the Coast Guard, and it was time to look for an on-shore challenge. She found such a challenge as mathematics teacher and "curriculum and instructional leader" at the East Lyme High School in East Lyme, Connecticut.

Linda has ancestors from both the land of Christopher Columbus, on her mother's side, and Leif Erickson from her father's. Her pioneering work and courage at sea coupled with her sense of adventure is a continuation of this heritage.

She has been an inspiration to all women seeking equity, choice, achievement and fulfillment in their careers. The daughter of Mr. and Mrs. Thomas Johansen of Dartmouth, Massachusetts, has carried on the tradition of her ancestors.

Well done, Linda!

THE HELGELANDS OF NEW BEDFORD: THE EBB AND FLOW OF THE TIDES OF LIFE

WHEN WE ARE CHILDREN, certain grownups are special to us for a variety of reasons. It may be because they smile or speak to us warmly or simply make a point of always recognizing us in some friendly way. Such a woman in my memory was Mrs. Pauline Helgeland. When I was young, I found her to be an especially open and caring woman who had generosity of spirit and who made me feel welcomed and accepted. I remember my mother always had something nice to say about her and termed her a "real lady."

I knew her from the church. She would sometimes invite the youth group to her home for a Sunday evening get-together. Those evenings were very special and in some ways took the place of dating in those innocent days of the early 1950s. Ten or twelve church teens would meet for dessert and coffee, games and discussions. It was our social life, and we giggled and acted about as silly as most young teens did in those days, but we were also looking for meaning in our lives through our faith and an understanding of the world in which we lived.

It was especially pleasant to go down to Mrs. Helgeland's home on Orchard Street, which to me was a palace. It was a lovely home, warm and welcoming, with a porch and a large living room. The kitchen was always warm with the fragrance of hot coffee and something in the oven that promised to be delicious. She was busy, but never too busy to give a cheery greeting. Occasionally her husband was home, but he said very little as was the case with their son Walter, who was friendly with an infectious smile but a bit shy and considered "a brain" in math and science in high school. She would mention me to her husband, who would acknowledge the introduction, then turn away sadly. The words, "This is Astrid Tollefsen, Sigvart's daughter," would bring sad looks to many faces as they were reminded of their own vulnerability at sea. Fishermen were not comfortable with the children or wives of their lost colleagues. It was too much a reminder of what could happen.

The Helgelands were active at the Elim Baptist Church and, although they attended the Trinity Lutheran Church for a while, Mrs. Helgeland liked adult baptism and returned to Elim where she also liked the new minister. The Lutheran church was very strict at that time, but so was Elim. I can't imagine any church being more strict than Elim, but some thought differently.

Pauline Helgeland came from Årstad in Southern Norway, about an hour south of Stavanger, and her husband Oskar came from the Haugesund area. Oskar came to America in 1924. He had been orphaned at age sixteen, married at an early age and had three children before he emigrated. Just after his trip, his wife died from an illness in Norway, and his brother took care of his three children.

According to their son, Thomas Helgeland: "Mother came over in 1928 when she was twenty-six. She worked at homes as a housekeeper and a cook. She cooked also as a housekeeper because she cooked better than the cook." Oskar Helgeland met and married this capable woman and later Tommy was born. His other children came over when Tommy was about a year old, and the household was established. According to Tommy, "They were very practical in those years. My father was extremely kind; my mother a take-charge woman. Mother ran the family—now the women are running Norway and they deserve to run the country because they have been running the families for years. I grew up with his three children. He hadn't seen his kids for six years. They came over in 1930 but the girl died after only nine months in America as she had TB and a rheumatic heart. The oldest boy was a fisherman named Martin and he dropped out of school as moving had put him way behind in school. Christian also fished and did some electronics. He was an entrepreneur—and a very smart fellow. Both are dead now."

HIGH TIDE

TOMMY FURTHER RECALLS: "When father came up to New Bedford in 1937 to fish, we lived by Pope Beach in Fairhaven and liked it there, but we moved to New Bedford and rented a nice house on Orchard Street which we later bought. My father wasn't around much as he was fishing, but I remember him as a friendly man. He liked people and found them interesting. He was always bringing people home. 'Laughing Mike is coming,' he'd say. He had a soft spot for Norwegians whose families were not with them. He was very gentle and there was not an ounce of violence in him. My mother would give us a whack on our behinds once in a while. He was very tired when he came home from fishing.

"She was smart and vibrant and he was a great father. When he got sick and I was older, I got to appreciate that about him. Easygoing, he never would get an ulcer! Sometimes he wouldn't want to go fishing and my mother would say, 'You know you have to go. Many families depend on you.' He would never fight with her, but would give in.

"Mother felt being well-dressed was important, so we were always well-dressed. We had a big Chrysler, which gave the appearance of having money. From 1942 to 1948 we were moving up. We had a summer home and a car, but when Dad got sick it all went. He didn't put much into Social Security because he was a boat owner. He was sick for a few years and then died in 1950.

AND LOW TIDE

"MOTHER HAD THE BOAT but it was getting old. No one could make a go of it. Finally it was sold at auction to pay the bills. Mother sold the big house and bought a small house in the South End and worked in the schools as a cafeteria helper and also did housework. She was over fifty years old at the time. She then sold all her furniture and went to live with my youngest brother and his wife for a while, but later chose to live with a family as a housekeeper and cook in Florida. She came home when my sister was in college and lived with the Sig Midttun family, who owned the local bakery, for a couple of years. She struggled and would do anything for the kids to see that they got an education, and she paid room and board at Brown University for her youngest son, Walter and for her daughter Eleanor, who went to the University of Massachusetts in Amherst. She would give you the shirt off her back, and she was always proud of her work. She died in 1991."

—*Helgeland family archives*
Brian Helgeland as a grade schooler in New Bedford, circa late sixties.

Tommy's son, her grandson, Brian Helgeland, a film director and screenwriter, was quoted in a University of Massachusetts interview with the following words—words that referred to a fictional character but could have been written about his grandmother: "He had made great sacrifices for the one he loved and that allowed him to accept and live with the circumstances he ended up with."

TOMMY HELGELAND

I REMEMBER TOMMY VERY WELL. He was enough older that we all looked up to him, literally. He was tall, handsome and very pleasant, and we as young girls in the Sunday school stole glances at him when he was in his Navy uniform. But he broke all of our hearts when he brought his pretty Norwegian girlfriend to church and was soon engaged to her. She came from Haugesund and was a daughter of the Ulland family. Her father, an Evangelical preacher, was called Norway's Billy Graham. Tommy married and his life took another turn.

—*AT photo*

Tom Helgeland hits a high note at the annual Seaman's Bethel Memorial Service for lost seamen conducted on the New Bedford waterfront, 1996.

"One day," Tommy recalls, "someone in the choir said I had an exceptionally good voice, so I started to take voice lessons. Now my main interest in life is singing. I still study voice and go to seminars. I started to sing professionally thirty years ago— weddings, shows, operas—and went to music school at Oberlin College one summer. I have a large voice. My wife encouraged me to sing. There are proportionately more singers in Scandinavia than anyplace. The men are often tenors and I still sing professionally throughout the area. My son tried to get the singing job for me in 'L.A. Confidential.' He didn't succeed but he did get me a role singing in a Sylvester Stallone movie. I sang 'Ave Maria' just before the shooting. Look here—I still have my union card.

"I fished from the time I was sixteen on my father's boat *Lewis Thibeaut*, which was both a dragger and scalloper. Then I served in the Navy and went to college, two years to Southern Massachusetts Technical Institute. (Formerly the New Bedford Textile Institute, then SMU, now the University of Massachusetts, Dartmouth.) I graduated in 1971 with a B.A. in math and taught school for a while, and then went to work for the state, but I retired early because my wife was ill.

"She has a disease of the immune system—systemic lupus. She works hard and overcomes so much. We went to Norway in 1986 for her to say goodbye, then found renewed hope through advanced medicine in Boston."

KINA

I FIND TOMMY'S WIFE, Aud Karin, best known as "Kina," to be an intriguing woman. She is one of those rare people who resemble the proverbial artichoke: the more you peel back, the more delights you find. She has a great sense of humor and is more candid than most Norwegians. She is upfront and frank but with that little twist of humor that I find endearing and familiar. She has insight, great strength and the ability to live life to the fullest, despite the ever-demanding presence of lupus. I never talk with her that I don't laugh and learn something new and interesting—a new insight, an impression, a thought, or a new side to a complex matter. She gives a straight answer and has a comfortable personality. She is disarming and one of those special people I would like to know better.

THE FAMILY

TOMMY AND AUD KARIN have three children in whom they take great pride. "My daughters Katherine and Karen have worked so hard," relates Kina, "and have done so well. One daughter is a nurse anesthetist and well known in her field, and my other daughter is a nurse and has several children. We love taking care of our grandchildren. I give my daughters credit for their hard work and perseverance, and I am so proud of them."

The two daughters had a brother sandwiched between them and this middle child was named Brian. Tommy continues: "My son Brian is a screenwriter and very successful. He converts books into screenplays, writes screenplays

—Mery Vilhelmsen photo

Kina and Tom Helgeland (front) and Aleksander Hauge (left) with the Henry Pedersen family and Eleanor Helgeland, sister of Tom. They are seated at the head table in the Wamsutta Club after the Norwegian "Two Flags" concert in 1999.

The Helgeland children in July 1965. Brian's father points out that Brian has a gun in his hand and wonders if he might have had a screenplay in progress somewhere in his mind at the time.

—Helgeland family archives

and also produces and directs films. After college, he went to U.S.C. for a summer course in film writing. He borrowed the money and was out there for seven weeks. Caught the bug! Like his mother—hard-driving and works very hard."

A former employer related that Brian also worked on a fishing boat regularly and one day told him, "This is my last trip and I'm going to Hollywood to write." The owner remembers, "He read a lot on board and was a good worker—just a really nice guy."

BRIAN

"In California," his father continued, "he took a course and his teacher helped him out. He had no place to live and nobody to help. His teacher let him borrow his car and told him where he could find a decent place to live. He shared a room in Watts. He wrote a screenplay—a comedy about old people because he had worked in a nursing home. While in California he wrote a story about his grandfather for a contest. Somebody called, after he had returned home to Massachusetts, and told him he had won second prize and they would pay for his airfare back to L.A. They put him up in a hotel for a week, and that prize paid for an apartment. He tried to make it as a writer, but made nothing for a year. He got married to a girl from home, and she worked. Then he got an agent and wrote things I am not proud of—horrible pieces, blood and gore. 'They put bread on the table,' he said to me."

"Brian is very organized, likes his work and he is always pushing. I believe that his success comes from his ability to concentrate totally on what is at hand and when it is through, to relax completely. He never mixes the two. Most of us do, but he doesn't. Brian's wife is from Cape Cod and has a Norwegian and Finnish background. They have two wonderful children."

> *"He was cheerful and friendly in conversation, playful and youthful in his ways, and was much liked by the people."*
>
> —"The Saga of Harald Hardrager"

FROM NEW BEDFORD TO THE OSCAR

BRIAN HELGELAND WAS BORN IN 1961 and raised and schooled in New Bedford, where he was a member of the Elim Baptist Church. He was a member of the Norwegian community and is fondly remembered as a hard-working ambitious boy with an affable personality. And as did other Norwegian boys of that time, he "went out fishing" to make money to go to school, in this case graduate school. He didn't go away to college for his bachelor's degree but commuted instead to the nearby University of Massachusetts at Dartmouth. Friends have remarked that writing was not a passion until his early twenties. One former employer said, "He bought a book about scriptwriting and read it on the boat. He told me, I can do that!" But his mother said, "No, he always wrote from the time he was a kid and was a passionate reader."

Recently he went to Norway to the Haugesund Film Festival where he gave some insight into his field for aspiring writers. The Norwegians are very proud of his accomplishments and he along with his mother and father was featured in newspapers throughout that area. To the Norwegians it was a special time to have one of their own come back as a successful man.

Brian spoke recently of his work and career to a reporter for the Standard-Times: "Most of it, day to day, is hard work. But I think the last step is luck." And he described his long-term goal of "just directing my own stuff and not writing for hire anymore."

MOON TIDE: THE OSCAR

"The fairest cargo ship e'er bore, the gallant Harald homeward brings. Gold, and a fame that skald still sings.

—"The Saga of Harald Hardrager"

BRIAN TOLD ONE INTERVIEWER: "Winning an Oscar was always in the back of my mind. I didn't think it would happen so soon, but it was great to achieve that goal. Of course, as I was walking offstage I already wanted another one. Winning hasn't changed too much of anything." He further mentioned that after he received the Oscar for best screenplay for a film adapted from a book, for the 1998 film, "LA Confidential," he was a bit intimidated the next time he went to write and "it was only a letter." The first time he was recognized as a celebrity by a group of people was to him "a weird experience."

In Colorado, he told movie critic Marty Mapes: "I used to keep it (Oscar) on my desk and whenever I'd have to start typing or writing, I'd always look up and it would be there. So finally about a year and a half ago, I wrapped it all up in bubble wrap and threw it in the back of my closet, with all due respect

—Helgeland family archives

The Oscar is placed next to his other awards, including the infamous "Raspberry" for worst movie of the year, "The Postman." According to his father, Brian says that "displaying them both keeps me humble."

to it, but yeah, I couldn't look at it anymore. If I get another one, then I can bring it out."

Some of Brian's thoughts about life, opportunity and love as told to interviewers are—

On opportunity: "There are only a few real chances in life and what you do when they show up, whether you zig or whether you zag, in large part defines you and defines the form your life is going to take."

On the world: "The world is basically, I feel, a sad place. The only real weapons we have against this sadness are love and humor."

On work: "I write out of compulsion, I direct out of self-defense."

He seeks to direct the films he writes in order to maintain their integrity. Or as his mother candidly says, "He doesn't want anyone mucking them up."

Brian has told interviewers and members of his family that he would like to make a movie about commercial fishing in New Bedford, Massachusetts, his hometown. It is tentatively entitled "Finest Kind," and is an adventure film set against the backdrop of the commercial fishing world of New Bedford. He has expressed that he would like to shoot the entire movie in New Bedford.

Brian and his wife are raising two boys in Malibu, part of the Southern California film milieu. He has common-sense values and hopes for his sons, as he stated in the University of Massachusetts interview: "I would be happy if my boys ended up in Hollywood because that was what they really wanted. If they ended up there because it was the path of least resistance, I would be horrified."

—Helgeland family archives

Brian Helgeland holds his Oscar for best screenplay for L.A. Confidential, which was based on the novel by James Ellroy—after the ceremonies in 1998.

The Helgeland grandparents are frequent visitors and enjoy their California stays very much, as do other relatives. Brian often invites his relatives to his various film locations or shares special events in the film industry with them. His Norwegian common-sense values about family and living have prevailed in his life and he does not romanticize or idealize the glitzy Hollywood world of fame. He says about his work there in a recent interview: "You have to get past the romance and marquee value of it all to see if it's what you really want to do. Film is a harsh master. It is quite consuming, both in what you have to give to it and what it takes from you. George Bernard Shaw said it much better than I ever could: 'There are two tragedies in life. One is to lose your heart's desire. The other is to gain it.' If that doesn't scare you off, come on out!"

His advice to others: "There is no excuse for not doing the thing it is you want to do—especially when you are young and brave and foolish."

Young and brave, Brian, but I think not foolish!

BRIAN HELGELAND'S FILMOGRAPHY & AWARDS

Golden Globe, 1998: "L.A. Confidential," Best Screenplay Adapted From a Book.

The Academy Award, 1998: "L.A. Confidential," Best Screenplay Adapted From a Book.

"Man on Fire," 2004: screenwriter.

"Mystic River," 2003: screenwriter. Nominated for Golden Globe.

"Blood Work," 2003: screenwriter.

"The Order," 2003: screenwriter and director.

"A Knight's Tale," 2001: screenwriter and director.

"Playback," 1999: screenwriter and director.

"The Postman," 1997: screenwriter.

"L.A. Confidential," 1997: screenwriter.

"Conspiracy Theory," 1997: screenwriter.

"The Assassins," 1995: screenwriter.

"Highway to Hell," 1992: screenwriter.

"976-EVIL," 1988: screenwriter.

"Nightmare on Elm Street 4, The Dream Master," 1988: writer/screenwriter.

"Friday the Thirteenth," 1987: episode: "Mightier than the Sword," screenwriter.

KEEPING THE HOME WATERS SHIPSHAPE:
GAIL JACOBSEN ISAKSEN

KNOWN AS ONE OF FAIRHAVEN'S most industrious women, she can be seen running easily, daily, through the streets of Fairhaven. At first glance, one might think that this tall, shy, athletic, short-haired woman is still in her teens. On second look, one is immediately impressed with her focus and concentration and is delighted to experience her smile and wave.

Norwegian fathers often encourage their sons to enter the fishing industry and their daughters to become traditional wives of fishermen. But when a father has only daughters, what then? Fishing captain Leif Jacobsen had several daughters and, as most successful skippers, devoted his life to his work. He was a captain of the highliner *Pauline H*, respected in the community and beloved by his family. "He worked at sea, came in, unloaded the boat, said 'hi' to the family, worked on the boat to ready it for the next trip, and often left on the boat the next day," said two of his daughters. His family saw very little of him but his influence was profound.

When the time came, he encouraged his daughters to pursue extra schooling. One daughter, Sonja, went to beauty school and the other, Gail, went to a private junior college to be followed by a degree in medical technology at a local college. The assumption was that they were totally Americanized and that the fishing culture might not be part of their lives, but as with many assumptions, this was to prove false.

Sonja, who worked as a beautician, did what her friends had done—she married a successful fisherman who went on to be a boat owner and captain, and lived her life in the traditional Norwegian way. She raised a fisherman's family and the boat, family and church were the center of her life as it had been for her mother. Gail also married a fisherman, but her life took several

—*AT photo*

Three generations of the Isaksen family. From left, Gail Isaksen's husband Arne Isaksen with their son Max Isaksen and her father-in-law Jens Isaksen, in 1997. They are specialists in what their family did for hundreds of years in Norway—fishing.

turns and in many respects, it paralleled that of her father. As Gail recalled, "He was a work addict. He worked every day, all day and never found a way to relax and rest. He had no hobbies, took no vacations."

He made work and earning money his *'raison d'être.'* His only other interest outside of work and family was the church, and he contributed to that both in leadership and money. He understood commitment to work and one day when Gail was away at college, he and her mother planned to visit her there. Gail told them "she had work to do and was simply to busy to see them." He immediately understood and said to her mother, "She has work, that is what she has to do!" She was putting work before family just as he had done and he understood it.

She and her Norwegian-American husband, Arne Isaksen, who is part of a significant Norwegian family of boat owners and skippers, settled down to raise two children. She worked part-time, and also started to do volunteer work in the community. She says had she been a man, she "probably would have carried on the tradition of fishing." She enjoys her volunteer work and finds she prefers "hands-on" work. She chooses to do

Leif Jacobsen, skipper of the dragger *Pauline H.* His boat was known as a "highliner" and fishermen vied to be part of his crew. A hard-working and industrious emigrant from Karmøy, he enjoyed the reputation as a fine skipper, church supporter and upstanding member of the community. He was father to three daughters.

necessary work herself, when possible, rather than delegate it to others. In the tradition of the Norwegians, she enjoys physical work and exercise.

She has been running throughout Fairhaven for many years. And it was on these runs that she gleaned an intimate view of the community to which she was devoted. She somehow never found her saturation point in work, so what better than improving the town she loved so much? Initially she acquired and managed real estate, but later became more involved with the Euro Ship Store and improved and enlarged it.

—Courtesy Sonja Jacobsen Sovik

Gail Jacobsen Isaksen in her Fairhaven High School graduation photo. Her love for the school has been demonstrated by her extensive fundraising for its current needs.

She then started to buy and renovate older buildings and gave them a renewed life and also expanded the Euro Ship Store into an impressive retail store for Norwegian exports and clothing. A restaurant was next on her list and later the renovated one of Fairhaven's most nostalgic buildings which formerly housed a neighborhood drugstore. This latest venture is an upscale Norwegian retail store for Norwegian imports, which includes gifts, clothing, toys and, of course, sweaters. The upper floor will someday become a community gathering place and function room.

She continues her volunteer work on boards and projects within the area and is particularly proud of her work with her public high school alumni organization which has raised hundreds of thousands of dollars to help the school.

She also has had active leadership roles on nonprofit boards of directors which are allied to the sea, such as the Whaling Museum of New Bedford. Recently Gail was honored in a special ceremony and banquet by the Fairhaven Improvement League for her volunteer and professional work enhancing and improving the community.

She feels that the Norwegian always thinks about "hard times around the corner," and never splurges on self or family. Her contribution to the community is in time rather than financial gifts. She will give of her wealth to the church and to organizations where "she knows exactly how her gift will be used and trusts this use," but she needs to feel that her money goes directly to the work of an organization rather than overhead. It is natural that a hands-on person would feel this way and she would paint thousands of square feet of a building herself rather than depend on someone else.

So how does this workaholic relax? In the good old Norwegian tradition, she sails—most often in her 1974 sailboat in the Buzzards Bay harbors and inlets, and while sailing perhaps dreaming about her next project or the work she will be doing the next year.

Just as her father and relatives dreamed their dreams on their many boats on the same waters for many years, so will Gail Isaksen continue to work and eventually, she will leave her community a much better place because of her dreams and commitment.

So if you are in Fairhaven and see a tall lean woman run by, give her a wave and a thank-you. She deserves it.

THE PREVAILING WINDS OF FAITH:
THE REV. MR. HENRY ARNE PEDERSEN

THE ROAD TO FAITH sometimes takes unexpected turns and directions. The following story of one member of the Norwegian community in Greater New Bedford is a personal narrative of such a road to faith and service.

I knew this man in his earliest years and later as a teenager when we attended the same school, church and youth group meetings during the school year. In school he was a popular, funny, very intelligent and we thought, aspiring thespian. With generous parents, a handsome appearance and a sometimes independent attitude, he would have been the one I would have least expected to devote himself to Christian service.

He was a bit of a "wise guy," but today he is just wise, a treat to listen to when in the pulpit and a source of great humor and sensitivity to his friends and family, and it has been a joy to rediscover him after many years. This is his story in his words and with his favorite Bible verses.

> *"Mightier than the thunder of the great waters, mightier than the breakers of the sea—the Lord on high is mighty."*
>
> —Psalm 93:4

HENRY'S LIFE

"MY FATHER, ARNE P. PEDERSEN, was born in 1902 and came from the island of Vega in Helgeland in Northern Norway, north of Trondheim. He was one of nine children and was the youngest of three males. There was only so much room on the island, so he went to sea in the Merchant Marine when he was young.

There were some American connections already. His mother had a brother who had settled on Vashon Island near Seattle. They were farmers: strawberries, currents, and cherries. He also had an uncle on Nantucket; a yachtsman called 'Captain Pete,' who repaired yachts and had a little boathouse. His name was Peter Heinrick Pedersen and he was known as a colorful character. My father was on merchant vessels and traveled several times to Boston and visited his uncle on Nantucket. Captain Pete persuaded him to 'come over,' and so he did, and he started yachting in Nantucket. He was the skipper of a yacht for an industrialist from New Jersey."

NANTUCKET LOVE STORY

"NANTUCKET WAS THE PLACE where my father met my mother Anna K. Nilsson of Gustavsberg, Sweden. Mother was completely alone and had no relatives in this country. She had had a boyfriend from Sweden living in the U.S.A., and he convinced her to come over, but while on the boat she decided it wouldn't work out. Her reason for emigrating was gone.

"She was a Baptist in Sweden, and in the Bible study group on the ship, she met a Swedish dentist and his wife from Quincy, Massachusetts. They took her under their wing, and she lived at their home as a domestic. Because she had worked at a hospital in Sweden, she later answered an ad for a hospital job in Nantucket. She could speak very little English, and my father could speak very little English, so when they met one day in Nantucket, it was

—Barbara Simonson Medhaug archives

The F/V *Pelican*, once owned by the Pedersen family, is shown here in New Bedford Harbor.

natural they would be drawn together. They could understand each other! They took a night school class in English together, fell in love and married.

"He then started to fish out of Nantucket and joined up with a businessman from New Bedford who dealt with fishing supplies. My father started to skipper the boats. They kept building new boats and started up a fleet of boats where he was half-owner. He moved to New Bedford in the late twenties. My father had both draggers and scallopers. His boats were named the *Anna, Charles Beckman, Penguin, Pelican,* and *Porpoise.*

They finally ended their partnership because my father had a bad heart, and he decided to shift gears completely. After the heart problems, when he was semi-retired, he gave the skippers an opportunity to buy into the boats gradually. All of the mates were Norwegian and his crews, who had stayed with the boats for a long time, were very loyal to the boats. The boats made money, and the men were treated decently. The skippers in those days worked together and assisted each other and communicated by code where the fish were, and they cooperated with each other.

"During the war years, my father had a plaque given to him for scouting submarines. He talked about going in and reporting the sighting of a submarine on one occasion.

"The *Penguin* was tragically lost at sea in the fifties and just disappeared off the face of the earth. Nothing was ever heard of it again—no wreckage or anything. He testified in the inquiry concerning it."

THE STORM

"OFTEN MY FATHER got caught up in a storm or bad weather and had to be awake most of the time. This was especially true before good communications were developed. Father once recalled being on deck while his mate was at the wheel. He looked over the side and looked down a hundred feet. They were right on the crest of a wave. He told me he didn't know what to do. If he had said something or the boat moved one millimeter, he and the boat would have been gone. They just kept going on the crest and made it OK. I always thought he had exaggerated until I read recently a Coast Guard oceanographer's statement regarding the height of some waves.

"Only be careful, and watch yourselves closely so that you do not
  forget the things your eyes have seen or let them slip from your
  heart as long as you live.
Teach them to your children and to their children after them."

—Deuteronomy 4:9

"We had several sets of friends. We were close to the Helgelands, the Rasmussens, and Joseph Isaksens, We attended the Swedish Church but went to special meetings and bazaars at the Norwegian Church. My sister played the piano there on occasions. It was almost like a little barn with a pot-bellied stove, and when they did the Christmas thing it was lots of fun as they would dance around the tree. At Christmas the Norwegians would have parties at a couple of halls near the hotel. The families had children our age, so it worked out well. Also at Christmas we would visit the different families at their homes and play games. The Midttun family who owned the Norwegian bakery was our next-door neighbor. We would share our fish with them, and they would share their baked goods with us. This was in the days before freezers became commonplace.

"My mother used to love to visit the different homes of her friends where they would do needlework for the bazaar at the Swedish Church. Then they got a new minister who outlawed the bazaars because he felt they were not Christian things to do. She was very sad about that as it meant a lot to her to lose this social side of the church.

TRIPS TO NORWAY

"WE WENT BACK after the Second World War as a family in 1947—a bit of showboating. We brought a car with us and to get to the island you had to take one of two boats. We didn't know about the ferry, but we just assumed that both boats were large enough to take the car. So we went on the steamer. We had a big '47 Oldsmobile. They put oil drums down on the deck, put the car on them and tied the car down to bring it to the island. We brought it back on the ferry. The road on the island was narrow. Ours was the third car on the island. If we met anything, we had to back up and let the horse and wagon go past.

"My father's family had done fairly well by Norwegian standards, and he felt he needed to show them he didn't make a mistake by leaving Norway. The children used to argue about who was more closely related to me. Everyone on the island, it seemed, was related in some fashion. Cousins often marry cousins still.

On a trip I took in 1988, I found my Swedish cousins to be great fun, but they were not Baptists. Swedish Baptists tend to be more serious. In Norway, my sense was that my being a clergyman prevented them from being as open with me. That was not considered in Sweden. There was a time when church and state as one was a very strong concept, but not so much now. In 1947, one cousin in Norway had been confirmed the spring before we got there, and everyone was still ecstatic. There were formal pictures of her confirmation dress, and she actually put it on again so my father could take pictures of her. It is very important in the Norwegian Lutheran Church and people can still tell who was confirmed with them at the same time.

—AT photo

Henry Pedersen talks with old Sunday school friend Beverly Berg Dirksen at the Seaman's Bethel in 1998.

"In 1988 I went to church in Norway. They had baptisms while I was there and even with that, with people in traditional costumes, there were very few people in the church. I would have thought that this would have been a big family time to gather. More people were at the party after. Nowadays at weddings there are few people in the church, but when you go to the reception hall, it is loaded with people. My feeling is that most people ignore the church in Norway.

"I really see my faith and my identity as being more universal than being a Baptist. Baptist is just the club that allows me to function in an orderly fashion. "I believe that God had a plan for my life and I feel confident that the plan was for ministry, whatever the garden was that I grew up in. Actually both Elim and the Lutheran Church in Fairhaven at the time were quite pietistic and, I think, that is still the influence that prevails in my life. I believe that my mother's influence gave me the structure from which to function, and my father's influence gave me the impetus to not be restrained by that structure.

FATHER

"As I picture my father, I picture someone who was not church-related but, in essence, had a natural kind of piety. I remember going over to Oak Bluffs once on a sport-fishing boat. Early in the morning I would be on the deck with him as the sun came over the horizon, and he would say, 'Good morning Mr. Sun,' kind of like a Saint Frances type of thing when he could commune and appreciate God. He was a fun-loving guy as well as being honest and open. I believe that my father had a dream that we could somehow work together in some kind of business connected with the fishing industry without actually fishing. I was scheduled to go to Bryant College to get a business degree when I shifted gears and headed for Bethel College and the ministry.

TISPAQUIN

"IT WAS AT A YOUNG PEOPLE'S SESSION at our church camp, Camp Tispaquin, in Middleboro, the summer after I graduated from high school, when I made a decision about my life. One of the speakers mentioned in his sermon the possibility of asking God what He wanted for your life. So I began praying about it, and felt a strong call to go into some kind of full-time ministry. I sought advice from those who were leading the camp, and they encouraged me to apply, even though it was quite late, to go to Bethel College and Seminary in St Paul, Minnesota, which was the Baptist General Conference college. Neither of my folks was very happy with my decision. They did support me in it, however, so I applied and was accepted. I don't believe I realized it consciously at the time but, unconsciously, I knew that my father and I could never work together. We were too much alike and both of us were too bullheaded. I believe that it would have been a disaster as I look back on it.

"I'm sure that both my father and mother had an influence on my going into the ministry but probably not a direct one. The leading grace of God works in wonderful and mysterious ways. I can't explain why—when my parents asked me what I wanted for a high school graduation present—I told them a Thompson Reference Bible. If you had known me in high school, you could not picture me asking for something like that."

MY MINISTRY: NAVAL CHAPLAIN

"AFTER COLLEGE, marriage to a Norwegian woman from the Midwest and seminary in Philadelphia, the Navy gave me the opportunity to go to sea and be in the ministry at the same time. I felt a call to the military chaplain corps and had been impressed with the few military chaplains I had met. I actually sought out chaplains in each of the branches while in seminary to see if I could get a feel for the direction that God wanted me to go. I had a picture of myself being very seasick onboard ship and being quite ineffective, but at some point I left that concern with God and made the plunge into the Navy. I never did get sick. I enjoyed Navy life. (*His Norwegian heritage won.*)

"I was a lieutenant commander in the regular Navy when I resigned, and was due for another sea billet and I had a love/hate feeling toward that. I hated the thought of being away from home and my family—we had four children. On the other hand, I loved the opportunities for ministry that this life gave me. I had discussions with the detailer and the Chief of Chaplains Office about future assignments. Because I had been pegged as a viable preacher, I was going to be assigned duty at one of the chapels.

"I had a master's degree in counseling and wanted to be assigned a duty where that would be my major focus. It was becoming more and more difficult counseling men who were in the service and objecting to our nation's involvement in Vietnam. I had been doing some thinking on my own and had pretty much come to the conclusion that it was a mistake for us to be there. I found myself pressing the envelope with some of the Navy's rules and I wondered how long I could do that and still be promoted in the Navy. War or near war gave me a sinking feeling in my gut—one that said that this is not the way it is supposed to be. I am not an isolationist, but I am also one who doesn't think that we have to be the protector for everyone in the world, whether they want it or not. It seems to me that there is a bit of arrogance when we say we know what is best for everyone.

THE PRISON MINISTRY

"I LEFT THE NAVY and went into the prison ministry and there was a sense of fulfillment in my life. It also offered me a security for my family that the church couldn't offer, and I was able to put four children through college. There was a time in my prison ministry when I felt that I could influence the whole prison movement toward some sort of decency and constructive purpose. I quit thinking that at some point. All I could do was try to do the best where I was planted at any given time for that given time. I feel that I did just that. Another aspect of prison ministry is that, for me, it was a one-on-one ministry. I felt that I could have an influence on individuals—inmates, inmate families, and staff. I was able to support many individuals through some trying times. I saw lives change, and I was able to experience God in many wonderful ways. I think that the greatest lesson I learned from the prisoners is that there is not much difference between people on the outside and those inside.

—Pedersen archives

The Reverend Mr. Henry Arne Pedersen in 2004.

"I consider myself someone who is willing to take a creative risk and that might come from the adventuresome Norsemen.

"Are you willing to ask God, "What do you want from me"?

Recently in 2004, Henry wrote a sermonette for his newsletter about his life choices and he transformed it into a challenge for all.

"Peter received God's call standing in the midst of fish with Jesus on his fishing boat. I graduated from high school in June of 1953 and was scheduled to head for college in a few weeks. I wasn't very enthused about it, and I would have preferred to go fishing—but my father was insisting I give it a try. I was attending a week at a Christian youth camp when I heard a question asked by the minister, 'Have you ever asked God what God wants for your life?' I had never done that and I wasn't sure that it was necessary, but the question kept pounding in my head until I decided that asking the question couldn't hurt and so I asked it. God's answer changed my life forever. I heard God telling me, 'I want you in ministry for and with me.' I asked God 'What kind of ministry?' God told me 'Don't worry about that, I'll let you know when the time comes for you to know.'"

"That was fifty years ago and God led me to several schools to prepare myself. God led me to be commissioned as an U.S. Navy Chaplain. God led me through more schooling. God led me to become a chaplain in the federal prison system. God led me to pastor several churches. God is till leading me and you know what? I don't know where or what God wants me to do next, but I can say with Paul, "Here by the grace of God I am what I am, and God's grace to me was not in vain."

"So I would ask you today, 'Is God calling you?' God might want you to stay physically, but leave behind attitudes, baggage, prejudice, or old habits. God might want you to still go to the job you went to yesterday—but as a new person. Are you willing to ask God 'What do you want from me?' I still do."

> *"The man who thinks he knows something does not yet know as he*
> *ought to know.*
> *But the man who loves God is known by God."*
>
> —1 Corinthians 8: 2–3

Svein and Ketil Berg, Uncle Kristian Berg,
Kjersti and Mary Ann Berg (right) with
friends at a dinner with their cousin,
Kristian, in the early nineties in Norway.

—K. Simsarian photo

DR. KRISTIAN THOMAS SIMSARIAN: AMERICAN *PENDLER*

"When I was a child, I spoke like a child, I thought like a child, I reasoned like a child. When I became a man, I put aside childish things."

—1 Corinthians 13:11

As generations move along, the Norwegian lifestyle is modified and diluted many times as it is fuses with different American values. Like the process of natural selection, some stays and some goes. This is especially true for those who have a mixed ethnic identity. Norwegian-American children do not always marry Norwegians and their children, and their children's children feel less and less the call of Norway as the motherland.

Therefore a grandchild of a Norwegian emigrant, who is simply one-fourth Norwegian, might not be expected to have more than a cursory Scandinavian interest.

Not the case with this man, I realized, as I sat in a room at the Royal Institute of Technology in Stockholm, Sweden, on a damp March day in the year 2000. Kristian Thomas Simsarian was starting out the new millennium by defending his doctoral thesis in computer science. The research was done on integrating computer science into other disciplines. I understood only the first paragraph of his thesis.

—LaPorte Photo.

Kristian's parents, Astrid and J. Russell Simsarian, in 1965. Lieutenant Simsarian always said that his name sounded more like Sorensen when he was introduced to Astrid's Norwegian grandmother.

He was standing in the front of the room in his suit and tie, looking poised, dignified and confident, while four men, all Ph.D.s, specialists in their field and flown in for the occasion, examined, challenged and questioned him on his research. They had come from Italy, Germany, Denmark and Northern Sweden and were tough on him, posing questions and counter-questions for a seemingly endless time, before retiring to deliberate in another room.

—AT photo

Representatives from the Royal Institute of Technology, Stockholm, and the Swedish Institute of Computer Science congratulate a beaming Dr. Kristian Simsarian just after his successful doctoral examination.

During the break, I nervously talked with this young man, my son, who assured me the outcome of the deliberations would be fine. I spied the champagne in the corner as well as canapés, and thought 'what will we do with this if he doesn't pass?' Since I couldn't understand what they were discussing, I couldn't evaluate the situation.

The men came out of their deliberations, and my son stood before them in front of the room, as they told him of their decision. His work had been accepted. He was now a Ph.D.

—Cawpaqua Photo

Kristian about to be graduated from Deerfield Academy in 1984.

While he was accepting congratulations from the assembled group and receiving flowers and gifts, I sat and thought about his life: My Norwegian, Yankee, German and Armenian son. How had he arrived at this point in his life, speaking fluent Swedish and living and working in Scandinavia as a doctor in computer science (engineering.) I laughed to myself when I thought of his early math work in the first grade.

Born in Rhode Island, raised in Ohio and Laguna Beach, California, he had traveled east to Deerfield Academy, in Massachusetts, on a partial scholarship when he was fifteen years old.

After graduation, he went on to Columbia University's School of Science and Technology and graduated in 1988. During those years he also worked in New York City and Switzerland.

In his high school and undergraduate college years, he had summer jobs as surveyor, pool guard, swimming instructor, and sandwich maker. He earned his own money as a preteen to raft down the Colorado, hike at Yellowstone, ski at Big Bear, ride horses in Mexico, and parafly in Mazatlan as well as to attend camp in the summer. When he was ten to twelve, he worked as a volunteer with Vietnamese refugees, as a teacher-helper with Japanese students in a summer program and as a junior counselor at a YMCA camp. At fourteen he was a volunteer with a YWCA daycare center.

He learned early how to set a goal, plan how to finance it and in the end achieve it. He always worked to get where he is today, but also, when he was a very young boy he waited endless hours at the Boy's Club each evening until I could pick him up after my work. There was no daycare in the early seventies for a divorced working mother.

In graduate school at the University of Virginia, he earned a full fellowship from Mobil Oil. That gave him the opportunity to spend fulltime on his research.

I will always remember his youth and the discussions I had with other parents who felt the focus for their children should be on beach and surfing. It is difficult in California to raise a child who can learn to balance work and fun. And I recalled his preteen year as an amateur magician and how this little hobby helped him develop as a speaker. I remember fondly those enjoyable summers when he was part of the Laguna Beach Pageant of the Masters, a summer festival featuring tableaux of living paintings.

But most of all when I think of my son growing up, I think of him as a two-and-a-half-year-old, unscrewing switch plates—to my horror—or putting the rug cleaning machine together and at eight, installing a whole new garbage disposal or fixing the TV. There seemed to be nothing he couldn't fix. He just knew how to do it and when I think of this, I also think of the Norwegian fishermen who often had to have the 'know-how' to make emergency repairs on their boats. This quality seems to be in the genes.

I am very proud he has undertaken to live a responsible life. He takes responsibility for all his actions and he responds in measured, mature ways, including decisions about his environment, work, wealth, charity and relationships. He sees life in global terms and firmly believes in international negotiation, and he carefully avoids work that has anything to do with war because he is committed to peaceful ways to settle conflicts. He finally left the robotic field with the comment, "Every time I build a robot, there is always someone out there trying to put a gun in its hand."

SWEDEN

WHY HIS FOCUS ON SCANDINAVIA? The only holiday we celebrated in a Norwegian way was Christmas. I told him many times about my first Christmas in Norway and always wanted him to share in it somehow. He had some Norwegian friends in California when he was young, and they invited him to take Swedish lessons, as there were no Norwegian lessons nearby. He did, and I remember saying to him, "Why do you want to learn Swedish? You will never have any use for that."

While he was teaching at the University of Edinburgh, I flew over and we went to Norway together for him to meet his Norwegian relatives.

He loved it and was very impressed with his grandfather's hometown of

—*AT photo*

Kristian meets his Tante Marie Berg just before her death in 1991 in Norway.

Skudeneshavn. He loved the closeness and warmth of the people, and he seemed to really enjoy his days in Norway, but he did remark that everyone he saw looked like his mother at a different age and wasn't sure he liked that reminder too much!

When the opportunity came to work and study in Sweden, Kristian took it and I was thrilled that he would be able to explore his roots a bit more on excursions to Norway. In his seven years of work and study he did just that, through Telemark skiing, hiking, driving, boating, biking, touring, camping and visiting family. He loves the rugged out-of-doors with its challenges and could converse easily with his Scandinavian friends and developed close ties with family members.

He spoke Swedish fluently and understood Norwegian. When in Norway he would speak in Swedish and be answered in Norwegian.

A true *pendler*, as well as lecturer, author, international workshop speaker, and scientist, he is now back in California and working for an international company. He is also restoring his old Victorian home, a "Painted Lady," and makes full use of his mechanical skills. I fully expect him to return to Europe sometime in the not-too-distant-future, as he is a man of both America and Europe.

When I picked up his thesis and read the acknowledgments, I felt the tears well up in my eyes—he thanked his mother for his success. Life does give us some special gifts to cherish! I remembered his youth and his tongue-in-cheek sense of humor, such as the letter he wrote me from Deerfield: "So, Happy Mother's Day! It must be nice to have a special day all to yourself or at least

Kristian was born while his uncle, Navy Lieutenant Thomas Severt Tollefsen, first-generation Norwegian-American on his father's side, was on dangerous duty battling Viet Cong forces in Vietnam's Mekong Delta. He was commanding officer of a unit of hydro-jet river patrol boats, which protected the vital water gateway to Saigon. Tom earned the Bronze Star with Combat V for Valor. He was the first river patrol unit commander since the Civil War.

dedicated to you. Too bad there is no Fantastically Spectacular Son Day or Truly Devoted To Their Parents Boarding School Students Day."

We say that the more things change, the more they stay the same. A *pendler*, just as were his early relatives from Ferkingstad on Karmøy, the home of the Vikings, going back and forth is in his blood and his genes. And I am thankful that while he lives in these different worlds, he is doing work that will improve the world.

Now, I will get up from my chair and congratulate my son, today a distinguished man surrounded by other distinguished people. I must not show my pride in him too much or how much I love him, as I don't want to embarrass him. Doctor of Philosophy or not, to me, he will always be my boy. His grandfather, Sigvart Tollefsen from Skudeneshavn, would be very proud today!

And to Kristian, I will say: 'You did it all yourself. I just enjoyed the ride.'

—Simsarian photo

Kristian, now an official PhD., in Stockholm dressed in the proper attire with formal black tux, tails and a traditional large hat. He stands on the famous stairs of Stockholm's Old City Hall where the formal ceremony was held and from where we most often view the Nobel Awards ceremony. The Nobel Prize banquet and Kristian's graduation banquet were held in the famous golden hall where about eighteen million pieces of gold and colored-glass mosaics cover the walls.

20

In Dry Dock

The altar of the Karmøy Fisherman's Memorial and the sea.

"Tønnes Olsen"

But a Karmøy son with fish in his soul
  needs to work the Norsemen's role.
So I went fishing on Georges Bank
  met Norwegians and joined their rank,
scalloped from New Bedford town
  many languages there I found.
But at bars where fishermen gathered
  Skoal was the word that really mattered.
But that was a long time ago,
  Yes, that was a long time ago.

—Photo and poem by Aleksander Hauge

A FTER A LIFETIME OF WORKING on the sea and having the boat itself as the core of their lives, the older fishermen are now retired and at home. Some take a trip out to sea once or twice a year, just to be part of it all again and to earn good money—but it is not the same as "in the old days."

As for many who did not survive the sea, their injuries, or health issues, their widows still lead quiet lives in the New Bedford area or in Seattle or Norway. They are often seen in church or at their children's or grandchildren's rites of passage. Some remarried, others did not. If they remarried, it was most often to a fisherman who was a widower.

The retired men live off their savings (often substantial), their fishermen's pensions (surprisingly small), and their Social Security checks. Some have benefits from

—*AT photo*

The late Sarah (Sally) Tonnessen and sister, the late Dorothy Johannessen, at Sally's waterfront home in Fairhaven, 1996. Dorothy was my first employer and Sally our long-standing friend.

Norway, and many received letters telling them they needed one or more trips to qualify for their union pensions. Most did not know when they left America that they lacked final qualification, or that one more trip would mean a life-

—*AT photo*

The late Gunnar Haines and Eleanor (Isaksen) Haines at their home in Mattapoisett in 1997.

—*AT photo*

Elbjorg Tjorvold of Norway and Barbara Simonsen of New Bedford enjoy a post-concert dinner at the Wamsutta Club, New Bedford, 1999.

time of security. The Norwegian fishermen rarely questioned the letters or challenged the decisions. They were hesitant to question what they perceived to be authority.

Others who came in the late fifties and sixties own or partially own several boats. They are affluent and live in impressive homes. Because their incomes still depend on the available fish, they tend to go through both good and better times as compared to other fields. They have made more money than most of them knew was possible as youths in Norway.

Several have become more involved in the greater community, but most limit their activities to the Norwegian community. Most who had little time for their children when they were working out to sea, say they enjoy their grandchildren now very much.

The boats are very large, technical and impersonal today. They cost several millions of dollars to build and they can generate a great deal of money for their owners when the government allows full access to the fish. The crews generally are not Norwegian unless they are the sons or relatives of the owner. The shipboard meals—once wonderful dishes produced by Norwegian cooks, and a real morale factor on the boat—now come out of a microwave.

Gone are the days when the food was cooked in the same area where the fishermen slept, played cards and lived. Gone is the camaraderie of the young Norwegian men, the aroma of the Norwegian foods mixed with the smells of the boat, the wet clothing and boots that were never changed. Now there are showers, toilets, private berths and all the niceties of home. The sea still exacts its toll, but today, with better equipment and navigational tools, storms very often can be predicted as easily as finding fish.

"My soul is full of longing for the secret of the sea, and the heart of the great ocean sends a thrilling pulse through me."

—Henry Wadsworth Longfellow

KEEPING IN TOUCH

THE RETIRED FISHERMEN are literally "fish out of water" and almost all find it necessary to meet with each other daily to discuss old times. Tales of their accomplishments tend to magnify with each passing year. In Norway, on Karmøy, they meet at the Fisherman's Museum, where they sit framed by their fishing photos and other memorabilia. They drink coffee, eat waffles and talk exclusively with those who share their experiences—those who fished from Norway and those who fished from America.

—*AT photo*

Two retired fishermen from the New Bedford fishing fleet, Erling Sjoen and Larry Sanhåland, at the fisherman's museum on Karmøy.

—*AT photo*

Rogaland Fisherman's Museum on Karmøy, where the retired fishermen come and eat waffles, drink coffee and tell their tales.

They have a favorite restaurant on Karmøy where they meet each morning for coffee, cigarettes and stories. It is a ritual to go there daily, arriving about eleven in their 1958-73 American cars and leaving a few hours later to have lunch *(Middag)* with their wives. They talk with great nostalgia about the old days together. Theirs is very much a private men's club. Visitors are not really welcomed and are examined with some curiosity.

In Fairhaven they can be seen at Fort Phoenix sitting in cars, smoking and sometimes drinking coffee. They share news from Norwegian newspapers and the Internet as well as letters and phone calls from Norway. They exchange stories with those who have recently returned from Norway and often talk about their next trip there. There is always great interest in who is

Old painting of Norwegian home in the nineteenth century. Most likely it was in Skudeneshavn as it is rather typical of homes in Southwest Norway.

—*AT photo*

The old section of Bergen, Norway, in 1992. Norwegians would remember lovely places like this when they were in their new country. Bergen was once a member of the Hanseatic League and a valued trading partner in Europe. Her historic cosmopolitan roots coupled with her unique architecture marks her as a unique city in Norway.

ill, who has died, and who is still working. Some have computers and relate the latest news from Norway. The most popular Web site invariably is the one operated by the *Haugesunds Avis*, a newspaper for the Haugesund area.

"I never was on the dull tame shore, but I loved the great sea more and more."

—Bryan W. Procter, "The Sea"

There they sit and watch the boats coming in and out of New Bedford Harbor. They estimate the haul, remark on the condition of the boat, talk about the trip and the weather and relive their days as fishermen. Always the weather is the focus of conversation, as it is with many Norwegians.

Some of the older men go to the local boat settlement house to talk about the old days and watch the younger men coming in and out. They sometimes ask questions of these men or try to get a good conversation going. Some of the younger fishermen, especially those of Norwegian ancestry, talk to them, and others look at them as curiosities. Some still meet in one or two bars in town. Others walk a bit around New Bedford, and many still go to events that New Bedford and Fairhaven have to offer such as parades, street fairs, the Fisherman's Memorial Service, the Blessing of the Fleet and other activities where they might see old friends.

Some have money to burn, but too many live on marginal incomes. Some still live in rooming houses and others in lovely homes. Some never go back to Norway and others go each year. There is a great divide in the standard of living among the fishermen.

Seamen's Bethel pulpit and cenotaphs shown in a commemorative 1984 envelope and stamp.

—AT photo

Seamen's Bethel cenotaph memorializing the fishermen out of New Bedford who were lost at sea. Many Norwegian names are listed.

—*AT photo*

The Annual Seamen's Bethel Memorial service
for lost fishermen held on the State Pier in New
Bedford, 1996. Tom Helgeland and Roy Enoksen,
both board members, are in the background.

—*Magne Ådland archives*

Magne Ådland in Norway today.

Many have second homes in Norway; all have relatives there. In almost
every conversation, it seems, among Norwegians in Fairhaven there is a reference to a friend who is coming or going to Norway, or to Norwegians who
are coming here to visit. For many it is just as easy to go to Norway as it is to
New York.

—*AT photo*

Ike and Evelyn (Rasmussen) Isaksen at their
home in Fairhaven in 1997. He operated a
large fish store in California with her
brother, Einar Rasmussen. The Rasmussens
attended the Elim Baptist Church when I
was a child.

—*Medhaug archives*

Lise Stol Medhaug with an American
Embassy representative at the reception
following the Karmøy Fishermen's
Memorial dedication at the Karmøy
Kommune building, 1992.

HOMES IN NORWAY

LARGE HOMES WERE BUILT in Norway with both New Bedford and Alaska/Seattle money and they are well tended by the wives and families. In Norway such homes have a strong influence of American styling and often are ranch-type homes. Much on Karmøy itself has a New Bedford-Fairhaven flavor to it. Shops, homes, restaurants, drive-ins and clothing seem to be influenced in some way by life in New Bedford. There are similar foods, cars, music—especially music—and the language still shows the influence of the fifties and sixties in New Bedford and Seattle. The clothing and watches often reflects that era. Those who worked in Alaska often wear watches made from nuggets of gold with Alaskan symbols on them. The vernacular of those times oftens permeates their speech.

Today on Karmøy, for instance, many of the younger retired fishermen work full- or part-time. They work on boats associated with the oil industry all or part of the year, or they own businesses, and, in one case, design equipment for the quick rescue of men from oil rigs. Some of the men who live in Norway have small homes in Florida where they spend the winters.

Prosperous Norwegians travel a great deal these days and many are seeing the world during the winter, so they can leave the snows of Norway behind. Others have pleasure boats that serve also for day fishing when they feel the need to go back to sea. Others still proudly drive their meticulously kept 1960s American cars or others may bring them just for a Sunday drive.

—Alf Isaksen archives

Alf Isaksen in Norway today with his American car. He takes it out on special occasions and describes it as: "A 1966 Chevrolet Malibu with a 283 engine that has 195 h.p., which we bought new from George O'Hara in New Bedford in 1966. The engine has newly been rebuilt and the car has also been repainted, in the original color."

—AT photo

Karl Johann and Berit Melkevik at a 1998 party at *Little House*, my rental home in Skudeneshavn. He fished out of New Bedford for many years but returned to Norway and owned a grocery store there. He missed Fairhaven and his friends very much and they both love to visit America.

458

One example of retired life is the Egil Ellingsen's in Seattle. He says of their retirement: "For the past ten years, Kitty and I have traveled extensively throughout the U.S. and abroad. On many of these trips we have been fortunate that our children and grandchildren have joined us in Norway, Canada, the East Coast, Florida and Arizona. What wonderful memories we share and we reminisce of these times together."

NORWAY TODAY

NORWAY ITSELF HAS CHANGED much since these men left to make money in America. They left a poor country and are now living in the second wealthiest country in the world. According to a 2001 feature story in the Los Angeles Times: "A United Nations report named it the top place to live. And the once-poor nation is dedicated to spreading its now substantial wealth." The journalist, Times staff writer Carol A. Williams, went on to point out that in Norway, "Lifelong financial security is guaranteed, no matter how many layoffs, stock market crashes or catastrophic illnesses come your way. Consider the psychological well-being of belonging to a country where no one is homeless or hungry, where women and men are equal, where a pristine environment is reverentially protected and where sharing the wealth with the world's less fortunate is a moral obligation. Norway's North Sea tracts have proved to be a bountiful source of the precious commodity (oil), turning this country once dependent on fishing and farming into the number-two oil exporter in the world. Even with fluctuating oil prices, Norway has skillfully managed the state-owned industry and amassed a public fund of $60 billion."

Retirees and their families have very good lives in Norway, and benefits that we can only dream of in America. Yet, work is admired and many go on working—they simply work because they enjoy it.

MEMORIES

ONE MAN, SIMON VEA, on Karmøy, has thousands of photos he took over the years. They fill the walls and ceilings of an attic and many walls and bookcases in his house. He lives with his memories of being away from home and family for most of his working years.

Some men have had to adapt to living at home again. The wives do not relinquish their authority over the house lightly and that may be one reason why the men still feel the need to share hours with each other daily. I suspect they feel like they are in between trips much of the time.

Some live in nursing homes. I vividly remember visiting a friend of my father's, a retired fishing captain named Bernard Tom Larsen, in a nursing

—AT photo

Part of Simon Vea's attic gallery. Photos kept his life vivid and real to his Norwegian family when he fished off the shores of North America.

home just before his death a few years ago. He lay there quietly, very wrinkled and pale against the white sheets. I looked at his small living/dying space and saw only two personal treasures: a photo of his boat and a photo of his island, Utsira, near Karmøy. Those were the two cherished memories he chose to have at his side. He had his ashes scattered in the sea.

"Your path led through the sea, your way through the mighty waters."

—Psalm 77: 18-20

THE CEMETERY

MANY SUCH MEN are now part of the sea, while others rest in Fairhaven's beautiful Riverside Cemetery. This cemetery, perhaps one of the loveliest in

—AT photo

The Falnes Church in Skudenes, the church home of my family since it was built.

—AT photo

Papa'sma and Grandfather's grave along with David Tollefsen's ashes by the main path at the Falnes Church graveyard.

America, has many gravestones with Norwegian names on its landscaped hills. The graves are lovingly tended, and fellow Norwegians attend the funeral services of their brother fishermen. They take this ritual very seriously and it is important to them to participate in these observances.

Skippers often have a photo etching of their boat on the gravestone itself. They seemingly do not wish to distinguish the boat from their own being, even in death, which is somewhat a reminder of the early Viking rituals

In Norway, they are buried in their extended family plots. There is a memorial to honor lost fishermen at the Seaman's Bethel in New Bedford, one in Seattle and one also on the island of Karmøy in Norway, to honor those from that island lost to the sea in America.

The bell tower and hymns from this memorial give the relatives and friends of the lost men a place to meditate and grieve, as well as a place for others to learn.

"Tønnes Olsen," by Aleksander Hauge

To the graveyard I did wander
to give my greetings to mother and father.
Went for a walk on Akra's sand
and saw the sunset by Nyvingen.
Heard the lapvings and birds of the bay
and thanked God for all of my days,
and thanked God for all of my days."

The Karmøy Fisherman's Memorial.

—A. Hauge photos, 2003

The Memorial Is Dedicated

—Photo by Lise Medhaug

People flock to the dedication and view it from the rocks in the summer of 2002 on Karmøy.

—Photo by Lise Medhaug

The Memorial is dedicated by distinguished Lutheran clergy.

—Photo by Lise Medhaug

Names of Karmøy fishermen who died at sea in America include my father and three uncles.

The older fishermen still "walk the walk" of the mariner and still never look quite comfortable in town clothes. They enjoy being together, but most would rather be out to sea, where their adventurous lives were lived.

Despite their years, despite their problems, despite the dangers they endured, when they smile, one can still see that beautiful look of youth and imagine the blond hair blowing in the wind with the salt on their faces. One can still see the sense of adventure in their eyes. Despite all of the dangers, I believe, most would not have lived any other way.

They lived lives that will never be replicated—in two countries that will never again be the same.

In Memoriam

SCANDINAVIAN FISHERMEN
WHO LOST THEIR LIVES
WHILE FISHING OUT OF THE PORT
OF NEW BEDFORD 1931–1990

1931	*Mary*	Tobias Tollefsen
1938	*Valencia*	Sigvart Tollefsen
1947	*Margee & Pat*	Bjarne Tollefsen
1949	*Ramona*	Alf Josephsen
		Augusta Carlsen
		Carl Naley
1949	*Gayhead*	Karl Haakonsen
		Jacob Helgesen
		Ragnvald Abelsen
		Sivert Petersen
		Hans Johansen
		Targe Pedersen
		Peter Apeland
1950	*Four Sisters*	Gunnar Pedersen
		Martin Johnson
1950	*William J. Landry*	Arne Hansen
1950	*Theresa A.*	John Hoaglund
1951	*Penguin*	Arne O. Knudsen
		Knut Matland
		Sigurd Matland
		Jon Aanensen
		Norman Hansen
1951	*Jerry & Jimmy*	Alfred Gaustad

1952	*Paolina*	Fritz Hokanson
		Harry Bjur
		Helger Johnson
1960	*Matilda S.*	Edward Sandve
1960	*Nancy Jane*	Osten Ostensen
1961	*Snoopy*	John Vestvik
1962	*Karina T.*	David Davidsen
		Karl Abrahamsen
1962	*Midnight Sun*	Arne Lindanger
		Sam Lund
		Torgils Holmen
		Jon Nilsen
		Magne Risdal
		Olav Ferkingstad
		Jens Ferkingstad
		Asbjorn Pedersen
		August Larsen
		Gordon Kallestein
1963	*Pauline H.*	Andrew Skeie
1964	*Lynn*	Arnleif Tollefsen
		Thurston Chelgren
		Haaken Gundersen
1967	*Crest*	Ludvig Peterson
1967	*Brighton*	Hobart Nillssen
1968	*Gailou*	Bjorn Eiriksson
1972	(no name listed)	Sigurd Berg
1973	(no name listed)	Ole S. Olsen
1975	*Eugene H.*	Lars E. Larsen
1984	*Commonwealth*	Jeffrey Nielsen
1989	*Act IV*	Kenneth H. Hansen
1990	*Blue Dove*	Kristian Hauge
1990	*Sol-E-Mar*	William A. Hokanson
		William A. Hokanson, Jr

2 I

~

Epilogue

MY VOYAGE

—AT photo

The Søregatå in Skudeneshavn on a cold winter morning in 1990.

"Write the things which thou hast seen, and the things which are, and the things which shall be hereafter."

—Revelations

"Each age, it is found, must write its own books; or rather, each generation for the next succeeding."

—Ralph Waldo Emerson

"Yes, it's hard to write, but it's harder not to."

—Carl Van Doren

~

My INTEREST IN EMIGRATION and my voyage of discovery may have begun when many thousands of Vietnamese refugees came to Camp Pendleton, California, in 1975. Camp Pendleton is south of Laguna Beach where I lived. At the time I was executive director of a YWCA and felt that there might be some way our YWCA could help the people living in the tent cites so close to us. I felt a responsibility to them, given our long involvement in the war and this being one more residual effect—coupled with the YWCA's commitment to women.

So I went down there with enthusiastic volunteers and developed an American acculturation program that lasted for about ten weeks. We got to know thousands of people, and became very friendly with those who helped us each week. I and the YWCA friends sponsored many of these refugees and we relocated about forty-five into our communities. A few became YWCA workers, and others lived in our YWCA building. Many have gone on to success, and their children went to college and moved into higher professions.

I found the experience fascinating and rewarding, but most of all I, as a result of it, became very interested in the concept of refugees and emigration. What is the difference? Refugees flee their country, usually for political reasons, because they feel their lives are in danger. Sometimes that is temporary and they return to their country when the problem has been resolved. An emigrant leaves his country under less severe conditions but with the feeling that he can make a better life in his chosen country. For some, economic conditions in their native lands are so poor that they have to leave to provide food for their families. At different points in history, Norway's emigrants faced such conditions. I think it is fair to term many of the Norwegian emigrants in the past century as economic refugees.

Norway is now a very rich country and is facing a large influx of refugees and immigrants. It is struggling to understand what being Norwegian really means. Does it include all of these people with different skin colors and religions from many different countries? Perhaps by understanding their own plight as refugees in the past, they can better understand their new immigrants.

With this background in mind, I began to look at my own family history through more enlightened eyes. But it wasn't until 1995 that my eyes really opened to the whole picture and what was to become a mission for me.

"WHEN I WAS OUT THERE . . ."

I HAD ALWAYS THOUGHT that the Norwegian emigration story should be written so that both the New Bedford area populace and the greater world where Norwegians live would better understand and appreciate this unique and courageous group. And I also knew that my experience was too narrow to launch this project. Basically, I had had too few experiences with the Norwegian side of my family, and yet I still knew there was something distinctive and special about these people and that they should be recognized.

Then, in one moment, in one evening in 1995, all at once—I knew absolutely what I had to do. It was a simple evening, dining by a warm fireplace with an old friend. We were playing catch-up, as we had not seen each other for thirty-six years and he began to tell me about his life. He talked about his joys, his tragedies, his sea stories and the lifestyle he had led by harvesting the seas. Then I heard him say these words: "When I was out there, fighting the waters. . . ." I remember looking up from my dinner and saying, "Fighting the Waters . . . what a wonderful name for a book." The whole concept flashed into my mind instantly. It would be a book about these men and women who came from Norway to build a life in America. It would be: the story of my father and thousands like him, and my story in a way, as well. The title over time was modified a bit from "fighting" to "following," but that was the beginning.

I didn't sleep much that night as I pondered the unknown. Where to begin, how to proceed, who to talk to, how to put it together? First I had to record all of the information this dear friend was telling me; then I needed to talk to others who had lived their lives on the sea. So I began to gather names and make phone calls to set up appointments.

The reception was not encouraging. I found Norwegian-Americans are shy about sharing their lives. Most declared that they had nothing to say—they had simply led their lives, nothing important, nothing different. But I persevered and found a few who, because of my Norwegian name or family, were willing to talk, probably more out of respect for my father's death at sea or curiosity than for any other reason. The Norwegians with whom I had gone to church when I was younger were the most giving and cooperative as were my Tante Ellen Thompsen, cousin Gunnar Berg, uncle David Tollefsen, all the Isaksens, Linda Risdal and others. And articles in a Norwegian newspaper and the New Bedford Standard-Times about my venture prompted some people who had a connection with New Bedford to contact me with wonderful stories.

When the fishermen talked, I listened, and gradually a plan for the book took shape. It became much larger than the lives and adventures of fishermen, extending to the emigration from Norway and the colorful culture the emigrants brought with them. Their culture affected everything they said and did and was the essence of their lifestyles and their particular acculturation to American life.

My first interview was very difficult, but challenging and exciting. A Norwegian friend went with me to bridge the gap somewhat but I was very nervous and unsure. But each interview got easier and brought new ideas and unknown paths to explore. Some interviews were served up with coffee and cakes and reminded me of youthful afternoon visits with my grandmother. Every interview I had with these men, and sometimes their wives, helped open up their world to me and gave me greater understanding of my father and his world, my heritage—a heritage I had known so little about and yet was very important in my life.

I remember my Uncle David's words when I told him of my plan. He slapped the table and said, "Finally you are going to know what you came from." The big advantage I had was that I was of two cultures and could look at this Norwegian culture with more objective eyes and also with an innate interest and perception.

As an elementary school teacher, I had taught that Norway was the "Land of the five F's." Fishing, Fjords, Farming, Furs, and Forests. Chalkboards illustrating this theme decorated the classrooms of America. Unfortunately that is as much as most Americans know about Norway and even that is anti-quated today.

Some say this project was a search for my father. In a way it was, but more than that it was as search for my identity and my roots. As in every search, we find things we can identify with and other things we cannot. We find truths, we find enlightenment and we find disappointments. I found all of those and more. Up to then I had always been on the outside looking in the window. Now I was in the living rooms and kitchens and very deeply into the most personal moments and experiences of people's lives.

Early into this project I was asked by Norwegian Public TV to narrate the New Bedford part of a project they were doing on the emigration. I gladly did that and it opened more doors to me. I was fortunate that there was growing interest in this work, especially in Norway, where there were several news-paper features and two TV interviews. It became almost too much, as it became difficult to shop without having people come over to talk to me, or look over and talk about me. I did not enjoy that kind of attention very much.

As a young girl I had tried to find, in childlike ways, identification with my father. I remember learning that the Norwegian princess was named Astrid. That was very special to me and gave me comfort in difficult times. I believed my father had named me after her. If I saw a photo of her or something written about her, I immediately identified with it. It was my secret tie to being Norwegian. Later I was to learn that King Harald of Norway was born within a few hours of my birth and that made it even more special. When I learned that both he and Astrid had, during the German occupation of Norway, spent their early childhood summers in South Dartmouth, Massachusetts, also as I had, I felt another tie to Norway. When one is without a father, and searching for the security that goes along with a very Norwegian name—the very thing that distances one from others in a Yankee world—a child may become highly romantic about ties to her father's homeland.

—AT photo

Emigrant Kina Ulland Helgeland, Fairhaven native Martha Johnson
Berg (half Swedish, and married to emigrant Gunnar Berg), and
second-generation Norwegian-American Carol Anne Tollefsen-
Hoaglund, three lovely ladies, two relatives and a friend who
supported me with their intelligence, wit and insight throughout this
book process.

Some have suggested that I have indeed a "romantic" view of this emigration. I would suggest that it is not my view that is romantic but the emigration
itself. Romance is made up of great courage, great adventures and feelings of
great loss and great love. The love of families, the love of the sea and the love
of two countries—and the great losses sustained certainly qualify this as a
romantic emigration.

Most authors have outlines; I did not. I developed a questionnaire that
served as a guide, but the story unfolded as the interviews were conducted. It
was only when I could see the interconnecting issues and patterns, and the
breadth of the material, that I began to see the widening scope. It was during
this period that I discovered the vital role of the wives, for instance, because
they spoke up during the interviews with their husbands.

My first research trip to Norway, when I could view the culture first-hand
and speak to those who had emigrated and returned was an enormously satis-
fying experience. I was warmly welcomed and accepted there and for the first
time in my life felt Norwegian. Recently a dear friend there was talking to me
on the telephone and she found out for the first time I was half-American. "I
never would have guessed," she said. "I just assumed both of your parents
came from Norway. You are so like us."

WELCOME TO NORWAY

I HAD TO INTERRUPT MY WORK for several years to care for my ill and
aged mother, fulltime. A few months after her death in 1998, I flew to Oslo

—AT photo

—AT photo

Little House among the tile rooftops of Skudeneshavn.

The large house in front of *Little House*—a gracious home with delightful, warm and friendly owners.

and took the train to Bryne to visit with my cousin Ketil Berg and his family. Then with his help, I went to Stavanger and sailed by ferry to Skudeneshavn.

I stood on the bow and thought about my mother and father and family. It was a windy, gray, damp day and I was a bit chilly—but in the distance, maybe a mile, there was a break in the clouds with sun streaks illuminating the red-tile rooftops of Skudeneshavn's white houses. The whole town was shining and sparkling as in a fairy tale. It felt as though God was pointing it out to me and saying, "Here is the magic town where you will find happiness."

—AT photo

—Mery Vilhelmsen photo

Johannes Hansen makes his famous waffles at his small waffle shop in the old section of Skudeneshavn. Circa 2000.

Author with author Jacob Johannessen in Stavanger, 1998.

470

I was welcomed at the ferry by a young man named Tor Magne Johannessen, who had corresponded by email about my project, and by the owner of the house I was to lease, Sigmund Wareberg. We all drove up to the hill in the old section of Skudeneshavn, the Søragadå. There they carried my heavy bags up by the white houses lining the steep, narrow, twisting streets—homes almost touching the street and set up against the rock. Standing outside one impressive and much-photographed house on Halvorsbakken was a very attractive, warm, friendly woman with a huge smile. She put her arms out to me and said, "Welcome to Norway!" And indeed I was welcomed, and the antique little house set into the rock behind their great house was a warm and wonderful source of inspiration and comfort to me during my three months there.

—AT photo

One of the many remarkable doors of Skudeneshavn.

One day as I was walking out of this magical place to go to town, a man turned and looked at me, and then looked again. He seemed a bit confused, I thought. I saw him the next day and he came over to me and said, "Tollefsen?" "Yes," I replied. "You gave me a shock yesterday, I thought I had seen a ghost. You look just like your great-aunt. Your face, your mannerisms, the way you move, your hands, your spirit. I thought I had seen Johanna and couldn't believe it." He made me feel part of the continuity of my father's family and heritage.

THE INTERVIEWEES

MANY OF THOSE INTERVIEWED did not want their names mentioned, because they were shy or because of the Norwegian tendency to confront each other about personal perceptions. This book is a perception based on interviews, experience and other research. Everyone has his/her own perception and this is mine. I hope that those whose names are mentioned and whose recollections are quoted, will not be criticized or confronted in any way. They offered valuable insights into the history of their people.

> *"I realized that an American regional novel always is resisted by*
> *the people of its locale, unless, of course, all descriptions are*
> *sweetness and light."* —Edna Ferber, "A Peculiar Treasure"

Others did not want some of the less favorable things about the community to be written, particularly concerning drinking. Yet many who didn't have this problem insisted I be honest about it. It is such an integral part of this emigration that I would have been less than honest not to write about it. Many families had to deal with it in one way or another and it is part of their world. My goal has always been to write a balanced perception of a people I greatly respect and love and whom I find fascinating. I made every attempt to deal with sensitive areas in an objective way.

At one point, I attended a funeral in America for one of my interviewees. As I looked around the congregation, I realized that I had very personal knowledge of the lives of the majority of the people there. It was an honor and also formidable responsibility, and I did not want to let them down.

BOATS

I HAD ALWAYS BELIEVED that the Norwegian loved the sea—that was a "given" in my knowledge. But I was to find out that the Norwegian loved his boat more. His boat was everything. The sea was something to contend with, to learn from, to have fear of, and to make a living from. Some men actually hated the sea and hated their work, but I never heard a Norwegian say he hated his boat. Boats large or small, fishing or pleasure have been and are a source of great love. The boat is of prime importance in his life. A Norwegian respected his boat, took care of his boat and trusted his boat to his success in life. He almost always had a picture of his boat prominently displayed in his home. Some of the women had a love/hate relationship with the boats because on one hand they took so much time and on the other hand brought so much wealth.

I found almost unbelievable courage among these men and women related to their lifestyle and boats, yet they took it all for granted. No one boasted of his or her achievements. (Of course there are always one or two exceptions!) Often I had to coax their stories out of them. There were great acts of heroism when all looked hopeless. I realized that the lore of the Viking age, when courage was the ultimate goal, permeated their lives at sea and at home constantly.

Men, traditionally in Norway, go out to sea for long periods of time and women are alone and manage the household. Men come back or are lost forever to the sea. Some men have gone away to America to fish for as long as twenty years and come back—it is their way of life. They trust their women to do as they should, no matter how long they are away, and trust them to do what they should do if their men should never come back.

In my family we have had five losses through drowning in one generation— more than most but less than some. Some families have not been touched by death at sea, but they are quick to tell me that in former generations their families had such losses.

Each death at sea teaches lessons that benefit all and those in the industry now have benefited greatly from this knowledge. I also found that this was a subject to be avoided, as it could be a reminder of what might happen to them.

In truth, I found some opposition to this project from unexpected sources. One

—AT photo, 1998

Berger Vikre stands below a picture of a boat at the Mælandsgården Museum, Skudeneshavn. The boat was built by his grandfather and my great-grandfather together.

went to great lengths for whatever reasons to oppose my work. Others would not cooperate because of their shyness or lack of self-worth. They didn't think their lives were important. Because of this reticence, really good and important stories have been lost to history as now many of these people are dead.

Several members of my family—particularly two aunts and two cousins— were very helpful and encouraging and picked me up when I felt down. The love and encouragement they gave me, despite being a bit shy about the stories of family life being published, will never be forgotten. I am also in debt to the City of New Bedford under the leadership of Mayor Frederick M. Kalisz Jr. for extending encouragement, hospitality and warmth to me.

I found enthusiasm, willingness to help, and some who assisted financially, in the Norwegian-American and New Bedford communities. The Norwegian government, the *Nordmans' Forbundet*, whose goal is to promote culture, and later, the Sons of Norway and the *Karmøy Kommune* also helped financially. Those who participated in the project—and they are by far the majority—have my eternal gratitude as they have made a contribution to the history of Norway and the New Bedford and Seattle areas for future generations. Those who helped had an understanding and appreciation of their history.

—*AT photo*

Corner of living room at *Little House* decorated beautifully by Randi Wareberg and cluttered by me. Her husband Sigmund kept the wood coming for the stove and it heated the house very well.

—*AT photo*

The antique bedroom at *Little House.*

I expected the Norwegians to be more jovial. I had not had enough experience with them to know of their perennial seriousness. There is some laughter, but not as much as I had anticipated. That is not to say there is no humor. Norwegians laugh at themselves in jokes. Generally, in my experience, on a one-to-one basis, Norwegians in Norway can be very humorous and respond with a great laugh. But in group settings they are more stern.

ACHIEVEMENT

I REMEMBER MY MOTHER encouraging us to achieve—because it would make our Norwegian family proud of us, she thought. What I have learned is that the more one does, the more one achieves, the more one stands out, the less one is acknowledged. This is where the American and the Norwegian part ways. I think this is where we most differ.

A friend in Norway once told me that her son had achieved great heights in the academic world and had received a great honor, yet she when she returned from the ceremonies she was not able to tell friends about it because they would look down upon her. One wonders what great accomplishments in the arts, sciences, literature and politics Norwegians could have achieved if this philosophy termed the *Janteloven* did not exist. Recognition is a basic need in life.

My Yankee mother always thought, and it could have been a remnant of her Quaker/Congregationalist background, that it was close to a sin to have too much money and that if people accumulated vast amounts of money, then it should be used to better society. We were taught that providing the best education for our children, with a little work thrown in by them, was very important, but that expensive cars and other symbols of wealth were frivolous and should be avoided. Many Norwegians, with some noticeable exceptions, also live more Spartan lives than many other emigrant groups, but they will often have very expensive cars.

> *"The poor man knows about the rich man but the rich man doesn't know the poor man."*
>
> —Old Norwegian saying

Money is interesting in other ways in that many Norwegians will save it and rarely spend it. Many in this emigration live simple lives but have accumulated wealth that could be used to improve society or establish foundations for medical research, the arts, history and such. But this is rarely done. They often give generously to their church. Norway itself squirrels away its oil revenues, and teachers there will tell you that is often difficult to obtain essential supplies for teaching, despite the fact that Norway is one of the wealthiest countries in the world.

Generally speaking, I found in my research in Norway that people there were friendly, helpful and enthusiastic about my work. One of the wonderful side effects of this book was that I widened my circle of friends and got to know relatives in Norway. I really enjoyed my time there and the people I met. They accepted me as one of them and not as half-Norwegian. To them I had come home to where my ancestors had lived since the beginning of time. I was just one more Norwegian *pendler*. And in many ways, I was very like them in temperament, appearance, and outlook. I identified with them greatly and was very honored to be accepted by them so unconditionally. There are several wonderful friends there, men and women, who are at the top of my telephone list and whom I miss when I am in the States. These are people with whom I can talk, laugh and share life's experiences in a very easy and comfortable way.

—AT photo

Randi and Sigmund Wareberg enjoying waffles and coffee in their hospitable kitchen.

I attended a funeral for my father's cousin, Gunvald Andersen, on my third trip to Norway in 2001. Just to walk to the church and to see my ancestors' memorial stones on either side of the path and to be part of the beautiful service and the burial was a memorable, but bittersweet experience for me. I was experiencing the tradition of the town of my father, in the church of my father, and unfortunately, the death of his cousin. Later I was to meet many wonderful relatives of this gracious lady. It is the only

—AT photo

Part of the interior of the Falnes Church, serving Skudeneshavn, where all my ancestors, including my father, were baptized and confirmed. Many family members are also buried in the church yard.

totally traditional Norwegian funeral I have been to, and it was very meaningful, and, where everyone, but me, knew what to do and did it in unison. Again I felt part of the continuity of life and spirit in Skudenes and my family's place in the community.

Later there was a luncheon at her home with many family (some of whom I had never met) and friends who one by one at their own prompting got up and spoke of her and her life. Many brought fabulous cakes to display and share with the group. It was a very warm and special experience for me.

During one of the speeches, I had a reflection of similar such meetings during my childhood when people stood by a dining table and gave long speeches in Norwegian. I knew then that I had attended such long-forgotten Norwegian activities when I was very young.

Many have helped me with this book in time, effort and insight. My son Dr. Kristian Simsarian traveled to Norway while he was working and studying in Sweden and did some initial interviewing for me. I found his interviews fascinating as they differed from mine in several ways and elicited good objective information I probably would not have been given. My thanks to him for his efforts on my behalf.

He is an excellent interviewer and certainly a better listener and less a talker than I. He also lent me his apartment in Stockholm for a whole winter and it was there where I started to write on the computer without telephones ringing or any other disturbances. Once I had accomplished my goals for the week, I would reward myself by going into the city to a museum, concert, opera or just walking around. A magnificent city where I participated in celebrating the Millenium.

—*AT Photo 1998*

Kristian Simsarian visits Norway in 1998
and enjoys the "magic table" with Signe
Høines at his great-grandfather's ancestral
Høines home in Skudeneshavn. He dubbed
it the "magic table" because it appears laden
with food and goodies from seemingly out
of nowhere and is always a wonderful and
delicious surprise for him.

—*AT Photo*

The late Tobias Høines, my father's first
cousin, relaxes at his home at the Høines
farm in Skudeneshavn, 1998.

I found myself changing personally during this project. I went back to my maiden name and I felt very good about that. I was myself again.

The men, I found, tended to be quiet and shy at home and to keep their feelings to themselves, but there were some noticeable exceptions. I had experienced this quietness with my brother when we were growing up. Momma always said he was "just like his father" in that way. Poor Momma, neither of us were like her family and we must have been difficult for her to understand but she was always there to support and love us anyway even though, I think, we must have been a mystery to her.

In interviews, one is constantly looking for linkage, ideas to go into new and unknown areas. When I interviewed, I looked actively for those little byways that were critical to discovering new thoughts, paths, and ideas. It is often not the initial answers I got that were important, but the information that I somehow linked . . . a new path . . . that was the most interesting.

As one woman said to me, "It will be your story and no one can write it like you." I hope I did that. But mostly, I had to write it because it

—*AT Photo*

Barbara Simonsen Medhaug was very supportive and helpful during the entire book project. She has my eternal thanks.

—*AT photo*

Two wonderful supporters, Mery Stol Vilhelmsen in Norway and Ellen Risdal Isaksen in Fairhaven. I knew neither before this project, but they opened their hearts, gave me encouragement, assisted in many important ways and made it possible for me to write this book. Special thanks!

was a mission for me. I couldn't stop. I gave up my consulting firm, as there was no time for it. I took on this project as a leap of faith. And I thank God for that and for the courage to continue despite long odds. When I needed help, it was always there, whether in the form of an idea, an insight, a new path, a gift or some kind words.

Publishing was not a friendly experience but it was an educational one. I became very distanced from publishers after two bad experiences. As chaotic as publishing was, I never knew when I started to write how exhilarating writing could be. I had no idea that on some days the words and ideas would come so fast that I could hardly get them onto the keyboard in time. I would feel a great sense of achievement and almost a thrill. In contrast, re-editing and re-writing have to be most tedious, boring and frustrating tasks in a creative enterprise. I finally had experienced the wonderful surge of creativity in work and it did eventually overcome the boredom of the rest of it.

This project started to expand as it went on. I asked Norwegian balladeer Aleksander Hauge to write music for a CD to go along with this book and to be used as an insert. He wrote beautiful music but since the original book publisher went out of business and the book delayed, Aleksander's CD was produced earlier. Excited by the content of this project and his CD, he went on to spearhead a memorial on Karmøy for lost fishermen who died in America's waters. I helped to raise money for this in Massachusetts.

I spearheaded two cultural events in the New Bedford community, including two concerts with Aleksander Hauge and a 17th of May celebration. For me it was a way of paying back those who had helped me with my project and also a way of bringing excellent Norwegian music

—*Rune Håkonsen photo*

Aleksander Hauge sings one of his meaningful songs on Karmøy in 2000.

Lars Roar Fure, formerly with the Norwegian Consulate in New York and now a senior advisor with the Ministry of Foreign Affairs in Oslo. His support was invaluable.

to the community in addition to raising money for the Karmøy Memorial. Many of the older people in the community were deeply touched by the first concert, and this, in itself, was a great reward to me. I felt I had honored my grandparents in this work, and it was a labor of love and a gift from me and some of my cousins to their memory. I am indebted to them for their enthusiasm, cooperation and moral support.

Gunnar Berg assisted the Norwegian Consul for the 17th of May program, and he was of great help to me. Carol Anne Hoaglund-Tollefsen was extremely helpful with the concert and assisted very professionally with one of the readings and organization. The Reverend Mr. Henry Pedersen, an old childhood friend, assisted in both events and was much appreciated by the audience. A large group of volunteers led by Sonja Sovik, Gail Isaksen and Ellen Isaksen helped in many ways including preparing and serving the delicious food and they have my appreciation and thanks.

The Mayor of New Bedford, the New Bedford City Council, the Massachusetts State Legislature and the Governor of Massachusetts all recog-

Standing in front of New Bedford City Hall before the flag-raising ceremony on the 17th of May, 2001, are the Honorable Frederick M. Kalisz, Jr, Mayor of New Bedford, author Astrid Tollefsen, Norwegian balladeer Aleksander Hauge and Lars Roar Fure of the Norwegian Consulate in New York City.

—AT photo

My lovely friend Evva
Meyer Larson wears my
bunad to a Norwegian
special event in New
Bedford.

nized the Norwegian community at the 17th of
May celebration. The mayor of New Bedford had
a flag-raising ceremony at the New Bedford City
Hall and we were all honored to have the
Norwegian consul from New York, Lars Fure,
attend and speak. It was both an exhausting and
exhilarating experience and one that few who
attended shall forget.

I hope this book will inspire a Fisherman's
Museum and monument to be built in New
Bedford or Fairhaven in the near future. Another
personal dream is to have the creation of a sculp-
ture of a woman and her children waiting for the
boat of her fisherman husband and father to come
back into port. Ideally this would stand at Fort
Phoenix, where women have waited throughout
the past century and longer.

I experienced some really wonderful people
on this voyage and through them glimpsed some
exciting, soul-searching, courageous and
admirable chapters of unique lives. I hope you
enjoyed meeting them also.

PAPA

MY SECOND INTERVIEW was with Jens Isaksen, who as a child in Norway
had lived across the street from my family in Skudeneshavn. After we talked,
we went down to the docks together in Fairhaven
to see one of his boats. This was my first visit to a
dock with a Norwegian fisherman. As we returned
and walked back to the main street, I thought, *This
is what I would have done with my father*, and I
remember smiling at Jens and thinking my father
might have been like him, as he also was known to
be a strong, quiet, kind and gentle man. That was
a very special moment for me.

Had my father lived, our family life would
have been very different. We would have been
more affluent with less worry and anxiety
throughout my formative years. My mother
would have been healthier and happier and would
have been able to walk into a store and purchase a

—AT photo

Rodman School friend
Kirsten Lindoe (Smedsvik),
now living in Haugesund.

—*AT photo*

Accomplished, confident, lovely and capable, Ida-Kristin Bleivik of Haugesund—a shining example of the modern Norwegian woman. She rescued me when I got into difficulty with my car in Norway by stopping, taking charge, getting help and generally assisting me with her cell phone and knowledge of community. She didn't leave until I was ready to drive away. It meant a lot to me to have this kind of help from a gracious stranger.

desired item for herself, something she never, never was able to do after Papa died—not until her senior working years.

I would have had more self-esteem, understood men better and most likely would have married young to a fisherman and lived that lifestyle. My life would have been considerably narrowed and I, perhaps, would never have experienced the travel, education, worldwide friendships, outreach, recognition, achievements and the wonderful experiences I actually have had. My brother would have lived and loved his life on the sea to be sure, but maybe on a fishing boat rather than a U.S. Navy vessel. We would have been able to speak Norwegian.

I have one memory of my father's influence and consequently one quality that has been with me throughout my lifetime. There was a day just before Papa died when he wanted to take me for a walk. I can position the time accurately, because Momma had a carriage with her and my brother had just been born two months before Papa died. There was an argument. He wanted to take me for a walk up the street, and Momma didn't want him to and chastised him for letting me run free and thereby putting me in danger. But he took me anyway, holding my hand until we came to the corner. And at the corner he showed me the difference between the sidewalk, the curbstone and the street. "The street is black," he said. "See this stone—this is where you stop and put your feet—right here—on the edge and wait for me. I will come and bring you across the street." So we crossed the street and walked along hand-in-hand again and halfway down the block (where Momma couldn't see us) he let go and I knew then I could run and as I ran down the sidewalk, I also knew he was behind me and would pick me up if I fell and that I was to look for the stone. And I saw it in the distance and ran to it and stopped on it and firmly planted my feet on it, and then I turned and saw Papa and smiled up at him. He came up to me, held my hand and said, "Astri, you are my good girl." I was so happy that I had done it right.

In this one lessen I learned how to be trusted and to trust, how to have freedom in life while always recognizing the curbs, and how to stop at a curb until I could safely go on. I learned that love and trust have responsibilities attached, and I learned what it felt like to have someone have faith in me.

After he died, I was back in the harness and leash, even to the extent that when we were in a backyard with other families or children, my leash was attached to a rope, which was attached to the clothesline. I was not to experience that wonderful freedom, faith and trust again for many many years, but when I was on my own and had freedom, I was able to recognize the curbs in life.

And so it is, I observed, with Norwegian children in Norway and, therefore, I think this is one of the answers as to why Norwegians are independent and also have great courage as adults. They learn about freedom, curbs and responsibility very early in life and are trusted by their parents to exercise care in this freedom.

Did I find Papa while writing this book? I learned about his culture and heritage and my place in it. In that, I found what he would have wanted to pass on to me. Perhaps he has been walking behind me all my life protecting me— I would like to think so.

I know that by following the waters and being guided by our mutually shared ideals, I indeed fulfilled my destiny. I hope that Papa would still say, "Good girl."

Tusen Takk (Thank You)

Astrid Tollefsen
West Barnstable, Massachusetts, 2004

Acknowledgments

M<small>Y</small> <small>DEEP APPRECIATION</small> to these people & organizations

Life experiences:

Aastein Aase
Aleksander & Anne Hauge
Alf & Tove Isaksen
Anonymous - (3)
Arne Olsen*
Arnleiv Jensen
Barbara Simonsen Medhaug
Berit & Magne Nes
Berit & Malvin Kvilhaug
Bernard Olsen
Bjorne Sjoen & family
Bradford Hathaway
Carol Gallop Berg
Carol Ann Tollefsen-
  Hoaglund
CDR Thomas Severt
  Tollefsen, USN (Ret)
David* & Marie Tollefsen
Didrik Didriksen*
Doris Gustafson Bendiksen
Dorothy & Ivar Olsen
Dorothy Johannessen*
Dr. Robert Bendiksen
Egil & Kitty Ellingsen
Eleanor & Karin Hansen
Eli Syre
Ellen Gurie Tollefsen
  Thompsen*
Ellen Simonsen
Ellen Skaar
Evie Olden
Florence Lekom
Gail Jacobsen Isaksen
Gunleif* & Helen*
  Wilhelmsen
Gunnar & Martha Berg
Gunnar Fagerland
Gunnar* & Elinor Haines

Håkon Eilertsen*
Harald Mannes
Harriet Johannessen
  Didriksen
Ike & Evelyn Isaksen
Jack* & Ruth Ostensen
Jacob Jacobsen
Jacob Johannessen
Jakob Stol
Janna Isaksen
Jens* & Marlene Isaksen
Johanna Risdal
John & Ellen Isaksen
Judy Simonsen Ferreira
Kaare & Sigrun Ness
Karl Johann & Berit
  Melkevik
Karl* & Marthe Berg
Kirsten Lindoe Smedsvik
Kitty & Egil Ellingsen
Kris "Pase"* & Mrs.Olsen
Lars Roar Fure
Lauritz Eidesvik
Linda Johansen
Linda Risdal Knott &
  Spencer Knott
Lise Stol Medhaug & Mery
  Stol Vilhelmsen
Magne Aadland
Margie Thompsen
  Gustafson*
Mr.* & Mrs. Arnold Veek
Mr. & Mrs* Kristoffer
  Birkeland
Mrs. Simon Johansen
Mrs. Liv Haines
Muriel Caswell Tollefsen
  (Boffoli)*
Oddvar Solstad (Moe)

Peder Eliasen
Ralph Brown
Robert Nesse
Roy Enoksen
Sandra Olsen DeMoranville
Sara (Sally) Tonnessen*
Serine Matland
Severin Haines
Sigrid & Gunnar Gundersen
Sonja Jacobsen Sovik
Stephen Small
Sverre Mannes
The Berg Sisters: Betsey,
  Beverly, Kathy & Nancy
The Reverend Dr. Gordon
  M. Torgersen
The Reverend Mr. Johnnie
  Glad
The Reverend Mr. Henry
  Pedersen
Thomas & Kina Helgeland
Toni Isaksen Johnson
Tor Tollessen
William Olden

Support from the media:

Haugesunds Avis (Bjarte
  Amble)
Karmøy Bladet: Lovise
  Johannessen
New Bedford Standard-Times:
  William Kennedy,
  Publisher & President.
  Writers, Jack Stewardson,
  Joanna Weeks & former
  editor, Brad Hathaway
Norway Times: Espen
  Tjersland

483

The Advocate, The Barnacle,
   The Wanderer
TV Haugaland: Øyvind
   Fjeldheim, Eirik Davidsen,
Eirik Hustvedt
TV Station 2, Bergen,
   Norway: Karl Johann
   Paulsen
Viking Magazine, SON
Western Viking, Seattle

Cooperation:
Arne Langheller
Dr. & Mrs. Dan D.
   Daatland
Dr. Hans-Eirek & Lilian
   Aarek
Dreyer Books, Stavanger
Elisabet Middleton
Ellen-Carin Piaskoski
Hans Storhaug
John Allan Bakke,
   Karmøy Kommune
Kristin Brudevoll
Laila Stange
Lars Fure
Leif Meling
Nordmanns-Forbundet
Norwegian Consulate, New
   York City
Randi & Sigmund
   Wareberg
Sons of Norway
Sons of Norway,
   Norumbega Lodge
Svain Langheller
Sigurd Johannessen
The Ketil Berg Family
The Norway Club, San
   Francisco
The Tobias Hoines Family
Tor Magne Johannessen
Trinity Lutheran Church,
   Fairhaven
The Reverend Mr. John H.
   Niemann)
Winifred Caswell Johnson*

**Encouraging friends &
relatives:**
Aleksander & Anne Hauge
Ann & William C. Arthur
Barbara Ballard

Dr. David S. Martin
Siat Vincent
Edward D. Simsarian
Elizabeth Clark
Elizabeth Ohman Bard
Evangeline Smedley
Evva Meyer Larson
Greta Garten Jelleson
Harald Koksa
Janet Judge Castle
Joan Currie
Joan Halliday McFadgen
Mary Cockrell Ehrendreich
Mary T. Douglas
Maureen Ronan
Peg Urquiola Marquis
Randi & Sigmund
   Wareberg
Siat Vincent

Translators:
Gunnar Berg, Aastein Aase
Rune Haakonsen, Barbara
   Simonsen Medhaug,
   Aleksander Hauge

Copy Editor:
Linda Risdal Knott

Misc. editing:
Elizabeth Ohman Bard,
   Evva Meyer Larson

**Misc. cultural & technical
information:**
The Soviks, Ellen & John
   Isaksen, Gunnar Berg,
   Barbara Medhaug, Mery
   Vilhelmsen, Alf Isaksen,
   Aleksander Hauge

City of New Bedford:
Mayor
Frederick M. Kalisz, Jr.
Steve Furtado
Arthur Motta

Karmøy Kommune
Mayor of Karmøy:
Ordfører: Kjell Arvid
   Svendsen

Karmøy Fundraising:
Lise Stol Medhaug.

Special contributions
Cover Painting: "Sailing
   into Skudeneshavn", 1902,
   Gunvald Falnes. Owner:
   Dr. Inge Gilje,
   Haugesund.
Photo: Gunleif Wilhelmsen
   (1975) By James
   Nachtwey/ VII (Paris)
Painting: "Waiting for
   Papa" © Magne Adolfsen,
   Kvitsøy, Norway
Illustrations: USCG Ships,
   George E. Bieda:
   Windjammer Arts
New Bedford Scenes: Artist,
   Arthur Moniz
Selected vessel photos: Mr.
   Steve Kennedy, Cape Cod
Musical lyrics, poetry,
   Karmøy Fisherman's
   Memorial photos:
   Aleksander Hauge
Motif: Evangeline Smedley,
   Santa Barbara, California
Poem: "Amerika"
Mery Stol Vilhelmsen
Rosemaling Motif: Joan
   Dahl, "Norwegian Trolls
   & Rosemaling Vol.1"
   www.rosemal.com

Book design with thanks:
Publisher's Design &
   Production Services, Inc.
   Sagamore Beach, MA.

Special thanks to:
To my esteemed editor:
Mr. William J. Breisky
A friend
My son, Dr. Kristian
   Thomas Simsarian
& always, Momma*

*Now deceased

My apologies for any
omissions. It was my intent
to include all.

Style Notes

AND DISCLAIMERS

1. Fishing vessels are in most cases designated by name only—assuming the F/V.
2. Language of the interviewees is as close as possible to their actual syntax, usage, grammar, cadence and rhythm patterns. Some editing was done for clarity only. I felt it important to the integrity of the book to show, whenever possible, the essence of the people of this emigration by keeping their language their own. Interviews were done face-to-face, or by mail or email, as noted. Norwegians, for instance, are apt not to use "the," "an" or "a" and often use "was" instead of "were" as it more closely mimics the Norwegian usage. I only wish I could have captured the delightful lyric speech rhythms for the reader, especially from the people of Karmøy.
3. I often used a tape recorder, but found that my written notes were sometimes better as the tape recorders proved unreliable when there was background noise or when several people with accents were talking at once. All quotes have been kept as accurate as possible within these constraints. It was my goal to capture the essence of the interview and to include it within the appropriate topic. Some chapters include segments of interviews which are designated according to subject matter. Material was also gleaned from conversations and remarks.
4. I have attributed interviews to the interviewees when possible. I tried to withhold attribution when the interviewee wished his or her name not be mentioned. I have used more names than I wished to use because all professional editors who looked at this book insisted that names of people be included for veracity. It was not my intention to use any names of people who wished otherwise and I hope I did this according to our mutual understanding. I sought to exclude names on any or all materials where their use might cause embarrassment to the parties involved.
5. I thank all of the interviewees for candidly sharing their life experiences with me. Some would give information only if their identities were not revealed. I tried to honor each of these verbal agreements, but if I have erred, I ask your forgiveness as it was not intentional. Some interviews were not used because the material was considered redundant or had appeared in other works.

485

6. I used the word "emigrants" rather than "immigrants" in most places as it is my perspective that these people emigrated *from* Norway and being "*from* Norway" was the most important element of their emigration. Also they often went back and forth, so they were not truly the "immigrant" we know from many other countries. They were more realistically "*pendlers*" or commuters or in some cases economic refugees, and I feel that the word emigrant more aptly describes them. The Merriam Webster dictionary defines "emigrate" as: "to leave one's place of residence or country to live elsewhere."

7. Numbers were spelled out in the text except when they came from quoted materials where they were not spelled out. I used them as they were written.

8. Photos were given to me by many people and most photos did not have names or identification on them. I have designated them as general fishing photos and given credit only when I was sure of its origin. In many cases a photo was given to me by one person, but could have been taken by another. Photos may be misattributed because of this. If this is applicable, I apologize. These private photos are mainly from:

Aleksander Hauge and friends	Mary Stol Vilhelmsen
Alf and Tove Isaksen	Otto Olsen
Arnleif Jensen	Ralph Brown
Barbara Medhaug	Serine Matland
Carol-Anne Tollefsen Hoagland	Simon Vea
Ellen Tollefsen Thompsen	Sonja Sovik
Evie Olden Schein	Stephen Small
Gunnar Berg	Sverre Mannes
Harald Mannes	The daughters of Olaf Berg
Janna Isaksen	The Henry Simonsen family
Jens and Marlena Isaksen	The Thomas Helgelands
John and Ellen Isaksen	Tobias Hoines
Linda Risdal Knott	Toni Isaksen Johnson
Lise Stol Medhaug	William Olden
Magne Ådland	The term "AT photo" designates a
Marie Tollefsen	photo taken by the author

9. Errors happen under the best of conditions, but can more easily occur when there are several computers and one is working in different countries with different software. I ask for the reader's indulgence and forgiveness for any unintentional mistakes or errors.

10. Spelling accuracy is difficult with foreign names because of the extra symbols used and my lack of Norwegian language skills. Whenever possible the correct letters were used and they have been checked. However, I am sure that there are incorrect words and ask your indulgence and understanding of this problem. Although different Norwegians have checked different chapters, I fully realize that I am vulnerable in this area. Often I found that when I had changed a word and saved it, it popped up again when the program was reactivated. This seems to be a glitch in either my hardware or software, and I was constantly finding

errors that had been corrected, in some cases several times. There may be more. This has been a particularly frustrating problem for me. Please accept my apologies.

11. This book is my truthful perception at this point in time, based on interviews, conversations, readings, travel and life experiences. It is an oral history primarily and recorded in the words of those who lived it. You might say, "I don't remember the incident like that." That is a normal reaction as described by a New York Times, April 5, 2004 opinion piece called, "The Fog of War," by Daniel L. Schacter, a professor of psychology at Harvard and the author of "The Seven Sins of Memory: How the Mind Forgets and Remembers." He wrote: "the way the brain stores and retrieves information, research shows, can sometimes lead people to hold different memories of the same event. Transience, mis-attribution and bias occur even when we do our best to recollect the past accurately."

12. Stories from the interviewees are based on their perceptions and memories as is appropriate to an oral history. They are the truth as they remember it. Some of the stories come from their youth as they experienced it. The war years, in partic-ular, because of the trauma is very vivid in their minds. The reader, however, must remember that these particular stories are born of youth and represent memories of youth.

13. This book was not written to be an academic book; indeed, I have personalized much of the material in order to make it more readable and interesting for the average person. I feel it could, however, be helpful as supplementary material in course work dealing with migration studies, Norwegian life and culture, and the fishermen of New Bedford and Alaska.

14. The reader may question how I can remember so many things about my early childhood. To some it may seem impossible and indeed even my own mother questioned it. All I can say is—I do remember it well. It may be because the trauma surrounding my father's death makes these early events very vivid to me. I answered my mother's question by drawing a floor plan of our first home and pointing out to her where the different furniture was located. She finally realized that I did remember, and she didn't question it again.

As I get older, I can't remember where I left my keys or glasses, but my child-hood events are very real to me and according to my mother's girlfriend—very accurate.

~

Chapter Notes

Foreword

1. Lars Fure, formerly with the Norwegian Consulate in New York and now with the Norwegian Ministry of Foreign Affairs in Oslo, helped to support this project and was very kind to write the foreword for this book. He worked with me on the 17th of May festivities in New Bedford. He is a dedicated professional and a very well educated man who is a credit to the Norwegian Foreign Ministry and consequently Norway itself.

Prologue: Two Houses, Two Shores

2. This prologue, which introduces one Norwegian woman (my grandmother) and her family, was written to set the tone for the events that follow. Her former home in Fairhaven, which we thought might be demolished, will now begin a new life. Purchased by one of Papa'sma's great-grandchildren, it will be refurbished and become home to a new generation—thus increasing its lifespan to several hundred years.

3. "Skudeneshavn" has gone though various spellings and more recently, Skudesneshavn, as it is known to the older emigrants. *Havn* means harbor, so it is not correct to refer to it as Skudeneshavn harbor, hence the word "waters" is used. Other areas of the town not directly on the water are often known as Skudenes. It has developed into a lovely, quaint seaside tourist town, which is very popular with Europeans for fishing, sailing and as a launching place for other Norwegian tours. There is a large festival around the time of our Fourth of July, which is well worth attending.

Chapter 1: The Baptismal Waters

4. The Statue of Liberty information is from the Vigsnes Copper Mine Museum (*Vigsnes Grubemuseum*) on Karmøy and from conversations with its founder,

Aleksander Hauge. The Vigsnes copper mine museum has added a replica of "Miss Liberty" to its display. A member of the National Park Service in New York City told me that a rock from the mine on Karmøy is on display today on Liberty Island.

5. Information about Ellis Island is from the National Park Service and *Ellis Island, Gateway to the American Dream*, Pamela Reeves, Barnes and Noble Books, New York, 1998. Members of the National Park Service were very helpful to me.

6. Martin Isaksen owned *Cristeen* from 1936-1958, and sold it upon his retirement at age seventy-one. Renamed *Christeen*, it is now harbored in Oyster Bay, N.Y., where it is preserved by *Christeen* Oyster Sloop Preservation Corporation. Built in 1883, and the oldest oyster-harvesting sailing vessel of its kind in this country, *Christeen* is the only Maritime National Historical Landmark on Long Island and the oldest documented American vessel still operating in the United States. *Christeen* survived six major hurricanes and two sinkings. Toni Isaksen Johnson writes that: "*Christeen* made fifty-four trips in 2002 including a wedding on board."

7. Re. Jensen: I have used "Mother," instead of "Mamma"—as he spells it—in this chapter, because the spelling may be confusing to the reader. The traditional spelling of "Momma" is used elsewhere for other references.

Chapter 2: Yesterday's Tides

8. For more information about emigration to America, see *The Promise of America* homepage: *http://www.nb.no/emigrasjon/emigration/* and *The Sloopers; Their Ancestry and Posterity; The Story of the People on the Norwegian Mayflower—The Sloop, "Restoration,"* by J. Hart Rosdail, 1961. Website: *http://www.wheelerfolk. org/slooper/society/main.htm*

9. This illustration is a good example of the work done by New Bedford artist Arthur Moniz who has been painting for over twenty-five years. He studied at the Massachusetts College of Art and the School of the Museum of Fine Arts in Boston. Mr. Moniz paints in all media—oil, acrylics, egg-tempera and watercolor. His paintings are highly detailed with a feeling of quiet calm to them. He has had many significant one-man shows, and his work is especially well loved in Japan. His paintings are in the permanent collections of the Imperial Palace, Tokyo; the John Manjiro House (Museum), Tosashimizu, Kochi, Japan; and the John Manjiro Society, Tokyo. Recently, he has developed a style of painting he calls graphite watercolor. These are extremely meticulous pencil renderings over which are added transparent watercolor washes. His studio is located at 26 Centre Street, New Bedford, MA 02740. Source: *www.ultranet.com/~a-moniz*

10. From a New Bedford Standard-Times article by Earl B Dias: "Unquestionably, Fairhaven's most famous native son is Henry Huttleston Rogers, the Standard Oil magnate who became one of the most powerful tycoons of his day. Born in 1840, Rogers lived during his childhood and early youth in the house at 39 Middle Street, which still stands today. A member of the first graduating class of Fairhaven High School, Rogers, after completing his secondary school studies, worked as a clerk in a grocery store, then as a baggage master for the Old Colony Railroad, and, at the age of twenty, left to seek his fortune in the oil fields of

Pennsylvania. By the time of his death in 1909, he had amassed a fortune of more than $100,000,000, but despite his rise in the world, he never forgot Fairhaven, which he once called 'the dear old town which for 200 years has been the home of a continuous line of some of my ancestors.' During his lifetime he spent many happy hours in Fairhaven at his elaborate eighty-five-room mansion near Fort Phoenix, and he bestowed on the town such priceless gifts as the magnificent Fairhaven High School."

11. Material re. Mrs. Broughton from *Some Memories of Cara Leland Rogers Broughton, The first Lady Fairhaven,* Mabel Hoyle Knipe, Fairhaven, Massachusetts, March, 1984.

12. Thank to Carolyn Longworth, Library Director, Millicent Library, Fairhaven, for her telephone help re. Fairhaven's history.

13. The cover print shows the New Bedford Ship Supply as owned by the Tonnessen family. Today there is a pocket park across the highway from this store, and it is beautifully situated by the waterfront with gardens and seating. Named Tonnessen Park, it was built in memory of Rasmus Tonnessen and has a view of the New Bedford Ship Supply as well as part of the harbor. The park is a reminder of the influence of Norwegians in the area and, in particular, the Tonnessens. It is a place to sit, relax, and ponder, and a place from where one may view the hustle and bustle of the waterfront and the boats.

14. Many neighborhoods were torn down by planners who, in my opinion, did not have good historical perspective. Many unique buildings were lost. It shocks returning residents even today. I like to think that the Elim Baptist Church was very courageous in preserving its building when it said "no" to this plan. It now stands as an island of independence and as a monument to the wise separation of church and state.

   After the destruction, *WHALE* was founded. The Waterfront Historic Area LeaguE *(WHALE)* was founded as a non-profit, membership-based corporation dedicated to building the future on the best of the past. WHALE's mission is simple: "Preserving, protecting and restoring historic structures and sites of the New Bedford Region. Its vision is a harbor and working waterfront reunited to its historic districts and downtown." (From the WHALE website at: *www.water-frontleague.org*)

Chapter 3: Charting New Waters

15. Materials in this chapter are taken from personal memories, conversations with relatives and friends of my mother, and articles from the New Bedford Standard-Times about the loss of the *Valencia* and death of Captain Sigvart Tollefsen. Information was also obtained from interviews with relatives in the USA and Norway, and the son of a survivor in Norway. The late Tobias Hoines, Skudeneshavn cousin, was very helpful. Family history was taken from genealogical records.

16. I have written about practical jokes in this chapter as they pertained to my father. However, I have learned over the years that practical jokes are common among Norwegians and refined to a high degree. My understanding is that there was so

little entertainment and so little money there that people had to entertain themselves, and they did that through music and also practical jokes.

17. From a November 1999 article in USA Today entitled: "1938 Hurricane Left Mark on New England": "The hurricane that hit New England on September 21, 1938, was the region's worst so far this century. The storm killed at least 600 people and did at least $306 million in damage in 1938 dollars, which would equal about $3.5 billion in today's dollars. Afterward, people talked about the 'tidal wave' that swept away hundreds of beachfront homes. Oceanographers try to stay away from the term 'tidal wave' because large waves have nothing to do with tides. Oceanographers and geologists use the Japanese word '*tsunami*' for what are often called 'tidal waves.' Undersea earthquakes or landslides cause these waves. What happened in the 1938 New England hurricane was 'storm surge.' But, in this case, 'tidal wave' in the general sense of something out of a horror movie seems appropriate. On Long Island and the southern New England coast, the surge was between 12 and 16 feet. The water swept away huge, solid, stone houses that had stood near beaches. Wind gusts up to 183 mph were measured at the Blue Hill observatory outside Boston. A good book about the storm is Everett Allen's *A Wind to Shake the World*, published by Little Brown in Boston in 1976. Allen had just started his first job as a newspaper reporter when the storm hit September 21, 1938. In addition to his own experiences, Allen tells the stories of scores of others caught by the storm and gives a good overview. In 1988, the American Meteorological Society published a 128-page book, *The 1938 Hurricane: An Historical and Pictorial Summary*. Information about obtaining it is available from the Society at 45 Beacon Street, Boston, MA 02109-3693."

18. Almost any major library has copies of The New York Times on microfilm back into the 1930s. Looking at the issues beginning the day of the storm, September 21, and for the next week, is fascinating. Public Television's *The American Experience* series includes "The Hurricane of '38," which is mostly interviews with survivors and some film from 1938. To buy a videotape, call PBS Video at 1-800-328-7271.

19. Summary: Widespread inland flooding, high winds inland, with severe coastal flooding.
Public Impact: 564 deaths, 1,700 Injured, 2,600 boats destroyed, 3,300 damaged. Homes/Buildings: 8,900 destroyed, 15,000 damaged. Catastrophic fires touched off by power lines in Connecticut. *Southern New England Tropical Storms and Hurricanes*, by David R Vallee and Michael Dion, National Weather Service, Taunton, MA.

20. The year 1966—Completion of the Hurricane Barrier protecting the inner harbor of New Bedford. It is 9,100 feet long and stands twenty feet above mean sea level.

Chapter 4: The Explosive Waters

21. Information in this chapter is from interviews in Norway and America. Also ODIN (Official Norwegian information on the Internet), "The History Channel"; visits to the Resistance Museum in Oslo; the Cabinet War Rooms in London. Some personal and family experiences were valuable.

Chapter 5: Sailing a True Course

22. The Berg segment of this chapter is from his daughters via phone and letters and also from New Bedford Standard-Times articles supplied by the Berg family. Copies of diary entries from Aletha Berg and photos were supplied by the Berg family. The Standard-Times had no file on the Berg family.
23. Disclaimer: There is no intention on the part of the author to accuse, indict, hurt, or in any way defame the Fisherman's Union in this story. It is based on information from newspapers and the Berg family. The story was based on available information only. I was unable to find additional information but that does not mean that it does not exist.
24. The Simonsen section was from the New Bedford Standard-Times, materials from his wife and daughter, as well as from an interview with a member of the crew, Karl Johann Melkevik, and newspaper articles and information on the Internet from Canada.

Chapter 6: The Emigrant Wave

25. This chapter is based on personal interviews and letters in America and Norway. From the New Bedford Standard-Times, September 27, 2000, regarding Lincoln Park: "The former amusement park, which closed for good in 1987, was once the hub of summertime fun on the South Coast. The park was opened in 1894 by the Union Street Railway as a way of attracting ridership on trolleys between New Bedford and Fall River. In its heyday during the '40s, '50s and '60s, people met their spouses there, the Comet roller coaster thrilled thousands, and performers like Connie Francis and trumpeter Jimmy Dorsey entertained audiences in the old ballroom."

Chapter 7: Hurricane Carol

26. This story is based heavily on a feature article written by the very talented Jack Stewardson of the New Bedford Standard-Times, who in my opinion makes the waterfront come alive with his spirited and fascinating writing and research. I am very indebted to him. Also thanks Carol Anne Tollefsen-Hoaglund for her hurricane memories and to Sandra DeMoranville for her recollections of her father.
27. Noman's Land, according to Wampanoag tribal history on the Internet, came into being when Moshup was building a bridge from Aquinnah to a nearby island. He was carefully placing huge boulders in the sea when a crab caught him by his big toe. In a fit of anger, Moshup threw the crab into the water, along with some of the boulders. This came to be the island of Noman's Land today whose name reportedly comes from the Indian name *Tequenoman*. The shores off Noman's Land are a favorite Wampanoag fishing spot.

Chapter 8: Discovering my Heritage—Faith

28. This chapter is based on my memories, newspaper articles about The Rev. Dr. Gordon Torgersen, and some recollections of other Elim youth.

Chapter 9: Secrets of the Deep

29. Interviews for this chapter included: Kaare Ness, John Isaksen, the late David Tollefsen, the late Jacob Ostensen, and more.

Chapter 10: The Treacherous Shores

30. This chapter is based on interviews with many fishermen and their families. Because of the sensitiveness of the subject mater, all names have been withheld to protect the privacy of the interviewees.

Chapter: 11: Discovering my Heritage—Norway

31. Christmas was at the home of Kristian and Marie Berg and their son Ketil in 1960 on Askøy, Norway, an island just off the coast of Bergen. Greta Garten Jelleson still remembers this as her definitive Christmas. Each Christmas thereafter, I have made Norwegian waffles and thought of Tante Marie and her family and that wonderful Norwegian Christmas.
32. Conversation with Trygve Lie, December 1960, train from Oslo to Bergen.

Chapter 12: The Language Whirlpool

33. Most cultures teach other languages, but we have few people who are academically bilingual. The ability to communicate with others abroad is necessary for good communication, understanding, and the sharing of experiences.

Chapter 13: Homeport

34. The term "exilic" means self-imposed absence from one's country, the condition or a period of living away from one's native country. Exile is a form of this word. There are many terms referring to people who come from other countries to settle in another. Some are: emigrants, exiles, political or economic refugees, displaced persons, or victims of a diaspora. But all have one thing in common: the people have relocated and have to adjust to their new environs. Some can never go back and others may. But their lives will never be the same. Sometimes it is but a thread that distinguishes one from the other and in all cases there is the pain of separation and sadness for those who were left behind. There is also a group of residents in the new land who must adjust, must accommodate and alter their lives to some degree as well. The great movements of peoples in the twentieth century and most likely the twenty-first century is perhaps one of the great events in the history of the world and its culture.
35. Marriage: The New Bedford area still has strong ethnic identities when compared to other parts of the country. People are often known by their family's original ethnic tradition. Although the early Norwegian emigrants primarily married Norwegians in the first third of the century, marriages to other northern Europeans such as Germans and Swedes as well as Yankees also occurred with increasing frequency up to the mid-century. The second generation of the original New Bedford Norwegian pioneers tended to marry more non-Scandinavian

local people and the children of the final emigrants, those coming over after 1955, often did not marry Norwegians. Some second and third-generation members married into other ethnic groups, races or religions. Many changed their religion to correspond to their spouse, as when the spouse was Roman Catholic, and sometimes a spouse became a Lutheran. Marrying a Norwegian or another Scandinavian in present generations often has become the exception rather than the rule.

Chapter 14: The Perilous Waters

36. Materials for the story are from the New Bedford Standard-Times, members of the Risdal (extended) family, and others related to the events. including Pastor Johnny Glad in Norway. The interviews in this chapter were conducted from 1996-2000 and were held in New Bedford, Fairhaven and Norway in person and by phone. Winter 2000 interviews were conducted via telephone from Sweden to Norway and Fairhaven. Special thanks to Ralph Brown, formerly with the U.S. Coast Guard, and Brad Hathaway of the New Bedford Standard-Times for their recollections of this loss. Also special thanks to Aleksander Hauge for his moving music and lyrics in *The Ballad of the Midnight Sun*, a song which represents "everyman" and no one specific man on the boat. I regret that only some photos of the lost men were available to me for reproduction. Some material was para-phrased from the Norwegian documentary, "The Last Emigration," 1996, Bergen, Norway, TV Channel 2.

37. The trial and language: I was in a courtroom in Massachusetts in 1999 when there was a housing case with three visiting Irish defendants, two East Indian plaintiffs and one Puerto Rican witness. All had very limited American-English skills. I watched the judge as he became more and more frustrated and finally simply ruled in favor of the Irish, even though it was clear that they were at fault. He simply gave up. He couldn't understand the stories of anyone present.

Chapter 15: Working the Waters

38. The wonderful photo on the first page of this chapter, which in my opinion shows the soul of the fisherman, is one of the best studies I have ever seen and it came to this book in a circuitous way. I needed a good photo of Gunleif Wilhelmsen, so I got in touch with his son and he wrote me this letter:

"Hi, Becky told me you were looking for some pics of my Dad. This is a great one and it was taken by James Nachtwey on a trip aboard the *Ocean Gem* around 1975. He wrote an article on that trip that appeared in the Providence Sunday Journal around that time, but this picture was not in it. I'm giving you his name in case you need to credit him....Richard Wilhelmsen."

So I began my search for James Nachtwey and it turned out to be a very pleasant journey. I finally contacted him and then he wrote me that he did warmly remember Gunleif and his trip on the *Ocean Gem*. Here is a little about this amazing man, from various web pages:

James Nachtwey/VII grew up in Massachusetts and graduated from Dartmouth College, where he studied art history and political science, in 1970.

He worked aboard ships in the Merchant Marine, and while teaching himself photography, he was an apprentice news film editor and a truck driver. In 1975 he took a fishing trip with Gunleif Wilhelmsen and photographed it for the Providence Journal. He gave this photo to Gunleif. To me it tells the whole story of the fisherman. When one looks at Gunleif's eyes, one can see the pain, apprehension, gravity, knowledge, security, professionalism and thoughts of a fishing captain as he goes out to sea.

Mr. Nachtwey, a world-renowned combat photo-journalist, has won numerous awards and honors including The Common Wealth Award, Martin Luther King Award, Dr. Jean Mayer Global Citizenship Award, Henry Luce Award, Robert Capa Gold Medal (five times), the World Press Photo Award (twice), Magazine Photographer of the Year (seven times), the International Center of Photography Infinity Award (three times), the Leica Award (twice), the Bayeaux Award for War Correspondents (twice), the Alfred Eisenstaedt Award, the Canon Photo Essayist Award and the W. Eugene Smith Memorial Grant in Humanistic Photography. He is a fellow of the Royal Photographic Society and has an Honorary Doctorate of Fine Arts from the Massachusetts College of Arts. He is the World Press Photo Foundation's Pictures of the Year, International: Magazine Photographer of the Year–2003-2004. VII Photo agency is located at 58 Boulevard Latour Maubourg, F-75007 Paris, France. James Nachtwey is a generous, friendly and warm human being, and I feel so honored to have his work in this book.

Many thanks to him for this gesture.

39. I chose these men for this chapter because they represented the hard-working everyday fishermen and skippers who are the backbone of the industry.

a. I conducted in-person, first-hand interviews with Helen Veek Wilhelmsen, her brother, Mr. Arnold Veek, and his wife, and Gunleif Wilhelmsen, 1999, with follow-up interviews.

b. Sverre Mannes, interviewed in Norway, 1998.

c. Anonymous in 1999 who just wanted to tell me his story freely without having his name attached.

d. Stephen Small, grandson of Hans Haram, was interviewed in 2001 in Maine.

40. Today's fishing industry (current information 2004): "The seafood industry spawns $850 million in related sales per year and provides more than 3,500 people with jobs," Mayor Frederick M. Kalisz Jr. told the New Bedford Standard-Times in 2004.

Figures/Facts about the New Bedford Fishing Industry from the National Park Service:

The New Bedford fishing fleet includes 113 scallop vessels (fish primarily for scallops), 150 draggers or ground fish vessels (fish primarily for cod, flounder and haddock), 50 smaller vessels or day boats, lobster vessels and quahoggers.

The average annual income for fishermen, according to 1997 employment records, is $43,833.

New Bedford is home to New England's first electronic display auction process, whereby fish buyers have the ability to bid on fish directly from a closed-loop system of purchasing and selling, known as the Whaling City Display Auction and BASE (Buyers And Sellers Exchange).

New Bedford won the top-valued-port-in-the-nation status from 1983 to 1991. It remains the richest on the east coast with a total landing value of $90 million from the 40 million pounds of seafood landed in 1997.

Over 60 businesses registered as buyers and processors of seafood operate out of New Bedford.

Over 8.6 million pounds of ground fish species of haddock, cod and flounder was landed in New Bedford in 1997, worth over $10 million.

Statistical Information:

The New Bedford fishing industry makes up one-third of the city's economy, generating $4 on land for every $1 in landings. The average days at sea for a ground fishing vessel (fish primarily for cod, flounder and haddock) from New Bedford is eight days with a three-to-five-man crew working a variety of shifts as they tow their nets for two to three hours at a time.

The price for sea scallops in 1938 was 14 cents a pound, compared to today's $6.66 a pound.

The sea scallop fleet (fish primarily for sea scallops) fishes for much longer periods, up to 18 days at sea with their seven-man crews, tow two heavy steel 15-foot dredges along the sea bottom where scallops are found.

The sea scallop still remains the most valued catch of New Bedford fishermen, accounting for $44.9 million from 6.7 million pounds landing in 1997.

The top national average occurred in 1990, when over $160.4 million worth of seafood was landed in New Bedford as recorded by the National Marine Fisheries Service.

Up to 40 percent of the fishermen labor force is over 45 years of age. Forty-four percent were born outside the United States, with two-thirds immigrating since 1960.

Well-developed shoreside seafood processing, marketing and delivery channels are world-renowned. Each day a wide variety of fish is landed, processed and trucked to major U.S. cities, as well as exported to many parts of the world.

Chapter 16: Finest Kind

41. Based on in-person interviews with Kaare Ness in Massachusetts and Norway. Although Kaare Ness did not name Trident Seafood specifically, he is one of the founders. The Trident website states: " 'It started with one boat,' says Trident Seafoods President Chuck Bundrant, glancing at the etching of the 135-foot *Billikin* that hangs above his desk. 'We asked why we couldn't catch crab and process crab on the same vessel. They said it wasn't going to work. That was in 1970.' Chuck Bundrant was an Alaska king crab fisherman; so were Kaare Ness and Mike Jacobson, who would soon become his partners....These fishermen understood that the key to their future lay beyond the docks where the boats simply unloaded the catch. Together they built the *Billikin*, adding crab cookers and freezing equipment necessary to process their own finished product. They embarked on a new course for themselves and ultimately the Alaska seafood industry...Trident Seafoods was founded in 1973, and the young corporation hooked its future to the bounty of Alaska's fishery resources and the demand for

quality seafood that was building worldwide. It began with one boat. In the year 2000, Trident Seafoods was processing more than 250 million pounds of finished products and employing 4,000 people, making Trident Seafoods Corporation the most successful privately held, 'all-American-owned' seafood processor in Alaska and the Pacific Northwest."

Trident web is: *http://www.tridentseafoods.com/navigate.asp?SecVar=b& SubSecVar=b3&SubSec2Var=*

42. Harald Mannes: Interview in Norway, phone, and information from newspapers.

43. Andrew Olden: Letter from his son William and conversations and letter from his daughter Evie Olden Schein. Other information from the New Bedford Standard-Times.

44. Mathias Bendiksen: letter and interview with son Robert and Mathias' wife, Doris.

45. For readers interested in knowing more about Norwegian seafaring history and culture, I would encourage them to read the Icelandic Sagas. Iceland at one time was part of Norway, so these Sagas also are Norwegian history. One website for the Sagas in English is *http://www.simnet.is/gardarj/folk/sagas.htm*

Other sites may be found using the search word Saga. Books on the Sagas are listed on book websites such as Amazon.com or Barnes and Noble. The search word Saga will bring you to them. They are fascinating stories that show where many of today's cultural traits and values originated.

Chapter 17: Discovering My Heritage—The Navy Years

46. Personal memories of my Navy experience in New York City, 1963-65.

Chapter 18: Beckoning Waters

47. Skudeneshavn, 1997, interviews by Kristian Simsarian with Peder Eliasen, Magne Aadland, Sverre Mannes, the Melkeviks and the Alf Isaksens.

Other interviews included Lise Medhaug, two anonymous, Jakob Stol, Kaare Ness, Egil and Kitty Ellingsen, and various people who left New Bedford.

Egil and Kitty Ellingsen's memories came from a long email sent to me by the family. The memories of the war years come from a telephone conversation, as did several miscellaneous remembrances. Their letter was edited very little and sections were divided between chapters. Sadly, no photographs were forthcoming.

Chapter 19: The Following Waters

48. Gail Isaksen: Interview in Fairhaven 2001, as well as newspaper materials.

Linda Johansen: Interview in Connecticut in 1997 and discussion with her grandmother.

Henry Pedersen: Letter and interview, 1997.

Thomas and Kina Helgeland interviews and newspaper articles about Brian, 1997–2002.

Kristian Thomas Simsarian: Mother's memories, with supporting materials.

~

49. Introductory photo: The statue of Marilyn Monroe is in the background of this photo. Her father, Martin E. Mortensen, a seafarer, was briefly married to her mother, according to one author, and is reputed to be a native of Haugesund. One book written about her described a phone call from her father when she was an adult. Although they didn't meet, she recalled that they spoke a bit, that he expressed pride in her, and that he had a funny way of speaking English.

50. Many celebrities over the years have had Norwegian roots. I recall that in May 1975, I had a long conversation with the Emmy Award-winning Sally Struthers, whose mother's family was from Kristiansand. Sally told me about her Tante Astrid and expressed pride in her Norwegian heritage. The Academy Award-winning Renée Zellweger also has a mother from Norway and speaks of her often in interviews. There are too many Norwegian-American people of achievement to recognize in this chapter, but they are numerous and excelling in their fields of endeavor.

Chapter 20: In Dry Dock

51. Interviews were held in Norway and the New Bedford area, including some anonymous old-timers in Fairhaven and the late Arne Olsen. The words of retired fishermen in Norway, the late Didrik Didriksen, Sverre Mannes, men at the fishing museum on Karmøy and more are in this chapter. Special thanks to Aleksander Hauge for his stunning photos of the Karmøy Fisherman's Memorial and also to Lise Medhaug and Dr. Hans Eirik Aarek for their photos taken on the day of dedication.

Chapter 21: Epilogue

52. Personal thoughts about the years researching and writing this book:
     This was a time of expectations, creativity, generosity, disappointments, broken promises and achievement. There were many cases of generosity from people and organizations, and they more than balanced those who were armchair critics or skeptical bystanders. It is difficult to go forth on an adventure and long-term work of this size. There are days when you want nothing more than to throw it all out the window and get on with your life, but a kind and encouraging word here and there can bring you right back to a new thought and direction. I thank those who did that: kept their word to me, encouraged my work, and helped preserve a part of history. Special thanks to Aleksander Hauge for his good information, great photos, encouragement, island area tours, and inspirational music. Some people wished to remain anonymous as they felt this was the only way they could talk freely. This information was critical to the book. My thanks to them again for their generosity. My thanks to all who helped this book become a reality.

53. *Legacy and Folklore* are supplementary materials reflecting the culture and history of the Norwegian emigrants. The two lighthearted discourses on "Vikings and the Cowboys" and "Vikings and the Fishermen" are simple exercises in observation and a bit of fun on my part.

Men and Their Boats

54. Photos are from many sources, including the fishermen and boat owners. Special thanks for the photo of the F/V *Sippican* to photographer Ivan Flye, "The Pictorial Studio," Newcastle, Maine, whom I failed to locate. Special thanks to Arthur Moniz for his fishing boat print and to Steve Kennedy for his great photos of fishing boats. Also a "thank you" to Harald Koksa, and the Norwegian American Line museum for information about the NAL liners.

Bibliography

55. This list of books and materials may be useful to the reader.

Appendix

56. These documents were given to me on behalf of the Norwegian community during the 17th of May celebrations in New Bedford in 2001.
57. The Coast Guard report is representative of a typical U.S. Coast Guard report. Although there were many more crews and boats lost, only a few are listed in the Internet version of lost ships, which includes vessels from all over America. Website: *http://www.webandwire.com/coast%20guard%20casualty%20page.htm*
58. Fisherman's Museums: Other cities have created them successfully and so can New Bedford. It is my hope that the New Bedford area will have a fisherman's museum in the near future. I further hope that someone will try to rescue a wooden boat now, so that it can be restored as a living museum later. It would be a tragedy to lose this important part of New Bedford's history or to see another city—such as Mystic, Connecticut—add it to their museum. I hope that the people of New Bedford will have twenty-first-century vision and not let this happen to their history a second time.
59. Photos in this book: Every attempt has been made to contact the owners of photos. Some people are gone and some businesses are closed. If I have over-looked anyone, I deeply regret it. It was not intentional. I ask your forgiveness and will attempt correct attribution in future editions of this book. Many photos are now in the public domain.

Bibiography

1. Arnett, Peter. *Live from the Battlefield*, Simon and Schuster, 1994.
2. Braynard, Frank O. & William H. Miller. *Fifty Famous Liners*. Patrick Stevens Limited, UK, 1982.
3. Cohat, Yves. *The Vikings, Lords of the Sea—Discoveries*. Harry N. Abrams Inc., Publishers, 1992. (Translated from the French)
4. Ditlevsen, Tove. *Early Spring*, translated by Tiina Nunnaly. The Women's Press Ltd. 1967.
5. Gjersvik, Martin. De som dro fra Karmøy til Amerika. (Those who went from Karmøy to America.) Worums Trykkeri A/S., Haugesund, Norway, 1984.
6. Hamilton, Edith. *Mythology, Timeless Tales of Gods and Heroes*, Little, Brown and Co., 1942.
7. Hanson, Katherine (editor*). An Everyday Story: Norwegian Women's Fiction*, Seal Press, Feminist Publishers, 1984.
8. Hauge, Aleksander. *Vigsnes Kopperverk (The Vigsnes Copper Mine)*, Dreyer Bok, 1986.
9. Ibsen, Henrik. *The Wild Duck*, Ivan R. Dee, Inc., 1990.
10. Langheller, Svein Ivar et al. *SKIP, Om Skipsbyggingstradisjoner, Fartoyvern, Ungdoms–Prosjekter og Bygging Av Nye Treskip*, with summary in English, Lokal Historisk Stiftelse, Tysvaer, 1997.
11. LeCarre, John. *The Secret Pilgrim*, Alfred A. Knopf, New York, 1991.
12. MacLeish, William. *Oil and Water*, The Atlantic Monthly Press, Boston, New York, 1985.
13. Reeves, Pamela. *Ellis Island, Gateway to the American Dream*, Barnes and Noble, *1998*.
14. Rolvaag, Ole Edvart. *Giants in the Earth*, Harper Collins Publishers, Perennial series, 1999.
15. Sande, Lars Chr. (editor). *Norsemen Follow the Trail*. English translation (abridged) of "*De som dro ut*", Dreyer Press, Stavanger, Norway. (no date)

16. Scott, Paul. *Jewel in the Crown*, University of Chicago Press. Reprint edition, 1998.
17. Vanberg, Bent. *From So Many . . . For So Few*, Sons of Norway, Heritage Productions.

Magazines

1. *Esso, PERSPEKTIV, 1997, ESSO*, Norge, AS. Oslo, Norway.
2. National Geographic, *In Search of the Vikings*, May 2000.
3. New Yorker Magazine, April 23, 2001. Louis Menard, *"She Had to Have It"* (Hetty Green)

Norwegian-oriented books in print of special interest

1. Bojer, Johan. *The Emigrants*, Greenwood Press. Reprint,1974.
2. Bryan, George B. *An Ibsen Companion: A Dictionary-Guide to the Life, Works, and Critical Reception of Henrik Ibsen*, Greenwood Press, 1984.
3. Fuegner, Richard S. *Beneath the Tyrant's Yoke: Norwegian Resistance to the German Occupation of Norway, 1940-1945*, Beaver's Pond Press, 2002.
4. Gaarder, Jostein. Paulette Moller, Translator. *Sophie's World: A Novel About the History of Philosophy*, Publishing Group, 1996.
5. Lovoll, Odd Sverre et al. *The Promise of America*, University of Minnesota Press, 1985.
6. Lovoll, Odd Sverre. *The Promise Fulfilled: A Portrait of Norwegian Americans Today*. University of Minnesota Press, 1998.
7. Mauk, David C. *The Colony That Rose from the Sea: Norwegian Maritime Migration and Community in Brooklyn, 1850-1910*. University of Illinois Press, 1998.
8. Qualey, Carlton. *Norwegian Settlement in the United States*, Norwegian-American Historical Association, 1901.
9. Rolvaag, O.F. (Nora O. Solum, translator). *Peder Victorious: A Tale of the Pioneers 20 Years Later*, 1st Bison Book. Ed, 1982.
10. Semmingsen, Ingrid. (Einar Haugen, translator). *Norway to America: A History of the Migration*, University of Minnesota Press, 1980.
11. Veblen, Thorstein. *Norwegian-American Studies*, (Vol. 34), Norwegian American Historical Assn, 2001.
12. Zempel, Solveig (editor). *In Their Own Words: Letters from Norwegian Immigrants*, University of Minnesota Press, 1991.

Books about commercial fishermen

1. Bartlett, Kim. Nubar Alexanian (Photographer), *The Finest Kind: The Fishermen of Gloucester*, W.W. Norton & Company, 2002.
2. Carey, Richard Adams. *Against the Tide: The Fate of the New England Fisherman*, Houghton Mifflin Co., 1999.
3. Greenlaw, Linda. *The Hungry Ocean: A Swordboat Captain's Journey*, Little Brown & Company, 1999.

4. Junger, Sebastian. *The Perfect Storm: A True Story of Men Against the Sea*, W.W. Norton & Company, 1997.

5. MacLeish, William H. *Oil and Water*, Atlantic Monthy Press, Boston, 1985.

6. McCloskey, William. *Highliners: The Classic Novel about Fishermen of Alaska*, The Lyons Press, 2000.

7. McCloskey, William. *Their Fathers' Work, Casting Nets with the World's Fishermen*. International Marine/Ragged Mountain Press, 1998.

8. McCloskey, Willliam. *Fish Decks: Seafarers of the North Atlantic*. Paragon House Publications, 1990.

9. Pierce, Wesley George. *Going Fishing: The Story of the Deep-Sea Fishermen of New England*, McGraw-Hill, 1989.

10. Playfair, Susan R. *Vanishing Species: Saving the Fish, Sacrificing the Fishermen*, University Press of New England, 1st edition, 2003.

Books of interest to women

1. Aasvik, Hanna. *War and Innocence: A Young Girl's Life in Occupied Norway*, Hara Publishing, 2000.

2. Brundland, Gro. *Madam Prime Minister: A Life in Power and Politics*, Farrar Straus & Giroux, 2002.

3. Brunsdale, Mitzi. *Sigrid Undset: Chronicler of Norway*, (Berg Women's Series) Publisher: Berg Pub Ltd. February, 1989.

4. Gullestad, Marianne. *Kitchen-Table Society: A Case Study of the Family Life and Friendships of Young Working-Class Mothers in Urban Norway*, Universitetsforlaget; 1984.

5. Jochens, Jenny. *Women in Old Norse Society*, Cornell University Press, 1996.

6. Lagerquist, L. Deanne. *In America the Men Milk the Cows: Factors of Gender, Ethnicity, and Religion in the Americanization of Norwegian-American Women*, (Chicago Studies) Carlson Publications, June, 1991.

7. Lurie, April. *Dancing in the Streets of Brooklyn*, Delacorte Press, 2002.

8. Morgan, Patti Jones. *Island Soul: A Memoir of Norway*, Double SS Press, 2000.

9. Schultz, April R. *Ethnicity on Parade: Inventing the Norwegian American Through Celebration*, Univ. of Massachusetts Press, 1995.

10. Solbakken, Elizabeth. *Redefining Integrity: The Portrayal of Women in the Contemporary Novels of Sigrid Undset*, Peter D. Lang GmbH Series, European University Studies, 1992.

11. Undset, Sigrid. *Kristian Lavransdatter* (combined volumes), Alfred A Knopf, 1972.

Websites readers might enjoy

1. A colorful website about fishing in the Lofoton Islands and trading routes to other parts of Norway. *http://www.ub.uit.no/northernlights/eng/hansa.htm*

2. A good Norwegian site for general knowledge and especially for tourists: *http://www.gonorway.no/index3.html.*

3. City of New Bedford Official Website: A comprehensive site. *http://www.ci.new-bedford.ma.us/*

4. Ellis Island National Park Service. *http://www.nps.gov/stli/serv02.htm*
5. Great Norwegian geneology site *http://digitalarkivet.uib.no.*
6. In-depth information about Norwegian names, emigrant ships and other genealogical information. *www.norwayheritage.com/ships/names.htm#name*
7. King's Advice (technical skills of the Vikings) *http://www.mnh.si.edu/vikings/voyage/subset/greenland/sagas.html*
8. Lost at Sea. A particularly good website about fishermen from Nova Scotia. *http://www.lostatsea.ca*
9. Millicent Library, Fairhaven, MA. A very interesting and informative site. *http://www.millicentlibrary.org/*
10. Norwegian Bokmål language. All about this language. *http://anubis.dkuug.dk/jtc1/sc22/WG20/docs/n854-Bokmal.htm*
11. Official Norwegian government information website ODIN. *http://odin.dep.no/odin/engelsk/index-b-n-a.html*
12. Norwegian holidays. *http://www.mnsu.edu/emuseum/history/mnstatehistory/nw_holidays.html*

German websites concerning Norway and WWII

1. German Coastal Defence in Norway during WW II, By Bjorn Jervas. http://www.feldgrau.com/norwcoast.html
2. Norwegian Collaborationist Forces During WWII: *http://www.feldgrau.com/a-norway.html*
3. Norwegian Volunteers in the German Wehrmacht in WWII, by Marc Rikmenspoel and Jason Pipes. *http://www.feldgrau.com/norway.html*
4. The Invasion of Norway: *http://www.feldgrau.com/norwegian.html*

Norwegian Heritage Day
Recognition

The
Commonwealth of Massachusetts

Jane Swift
— Governor —

to

NORWEGIAN HERITAGE DAY

*In celebration of the contribution of Norwegian-Americans
to the fishing industry of New Bedford*

which is deserving of recognition by all the citizens of Massachusetts,

this ___nineteenth___ day of ___May___ in the year _2001_ .

Governor

CITY OF NEW BEDFORD

IN CITY COUNCIL

February 22, 2001

RESOLUTIONS HONORING THE NORWEGIAN-AMERICANS OF THE GREATER NEW BEDFORD COMMUNITY

WHEREAS, On May 17, 2001, the Norwegian-Americans of the Greater New Bedford Community shall celebrate Norwegian Heritage Day on the anniversary of their native country's independence; and

WHEREAS, This celebration will be honored by the presence of the Norwegian Consulate General and other honored guests from Norway; and

WHEREAS, The proceeds from this celebration will go to the erecting of a memorial on the Norwegian Island of Karmoy, honoring the lost Norwegian fisherman from New Bedford; and

WHEREAS, Astrid Tollefsen has compiled a history of the Norwegian-Americans in the book <u>Following the Water</u>; and

WHEREAS, The Norwegian-Americans have been immigrating to the New Bedford Community since the early 20th Century; and

WHEREAS, The Norwegian-Americans are responsible for the establishment of the scallop and fish industries in the Greater New Bedford Community; and

WHEREAS, The Norwegian-Americans have contributed to the well-being of the entire Country, even contributing their services during times of war; and

WHEREAS, The Norwegian-Americans of the Greater New Bedford Community have continually proved themselves to be upright citizens:

NOW, THEREFORE, BE IT RESOLVED, That the New Bedford City Council honors the **NORWEGIAN-AMERICANS** of the **GREATER NEW BEDFORD COMMUNITY,** and extends sincere best wishes for their continued success and happiness in all their endeavors; and

BE IT FURTHER RESOLVED, That a copy of these Resolutions be forwarded to Astrid Tollefsen on behalf of the Norwegian-Americans of the Greater New Bedford Community.

Offered by:

_____
George Rogers, Councillor At Large

_____
Denis Lawrence, Jr., City Council President

_____
Dennis W. Farias, Councillor Ward One

_____
John T. Saunders, Councillor At Large

_____
George N. Smith, Councillor Ward Three

_____
Jane L. Gonsalves, Councillor Ward Five

_____
Joseph T. Andrade, Councillor Ward Four

_____
Victor C. Pinheiro, Councillor Ward Six

_____
David Alves, Councillor At Large

_____
Brian K. Gomes, Councillor At Large

_____
Paul Koczera, Councillor Ward Two

City of New Bedford
Mayor
Frederick M. Kalisz, Jr.

OFFICIAL PROCLAMATION

WHEREAS: *To honor those Norwegian Americans who were lost at sea while fishing off New Bedford Shores;*

WHEREAS: *To recognize the contribution of these Norwegian Americans made to the establishment, growth, vigor and profit of the fishing industry and its collateral industries in New Bedford, which is now the second largest port in the United States;*

WHEREAS: *To recognize the service they performed during the first world war, second world war and in other wars by serving in the United States Military and if not in the military in the Second World War by serving as scouts for the **US NAVY** to locate, identify and report German submarines off the coast of New Bedford;*

WHEREAS: *To recognize that the Norwegian Americans have contributed to the economy and their neighborhoods by their thrifty, responsible, and conservative life styles in their homes, churches and community. Their contributions to the Greater New Bedford area include: building and supporting churches, improving neighborhoods and educating their children as well as passing on their trades to their children; and*

WHEREAS: *In particular the women in the Norwegian American community who by their patience, skills, strength and support were able to keep the families together by themselves through long periods of time alone and when tragedy struck, all alone. Their strength, courage and fidelity coupled with their husbands skills and hard work made this emigration a success.*

NOW THEREFORE, I, FREDERICK M. KALISZ, JR., *Mayor of the City of New Bedford, do hereby proclaim this Seventeenth day of May in the Year of the Lord A.D. 2001, to be*

NORWEGIAN HERITAGE DAY

and urge all the citizens of New Bedford to take cognizance of this event and participate fittingly in its observance.

Frederick M. Kalisz, Jr., Mayor

Massachusetts House of Representatives

Resolutions

**HONORING THE NORWEGIAN-AMERICANS OF THE
GREATER NEW BEDFORD COMMUNITY.**

WHEREAS, ON THE OCCASION OF THE ANNIVERSARY OF THEIR NATIVE COUNTRY'S INDEPENDENCE, NORWEGIAN-AMERICANS OF THE GREATER NEW BEDFORD COMMUNITY WILL CELEBRATE NORWEGIAN HERITAGE DAY ON MAY 17, 2001; AND

WHEREAS, THE NORWEGIAN CONSULATE GENERAL AND OTHER HONORED GUESTS FROM NORWAY WILL JOIN WITH THE NORWEGIAN-AMERICAN COMMUNITY TO CELEBRATE THEIR NATIVE COUNTRY'S INDEPENDENCE; AND

WHEREAS, A MEMORIAL WILL BE ERECTED ON THE NORWEGIAN ISLAND OF KARMOY HONORING THE LOST NORWEGIAN FISHERMEN FROM NEW BEDFORD; AND

WHEREAS, ASTRID TOLLEFSEN HAS COMPILED A HISTORY OF NORWEGIAN-AMERICANS IN HER BOOK, *FOLLOWING THE WATERS*; AND

WHEREAS, NORWEGIAN-AMERICANS HAVE BEEN IMMIGRATING TO THE NEW BEDFORD COMMUNITY SINCE THE EARLY 20TH CENTURY AND ARE RESPONSIBLE FOR THE ESTABLISHMENT OF THE SCALLOP AND FISHING INDUSTRIES IN THE GREATER NEW BEDFORD COMMUNITY; AND

WHEREAS, NORWEGIAN-AMERICANS HAVE CONTRIBUTED TO THE ADVANCEMENT OF OUR COUNTRY INCLUDING, BUT NOT LIMITED TO, ANSWERING OUR COUNTRY'S CALL TO ARMS TO DEFEND THE PRINCIPLES OF DEMOCRACY; THEREFORE BE IT

RESOLVED, THAT THE MASSACHUSETTS HOUSE OF REPRESENTATIVES HONOR THE NORWEGIAN-AMERICANS OF THE GREATER NEW BEDFORD COMMUNITY AND EXTENDS ITS SINCERE BEST WISHES FOR THEIR CONTINUED SUCCESS AND HAPPINESS IN ALL THEIR FUTURE ENDEAVORS; AND BE IT FURTHER

RESOLVED, THAT A COPY OF THESE RESOLUTIONS BE FORWARDED BY THE CLERK OF THE HOUSE OF REPRESENTATIVES TO ASTRID TOLLEFSEN ON BEHALF OF THE NORWEGIAN-AMERICANS OF THE GREATER NEW BEDFORD COMMUNITY.

HOUSE OF REPRESENTATIVES, ADOPTED, MAY 10, 2001

Thomas M. Finneson
SPEAKER OF THE HOUSE

Steven T. James
CLERK OF THE HOUSE

OFFERED BY:

REPRESENTATIVE GEORGE ROGERS

REPRESENTATIVE JOHN F. QUINN

EDWARD M. KENNEDY
MASSACHUSETTS

United States Senate

WASHINGTON, DC 20510–2101

May 17, 2000

City of New Bedford
Fisherman's Memorial Committee
New Bedford, MA 02470

Dear Friends:

It is an honor to offer my greetings and best wishes to everyone gathered today for the first Norwegian Heritage Day in New Bedford. I wish I could be with you to commemorate and celebrate this important occasion.

It is fitting to pay tribute to the many contributions of the Norwegians to the City of New Bedford and to the Commonwealth of Massachusetts. I specifically applaud their commitment to the fishing industry. We take pride in New Bedford's history as one of our great fishing ports, and all of us are proud of the extraordinary dedication by the Norwegian community to its fishermen.

In addition, I would like to recognize Janna Isaksen, a Norwegian-American who is in the audience today. It was with great courage that Janna persevered during World War II. Janna is truly a model to us all and is a proud representation of the best that Norway has to offer.

With best wishes and warm regards on this special day,

Sincerely,

Edward M. Kennedy

Sample Coast Guard Reports

Address Reply to:
COMMANDANT   MVI
U. S. Coast Guard   8 August, 1950
Headquarters   File: (FV FOUR SISTERS
Washington 25, D. C.   a-1 Bd)

From: Chief, Merchant Vessel Inspection Division
To: Commandant
Via: Acting Chief, Office of Merchant Marine Safety

Subj: FV FOUR SISTERS; sinking of with loss of life of crew in the vicinity
      of Nantucket Shoal area during April, 1950.

1.   Pursuant to the provisions of Title 46 C.F.R. Part 136, the record of
the Marine Board convened to investigate subject casualty, together with its
Findings of Fact, Opinions and Recommendations, has been reviewed and is forwarded herewith.

2.   The motorboat, FOUR SISTERS, 43 gross tons, 64.6' in length, wood hull,
built in 1926, was regularly employed as a commercial fishing vessel out of
New Bedford, Massachusetts. This vessel with approximately 700 gallons of
scallops on board was proceeding to Pollock Rip in order to make the Woods Hole
market and was last sighted at about 0600 on 7 April, 1950, in a position near
No. 10 Buoy east of Nantucket. It is presumed that the FOUR SISTERS foundered
with the loss of all persons on board. On 7 April, 1950, the wind velocity
in the area of the casualty reached as high as 52 miles per hour with occasional
gusts of 65 miles per hour.

3.   As a result of this casualty the following crew members lost their lives:

    Gunnar Pedersen   Victor Boine
    Martin Johnson   James Morrison
    James Lopes, Jr.   George St. Clair
    Manuel Moniz, Jr.   John Correia, Jr.
    Louis Boine   Kenneth Dyer

4.   The Board made the following Findings of Fact:

    "(1) That the FOUR SISTERS of New Bedford, Official No. 225463, of 43
    gross tons, was owned and operated out of New Bedford by Abram H.
    Reservitz, Master Gunnar Pedersen.

    (2) That the vessel was a wooden hull built in 1926 in Thomaston,
    Maine.

    (3) That the vessel sailed from New Bedford on March 29.

    (4) That the FOUR SISTERS was last sighted on the morning of 7 April
    at about 0600 in a position near No. 10 Buoy, east of Nantucket.

Chief, MWI Division to
Commandant

MWI
8 August, 1950
(FV FOUR SISTERS e-1 Bd)

(23) That on April 7 at the Weather Bureau Station at Nantucket the wind velocity was as high as fifty-two miles per hour with occasional gusts to sixty-five miles per hour.

(24) That the Weather Bureau considers their coastal forecast ordinarily to cover water to a limit of about twenty-five miles offshore.

(25) That a representative of the fishing industry understood the coastal forecast to cover only ten miles offshore.

(26) That the storm warnings issued by the Weather Bureau are broadcast over commercial radio stations WBZ, WEE, WHDH and WCOP.

(27) That northeast storm warnings were continued south of Boston on the morning of April 8.

(28) That the storm warnings were changed to small craft warnings at 5:00 a.m. on April 9.

(29) That ships offshore southeast of Nantucket reported winds as high as Beaufort force 11.

(30) That the Master of the Fishing Vessel FRIENDSHIP reported winds seventy-five to eighty miles per hour, estimated, and seas of sixty to seventy feet.

(31) That the Master of the Fishing Vessel DAGNEY considered the storm too severe to attempt going through Pollock Rip Slue.

(32) That the FOUR SISTERS underwent major hull repairs from November 30, 1949, to January 31, 1950.

(33) That the vessel was hauled out of the water on December 14, her sheathing removed, her old planking removed, and the vessel was resheathed.

(34) That one section of the hull planking about five feet in length was replaced.

(35) That the planking of the vessel's hull was secured by nails.

(36) That the vessel's framing was made up of double three by six pieces sawn to shape.

(37) That the planking was two-inch hard pine.

(38) That the vessel was equipped with a wooden hatch cover over the fish hold which in turn was covered with a metal cover which fitted over the hatch and lapped down for about five inches, held down by a single hatch bar across the center.

- 3 -

Chief, MWI Division to
Commandant

MWI
8 August, 1950
(FV FOUR SISTERS e-1 Bd)

(5) That the FOUR SISTERS, in a radiotelephone conversation with the Fishing Vessel DAGNEY, asked the DAGNEY to pick up the FOUR SISTERS' buoy.

(6) That the FOUR SISTERS reported to the DAGNEY by radio that he was going to Pollock Rip in order to try to make the Woods Hole Harbor.

(7) That when the FOUR SISTERS and the DAGNEY departed at this time, the wind was blowing approximately thirty-five miles per hour.

(8) That when the FOUR SISTERS started for Pollock Rip, the weather was already too rough for fishing.

(9) That the FOUR SISTERS had on board scallops in the quantity of approximately seven hundred gallons.

(10) That the Fishing Vessel FRIENDSHIP was also in the vicinity at the time the FOUR SISTERS departed from the fishing grounds.

(11) That both the DAGNEY and the FRIENDSHIP run to the southward and returned safely to New Bedford.

(12) That Mr. Reservitz, the owner, first informed the Coast Guard that the FOUR SISTERS was overdue on April 9 at or about 1000.

(13) That on April 9 the Coast Guard searched by planes and vessels 4635 square miles.

(14) That on April 10, 6497 square miles were searched.

(15) That on April 11, 5001 square miles were searched.

(16) That on April 12, 2388 square miles were searched.

(17) That the total area searched was 21369 square miles.

(18) That on April 8 the Coast Guard had been engaged in a search in an area extending south from Pollock Rip Light Vessel for the Fishing Vessel WILLIAM LANDRY.

(19) That the beaches of Monomoy Island and Nantucket Island were kept under observation for several days.

(20) That the search by airmen and on the beaches disclosed no wreckage or equipment from the FOUR SISTERS.

(21) That small craft warnings were hoisted on April 5 at 6:00 a.m.

(22) That these warnings were kept up continuously until at 10:00 a.m. on April 7 they were changed to northeast storm warnings.

- 2 -

Chief, MVI Division to
Commandant

MVI
8 August, 1960
(FV FOUR SISTERS e-1 Bd)

(39) That the vessel carried one ring life buoy.

(40) That the vessel carried two fifteen-foot dories.

(41) That the vessel carried life preservers for each crew member.

(42) That the vessel was equipped with radiotelephone, a fathometer and a direction finder.

(43) That the vessel was equipped with one pump run off the engine plus two hand pumps of the handy-billy type.

(44) That the following-named men composed the crew of the Fishing Vessel FOUR SISTERS:

Captain Gunnar Pedersen, 923 Pleasant St., New Bedford, Mass.
Martin Johnson, 36 Elm St., Fairhaven, Mass.
James Lopez, Jr., 144 Mott St., New Bedford, Mass.
Manuel Monir, Jr., 92 Earle St., New Bedford, Mass.
Louis Boine, 32 Clover St., New Bedford, Mass.
Victor Boine, 32 Clover St., New Bedford, Mass.
James Morrison, 199 Ash St., New Bedford, Mass.
George St. Clair, 101 Main St., Fairhaven, Mass.
John Correia, Jr., 256 Chancery St., New Bedford, Mass.
Kenneth Dyer, 86 Laurel St., Fairhaven, Mass."

5. The Board expressed the following Opinions:

"(1) That the vessel foundered while en route from off Buoy No. 10, east of Nantucket Island, toward Pollock Rip on or about April 7.

(2) That the mail fastening of planking, including butts, was a poor type of construction in this vessel.

(3) That the search conducted after the vessel was reported overdue was thorough and adequate.

(4) That the above-named crew members are presumed to have been lost on or about April 7, 1960."

6. The Board made the following Recommendations:

"(1) That the Fishing Vessel FOUR SISTERS be officially declared lost at sea.

(2) That all vessels licensed for commercial fishing be brought under existing regulation for merchant vessels.

(3) Pending approval by the reviewing authority, no further action be taken and the case be closed."

- 4 -

Chief, MVI Division to
Commandant

MVI
8 August, 1960
(FV FOUR SISTERS e-1 Bd)

REMARKS

7. The Coast Guard has no statutory authority to officially declare the loss of a merchant type vessel at sea. The Coast Guard does have the authority to express its opinion that a vessel has been lost at sea which has been done in Opinion 1 of the Board.

8. Recommendation 2 of the Board states that all vessels licensed for commercial fishing be brought under existing regulations for merchant vessels. The safety requirements applicable to fishing vessels are at variance with those normally applicable to merchant type vessels. This is indicated by the fact that safety requirements are now subject to full statutory inspection and certification. Congressional bills encompassing legislation suggested by Recommendation 2 of the Board are now before Congress for consideration and are as follows:

(a) HR 464 - A bill to apply the marine safety statutes and regulations thereunder to all seagoing motor-propelled vessels.

(b) HR 5384 - A bill to extend the marine safety statutes and regulations thereunder to seagoing motor fishing vessels of 15 gross tons or over.

9. Subject to the foregoing remarks, it is recommended that the Findings of Fact, Opinions and Recommendations of the Marine Board of Investigation be approved.

/s/ EDW. C. CLEAVE
EDW. C. CLEAVE

Ind-1
18 August, 1960
(FV FOUR SISTERS e-1 Bd)

From: Acting Chief, Office of Merchant Marine Safety
To: Commandant

Forwarded, recommending approval.

/s/ R. L. RANEY
R. L. RANEY

APPROVED 23 August 1950

/s/ A. C. RICHMOND
A. C. RICHMOND
Rear Admiral, U. S. Coast Guard
Acting Commandant

Sample List of Fishermen's Museums

USA

Fisherman's Museum, Mt. Desert, Maine

Pemaquid Point Lighthouse and Fisherman's Museum, Bristol, Maine

Fisherman's Museum, Reedville, Virginia

Fishermen's Museum, Jackson Harbor, Washington Island, Wisconsin

Canada

Fisherman's Museum, Musgrave Harbour, Newfoundland

Fisherman's Museum, General Delivery, Salvage, Newfoundland

Fisherman's Museum, Cemetery Road, St. Vincent's/ St. Mary's Bay, Newfoundland

Maritime Museums by Fisherman's Life Museum, Jeddore Oyster Ponds, Nova Scotia

Fisheries Museum of the Atlantic, Lunenburg, Nova Scotia

Main-a-Dieu Fishermen's Museum, Cape Breton

England

Fisherman's Museum, Clovelly, North Devon

Hastings Fishermen's Museum, Rock A Nore Road, Hastings, Sussex

Norway

Karmøy Fisherman's Museum, Åkrehamn

ABOUT THE TYPE

This book was set in Janson, a font that
is the faithful recreation of a great
seventeenth-century Dutch typeface cut by
Transylvanian Nicolas Kis. The strong main
strokes and fine hair strokes were influenced
by the art of copper engraving. It is noted for
its legibility as well as its elegance.